Motus Dei

ENDORSEMENTS

God is working in remarkable ways in parts of his world. Yet terms like *Church Planting Movements* and *Disciple Making Movements* have stirred strong debate in mission theology circles. Are we talking about the Spirit, who "blows where he wills," or cultural captivity to technique, strategy, speed, and scale? This book is important, whatever your perspective. And perhaps there is a third way. Despite the fact that God has chosen to work through movements at different points in history, the missiology of movements is relatively underdeveloped. The multiple authors in this volume help us take a step back from the slogans and action and ask, "What is actually going on here?" This reflective work is vital if we are to join in God's transforming work with humble boldness and find that third way.

PAUL BENDOR-SAMUEL, MRCGP, MBE | executive director, Oxford Centre for Mission Studies

There are more than three hundred thousand churches in the United States; that is twenty-three churches for every Starbucks. With so many good churches, most American pastors have never seen a movement of thousands of non-Christians becoming Christians. I wonder if that is why some church leaders have spoken out against movements. I listened as one critic referred to movements as "diabolical." He should not have said that. I forgave him. Another referred to the work of some missionaries as "gimmicks." I forgave him as well.

But in non-Christian countries, we are praying for movements. Movements are always an answer to prayer. I think of Samuel Zwemer, the great "apostle to Islam," who thanked God for five converts in his lifetime. Zwemer's prayer was Luke 5:5— "Lord, we have fished all night and caught nothing, but at your word we will let down our nets again." By a miracle, great numbers of fish filled the nets. Today, in a few parts of the non-Christian world, we are seeing what Zwemer longed to see. Let's keep praying to the Lord of the harvest. This is what *Motus Dei* is all about. Warrick Farah tells the story of movements in this superb book.

ROBERT A. BLINCOE, PhD | president emeritus, Frontiers US

As a local church missions pastor seeking to equip and send workers to the fields that are ripe for harvest, I find much of the movement literature communicates a simplistically formulaic methodology. This is not what you will find in *Motus Dei*. I am excited for this volume, which brings together theologians, historians, missiologists, and practitioners around the important topic of the movement of God.

REV. DAVE C. | global pastor, Park Community Church, Chicago, IL

Issues surrounding movements have risen to the forefront of missiology, creating a need for a more robust theology of movements. *Motus Dei* is a window into the dynamic discussion that is reshaping how the global church is fulfilling the Great Commission. If there was any one book that provides the clearest snapshot of the current "state of movement missiology," this is it.

TED ESLER, PhD | president, Missio Nexus

Any phenomenal movement of God that emerges with force and scale will attract both interest and critique. This volume is a comprehensive and reasoned response from a sterling collection of scholar-practitioners. Together they establish not only the plausibility of these ecclesial movements on the edges of God's kingdom, but help the reader envision how a fresh movement can arise in their own neighborhood, city, or people.

BRAD GILL | editor, *International Journal of Frontier Missiology*

Much missiological energy has been spent to explore Christ-centered movements of the past: the early Wesleyans of Britain and the US, Dalit groups in southern India, and peoples of the mountains of the India-Myanmar border to name a few. Can such movements occur today? *Do* they occur today? Building on the 2020 Motus Dei consultation, Warrick Farah and team offer a significant collection exploring the reality of current Christ-centered movements. Their documentation, explanation, analysis, and reflection, seasoned by some contributors with needed critique, help us take vital steps forward in our understanding. I warmly commend this important compendium.

DAVID GREENLEE, PhD | Operation Mobilization, missiologist and author

Clarity, information, and encouragement. This collection on kingdom movements provides all three. The international contributors exhibit extensive ministry experience and keen scholarly expertise. The wide-ranging topics—biblical-historical, missional-theological, analytical, practical—are addressed with substance. Perhaps best of all is the winsome approach that acknowledges missiological tensions and questions, all the while affirming the contemporary surge of peoples to follow Jesus. Many thanks to the Motus Dei Network for this timely and constructive publication.

REV. J. NELSON JENNINGS, PhD | mission pastor, consultant, and international liaison, Onnuri Church, editor, *Global Missiology*

Motus Dei is a breath of fresh air for the mission world, bringing much-needed empirical work to the phenomena of movements, where churches are planting churches. With baseline definitional work, missional theology, the exploration of movement dynamics, and case studies all in one volume, this book and the promise of ongoing research in future volumes is the place to go to better understand movements in order to wisely participate in what the Spirit is doing around the world.

ALAN JOHNSON, PhD | associate professor of anthropology, Assemblies of God Theological Seminary; coeditor of *Missiological Research: Interdisciplinary Foundations, Methods, and Integration*

As one who has spent decades in the worlds of both higher education and church planting, I highly recommend *Motus Dei*. It is well-researched, very informative, and extremely practical. *Motus Dei* would serve well as either a classroom text or a field handbook—a one-stop-shop resource on church planting movements.

BILL JONES, DMin | cofounder, Crossover Global; chancellor, Columbia International University

Motus Dei is the first report of a learning community of mission leaders and scholars in dialogue about how the Spirit of God has moved among them, creating households of faith, new generations of disciples, the multiplication of churches and seekers around the world. The goal of this community is to continue these conversations and to invite others participating with God in movements to join them. This book is an exceptional introduction.

SHERWOOD LINGENFELTER, PhD | provost emeritus, Fuller Theological Seminary, senior professor of Anthropology; coauthor of *Breaking Tradition to Accomplish Vision: Training Leaders for a Church-Planting Movement*

If ever there was an anthology whose "time has come," it is this compilation of reflections from leaders involved with movements of people to Christ from other religious backgrounds. The verifiable fact of large kingdom movements in the majority world needs to be taken seriously and celebrated. This volume sets the stage for their voices to emerge as part of Christ's global church and their indigenous experience of God in Christ to teach us all.

JAY MATENGA, DIS | director of Global Witness, World Evangelical Alliance; executive director, WEA Mission Commission

One third of the world's population does not have access to the gospel! One. Third. There is only one way so many will ever be reached, and that is through God-centered movements. This book contains all the information one needs to become versed in the importance and dynamics of contemporary movements. Comprised of writings by some of the most knowledgeable on the topic, the book is not only informative but also instructive, with helpful illustrative case studies. As Alan Hirsch notes in the afterword, *Motus Dei* is "packed full of movemental wisdom" that is so needful in understanding what it takes to reach the unreached today.

MARVIN J. NEWELL, DMiss | executive director, Alliance for the Unreached / A Third of Us

I highly recommend this book. *Motus Dei* captures all the very best and most current research on Disciple Making Movements. It looks back at the historic development of the field, and then forward, anticipating what is to come. As an edited volume, *Motus Dei* brings together premier scholars to offer a biblically astute, theologically robust, and culturally sophisticated analysis of Disciple Making Movements. It would be the "go-to" book for me on this subject.

GREGG A. OKESSON, PhD | interim provost and VP for academic affairs, Asbury Theological Seminary; author of *A Public Missiology: How Local Churches Witness to a Complex World*

In 1974, Ralph Winter's "hidden peoples" shook the mission world. Over the next three decades, "harvest field" research propelled missiology as a theological discipline. The corresponding, late-twentieth-century global advance is undeniable. In 2004, David Garrison's "ten universal elements" were equally seismic. Two decades into the twenty-first century, we are again witnessing the maturation of missiology relative to "harvest force" research. *Motus Dei* pushes our observations of multiplying movements from adolescence into adulthood as a discipline. The corresponding global advance is as yet unfolding.

NATHAN SHANK, PhD candidate | affinity global strategist— South Asian peoples, International Mission Board

Motus Dei

The Movement of God to Disciple the Nations

Warrick Farah | Editor

Dave Coles, James Lucas, & Jonathan Andrews | Associate Editors

WILLIAM CAREY PUBLISHING

Motus Dei: The Movement of God to Disciple the Nations

© 2021 by Warrick Farah. All rights reserved.

Unless otherwise noted, Scriptures are taken from from The Holy Bible, New International Version® NIV® Copyright © 1973 1978 1984 2011 by Biblica, Inc. TM Used by permission. All rights reserved worldwide.

Scripture quotations marked "ESV" are taken from The ESV® Bible (The Holy Bible, English Standard Version®), copyright © 2001 by Crossway, a publishing ministry of Good News Publishers. Used by permission. All rights reserved.

Published by William Carey Publishing
10 W. Dry Creek Cir
Littleton, CO 80120 | www.missionbooks.org

William Carey Publishing is a ministry of Frontier Ventures
Pasadena, CA 91104 | www.frontierventures.org

Cover and Interior Designer: Mike Riester
Cover image by Emily Jackson, unsplash.com
Copyeditor: Andy Sloan
Indexer: Rory Clark
Managing Editor: Melissa Hicks

ISBNs: 978-1-64508-348-1 (paperback)
        978-1-64508-350-4 (epub)

Printed worldwide

28 27 26 25 24   2 3 4 5 6   IN

Library of Congress Control Number: 2021944019

CONTENTS

INTRODUCTION

Motus Dei describes how God is working in our world through movements. But what kind of movements? People use the term *movement* to describe all kinds of groups of people that are growing and working together for a common goal. But we are not just talking about *any* type of movement.

We are talking about movements of the kingdom of God. Church planting movements. Disciple making movements. Movements in which King Jesus is made famous, and lives and communities are transformed by the gospel. Ultimately, we are talking about the *motus Dei*: Latin for the "movement of God."

We chose to call this book *Motus Dei* because we desire, first and foremost, to be rooted and grounded in the life-giving reality and character of God. We aim not simply for acceleration of fruitful ministry and multiplication of disciples, but ultimately for Jesus to receive worship from all peoples. We desire to join with God himself, through Christ, in his own movement to redeem the nations back to himself.

The Semantics and Discourse of Movements

When talking about movements, how precise does our definition need to be? Human communication often gets along sufficiently well without precise definitions of words. Think for instance of the word *culture*. The Bible has no word for culture, and even mission circles lack a universally accepted understanding of it. Yet we can still communicate quite well using this word—*culture*.

The same can be said in our dialogue on "movements." In *Motus Dei*, we primarily focus on a particular kind of movement observed in the world in the last few decades. In recent years, movements of disciples making disciples have been observed in many different contexts. They involve swift reproduction of disciples and multiplying groups of seekers or new believers who engage the Bible together and seek to obey its teachings. One specific and helpful definition of "Church Planting Movements" (CPM) comes from the 24:14 Coalition:

> CPM is a multiplication of disciples making disciples, and leaders developing leaders, resulting in indigenous churches (usually house churches) planting more churches. These new disciples and churches begin spreading rapidly through a people group or population segment, meeting people's spiritual and physical needs. They begin to transform their communities as the new Body of Christ lives out kingdom values. When consistent, multiple-stream 4th generation reproduction of churches occurs, church planting has crossed a threshold to becoming a sustainable movement. (Coles and Parks 2019, 315)

Yet, historically, we note that many peoples and places have been significantly impacted by Christ through a "movement" that does not exactly fit this definition. Our conversation on movements is still maturing; a broader or more analytical definition may be forthcoming. In Motus Dei, we intend to be specific, but also sufficiently broad to learn from other types of movements. For now, this definition from 24:14 best captures the essence of what we discuss in this book. Movements differ from revivals, evangelistic campaigns, mass conversions, and the so-called "church growth movement" of the previous generation (Garrison 2004, 23–25). None of those involve CPM's expectation of four or more generations of churches planting new churches and disciples making new disciples. They expand by addition rather than multiplication.

Any conversation, including this one on movements, inevitably develops a set of commonly used words and phrases, and our conversation on movements is no exception. Here are some important terms for our particular conversation:

- *Disciple Making Movements/Training 4 Trainers/Four Fields, etc.*: These are best understood as strategies or approaches to see movements occur. In other words, these are the processes, whereas movements are the result.

- *Oikos*: This Greek word is best translated "household." Because households in the New Testament context often included people beyond the nuclear family, the term has come to be used as "extended family" or even "a circle of influence." Scripture shows that most people came to faith in groups. Though these groups were not always members of an oikos in their world (e.g., Cornelius' relatives and friends), many today use the modern expansion of oikos to refer to them. When these groups respond and are discipled together, they often become a *church* (as we see, for example, churches built around an oikos, or home, in Acts 16:15; 1 Corinthians 16:19 and Colossians 4:15). This biblical approach also makes sense numerically and sociologically.[1]

- *Generation(s)*: In this context, this word is used to describe disciples making new disciples and churches planting new churches. When a church births a new church, that new church is the second "generation." However, sometimes this word is used with the more common definition of biological generations, as in chapter 19 on Iran and Algeria.

- *Person of Peace*: Proponents of this concept see Luke 10 describing a "person of peace" in Luke 10:5–7. This is a person who receives both the messenger and the message and opens his or her social network to the message of the kingdom.

---

1 This definition and the "person of peace" was modified from Coles and Parks 2019, 320–21.

Researching Movements

Movements can be viewed two ways: both as a reality happening in the world and as an approach to disciple making, church planting, and holistic community transformation. As you will see, movements, in this book, are a significant phenomenon. As such, they deserve to be studied, since they occur in different contexts. But the deeper question *Motus Dei* aims to answer is this: What factors are contributing to the increase of discipleship movements in the world today? And what can we, as the body of Christ, learn in order to see movements fostered more effectively among all peoples?

However, we don't aim to simply discover the right answers as much as to *ask the right questions*. To that end, this book is only a first step for the Motus Dei learning community. We envision a participatory, multiyear conversation—in which you are invited to take part. No single person or theory can adequately answer the questions we are asking. In missions, sometimes we look for the hero catalyst or the strategic silver bullet to unleash a movement of God. But we aren't simply looking for a technical solution, as if movement strategies could only be proposed and implemented by experts. Instead, we aim to mobilize the body of Christ—men and women, from all around the world—to work together to build a learning community of trust and curiosity that wants to know *what is going on behind what is going on* in movements.

A Brief Overview of the Book

Motus Dei aims to represent some of the best thinking and research on contemporary movements. The first section offers "**The Big Picture of Movements.**" Our volume opens with a primer from Warrick Farah to frame our conversation from the perspectives of history and theology, specifically ecclesiology. Farah also uses the lenses of sociology and mission praxis to take a deeper look at some of the movement theory in missiology. This explores how multiple perspectives can help our conversation mature, especially as we look simultaneously at movements in the New Testament and in our world today.

Next, Samuel Kebreab shares observations learned from researching disciple making movements in multiple settings for more than a decade. Kebreab's observations as a non-Western researcher and movement practitioner lay a vital foundation. It is important to note that the motus Dei conversation is inclusive and occurring not just among Westerners.

As you may be aware, movements and movement strategies are sometimes criticized, for various reasons. Dave Coles offers constructive and robust responses to the most common objections.

As we have noted, the last two decades have witnessed incredible growth of movements in the Majority World. More than 1 percent of the world's 7.8 billion people are currently reported to follow Jesus as part of a discipleship movement.[2] How should we understand the numbers and the sheer size of movements occurring today? Gene Daniels and Justin Long clarify vital issues related to these metrics and reports of church multiplication in non-Christian settings.

Next, the "**Missional Theology of Movements**" section offers an examination of discipleship movements from a biblical perspective. David Lim shows us how *oikos* church networks contribute to kingdom transformation. As one who attempts to harmonize issues that are sometimes kept apart in missiology, Lim has insights for the global church today. Craig Ott then shows what we can understand about movements specifically from the book of Acts.

One of the important issues in movement thinking is our understanding of what constitutes a church. Trevor Larsen shows us how *ekklesia* (Greek for "church") is formed in the movements he has been researching and leading.

Next, Michael Cooper takes us through the Gospel of John to show how John's missiological theology contributed to the incredible growth of the Jesus movement in Asia Minor during the first century. Finally, James Lucas tackles a narrative theology of biblical households and "people of peace," an important concept in movement missiology.

The chapters in the "**Movement Dynamics**" section consider some important realities and aspects of movements today. Steve Addison, who has written on movements for decades, discusses the life cycle of movements and factors that contribute to their rise and their fall.

To a large extent, our missiological discourse on movements has been dominated by male voices. As Pam Arlund and Regina Foard aptly demonstrate, female perspectives on movements have been neglected for far too long.

Paul Kuivinen displays how music and the arts play an incredibly important role in the missiology of movements. Complementing music and the arts is the world of digital technology. To that end, Frank Preston shows the importance of mass media in regard to movements.

Many have observed that the vast majority of movements currently occur in the Global South. How do issues of migration impact movements among refugees and asylum seekers in the Global North? Bradley Cocanower and João Mordomo share insights related to catalyzing movements in the diaspora.

The book then turns to "**Case Studies**." Despite their commonality, movements of disciples making disciples don't employ a cookie-cutter approach to ministry, and thus they don't all look the same. The case study section demonstrates the diversity of movements and the importance of context in our conversation. In that light, we look at the transference of spiritual DNA within

---

2 For example, see https://2414now.net/resources/#global-movement-statistics and http://www.missionfrontiers.org/issue/article/1-of-the-world-a-macroanalysis-of-1369-movements-to-christ.

East African movements, the incredible "Bhojpuri Breakthrough" in North India, a multiplication movement in Thailand, and the generational consequences of previous movements that swept through Algeria and Iran. As you will see, the case study section has been specifically designed to pair Western and non-Western authors together.

All of our conversation up to this point will be left hanging unless we consider **"Movement Leadership and Next Steps."** Through his empirical research, Emanuel Prinz describes the traits and competencies of effective movement catalysts. This will aid those considering leadership development and training.

Since many organizations are beginning to adopt a movement philosophy of ministry, Eric and Laura Adams explain how their organization has come to embrace a paradigm shift toward movement thinking.

Finally, our conversation shows that these twenty-one chapters really constitute just a first step. Nearly all of these chapters were presented in abbreviated form during the virtual Movements Research Symposium 2020, initiated by the Motus Dei Network. Together with the symposium listening team, Richard Grady offers a final chapter clarifying issues and imagining the further research that will be needed by the missions community in order for our conversation on movements to develop and mature.

Join the "Movements" Movement

Motus Dei is a learning community. We don't always see eye to eye on movements. You may note some tensions, even contradictions, between the perspectives of different chapter writers. We see this not as a weakness, but as a strength. God moves in different ways, and movements are different, just like so many other aspects of creation. As iron sharpens iron (Prov 27:17), we believe in the importance of this conversation and community engagement—to truly have fellowship with and learn from one another. If you have significant experience with movements and would like to join Motus Dei and become a part of our conversation, or if you have research you would like to share, please connect with us through http://motusdei.network. Additionally, if you would like to take an affordable, accredited online seminary course designed around this book, check out "Foundations for a Missiology of Movements," available here: https://masterclasses.ephesiology.com/courses/foundation-movement. As you read and reflect, may you be compelled in wonder and joy to join God's redemptive movement among all peoples today.

References

Coles, Dave, and Stan Parks, eds. 2019. *24:14 – A Testimony to All Peoples: Kingdom Movements Around the World*. Spring, TX: 24:14.

Garrison, David. 2004. *Church Planting Movements: How God Is Redeeming a Lost World*. Monument, CO: WIGTake Resources.

ABBREVIATIONS

ABMB	Algerian believer from a Muslim background
BDAG	Bauer, Danker, Arndt, and Gingrich (Greek-English Lexicon of the New Testament)
BJB	believer from a Jewish background
BMB	believer from a Muslim background
CLC	community learning center
CPM	church planting movement
CQ	cultural intelligence
CSV	comma-separated value (a computer file format)
DBS	Discovery Bible Study
DMM	disciple making movement
EMDC	Eurasia Media and Distribution Consultation
ESV	English Standard Version (of the Bible)
FJCCA	Free in Jesus Christ Church Association
GEN	Global Ethnodoxology Network
HC	house church
HCN	house church network
HoP	household of peace
HUP	homogeneous unit principle
IBMB	Iranian believer from a Muslim background
IMB	International Mission Board (of the SBC, see below)
IQA	internal quality assessment
MBB	Muslim background believer
MMO	movement-multiplication organization
MTDMM	media to disciple making movements
NAME	North Africa and Middle East
NG	New Generations
NGO	nongovernmental organization (usually a charity)

NKJV	New King James Version (of the Bible)
NT	New Testament
OFW	overseas Filipino workers
PMA	Philippine Missions Association
PoP	person of peace
PPOP	potential persons of peace
PTSD	post-traumatic stress disorder (post-traumatic stress syndrome in some sources)
SBC	Southern Baptist Church
SSA	sub-Saharan Africa
T4T	training for trainers (has other meanings in different contexts)
UNHCR	United Nations High Commission for Refugees (The UN Refugee Agency)
UPG	unreached people group
US	United States
UUPG	unengaged unreached people group

PART I
The Big Picture of Movements

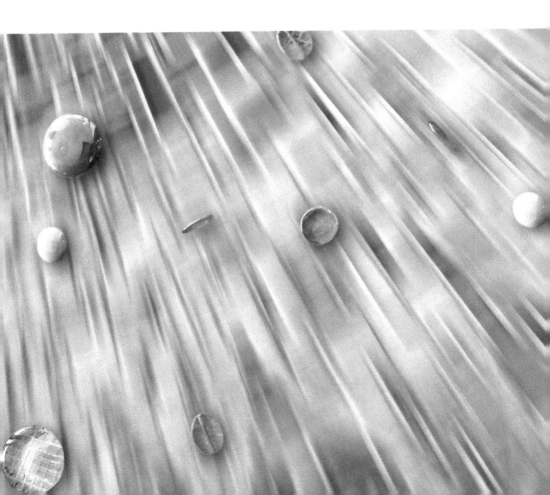

Movements Today: A Primer from Multiple Perspectives
Warrick Farah

The population of the world quadrupled in the twentieth century. Overall, Christianity kept pace with this growth, staying steady at around 30 percent of the global population. It is well known that the church has declined in the Global North and risen sharply in the Global South (Robert 2000; Johnson and Chung 2009). Yet, while tens of thousands of Muslims come to faith in Christ each year, another 35.5 million Muslims are born (Pew Research Center 2017). Tens of thousands compared to *millions*.

The situation is similar among Hindus, and even more problematic among Buddhists. The Center for the Study of Global Christianity estimates that the world's unevangelized population grows by around seventy thousand people every day (Johnson and Zurlo 2019). The harsh reality for those dedicated to seeing Jesus worshiped among all nations is that the world continues to become increasingly "unreached" each year (Parks 2017).

At the same time, the "movement" paradigm has become a significant trend in the evangelical missions community. Articles, books, and training events continue to appear in various mission circles. Mission agencies are dreaming big: An initiative was launched in 2018 to get people to pray that 10 percent of the Muslim world would become "reached" in the following ten years.[1] Sometimes it seems that *everyone* is talking about movements. Researchers have documented

---

1   See https://1010prayerandfasting.com/. Practically speaking, this means that around 19 million Muslims need to come to faith in Christ per year over the course of ten years. Consciously realized or not, such a bold prayer request presupposes an orientation toward movements.

the existence of over one thousand movements to Christ that comprise more than 77 million believers (Long 2020), the vast majority happening in places where there previously was no church. We are in the midst of a "movement" movement (Higgins 2018, 21).

Yet we do well to pause and reflect in the midst of all this action. What actually are these movements? How can we better understand movements, both as they occur in all their complexity, and yet also as a specific approach to ministry? Missiologists, theologians, movement practitioners, and even those new to the topic could benefit from a concise introduction to movements, written from a view that neither sensationalizes their emergence nor criticizes their existence.

I have outlined a missiology of movements, variously labelled church planting movements (CPM) or disciple making movements (DMM),[2] in a previous article (Farah 2020b).[3] In this initial chapter, I would like to go deeper. I want to briefly introduce movements from the perspectives of church history, ecclesiology, sociology, and mission practice. My intent is to develop a missiological framework for critical thinking about movements today.

A Historical Perspective

While it can be described in several ways, Christianity is *by nature* a movement. As a transglobal movement, it is the largest and most successful movement in history. Jesus started with twelve (Luke 6:12–16), sent out seventy (Luke 10:1–24), at Pentecost three thousand were added (Acts 2:41), and the numbers continued to grow daily (Acts 2:47). What began as a Messianic Jewish movement soon flowed into Gentile contexts as the apostles innovated their approaches to ministry (Acts 15; 1 Cor 9:21). In Acts 19:10, we read that "all the Jews and Greeks who lived in the province of Asia heard the word of the Lord" while Paul was in Ephesus for two years. As Andrew Walls states, "Crossing cultural boundaries has been the life blood of historic Christianity" (2002, 32). In all its diversity, including the various transitions it has gone through, the calling "to the ends of the earth" (Acts 1:8) has crossed more barriers and become "home" for more cultures than any other movement.

Multiplication in the Early Church

In the parable of the soils, Jesus himself teaches that the exponential growth of the "word of God" would occur in *some* contexts up to a "hundredfold" (Luke 8:4–8, 11–15). In the book of Acts, Luke often uses modifiers such as

---

2 Some use the label CPM as a result of a strategy like DMM or T4T (Coles and Parks 2019, 314–15). In this chapter, I hesitantly use the umbrella term "discipleship movements" to include CPM (and strategies that lead to CPM) as well as other movements like the Wesleyan Revival (Bevins 2019), which focused on discipleship but did not employ DMM or T4T. However, the term "discipleship" can indeed carry unhealthy baggage when associated with a passive process or with religiously consumeristic ecclesiologies.

3 Available here: http://ojs.globalmissiology.org/index.php/english/article/view/2309/5306

"greatly" (6:7), "daily" (16:5), and "mightily" (19:20) to highlight the dramatic nature of the growth of the early church. "Luke clearly makes a conscious effort to record the remarkable and pervasive spread of the gospel in fulfilment of the kingdom-growth motif in the Gospels" (Ott 2019, 112).

Michael Cooper believes that the book of Acts, along with Paul's epistles, records indigenous movements of Christ-followers that resulted in the multiplication of disciples who gathered in house churches: "Rather than a strategy for the expansion of the gospel, however, the CPMs in Acts were the result of faithful followers of Christ empowered by movement leaders to make more disciples, who assembled together in the homes of believers" (2020, 19). In other words, movements are not a *strategy*, but the *result* of a passion for Jesus demonstrated by making disciples.

In his letter to the Romans, Paul claimed that there was "no more place for me to work" (15:23) in the region from Jerusalem to Illyricum (Albania today), and that he desired to pass through Rome on his way to Spain (15:24). Craig Ott comments that Paul can confidently affirm that he had "fulfilled the ministry of the gospel of Christ" (15:19 ESV) only if he assumed that the churches he had planted in the region would continue to multiply and complete the work he had launched: "There is simply no other way to explain the dramatic numeric growth and spread of Christianity during the first centuries" (2019, 114).

Rodney Stark estimates that by the year AD 300 there were 6.3 million Christians in the Roman Empire (1996a, 7), while Cooper estimates there were around 5.5 million (2020, 32). Both estimate that this was around 10 percent of the total population, which is theorized by some as enough to create the tipping point in influencing the greater society (Xie et al. 2011; Cooper 2020, 29). The focus was not rapidity but more leaders equipping more believers for more works of service (Eph 4:11–12). As Paul seems to indicate in the prayer request of 2 Thessalonians 3:1, the "running ahead" *and* honoring of the "message of the Lord" is a biblical pattern for New Testament Christianity. Growth without health is not. "There must be a balance between evangelistic urgency and healthy maturational growth" (Ott and Wilson 2010, 77).

Yet we may also recognize that the early Christian movement was not necessarily a "CPM" as described by some CPM theorists today. It is anachronistic to read contemporary CPM/DMM strategies back into the Bible (Wu 2014). Historian Philip Jenkins remarks that the early Jesus movement did not coalesce into what we would consider the Christian church until around the year AD 200 (2018). The movements in the second century were still quite diverse (including many "Christian" groups that were later condemned as heretical by early church councils) and fluctuated with the ebb and flow of the times, including the sporadic persecutions and epidemics in the Roman Empire.

While faithful house churches read the biblical Gospels and Epistles (early Christianity was a distinctly "bookish" movement for its prolific use and study of texts [Hurtado 2016, 105]), the twenty-seven-book New Testament was not officially canonized until the end of the fourth century. This "movement" progressed in the second and third centuries, not primarily through organized evangelism and church multiplication strategies, but through a Christlike, countercultural lifestyle that was patient in the face of suffering and persecution (Kreider 2016, 9). Christian movements have not always remained in some places; they often decline and sometimes even die. The overall movement of Christianity is one of serial, not progressive, expansion (Walls 2002, 67).

Movement Ethos in Contemporary Missiology

In light of this, how did movement missiology begin to be incorporated into modern missionary strategy and goals? A generation after William Carey set off for India in 1793, mission societies struggled with the governance of new churches in many non-Christian contexts that had been established outside of "Christendom." As an administrative principle, mission leaders Rufus Anderson and Henry Venn are generally credited with the "three-self" formula, which meant that autonomous indigenous churches, *not foreign mission societies*, would themselves "become the means of missionary advance in the world" (Shenk 1981, 171). This three-self "formula" taught that churches should be self-supporting, self-propagating, and self-governing—in other words, free from colonial influence and dependency.

John Nevius adopted and taught this radically different approach to ministry in Korea in 1890, and added principles that Christians should be encouraged to remain in their pre-conversion social networks and that there be a discipleship program based on systematic Bible study (Handy 2012, 6–7). After this teaching, which catalyzed the Christian movement in Korea, the three-self formula came to be known as the Nevius Method (Ro 2000, 677). However, the traditional "mission station approach" persisted in many contexts (McGavran 1955, 68).

In the early twentieth century, Roland Allen further developed the Nevius method in his famous book *Missionary Methods: St. Paul's or Ours?* (1912). Allen pleaded with his contemporaries to break out of traditional approaches and to refocus explicitly on biblical principles that led to indigenous churches. At the same time, large numbers of peoples were coming to faith in some contexts, documented, for example, in the influential book by Waskom Pickett, *Christian Mass Movements in India* (1933).

In evaluating this book, mission anthropologist Paul Hiebert comments that these movements of multi-individual conversions had lasting results in both church formation and community transformation: "Pickett found that not only were people's lives transformed, but also their decisions were reinforced by their new Christian community. Individuals were not torn out of their social networks. Rather, whole communities were changed" (2008, 328).

Donald McGavran, father of the so-called "Church Growth Movement,"[4] was also strongly influenced by Pickett (Gallagher 2016, 66). McGavran took Pickett's ideas a step further toward a theory he called "people movements" (Hibbert 2012, 190), which was also based on phenomenological observation (McGavran 1955, 76). Alan Tippett also credits McGavran with coining the term "People Movement" and highlighting the significance that group ties play in initiating or constraining movements (1987, 253). In his book entitled *The Bridges of God*, McGavran sought to answer, "How do peoples, not just individuals, but clans, tribes, and castes, become Christian?" (1955, 1). He also coined the controversial "homogeneous unit principle" (HUP), which states that "people like to become Christians without crossing racial, linguistic, or class barriers" ([1970] 1990, 163).

As a strategy, René Padilla criticized the HUP as counter to the example of Jesus and the apostles, because it fails to take seriously the ministry of reconciliation and has "no biblical foundation" (1982, 29). Contrary to Padilla, however, the issue seems to be rather that people should be able to worship God in their own culture and not be forced into foreign expressions of the faith. Indigenous responses to the gospel will produce different cultural expressions of church that are both legitimate and necessary for the maturity of world Christianity. In other words, the pluriform nature of the church is a not a threat to biblical faith but embodies Christianity's very nature of continuity (Flett 2016, 19). McGavran's phenomenological observation is further balanced by the fact that while movements may begin in the same ethno-linguistic unit, they "rarely stop there" (Garrison 2004, 23). As noted earlier, Christianity as a movement is known for crossing boundaries and uniting diversity (Acts 11:20; 13:1; Gal 3:28).

In recent years, leaders like Bill Smith, Victor John (2019), David Watson (2014), and Ying and Grace Kai and Steve Smith (2011), among others, built upon these strategies for movements which yielded incredible numbers of churches planted and communities transformed. Today researchers, such as David Garrison, through his books *Church Planting Movements* (2004) and *A Wind in the House of Islam* (2014), have documented the rise of movements in the Global South. According to Garrison, "No one recalls who first coined the term 'Church Planting Movements,' though it appears to be a modification of Donald McGavran's landmark 'People Movements' adapted to emphasize the distinctive of generating multiplying indigenous churches" (2011, 9).

---

4 McGavran's original purpose of "church growth" within social networks led by unpaid leaders in house churches was later adapted for the goals of "church enlargement" for attractional and seeker-sensitive churches in the West. Lamenting this fact later in life, McGavran preferred the term "church multiplication" over "church growth" (Fitts 1993, 12). The Church Growth Movement eventually came to represent multiple schools of thought. Valid criticisms include the tendency towards pragmatic marketing programs, spreading religious consumerism, and an obsession with formulas and numbers.

In my view, though, CPMs differ from people movements. People movements tend to be linked strongly with favorable socio-political circumstances that facilitate their occurrence (cf. Montgomery 2020). CPMs might be better classified as "lay-led small-group discipling movements," where the small groups themselves multiply (at least up to four generations) and often in social networks. With or without favorable socio-political factors, the engine driving the CPM process tends to be easily reproducible churches with communal, interactive Bible study as their main liturgy (Farah 2020b, 3).

Motus Dei by Nature

It appears that the biblical data and the testimony of church history indicate that Christianity, *by nature*, is a movement (it is also much more than a movement). Indeed, "No people group or nation has become identified with Christ without a movement taking place among them at some point" (Lewis 2020, 8). Faithful disciples multiplied in the first three centuries without complex evangelistic strategies, and their multiplication resulted in more churches. When the modern missions era, between 1800 and 2000, witnessed an explosion of Christianity in the Global South, as well as when the church declined in the West during the end of the twentieth century, interest in studying biblical faith as a movement of God (i.e., *motus Dei*) was greatly renewed.

If biblical faith is indeed *motus Dei* by nature, then it necessarily provokes a missiological examination of elements that may inhibit movement in contemporary theology or Christian tradition. Are unbiblical doctrines and traditions preventing movements that need to be unlearned? In light of that question, here are six recurring missiological themes discussed in this section summarizing the history of discipleship movements that we may need to relearn today:

1) the immediacy of relationship with Jesus through the Holy Spirit, which empowers "ordinary" believers for ministry;

2) a willingness among leaders to innovate;

3) an emphasis on biblical principles for missionary methods;

4) the phenomenon of multi-individual conversions within social networks;

5) the centrality of Bible study in disciple making; and

6) the indigeneity of local churches, autonomous from outside dependency or control.

We now take a deeper look at this issue of ecclesiology.

An Ecclesiological Perspective

When discussing ecclesiology, theologian Howard Snyder reminds us that the church is a multidimensional mystery because it participates in the mystery of the Trinity, the mystery of the incarnational mission of Jesus, and the mystery of the sovereignty of God. He continues, "The church is also a mystery because its course through history is ambiguous.... It is not surprising therefore that the Bible gives no neat definition of 'church.' Instead it offers a wide range of images" (Snyder 2010, 1).

A classic work by Paul Minear identifies and describes ninety-six images for the church found in the New Testament ([1960] 2004). Minear's four "master images" are 1) the people of God; 2) the new creation; 3) the fellowship of faith; and 4) the body of Christ. While each of these images have reemerged at different times and places throughout history, and while no church is perfect, a mature ecclesiology would do well to incorporate all the biblical themes into the "mystery" of church (Antonio 2020, 176).

Ecclesiology Anchored in Deep Theological Identity

Inherent to this mystery is the diverse nature of biblical ecclesiology. Missional movement theorist Alan Hirsch notes that "ecclesiology (particularly in relation to the cultural forms of the church) is the most fluid of the core doctrines" of Scripture (2016, 143). Organizational changes occurred in the New Testament (NT) church whenever the shape of governance was hindering the spread of the gospel and the formation of churches. Thus, the "variety and flexibility of NT leadership seem to make any definitive statements on church governance or Christian leadership practice singularly unwise" (P. Shaw 2013, 138).

Ecclesiology is best understood not in a definition of functions, but in a robust "theological identity" (Van Gelder and Zscheile 2011, 165) that creates freedom for new expressions of church. As Jesus was sent into the world, so are we (John 20:21). Since the church is the *sent* body of the *sent* Christ, the church's theological identity is therefore missional by nature—meaning *sent* into the world. "This Spirit-led community possesses all the power of God's presence, even while it awaits the final judgment of evil that will lead to the creation of the new heavens and new earth" (Van Gelder 2000, 32).

Adaptive Ecclesiology in Christian, Post-Christian, and Non-Christian Contexts

In spite of the flexibility of biblical ecclesiology anchored in its theological identity, most ecclesiologies limit their descriptions of church in long-established *Christian contexts* that tend to be pastor-led, program-oriented, and building-centric. A more pressing question for us here pertains to an emerging ecclesiology in *non-Christian contexts* or frontier settings; in other words, an ecclesiology for least-reached places where there previously was no church. One bridge to this gap in the research is the "missional church" literature that describes ecclesiology in *post-Christian contexts* (e.g., Van Gelder and Zscheile 2011).

According to Michael Moynagh, post-Christian ecclesiology is a significant contemporary trend in theological studies. He uses the term "new contextual churches" as a way "to describe the birth and growth of Christian communities that serve people mainly outside the church, belong to their culture, make discipleship a priority, and form a new church among the people they serve" (2014, x). Through conversing with books like *House Church and Mission: The Importance of Household Structures in Early Christianity* (Gehring 2004), Moynagh shows how the NT church networked through homes, developed a "mixed economy" of ethnic homogeneity and diversity, and that emerging house churches reflected the structures of their sociological context.

Ed Smither similarly notes this feature of early church ecclesiology:

> As the oikos [Greek for household] structure was a natural medium for social networking in the ancient world and with the deliberate emphases by Jesus and Paul to minister from house to house, the house church model was central to mission strategy through the early fourth century. Even when we think about large Christian communities such as those at Rome, Carthage, and Antioch, we must envision a network of house churches. (2014, 154)

One recent treatment of emerging ecclesiology for churches in *non-Christian* contexts is the book *Seeking Church: Emerging Witnesses to the Kingdom* (Duerksen and Dyrness 2019). The authors use emergence theory "which stipulates that social communities arise over time in ways that reflect their interaction with specific historical and cultural dynamics" (2019, 25). While many churches are simply derivatives of a previous cultural expression of church, a church may emerge in a non-Christian setting according to specific cultural situations: "The persons of the church relate to each other and to God in the midst of their created space—that is, their situation in God's created order and what they have made of these gifts (i.e., their culture)" (2019, 154).[5]

Thus, as the early Jewish church used a model that was similar to the synagogue (Skarsaune 2008, 186), the early Gentile church instead adapted

---

5 However, inherent in this discussion is the authors' epistemological assumptions of the relationship between "form and meaning." The authors rightly argue that missiology has often used linguistic theory to describe the dynamic equivalence of meaning used in abstract communication while failing to apply those same standards to alternative forms of church, which is a community of actual people (2019, 21). However, in so doing, they seem to imply that form and meaning are arbitrarily related or completely separated, thus relativizing socio-cultural forms that the church can take. Others, such as Paul Hiebert, believe that form corresponds to meaning, and the strength of that correspondence varies from case to case. For Hiebert, a form-meaning *separation* stems from a dualistic mode of thinking inherited from and biased by Western culture. How we understand the form-meaning interplay (Farah 2020a) plays a large role in the ecclesiology of non-Christian contexts.

to the form of the Roman household, or *oikos* (e.g., Rom 16:5; 1 Cor 16:9; Col 4:15; Phlm 2).[6] According to context, emerging churches today in non-Christian settings will similarly adapt.

Multiplying Microchurches and Defining Church

The fluid house church, or "microchurch"[7] (Sanders 2019) model, seems an essential aspect for developing a movemental ecclesiology. Proponents of simple churches believe that the first-century church is normative for today and that "primitive" church structures are most often found in movements (Snyder 2010, 10). Similarly, Michael Cooper concludes that "the New Testament demonstrates the indigenous nature of the church, and this, no doubt, contributed to the rapid expansion of a movement of house churches throughout the Roman Empire" (2020, 184–85).

Alan Hirsch proposes that the body of Christ has the latent potential for movement built within (the essence of the church is missional), but often the church's theology, values, and structure inhibit or suppress that potential. According to Hirsch, the "apostolic genius" of NT ecclesiology for sustaining movements is described by

1) the absolute centrality of the person of Jesus Christ;

2) the priority of disciple making;

3) a missional-incarnational posture toward the world;

4) leadership that can both initiate movements (apostles, prophets, evangelists) and sustain movements (shepherds, teachers);

5) organic systems instead of hierarchical organizations; and

6) an outward-focused, inclusive community that can engage in risk and thrive in it (2016, 78ff).

This kind of "church as movement" ecclesiology contrasts from the "church as industrial complex" metaphor describing Christendom ecclesiology (Woodward and White Jr. 2016, 24). In order to recover the vitality of the early church, the NT and the vital role of the Holy Spirit must be the primary source for comparing institutional models with the ecclesiology of CPMs.

Large, previously existing churches and denominations can help catalyze movements (Shalom 2019; Larsen 2019). Additionally, other missiological studies, such as *Megachurch Christianity Reconsidered* (Gitau 2018), demonstrate how megachurches in the Global South provide stability for people in deeply volatile urban contexts and are not simply imports from the West. These

---

6   The actual history of this ecclesial development is more complex than these two forms, but the point remains.

7   Small, reproducing churches do not necessarily need to meet in homes, so "microchurch" might be a more accurate term than "house church."

important types of churches are also multiplying in various urban centers. The point, however, is that the movemental ecclesiology in CPMs is better described not in large institutions but in smaller, flexible structures. Large, stable institutions may occasionally be necessary to support smaller, more vulnerable churches in movements (Trousdale 2012, 116; Trousdale and Sunshine 2018, 129).[8]

As previously discussed, the NT presents a flexible ecclesiology and provides no neat definition of the form of church (Van Engen 2000, 193). However, it seems that there should be some biblical standard, such as Acts 2:42–47, or else the very idea of "church" itself becomes practically meaningless. To mitigate this issue, J. D. Payne discusses the need for an "irreducible ecclesiological minimum" to define church. This minimalist definition of a church is also helpful because adding any extra-scriptural requirements will possibly hinder the multiplication of indigenous churches (2009, 32). In other words, both *sub*-biblical ecclesiology and *extra*-biblical ecclesiology can be unsustainable for movements.

Missiologist L. D. Waterman defines church as

> "a significant group of Jesus' followers having an identity as a church (ekklesia) who gather together regularly on an ongoing basis, with recognized leadership under the headship of Christ, to worship God and encourage one another in obeying all his commands (including, but not limited to baptism and the Lord's Supper)" (2011, 467).

It is worth noting that minimalist definitions tend to focus on the *functions* of the church, not necessarily its *theological identity*. In any case, the irreducible ecclesiological minimum requires that a group of believers in Christ begin to self-identify as "a church," seek to learn and obey Scripture, observe baptism and communion, have recognized spiritual leaders, and realize their spiritual unity with other Christ-followers. However, it is important to realize that discipleship groups which eventually become biblical churches do not do so overnight. A mature ecclesiology presupposes mature disciples. Especially in movements, it is recognized that younger ecclesial forms often take time to mature into churches.

Toward a Movemental Ecclesiology on the Frontiers

In summary, most ecclesiologies describe the church either in Christian or post-Christian contexts. Even today, an ecclesiology especially for Africa (Lowery 2018) and Asia has not been "adequately articulated" (Ma 2018, 53). An area that needs more development in missiology is an ecclesiology in non-Christian contexts, especially of churches found in movements (see chapter 8 by Larsen in this volume). One key element of this movemental ecclesiology includes prioritizing the nascent NT forms of church which also emerged in non-Christian contexts and proved to be reproducible. As we have seen, the NT church:

---

8 There are other important ecclesiological issues to discuss concerning institutionalization and decentralization, but space precludes an adequate treatment here.

1) consisted mainly of flexible, indigenous microchurches or house church networks;

2) reflected the structure of its cultural and social setting;

3) was led by apostles, prophets, and evangelists, as well as by shepherds and teachers (Eph 4:11), not simply by pastors, like the contemporary church; and

4) identified theologically as a missional community of Jesus-followers created by the Spirit of God.

We are not surprised to find these kinds of biblical churches, rather than large institutions, to be the forms of church most easily reproducible and also most prevalent in discipleship movements today. Support and leadership from large institutions may provide a healthy stability to smaller churches that benefit movements, although traditional churches may often attempt to control or manage smaller church gatherings that are assumed to be under their "authority."

A Sociological Perspective

Because movements happen with *groups of people*, they may also be viewed through the lens of sociology. In fact, sociology describes how individuals become groups. With appropriate biblical discernment, social sciences help explain some of the means God uses to fulfill his purposes, both as described in the Bible and in our world today. God works through social conditions to bring about faith in Christ, and these conditions can be studied sociologically (Montgomery 2012, xvi). This section introduces some brief sociological theory to examine the dynamics of movements as the diffusion of religious faith across social networks.

Conversion, Social Networks, and the "Person of Peace"

Although most missiological studies of conversion have focussed on the micro-level of the individual (Farah 2013, 17), the group or societal level can reveal additional insights for understanding the phenomenon (Yang and Abel 2014, 150). Numerous sociological studies have demonstrated that social networks exert considerable influence on the life of religious communities (Everton 2015). For example, social networks often play a larger role in recruiting individuals to faith communities than does doctrine (Stark and Bainbridge 1980). Networks also serve as a primary vehicle for diffusing faith to a wider world (Collar 2013).

Missiological research has also shown that facilitating the movement of the gospel through natural social networks seems to be correlated with planting more churches (Gray and Gray 2010, 94). Granted that individuals have personal agency to follow Jesus, their social network powerfully influences them in ways they often do not realize.

One significant aspect of movement missiology has been the idea of the "person of peace" (Matt 10:11; Luke 10:5–6). In CPM/DMM literature, this person serves as a bridge or a gateway into a community or social network. Jerry Trousdale writes that "people of peace are God's pre-positioned agents to bridge the gospel to their family, their friends or their workplace" (2012, 90). However, it is debatable whether the person of peace idea is descriptive or prescriptive in the Bible. The understanding of precisely who constitutes a person of peace is ambiguous, and thus some fear that it could lead to a simplistic strategy for church planting (Matthews 2019). Nevertheless, the person of peace principle has been well documented in the phenomenology of movements (Garrison 2004, 45, 213).

This person-of-peace principle seems to match a key aspect of social network theory, where social entrepreneurs, or "brokers," act as bridges that fill "structural holes" (Burt 1992). When brokers step into these gaps between networks they are "creating change and movement" (Kadushin 2012, 66). These "bridge people," or "people of peace," connect people together to facilitate the diffusion of new ideas into new networks. What may or may not be a biblical principle is an observable phenomenon in movement dynamics. It isn't wrong to search for these types of people.

Sociologist Rodney Stark summarizes, "Successful movements discover techniques for remaining open networks, able to reach out and into new adjacent social networks. And herein lies the capacity of movements to sustain exponential rates of growth over a long period of time" (1996a, 20).

The "Right Set of Circumstances" and Social Structure

Christians believe the ultimate source of fruitful ministry is the Holy Spirit. But just as a sailboat needs to be properly prepared to sail, we may ask, "Is my ministry positioned to move the way he blows so that it can become a movement of God?" (Smith 2013, 29). However, we may further question if movements can happen in *any context* if the Holy Spirit moves and our ministries are correctly "positioned." Clearly, many peoples and places are resistant to Christian ministry of any kind (Woodberry 1998). To answer these types of questions, social scientists often speak of social movements requiring "the right set of circumstances" (Conley 2011, 606). In other words, movements are facilitated by the right leader with the right innovation being in the right place at the right time. Successful movements often spread in the midst of an unpredictable and complex group of conditions. The "tipping points" of when movements begin to take off and grow exponentially are almost impossible to forecast and are best discovered in hindsight (Kadushin 2012, 210).

For example, the majority of documented movements happening today are found in rural, developing areas within the Global South and are comprised of microchurches. In other words, the types of contexts in which movements are *most likely* to occur are in so-called peasant societies (Hiebert 2008, 123), where extended families are more or less intact and people don't already juggle competing identities and issues of multiple belonging. CPMs are also *most likely* to be comprised of simple churches and are occasionally supported (but not controlled) by larger institutions.

Thus, movements seem to be constrained by one or two limitations: 1) hierarchical or institutional ecclesiologies; and/or 2) urban and complex postindustrial societies. However, several movements in Asia have gained a foothold in cities (e.g., Kai and Kai 2018, Kindle 151; John and Coles 2019, chap. 8). The movements there tend not to be city-wide, however, but within ethnic burrows or urban enclaves within cities. In fact, several movements that started in rural areas have eventually moved into urban enclaves as the people did.

This begs further questions about where movements are most likely to occur: Are movements constrained in the West by the breakdown of the oikos in post-Christian societies within an increasingly individualized world? Has the West been inoculated to movements from the blight of Christendom? Does the rationalistic, Enlightenment worldview of the West suppress the possibility of movements in which the supernatural plays a key role (Trousdale and Sunshine 2018, 226)? What role does privatized media play in secularized individualism, as well as sporadic times of "social distancing" due to biosecurity events such as the COVID-19 pandemic?

In reality, not much missiological research has been done on these types of structural-contextual-sociological issues, and we still have much to learn. But the point remains for movements—both context and circumstance matter. And finally, the unpredictable movement of the Holy Spirit is the ultimate deciding factor (John 3:8).

Discovery Bible Study, Ritual, and Energy

Clearly, movements involve much energy from people who join and further propel the movement forward. In terms of positive emotional energy, movements both create energy and require energy from participants. One of the tools used to accomplish this in many discipleship movements is Discovery Bible Study (DBS). In a sociological perspective, DBS may be thought of as a liturgical ritual that creates and maintains energy for discipleship groups and movements. DBS and abundant prayer act as symbols of group membership in DMM/CPM strategy.

As rituals, DBS and communal prayer are highly interactive because they emphasize inductive learning and active participation. Done regularly, DBS becomes an "interaction ritual chain" in which people continually move toward situations that provide emotional energy (Collins 2014, 158). It is not simply that people become excited through the liturgical repetition of a DBS formula, but that the Holy Spirit animates disciples as they practice NT patterns of following

Christ, who is actively working in the community. Within the dynamics of a movement, the social expectations are such that everyone, not just the leaders, are responsible to the ministry.

Perhaps because there is no formal equivalent in non-Christian faith traditions, DBS and a communal piety expressed in prayer, fasting, and local worship music seem to create positive experiences for new believers in those contexts. The Holy Spirit stimulates novel and exciting energy through group interaction around the "living and active" Word of God (Heb 4:12). While the early church gatherings also seemed to be highly participatory (1 Cor 14:26–33), other types of discipleship movements may also interact with the Holy Spirit and Scripture (other than via DBS) to propel a movement through a community. The principle seems to be that genuine discipleship movements involve a deep, experiential spirituality around the gospel, and likewise that a deep gospel spirituality may lead to discipleship movements as well.

Obedience-Based Discipleship and "Strictness"

Successful movements grow because energy turns into activity from participants. Particularly for discipleship movements, the DMM/T4T strategy prioritizes obedience-based discipleship over knowledge-based discipleship (Smith 2011, 71; Watson and Watson 2014, 39). Obedience-based discipleship seems to have started as a counterbalance to the rationalism and individualism inherent in Western educational forms of discipleship (Pratt 2015, 5). For proponents of obedience-based discipleship, accountability to biblical commands such as evangelism and godly behavior is biblically preferred over merely cognitive "discipleship" centered around the transfer of information. This accountability creates an environment where following Jesus is a matter of serious life transformation. The Watsons note that the "Modern church has made the Christian life too easy for its members" (2014, 39). According to Mike Breen, Jesus' combination of "high challenge" and "high invitation" for his followers is essential to creating missional movements, as Christians are discipled to be active producers and not passive consumers of their faith (2017, Kindle 260ff).

Interestingly, a well-known sociological paradox observes that "religions that demand the most from their members often grow the fastest, but as religions become large and successful, they tend to become less strict" (Conley 2011, 583). While it may not seem rational for people to join a community that demands much from them, "strict" churches are often "strong" because they achieve high levels of commitment which provide mutual benefits to members (Iannaccone 1994). "Strictness" also reduces the number of "free riders" who contribute little to the community and thus reduce the average level of participation, enthusiasm, and energy (Everton 2018, 19). As movements grow, the challenge is to see accountability, knowledge, and faithfulness in their proper balance.

Identity and Insiderness

Andrew Walls has famously stated that throughout history, disciples of Jesus tend to be indigenously "at home" in their context *and* paradoxically "pilgrims" at the same time (1996). This reflects the scriptural paradox: simultaneously *in* the world, but not *of* the world (John 17:15–18). In other words, there must be a "medium tension" with the surrounding context: distinctive, but not absolutely foreign (Stark 1996b, 137). This tension necessarily relates to the ways movements are able to grow within certain contexts. New believers must find that balance of being inside the context in some way ("in the world"), but also outside in some way ("not of the world").

Without minimizing the belief contents of a religion, sociologist Robert Montgomery states that "people will be receptive to or resist a new religion according to whether they perceive that it enhances or detracts from an aspect of their social identities which they value" (2012, 268). Looking at this macro-level of analysis, contexts which are more resistant to the gospel are likely places where biblical faith is perceived negatively, whereas places that have witnessed significant movements have perceived the novelty of faith in Christ positively.

Yet it is not simply a binary issue. Leadership and contextualization loom large in this conversation. One way to understand movements is "The Complexity of Insiderness" model, which demonstrates the diversity of ways new believers in frontier contexts relate to their previous faith traditions (table 1.1). As the common aphorism states, "All models are wrong, but some are useful." With that in mind, the columns in table 1 represent different aspects of the religious context of a setting. For example, Exiles and Cultural Insiders are usually not socially *inside* their context enough to maintain the kinds of relationships necessary for movements to occur. Similarly, Syncretistic Insiders are not theologically *outside* of their context enough to qualify as a biblically orthodox movement.

	Five Expressions of Insiderness	Cultural	Social	Communal	Ritual	Theological
	0. Exile (or Refugee)	o	o	o	o	o
	1. Cultural Insider	i	o	o	o	o
Movements	2. Sociocultural Insider	i	i	o	o/?	o
	3. Dual Belonging Insider	i	i	i	?/o	o
	4. Reinterpreting Insider	i	i	i	i	o
	5. Syncretistic Insider	i	i	i/?	?	i
	i = insider; o = outsider; ? = occasional exception or ambiguous					

Table 1.1 The Complexity of Insiderness (Farah 2015)

Movements, however, may be found in three kinds of "insiderness" indicated in table 1.1: Sociocultural, Dual-Belonging, and Reinterpreting Insiders (reality is more complex than this model suggests). Space precludes a longer treatment here,[9] but suffice it to say that these movements relate to their contexts in vastly different ways; insiderness is not a monolithic phenomenon. Movements are also often transitional in nature, and the dynamic process of relationship to context changes over time. It is also particularly important to distinguish between so-called "Insider Movements" and CPM: they are not the same. However, issues of identity and insiderness are crucial to the causes or hindrances of movements. In diverse and multifaceted ways, movements occur *inside* their people group or context and are not perceived to simply be foreign imports from the *outside*.

This section has briefly reviewed five characteristics of movements that attempt to explain, sociologically, how and why certain elements found in movements today contribute to their exponential growth. The final section will present an overview of movements from the perspective of mission practice.

A Practical Perspective

A practical axiom for leadership states that "a weakness is a strength overused." Many applications of movement missiology are biblical and inspiring. But in the implementation of strategy, movement practitioners and movement theory itself can become unbalanced by overplaying strengths. This may also happen if inexperienced practitioners misapply movement approaches. In this final section, I would like to point to a few practical overuses of movement missiology sometimes committed by novice Western missionaries who may lack adequate mentorship or have gaps in their understanding.

Activism and Patience

According to David Bebbington, activism (in addition to biblicism, crucicentrism, and conversionism) is one of the four characteristics of classic evangelicalism, as evangelicals recognize an "imperative to be up and doing" (1989, 12). Movements are a flurry of activity that can be described as activism. Movement leaders should be admired for their tenacity and grit: in times of political chaos and in natural disasters, practitioners are often found running into the suffering, not away from it. In addition, leadership coaching of movement leaders often involves a diagnostic on what practitioners need *to be doing* at certain stages of movement. Clearly, activism is not a flaw, but is one of the core competencies for followers of Christ (2 Tim 4:5).

However, mature movement practitioners realize that activism can lead to malpractice if not balanced by some important counter-practices and values. One practice is theological reflection. We must always be asking the question, What is going on behind what is going on? What does the Bible say about what

9 The full article is available here: https://www.ijfm.org/PDFs_IJFM/32_2_PDFs/IJFM_32_2-Farah.pdf.

I am doing at the moment? These kinds of pauses produce a godly patience and a dependence on the Holy Spirit. For immature Western missionaries attempting to catalyze movements, activism can also lead to task orientation in ministry that potentially dismisses hurting people who might not be "people of peace" or influencers in their community. For Jesus, the original movement catalyst, no one was invisible and the marginalized in society seemed to be of special concern for him. Movements tend to do a remarkable job of ministering to the oppressed in society. Finally, activism can lead to an unhealthy type of pragmatism. Of course, there are biblical reasons for certain kinds of pragmatism (1 Cor 9:19ff). Experienced movement catalysts know that an activism that prioritizes task over relationship and pragmatism over theology is corrected by a patient trust and reflective understanding that ultimately the movement is God's, not ours (Ps 46:10).

Obedience and Grace-Filled Holistic Spiritual Formation

Biblically speaking, discipleship is a process which affects the whole person. One way to envision this holistic process is by looking at changes in the behavioral, cognitive, and affective dimensions of humanity (Hiebert 2006, 29). In other words, following Christ should involve a redemptive, holistic transformation in each of these three areas: beliefs, behavior, and emotions. As mentioned previously, obedience-based discipleship focusses on the behavioral dimension. *Orthodoxy* (correct belief) is obviously important, but obedience is helpful to remind people of the importance of *orthopraxy* (correct behavior) in making disciples. (In addition to belief and behavior, the Bible also speaks of the need for *orthopathy* (correct feeling) for holistic spiritual formation [K. Shaw 2013].)

Those unfamiliar with actual movements sometimes assume that emphasizing obedience risks assuming that new believers will fail to understand the extravagant grace of God expressed in the gospel of Christ. As orthodoxy, orthopathy, and orthopraxy are integrated in ministry approaches, the danger for new believers to remain trapped in legalism is minimized. But of course, this is true everywhere. As witnessed in healthy movements, obedience functions in an environment of grace and holism where the gospel is the basis for all of discipleship and mission.

Formulas and Contextualization

Many movement strategies provide a clear roadmap for practitioners to follow in their disciple-making ministries. DMM, T4T, Four Fields, and others like them offer a simple "big picture" of goals and action points that many practitioners have found helpful in application. However, these strategies may be misunderstood as formulaic. For example, according to the Watsons, "there is a minimum DNA required for groups to replicate past the first generation" (2014, 145). New missionaries may incorrectly apply the DMM strategy as a simple DNA formula that must be followed precisely for a movement to develop.

Similarly, T4T is also sometimes critiqued for its "overly rigid methodology" and "inflexible evangelism scheme" (Terry 2017, 352) that can be misunderstood as failing to take context into account. However, elements in the strategy such as DBS help the movement become contextual (Farah 2020b, 5–6), and mature practitioners understand the importance of context. No two movements are the same. By looking closely at movements, one will see a great variety and diversity that reflects the incarnational nature of biblical faith. Yet there is a power in the simplicity of movement strategies that more complicated and sophisticated strategies seem to lack. Movement strategies have given practitioners tools for initiation and advance that were lacking in earlier less-well-defined approaches.

Simple Methods and Robust Theological Training of Leaders

The development of leaders is one of the great strengths of movements, partly due to the abundance of on-the-job training. It is far more effective to train potential leaders not in a classroom but when they are in the actual process of leading (Lausanne Movement 2004, 29). Clearly there are no shortcuts for spiritual maturity, but provided a quality mentoring and apprenticeship process, movements develop leaders similar to Jesus' pedagogy of following, experiencing, and doing. Similarly, in movements (DMM in particular), leaders spend much time leading with the Bible open in the DBS process. Movements are often Bible-centric rather than leader-centric, especially in oral societies. Garrison has noted that the authority of God's Word and the Lordship of Christ, not church planters, are "the parallel railroad tracks guiding the movement" (2004, 182).

And yet, as experienced movement catalysts know, DBS and frequent Bible studies are not a substitute for (formal or nonformal) theological training. For instance, DBS often follows a process of *knowledge* (What does the text say?), *comprehension* (What does it mean?), and *application* (How will I obey and who will I share it with?) of the biblical text. However, in Bloom's taxonomy of educational objectives, these are the lower processes of learning (P. Shaw 2014, 75). After comprehension comes *analysis* (What is the connection between this teaching and other teachings?), *synthesis* (What is the integration of this teaching and other teachings?), and finally *evaluation* (All things considered, how now shall we live in our context?). Standing alone, DBS is not a process that fosters the types of critical or analytical mental processing that is required for leaders to be able to handle complex issues in their context and to arrive at a place where healthy and robust "local theologizing" (Hiebert 1985) takes place.

While DBS majors in areas that theological training is lacking, the reverse is also true. The issue here is not one of balance but of integration. In the (online or face-to-face) classroom you might have all the answers, but it gets complicated by the brokenness of the world. Movement catalysts integrate on-the-job leadership development with deeper theological training for leaders (Kai and Kai 2018, 113; John and Coles 2019, chap. 11). (It does *not* follow that leaders also need an official degree or ordination.) Sadly, though, modern mission history of the past century and a half has too often *begun* by starting institutions like Bible colleges and seminaries and providing the tools for critical reflection, rather than beginning with the presentation and power of the gospel in a movement ethos followed much later by advanced theological reflection. Movements and theological training are not in opposition, but in the pursuit of "faith seeking understanding," faith comes first.[10]

Conclusion

Some ways of making disciples are more conducive to movements than other approaches, yet this doesn't mean that context is unimportant nor that traditional ecclesiology is heretical. Furthermore, this doesn't mean that bigger is better nor that numbers are necessarily a sign of success. The standard for ministry has been and always will be the revelation of Jesus Christ, and authentic discipleship movements only happen when Jesus is front and center. To that end, the relatively new missiological discourse around movements is developing and maturing.

While movements are an exciting reality in God's world today, and a promising approach to seeing lives and communities transformed among all nations (Farah 2020b), we still have much to learn. Mature missiology should be rich in disclaimers.[11] We must be able to nuance the discussion and provide people with tools for critical reflection, essential for our changing world and the dynamics of God's diverse mission. At the same time, it would be unwise to marginalize movement missiology or to assume movements are exaggerated or a passing fad. For those seeking to exalt Christ in mission, movements may well be a way of seeing biblical transformation occur on orders of magnitude greater than traditional approaches.

As this chapter has attempted to demonstrate, movements are a massive field of study that invites the integration of historical, theological, sociological, and practical inquiry. A multilevel and multidisciplinary research approach involving theologians, missiologists, social scientists, and practitioners is required to adequately meet this challenge. As participants in the mission of God to redeem the nations back to himself, we need to better understand how movements are happening and how they could be fostered more effectively.

Our aim is not to satisfy academic curiosity, but rather to provoke inquiry related to how God is at work in our world. Our research into movements is intended to steward this knowledge responsibly before the Lord, both in what is taught and how to better train those seeking to foster movements today. The following chapters offer some of the best missiological thinking in this exciting new conversation and concept that we are calling *motus Dei*.

---

10   This insight was given to me in a conversation with David Garrison.

11   This idea comes from email correspondence with Benjamin Hegeman.

References

Allen, Roland. 1912. *Missionary Methods: St. Paul's or Ours?* London: R. Scott.

Antonio, S. T. 2020. *Insider Church: Ekklesia and the Insider Paradigm.* Littleton, CO: William Carey.

Bebbington, David W. 1989. *Evangelicalism in Modern Britain: A History from the 1730s to the 1980s.* London: Unwin Hyman.

Bevins, Winfield. 2019. *Marks of a Movement: What the Church Today Can Learn from the Wesleyan Revival.* Grand Rapids: Zondervan.

Breen, Mike. 2017. *Building a Discipling Culture: How to Release a Missional Movement by Discipling People Like Jesus Did.* 3rd ed. Greenville, SC: 3DM.

Burt, Ronald S. 1992. *Structural Holes: The Social Structure of Competition.* Cambridge, MA: Harvard.

Coles, Dave, and Stan Parks, eds. 2019. *24:14 – A Testimony to All Peoples: Kingdom Movements Today.* Spring, TX: 24:14.

Collar, Anna. 2013. *Religious Networks in the Roman Empire: The Spread of New Ideas.* Cambridge: Cambridge University Press.

Collins, Randall. 2014. *Interaction Ritual Chains.* Princeton, NJ: Princeton University Press.

Conley, Dalton. 2011. *You May Ask Yourself: An Introduction to Thinking Like a Sociologist.* 2nd ed. New York: W. W. Norton.

Cooper, Michael T. 2020. *Ephesiology: The Study of the Ephesian Movement.* Littleton, CO: William Carey.

Duerksen, Darren, and William A. Dyrness. 2019. *Seeking Church: Emerging Witnesses to the Kingdom.* Downers Grove, IL: InterVarsity.

Everton, Sean F. 2015. "Networks and Religion: Ties That Bind, Loose, Build Up, and Tear Down." *Journal of Social Structure* 1 (16).

———. 2018. *Networks and Religion: Ties That Bind, Loose, Build-up, and Tear Down.* Cambridge: Cambridge University Press.

Farah, Warrick. 2013. "Emerging Missiological Themes in MBB Conversion Factors." *International Journal of Frontier Missiology* 30 (1): 13–20.

———. 2015. "The Complexity of Insiderness." *International Journal of Frontier Missiology* 32 (2): 85–91.

———. 2020a. "Hermeneutical Hinges: How Different Views of Religion and Culture Impact Interpretations of Islam." In *The Religious Other: A Biblical Understanding of Islam, the Qur'an and Muhammad*, edited by Martin Accad and Jonathan Andrews, 189–202. Carlisle, UK: Langham.

———. 2020b. "Motus Dei: Disciple-Making Movements and the Mission of God." *Global Missiology* 2 (17): 1–10.

Fitts, Bob. 1993. *Saturation Church Planting: Multiplying Congregations through House Churches.* Self-published.

Flett, John G. 2016. *Apostolicity: The Ecumenical Question in World Christian Perspective.* Downers Grove, IL: InterVarsity.

Gallagher, Sarita D. 2016. "Seeing with Church-Growth Eyes: The Rise of Indigenous Church Movements in Mission Praxis." In *The State of Missiology Today: Global Innovations in Christian Witness*, edited by Charles Van Engen. Downers Grove, IL: InterVarsity.

Garrison, David. 2004. *Church Planting Movements: How God Is Redeeming a Lost World*. Monument, CO: WIGTake Resources.

———. 2011. "10 Church Planting Movement FAQS." *Mission Frontiers* 33 (2): 9–11.

———. 2014. *A Wind in the House of Islam: How God Is Drawing Muslims around the World to Faith in Jesus Christ*. Monument, CO: WIGTake Resources.

Gehring, Roger W. 2004. *House Church and Mission: The Importance of Household Structures in Early Christianity*. Peabody, MA: Hendrickson.

Gitau, Wanjiru M. 2018. *Megachurch Christianity Reconsidered: Millennials and Social Change in African Perspective*. Downers Grove, IL: InterVarsity.

Gray, Andrea, and Leith Gray. 2010. "Attractional and Transformational Models of Planting." In *From Seed to Fruit: Global Trends, Fruitful Practices, and Emerging Issues among Muslims*, edited by Dudley Woodberry, 2nd ed. Pasadena, CA: William Carey.

Handy, Wesley L. 2012. "Correlating the Nevius Method with Church Planting Movements: Early Korean Revivals as a Case Study." *Eleutheria* 2 (1).

Hibbert, Richard. 2012. "Missionary Facilitation of New Movements to Christ: A Study of 19th Century and Early 20th Century China." *International Journal of Frontier Missiology* 29 (4): 189–95.

Hiebert, Paul. 1985. "The Fourth Self." In *Anthropological Insights for Missionaries*, 193–224. Grand Rapids: Baker.

———. 2006. "Worldview Transformation." In *From the Straight Path to the Narrow Way: Journeys of Faith*, edited by David Greenlee. Waynesboro, GA: Authentic Media.

———. 2008. *Transforming Worldviews: An Anthropological Understanding of How People Change*. Grand Rapids: Baker Academic.

Higgins, Kevin. 2018. "Measuring Insider Movements? Shifting to a Qualitative Standard." *International Journal of Frontier Missiology* 35 (1): 21–27.

Hirsch, Alan. 2016. *The Forgotten Ways: Reactivating Apostolic Movements*. 2nd ed. Grand Rapids: Brazos.

Hurtado, Larry W. 2016. *Destroyer of the Gods: Early Christian Distinctiveness in the Roman World*. Waco, TX: Baylor University Press.

Iannaccone, Laurence R. 1994. "Why Strict Churches Are Strong." *American Journal of Sociology* 99 (5): 1180–1211.

Jenkins, Philip. 2018. "When the Jesus Movement Became the Christian Church." *The Anxious Bench* blog, March 9, 2018. https://www.patheos.com/blogs/anxiousbench/2018/03/end-beginning-jesus-movement-became-christian-church/.

John, Victor, and Dave Coles. 2019. *Bhojpuri Breakthrough: A Movement That Keeps Multiplying*. Monument, CO: WIGTake Resources.

Johnson, Todd M., and Sun Young Chung. 2009. "Christianity's Centre of Gravity, AD 33–2100." In *Atlas of Global Christianity*, edited by Todd M. Johnson and Kenneth R. Ross, 50–55. Edinburgh: Edinburgh University Press.

Johnson, Todd M., and Gina A. Zurlo, eds. 2019. "Status of Global Christianity, 2020, in the Context of 1900–2050." In *World Christian Database*. Boston: Brill. https://www.gordonconwell.edu/center-for-global-christianity/wp-content/uploads/sites/13/2020/02/Status-of-Global-Christianity-2020.pdf.

Kadushin, Charles. 2012. *Understanding Social Networks: Theories, Concepts, and Findings*. Oxford: Oxford University Press.

Kai, Ying, and Grace Kai. 2018. *Training for Trainers: The Movement That Changed the Word*. Monument, CO: WIGTake.

Kreider, Alan. 2016. *The Patient Ferment of the Early Church: The Improbable Rise of Christianity in the Roman Empire*. Grand Rapids: Baker.

Larsen, Trevor, and A Band of Fruitful Brothers. 2019. "A Two-Rail Model for Existing Churches to Reach the Unreached." In *24:14 – A Testimony to All Peoples: Kingdom Movements Today*, edited by Dave Coles and Stan Parks. Spring, TX: 24:14.

Lausanne Movement. 2004. "Future Leadership." In *Lausanne Occasional Paper No. 41*, 41:1–50. Pattaya, Thailand: Lausanne Committee for World Evangelization.

Lewis, Rebecca. 2020. "Patterns in Long-Lasting Movements." *Mission Frontiers* 42 (3): 8–11.

Long, Justin. 2020. "1% of the World: A Macroanalysis of 1,369 Movements to Christ." *Mission Frontiers* 42 (6): 37–42.

Lowery, Stephanie A. 2018. "Ecclesiology in Africa: Apprentices on a Mission." In *The Church from Every Tribe and Tongue: Ecclesiology in the Majority World*, edited by Gene L. Green, Stephen T. Pardue, and K. K. Yeo. Cumbria, UK: Langham.

Ma, Wonsuk. 2018. "Two Tales of Emerging Ecclesiology in Asia: An Inquiry into Theological Shaping." In *The Church from Every Tribe and Tongue: Ecclesiology in the Majority World*, edited by Gene L. Green, Stephen T. Pardue, and K. K. Yeo, 53–73. Cumbria, UK: Langham.

Matthews, A. 2019. "Person of Peace Methodology in Church Planting: A Critical Analysis." *Missiology: An International Review* 47 (2): 187–99.

McGavran, Donald. 1955. *Bridges of God: A Study in the Strategy of Missions*. Eugene, OR: Wipf and Stock.

———. 1990. *Understanding Church Growth*. Grand Rapids: Eerdmans.

Minear, Paul S. 2004. *Images of the Church in the New Testament*. 2nd ed. Louisville, KY: Presbyterian Publishing Corporation.

Montgomery, Robert L. 2012. *Why Religions Spread: The Expansion of Buddhism, Christianity, and Islam with Implications for Missions*. 2nd ed. Black Mountain, NC: Cross Lines Publishing.

———. 2020. "Missions and Movements." *Sociology of Missions Project* (blog), March 23, 2020. https://sociologyofmissionsproject.org/2020/03/23/missions-and-movements/.

Moynagh, Michael. 2014. *Church for Every Context: An Introduction to Theology and Practice*. London: SCM Press.

Ott, Craig. 2019. *The Church on Mission: A Biblical Vision for Transformation among All People*. Grand Rapids: Baker.

Ott, Craig, and Gene Wilson. 2010. *Global Church Planting: Biblical Principles and Best Practices for Multiplication.* Grand Rapids: Baker.

Padilla, C. René. 1982. "The Unity of the Church and the Homogeneous Unit Principle." *International Bulletin of Missionary Research* 6 (1): 23–30.

Parks, Kent. 2017. "Finishing the Remaining 29% of World Evangelization." *Lausanne Global Analysis* 6 (3).

Payne, J. D. 2009. *Discovering Church Planting: An Introduction to the Whats, Whys, and Hows of Global Church Planting.* Downers Grove, IL: InterVarsity.

Pew Research Center. 2017. "The Changing Global Religious Landscape." *Pew Research Center's Religion & Public Life Project* (blog), April 5, 2017. https://www.pewforum.org/2017/04/05/the-changing-global-religious-landscape/.

Pickett, Waskom. 1933. "Christian Mass Movements in India." In *Christian Mass Movements in India.* Nashville: Abingdon.

Pratt, Zane. 2015. "Obedience-Based Discipleship." *Global Missiology* 4 (12): 1–10.

Ro, Bong Rin. 2000. "Nevius Method." In *Evangelical Dictionary of World Missions*, edited by A. Scott Moreau, 677. Grand Rapids: Baker.

Robert, Dana L. 2000. "Shifting Southward: Global Christianity Since 1945." *International Bulletin of Missionary Research* 24 (2): 50–58.

Sanders, Brian. 2019. *Microchurches: A Smaller Way.* UNDERGROUND Media.

Shalom. 2019. "The Role of Existing Churches in an African Movement." In *24:14— A Testimony to All Peoples: Kingdom Movements Today*, edited by Dave Coles and Stan Parks, 263–66. Spring, TX: 24:14.

Shaw, Karen. 2013. "Divine Heartbeats and Human Echoes: A Theology of Affectivity and Implications for Mission." *Evangelical Review of Theology* 37 (3): 196–209.

Shaw, Perry. 2013. "The Missional-Ecclesial Leadership Vision of the Early Church." *Evangelical Review of Theology* 37 (2): 131–39.

———. 2014. *Transforming Theological Education: A Practical Handbook for Integrative Learning.* Carlisle, UK: Langham.

Shenk, Wilbert R. 1981. "Rufus Anderson and Henry Venn: A Special Relationship?" *International Bulletin of Missionary Research* 5 (4): 168–72.

Skarsaune, Oskar. 2008. *In the Shadow of the Temple: Jewish Influences on Early Christianity.* Downers Grove, IL: InterVarsity.

Smith, Steve. 2011. *T4T: A Discipleship Re-Revolution.* Monument, CO: WIGTake Resources.

———. 2013. "CPM Essentials on a Napkin." *Mission Frontiers* 35 (6): 29–32.

Smither, Edward L. 2014. *Mission in the Early Church: Themes and Reflections.* Cambridge, UK: James Clarke.

Snyder, Howard A. 2010. "Models of Church and Mission: A Survey." Center for the Study of World Christian Revitalization Movements, 1–24. Edinburgh, UK. https://www.academia.edu/6940376/Models_of_Church_and_Mission_-_A_Survey.

Stark, Rodney. 1996a. *The Rise of Christianity: A Sociologist Reconsiders History.* Princeton, NJ: Princeton University Press.

———. 1996b. "Why Religious Movements Succeed or Fail: A Revised General Model." *Journal of Contemporary Religion* 11 (2): 133–46.

Stark, Rodney, and William Sims Bainbridge. 1980. "Networks of Faith: Interpersonal Bonds and Recruitment to Cults and Sects." *American Journal of Sociology* 85 (6): 1376–95.

Terry, George A. 2017. "A Missiology of Excluded Middles: An Analysis of the T4T Scheme for Evangelism and Discipleship." *Themelios* 42 (2): 335–52.

Tippett, Alan. 1987. *Introduction to Missiology*. Pasadena, CA: William Carey Library.

Trousdale, Jerry. 2012. *Miraculous Movements: How Hundreds of Thousands of Muslims Are Falling in Love with Jesus*. Nashville: Thomas Nelson.

Trousdale, Jerry, and Glenn Sunshine. 2018. *The Kingdom Unleashed: How Jesus' First-Century Kingdom Values Are Transforming Thousands of Cultures and Awakening His Church*. Murfreesboro, TN: DMM Library.

Van Engen, Charles. 2000. "Church." In *Evangelical Dictionary of World Missions*, edited by A. Scott Moreau, 192–95. Grand Rapids: Baker.

Van Gelder, Craig. 2000. *The Essence of the Church: A Community Created by the Spirit*. Grand Rapids: Baker.

Van Gelder, Craig, and Dwight J. Zscheile. 2011. *The Missional Church in Perspective: Mapping Trends and Shaping the Conversation*. Grand Rapids: Baker Academic.

Walls, Andrew. 1996. "The Gospel as Prisoner and Liberator of Culture." In *The Missionary Movement in Christian History: Studies in the Transmission of the Faith*. Maryknoll, NY: Orbis.

———. 2002. *The Cross-Cultural Process in Christian History: Studies in the Transmission and Appropriation of Faith*. New York: Orbis.

Waterman, L. D. 2011. "What Is Church? From Surveying Scripture to Applying in Culture." *Evangelical Missions Quarterly* 47 (4): 460–67.

Watson, David, and Paul Watson. 2014. *Contagious Disciple Making: Leading Others on a Journey of Discovery*. Nashville: Thomas Nelson.

Woodberry, Dudley, ed. 1998. *Reaching the Resistant: Barriers and Bridges for Mission*. Pasadena, CA: William Carey Library.

Woodward, JR, and Dan White Jr. 2016. *The Church as Movement: Starting and Sustaining Missional-Incarnational Communities*. Downers Grove, IL: InterVarsity.

Wu, Jackson. 2014. "There Are No Church Planting Movements in the Bible: Why Biblical Exegesis and Missiological Methods Cannot Be Separated." *Global Missiology* 1 (12). http://ojs.globalmissiology.org/index.php/english/article/view/1711.

Xie, J., S. Sreenivasan, G. Korniss, W. Zhang, C. Lim, and B. K. Szymanski. 2011. "Social Consensus through the Influence of Committed Minorities." *Physical Review E* 84 (1).

Yang, Fenggang, and Andrew Stuart Abel. 2014. "Sociology of Religious Conversion." In *The Oxford Handbook of Religious Conversion*, edited by Lewis R. Rambo and Charles E. Farhadian. Oxford: Oxford University Press.

2

Observations over Fifteen Years of Disciple Making Movements

Samuel Kebreab

I first heard the principles of Disciple Making Movements (DMMs) in 2006, while I was going through a disheartening season. I was serving our denomination as outreach coordinator in a church planting effort we had started among the Yoma[1] people, an unreached people group in Southern Ethiopia. We had aimed to plant one hundred village churches in fifteen years.[2] By 2006, our seventh year of engaging the people, we had planted only seven churches. I felt discouraged, and achieving our goal seemed far-fetched.

While attending DMM[3] training by David Watson and David Hunt, I felt their material made a lot of sense. They shared from their personal experience the outcome of DMMs: the planting of thousands of multigenerational[4] churches, with tens of thousands of Christ-followers. I began to feel a sense of hope that this could happen in our context if we attempted to implement the DMM principles they had outlined.

---

1 Pseudonym.

2 In DMM, a church is a group of baptized disciples who meet regularly for worship, studying the Bible, fellowship, and service. But at that point, I had not yet been exposed to DMM principles.

3 Trousdale defines a Disciple Making Movement as the spread of the gospel by making disciples who learn to obey the Word of God and quickly make other disciples who then repeat the process (2012, 16).

4 In DMMs, "generations" pertain to disciples and churches multiplying to produce more disciples and churches, which in turn multiply to produce more disciples and churches. This ongoing multiplication results in a multigenerational movement of disciples and churches in which one can trace the line of descent.

Soon after that, I began to train and coach our church planters, and the few young Yoma men and women who had come to know the Lord through the work of our ministry, using DMM principles. The work began to grow slowly but steadily, especially through the young Yoma men and women (who were themselves part of the Yoma community) as they began to reach their parents and other close relatives. By March 2009, these Yoma men and women were baptizing their close relatives and many others from the community. The number of village churches grew to fifty-four.

At the time of writing this chapter, this DMM among the Yoma people has continued for fourteen years. There are now 5,672 Christ-followers in 364 village churches, comprising seven generations of churches. Furthermore, in April 2020 the movement sent Yoma workers to a neighboring unengaged[5] unreached people group to engage them with DMM. This occasioned great celebration, as we witnessed a movement that had started in one unreached people group cascading to a DMM engagement in another unreached group, previously unengaged with the gospel.

My personal story stands as just one among thousands of DMM stories inspiring God's people to praise him as they learn of and experience his kingdom advancing—similar to the stories we read in the book of Acts. I have served for the past nine years as Africa Research Director for New Generations. This has given me opportunity to personally visit and closely observe movements in all five of our African regions. I also receive reports on DMMs, not only from our African regions but also from other parts of the world where we have DMM engagement.

In this chapter I will describe some of what our organization has observed through a fifteen-year journey. Since 2005, our organization has attempted to catalyze DMMs in fifty-six countries in Africa, South Asia, Southeast Asia, and the Far East. The movements we have seen happening bear the fingerprints of Jesus. When kingdom-minded people apply Jesus' mandates, God often births great movements.

Specifically, this chapter focuses on the outcomes we have observed from thirty-one African countries and one South Asian country. Only in those initiatives do we have sufficiently comprehensive research protocols, with research teams, to harvest and analyze data from 656 engagements in people groups, urban clusters, or social segment groups. We utilize both quantitative and qualitative measurement tools to measure and describe what we see God doing and to understand what we are missing or doing poorly. These fifteen years of research have given us much encouragement and helped us assist other organizations to improve as well.

5 A people group among whom no disciple making or church planting is happening.

Before sharing the data and the outcome of these years of partnering with God and over seven hundred ministries we serve in DMM work, I would like to describe the features of the DMMs we have researched.

Features of Disciple Making Movements

DMM is a term coined by New Generations to describe the spreading of the gospel with the intention of making disciples who learn to obey the Word of God and quickly make other disciples who then repeat the process, resulting in many churches being planted. A DMM is not primarily a strategy or program but rather a lifestyle and ministry philosophy which is based on kingdom values modeled by Jesus in the Gospels.

DMMs Depend Heavily on Prayer, Which Is Often Followed by Miraculous Signs

Every DMM we have the privilege of witnessing traces its origin to intense intercessory prayer and fasting.[6] Faith-filled prayers ask God to bring his kingdom into people's lives and whole villages and cities. This has resulted in transformed lives, communities, towns, and cities. Jesus taught his disciples to pray for God's kingdom to come; this crucial prayer produces kingdom results.

When Jesus' disciples went from village to village to proclaim the coming of the kingdom, he empowered them to show signs of God's kingdom presence among the people. They proclaimed the good news, accompanied by healing and deliverance. In DMM, we have seen the kingdom manifest its presence through healing, deliverance, and other miraculous signs alongside gospel proclamation. We estimate that miraculous signs have accompanied 50 to 70 percent[7] of occasions where movements have started.

DMMs Equip Ordinary People to Achieve the Impossible

DMMs are simple, scalable, and sustainable, partly because they usually start through committed and obedient ordinary people. Some of our successful movement leaders have been housewives, poor widows, bicycle taxi drivers, masons, farmers, and former commercial sex-workers. DMMs do not depend on highly skilled and educated outsiders to proclaim the message. They depend on obedient insiders who may not have any form of skill or education. They do not depend on resources sent from outside, but can be sustained through what local people can afford and generate (Matt 10:9–10). They do not lack workers to deploy, since workers rise up from within the harvest field itself.

However, this does not mean an absence of need for gifted and highly skilled outsiders in starting, promoting, or facilitating a movement. In DMM,

---

6 Our organization has many thousands of intercessors in the Global South who have dedicated themselves to pray for DMMs to flourish among the least-reached people groups of the world.

7 Based on information gathered from DMM reports.

an outsider serves mainly to equip ordinary people, who in turn do the job of initiating, promoting, and facilitating the work of the movement (Eph 4). The ministry model that depends on highly educated and highly paid clergy does not produce a simple, scalable, and sustainable movement.

DMMs are Holistic: Merging Compassion and Healing with the Gospel of Kingdom Transformation

We don't see a bifurcation between kingdom proclamation and compassion ministry in Jesus' earthly ministry. The Gospel writers tell us that Jesus came healing and preaching. When Jesus sent the twelve to the villages to proclaim the kingdom message, he gave them authority to heal and deliver people from demonic oppression. DMMs follow the principle of entering communities with genuine love expressed in compassion ministry. The compassion ministry we offer can range from healing and deliverance to providing means that benefit the welfare of the whole community, such as access to clean water, seeds, better health, better education, or skill development. Compassion ministry does not function as an end in itself but is integrated with our desire to see people reconciled to God. Compassion also helps us gain acceptance by the community and creates a willingness to hear our message.

DMMs Require Trusting God to Supply the Resources Locally

Luke 10 and Mathew 10 describe two vital resources God provides which enable DMMs to overcome both the cultural barrier and the cash barrier when entering a new field.

The first resource is God's pre-positioned person to bridge the gospel to their family, friends, community, or workplace. The Bible calls such a person a "person of peace" (PoP).[8] These people are generally receptive to the gospel testimony, hospitable, and willing to open their families to hear the gospel. The PoP, whether a man or woman, breaks the barrier of culture. As a cultural insider, they do the inside work of promoting the gospel in their family, community, and tribe, starting from day one.

The other provision pertains to field expenses. Jesus tells his disciples not to carry money when they go to the harvest field because everything they need will be provided to them in the field. This approach greatly minimizes the cash required to make disciples and plant churches. The traditional way of making disciples and planting churches costs a lot of money that must be generated from outside. In many cases, discipling a person to Christ requires a large sum of money. For example, David Barrett and Todd Johnson estimate the total expense per baptism in the United States to be $1.55 million (2001, 520–29). In our case,

---

8 We have examples of PoPs in the New Testament, such as the woman at the well, Zacchaeus, Cornelius, and Lydia. Jesus said that if a town or village had no PoP, the disciples were not to remain in that village (Matt 10:14).

all DMM expenses combined typically total far less than $100 for each individual baptized, and most of those resources are provided locally.

DMMs Depend on Lost People Discovering God in the Bible and Choosing to Obey What They Discover About God's Will in Every Passage

We believe God is already working in advance to prepare people's hearts (especially in the case of the PoP). Thus, the harvest worker's job is to help lost people discover the truth from the Bible and obey it.

We call this method Discovery Bible Study (DBS). A DBS typically takes place in a group setting and has four components: 1) The gathered group hears or reads a Bible passage or story in their own language, 2) each person in the group retells the message in their own words, 3) each one shares an "I will" statement, describing what they feel they should do in response to the passage and making a commitment to obey it, and 4) listing the people with whom they plan to share the passage they have learned. In this way, from day one we initiate the formation of disciples who have a lifestyle of obeying God and multiplying themselves.[9]

People may start to obey God at the individual level or in groups or as a community. We call a group that meets regularly to hear the Word of God with the intention of obeying it a "discovery group." In addition to studying the Bible together, a discovery group worships God together, prays and intercedes for their needs and the needs of their community, and supports each other. They also function as an accountability group to check if the members have carried out their "I will" statements and have shared with others what they have learned in the previous lesson.[10]

DMMs Involve Ordinary Disciples Making Disciples and Churches Planting Churches

One of the most important aspects of DMM is the multigenerational multiplication of disciples resulting in multiplication of churches, as more discovery groups transition to become multigenerational churches. This takes place intentionally, creating a movement that will have a longstanding result: reaching and transforming communities, people groups, affinity groups, towns, and cities. This happens through the proclamation, demonstration, and experience of the gospel. As the DMM progresses, most movements create their own organic structure that enables them to organize and at the same time sustain

---

9   In DMM we disciple people to conversion. This is modeled by Jesus who chose twelve disciples to be followers of him. But it was not until just before his death that the disciples began to confess Jesus as their Lord and Messiah and embrace following him even unto death. In some ministry models, people are asked to repent of their sins and confess Jesus as their Lord and Savior at the first encounter and then begin to teach them how to become a disciple in a discipleship class. I think this ministry model of discipleship is knowledge-based (we teach them to know how to become a disciple), but in DMM discipleship is obedience-based.

10 See Watson and Watson (2014), especially chapter 15, for an in-depth understanding of how a discovery group functions.

the movement of kingdom expansion. This differs from traditional methods in which church planters organize a new church in the form and structure acceptable to the mother church or denomination.

DMMs Require Courage and Sacrifice

Matthew 10:16–42 teaches us that suffering, persecution, and martyrdom accompany movements of kingdom advance. We have heard untold stories of sacrifice in our fifteen-year DMM journey. However, this has not discouraged the Christians in these movements; rather, it has emboldened them. Instead of killing movements, in most cases persecution has caused people to again count the cost of discipleship and press on to new opportunities to bring transformation in the hardest places.

Data Collection Method and Data Verification Process

Data Collection Strategies and Methodologies

Our organization has a data and research team comprised of eight people. Team members collect data and analyze the outcome of the DMM activities every quarter. We also collect DMM narratives from each region every quarter.

Numerical data is compiled and verified for accuracy at the regional level by the regional data officer and sent to the data team. Our quarterly data collection form contains fourteen elements. The numerical information is entered into a CSV sheet and compiled and analyzed through Chartio, a cloud-based data analytics software. We compile the stories and activity reports and analyze them to assess the nature of the movement and the life transformation happening among the people in the movement. As of the first quarter of 2020, we have DMM data for 655 people groups and seventy-seven urban centers and social segment groups—from thirty African countries and one South Asian country.

Data Verification Process, Both Quantitative and Qualitative Data

We have an ongoing method of determining the reliability and validity of data we receive from the regions. Before it reaches the data team, data sent from the field by the church planter passes through at least three reviewers: the area coordinator, the country director, and the regional data officer. Each person reviews the data for its reliability and accuracy. Questionable data is not submitted until verified.

Internal Audit and External Audit

Since 2012, we have been doing ongoing internal audits[11] by going to the field to do: a) quantitative assessments—to determine the number of churches and Christ-followers, and b) qualitative assessments—to assess the DNA of the potential or actual movement.

---

11 The internal audit is done by our organization and our partners.

In 2015, we invited an external audit to assess a country with remarkable outcomes. The International Mission Board's (SBC) Global Research Office performed that audit in 2016. The audited African country has many extraordinary Disciple Making Movements happening. The IMB team chose nine people groups (seven of which were Muslim background) to assess. The research group confirmed that strong DMMs are happening among these groups. A security-sanitized version of that 131-page assessment is available for Christian researchers and missiologists.

At this stage in our journey, we have started a comprehensive three-year process of internal audit which we call Internal Qualitative Assessment (IQA). We have designed the IQA to find out how much of the DNA of DMM has transferred from the first-generation disciple maker to the fifth-generation disciple or church.

2005-2020 Third Quarter Summary Outcomes from Five African Regions and One South Asian Region

New Generations, working with more than seven hundred African and South Asian partner organizations, has seen God accomplish the planting of 79,862 churches among 605 people groups and 51 urban centers and segments of society. Of the 79,862 planted churches, 29 percent of them have seen the majority of their members come from a Muslim background. The number of people who have become Christ-followers is 1,858,531, of whom 32 percent come from a Muslim background.

A total of 129 people groups, society segments, or urban centers have reached the DMM threshold; they have more than a hundred churches planted, four or more generations deep. Incredibly, the highest number of generations reached within one people group to date is thirty-four.

March 2005 to March 2020 New Generations Ministries Disciple-Making Movement 15-Year Outcomes						
Regions with hard data	Number of countries engaged with church planting	Total number of people groups engaged	Number of urban centers and social segments engaged	Total DMMs that reached movement stage (>100 churches and 4 generations)	Total number of churches planted	Total number of Christ-followers
AFRICA	30	349	64	115	57,057	1,601,815
SOUTH ASIA	1	306	13	13	18,874	181,917
TOTALS of hard data regions	31	655	77	128	75,931	1,783,732

Table 2.1 New Generations' 15-Year DMM Totals

Over the years, we have prioritized engaging unreached or *unengaged* people groups who have no "Jesus option." As a result, of the people groups we have engaged with DMM in the five regions of Africa and one region of Asia, the majority (61 percent) have been unreached people groups. We have intentionally made disciples in pioneer places amid people groups that had no or few disciples of Jesus Christ.

Analysis of the 129 Movements That Have Reached the DMM Threshold

The majority of the churches planted, and the majority of the people who have become Christ-followers, are found in these 129 movements that have reached the DMM threshold. The number of churches in these DMMs is 60,767: 76 percent of the total number of planted churches. The number of Christ-followers in these DMMs is 1,602,195: 86 percent of the total Christ-followers. Therefore, the 129 DMM movements offer a good representation of our organization's DMM catalyzing in Africa and South Asia. Let's look more closely at these representative movements. We have discovered the following:

1. Time period needed to reach DMM threshold. We found that on average it takes three and a half years (42 months) for a DMM engagement to reach the movement stage. The time ranges between 3 months minimum to 135 months (eleven years and 3 months) maximum. However, out of the 129 movements, 70 percent of them reached the DMM threshold in less than four years. We did not find much difference between people groups having more than 2 percent evangelical population and those having less than 2 percent evangelical population.

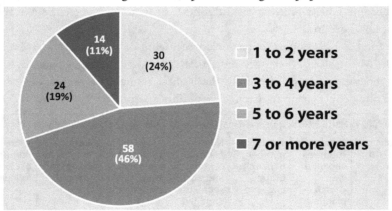

Figure 2.1 Number of People Groups Reaching DMM Threshold

2. Quantitative Relations between the PoP, DBS Groups, and Churches Planted. One of the elements we analyzed in the 129 DMMs was the proportion of PoPs to DBS groups. We intended to find out how many PoPs needed to be found for one DBS group to form. We found, through limited data from 2011 to 2017, in three sub-Saharan Africa (SSA) regions, that 1.3 PoPs needed to be found in order for one DBS group to start. In other words, for every four PoPs found, three DBS groups formed.

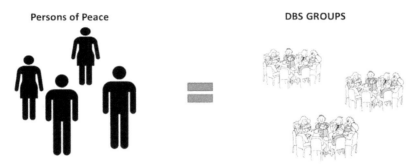

Figure 2.2 PoP per DBS

Secondly, we analyzed the proportion of DBS groups to the number of churches planted. We asked: How many DBS groups need to be established for one church to be planted? Based on five SSA regions plus the South Asia region, we found that 1.64 DBS groups were needed in order to plant one church. In other words, roughly three DBSs would end up becoming two churches.

Region	Number of DBS Groups Needed
Anglophone West Africa Region	2.64 DBS group for 1 church
Central Francophone Africa Region	0.99 DBS group for 1 church
East Africa Region	1.9 DBS groups for 1 church
Horn of Africa Region	1.2 DBS groups for 1 church
West Francophone Africa Region	1.4 DBS groups for 1 church
South Asia Region	1.7 DBS groups for 1 church
Average	1.64 DBS groups for 1 church

Table 2.2 Number of DBS Groups in Regions

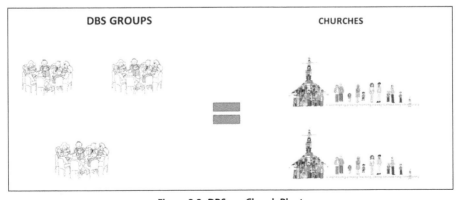

Figure 2.3 DBS per Church Plant

3. Correlations between the number of leaders trained and number of churches planted, and between the number of active coaches/trainers and number of churches planted. We analyzed in five sub-Saharan Africa regions whether we could see a correlation between the number of leaders trained and the number of churches planted. We also analyzed any correlation between the number of coaches/trainers actively training and diligently coaching Christ-followers and the number of churches planted.

We found a high positive correlation in both cases. The correlation coefficient between the number of leaders trained and number of churches planted was 0.85629. The correlation coefficient between active coaches/trainers and the number of churches planted was 0.887808.[12] This means that a greater number of active trainers and coaches results in more churches planted. In both cases, we found a statistically significant positive relationship, with p<0.001 value.

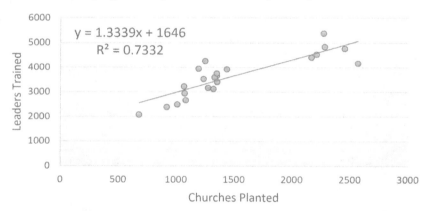

Figure 2.4 Correlation between Leaders with Church Plants

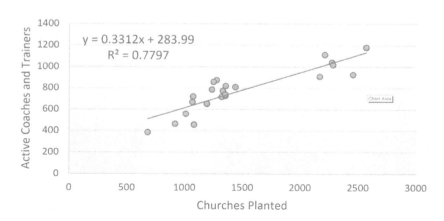

Figure 2.5 Correlation between Active Coaching and Training and Number of Churches Planted

---

12 The strength of correlation is strong if the result moves away from 0 to either -1 or 1.

A Summary of our Analysis

In our fifteen years on this Disciple Making Movement journey we have learned that kingdom advancement can only be realized through taking seriously the teaching of Jesus in the Gospels and committing ourselves to thoroughly obey him, whatever the cost may be. This has been confirmed to us by the outcome of multitudes from many "tribes, languages, peoples, and nations" becoming followers of Christ, and seeing the church of Christ formed in places and people groups previously categorized as unreached.

In the 129 movements, we analyzed the time required for a DMM engagement to reach movement stage (one hundred churches and four generations). We found that in most cases it took less than four years. We also analyzed the proportion of "persons of peace" to DBS groups, and the proportion of DBS groups to churches. We found that for each DBS group to be formed, an average of 1.3 persons of peace needed to be found. For each church established, an average of 1.6 DBS groups needed to be formed. In other words, roughly, the finding of four persons of peace will produce three DBS groups and three DBS groups will eventually transition into two churches. This "4→3→2" trend seems to be the rule in our case.

Figure 2.6 The 4–3–2 Model

The other thing we analyzed was the correlation between the number of people being trained, coached, and mentored to the number of churches planted. We found out that, in general, the more people are trained, coached, and mentored in DMM, the more churches are planted. As a succession of leaders emerges from a new generation of a movement, the leaders are trained and coached in DMM. In this way, the DNA of the movement continues.

Conclusion

According to Rick Wood, "Christian history demonstrates one certain reality; the only way that peoples are ever reached is through movements" (2018, 4). The Gospels and Acts also attest to this truth, as does our experience in the past fifteen years.

In Matthew 28:18–20, Jesus commands his disciples to make disciples of all nations. The book of Acts tells us how the disciples carried out this command. We read how that which started small, with the power of the Holy Spirit and the commitment of obedient disciples, became a movement that "turned the world upside down" (Acts 17:6 NKJV). God's kingdom impact was felt throughout the Roman Empire as generational leaders, disciples, and churches arose through the disciple-making process to carry on disciple-making from everywhere to everywhere.

While we don't claim DMM as the ministry strategy in the New Testament, DMMs do strive to function in the same spirit as that of Acts. We stand in awe to see multitudes from many people groups becoming followers of Christ, and we give credit to God for all the fruitfulness. We have learned firsthand that the harvest belongs to God, the means and principles for gathering the harvest come from God, and he is the one who sends harvest workers, even from the harvest field. We have learned that our part is to maintain a teachable and obedient heart that responds to the Spirit's prompting, as we work for God's name to be glorified among all peoples.

We know we are still novices and have a lot to learn from God and from his people. We also believe we have an obligation to share God's mighty work of salvation among multitudes of lost people, which has unfolded before our eyes through the DMM process. We know the work is vast and the harvest is great. Therefore, we desire for more of the body of Christ to join us in the DMM journey. We long to see DMMs unleashed throughout the world until the earth is "full of the knowledge of the Lord, as the waters cover the sea" (Isa 11:9).

References

Barrett, David B., and Todd M. Johnson. 2001. *World Christian Trends, AD 30–AD 2200*. Pasadena, CA: William Carey Library.

Robertson, Patrick, and David Watson. 2013. *The Father Glorified*. Nashville: Thomas Nelson.

Trousdale, Jerry. 2012. *Miraculous Movements: How Hundreds of Thousands of Muslims Are Falling in Love with Jesus*. Nashville: Thomas Nelson.

Trousdale, Jerry, and Glen Sunshine. 2018. *The Kingdom Unleashed: How Jesus' First-Century Values Are Transforming Thousands of Cultures and Awakening His Church*. Murfreesboro, TN: DMM Library.

Watson, David, and Paul Watson. 2014. *Contagious Disciple-Making: Leading Others on a Journey of Discovery*. Nashville: Thomas Nelson.

Wood, Rick. 2018. "Will We Hinder or Accelerate Movements? The Choice Is Ours." *Mission Frontiers* March/April 2018.

Addressing Theological and Missiological Objections to CPM/DMM

Dave Coles

In recent decades, many great works have been reported under the names "Church Planting Movements" (CPM) and/or "Disciple Making Movements" (DMM). Responses to these reports have ranged from great excitement to significant theological and missiological objections. In distilling a thorough review of articles and other discussion on the subject, I identified eight primary types of objections to the paradigms of CPM and DMM.

To assess which types of objections seemed most widely and strongly felt, I surveyed four networks of missionaries and missiologists, covering a wide range of theological and missiological perspectives. Respondents gave their opinion about each of the objections as stated below, based on a scale of 1 to 5, where 1 = Strongly disagree, 2 = Disagree, 3 = No opinion, 4 = Agree, and 5 = Strongly agree.

Responses from 102 individuals yielded these results:

1. "Rapid reproduction is never promised in Scripture and often results in shallow discipleship. Targeting rapid growth may frustrate workers and tempt them to exaggerate numbers." *Mean score—2.9/5*

2. "The CPM/DMM paradigm does not adequately include the biblical role of teaching by spiritually mature teachers." *Mean score—2.7/5*

3. "CPMs leave open a door for false teaching because of inadequate theological training for leaders." *Mean score—2.6/5*

4. "CPMs have inadequate ecclesiology. (Their 'churches' may not be real churches.)" *Mean score—2.5/5*

5. "The 'Person of Peace' strategy is not really taught in the texts of Matthew, Luke or Acts." *Mean score—2.28/5*

6. "'Obedience-based discipleship' is a dangerous paradigm, running the risk of bypassing grace and teaching legalism." *Mean score—2.22/5*

7. "Discovery Bible Study (DBS) is not a biblical approach to evangelism. The biblical pattern is proclamation." *Mean score—2.2/5*

8. "It is missiologically unwise, even dangerous, to have unbelievers studying the Bible without any mature Christian present to guide their study." *Mean score —2.18/5*

As I address each of these objections, I will use the most generic term—CPM—to mean "a multiplication of disciples making disciples, and leaders developing leaders, resulting in indigenous churches (usually house churches) planting more churches…. When consistent, multiple-stream fourth generation reproduction of churches occurs, church planting has crossed a threshold to becoming a sustainable movement" (Coles and Parks 2019, 315).

DMM is sometimes used as synonymous with CPM, but is more accurately understood as one of a number of *processes leading toward* a CPM.[1] Since objections often use the terms CPM and DMM somewhat interchangeably, my response will likewise minimize the distinction between the two, preferring the broader term: CPM. God is also working in other movements to Christ (including some described in this book) that don't fit the above definitions of CPM or DMM. This chapter will focus only on CPMs/DMMs and objections aimed at those paradigms.

Objection 1. Rapid reproduction is never promised in Scripture and often results in shallow discipleship. Targeting rapid growth may frustrate workers and tempt them to exaggerate numbers.

This concern includes four significant elements. I will address each in turn. First, "Rapid reproduction is never promised in Scripture." This is true. We do a

---

1 DMM "focuses on disciples engaging the lost to find persons of peace who will gather their family or circle of influence, to begin a Discovery Group. This is an inductive group Bible study process from Creation to Christ, learning directly from God through His Scripture. The journey toward Christ usually takes several months. During this process, seekers are encouraged to obey what they learn and share the Bible stories with others. When possible, they start new Discovery Groups with their family or friends. At the end of this initial study process, new believers are baptized. They then begin a several-month Discovery Bible Study (DBS) church-planting phase during which they are formed into a church" (Coles and Parks 2019, 315–16). Some other noteworthy processes leading to CPM include T4T, Four Fields, and Zúme.

disservice if we promise (or give the impression) that if anyone just does the right activities, a rapidly growing movement will result. The promises of Scripture passages such as John 15:5–8 and Matthew 13:23 focus on *abundant* fruit more than *rapid* fruit. Yet God's Spirit inspired Luke to report positively: "The number of disciples in Jerusalem increased rapidly, and a large number of priests became obedient to the faith" (Acts 6:7). The apostle Paul not only recalled rapid growth among the Thessalonians, but also asked them to pray for rapid growth in other locations as well. "Pray for us that the message of the Lord may spread rapidly and be honored, *just as it was with you*" (2 Thess 3:1).

Thus, rapid reproduction comes to us not as a promise, but as a positive value in New Testament kingdom advance. Whatever else we say about rapid reproduction, we do well to reflect the *positive* view portrayed by New Testament writers.

Second, "Rapid reproduction … often results in shallow discipleship." Shallow discipleship constitutes a sad reality throughout Christian history and in many parts of the Christian world today. A number of factors often contribute to inadequate discipleship. Among them could be named these four:

1. Weak initial commitment, with little or no connection to the lordship of Christ.

2. Profession of faith based on mere intellectual assent, rather than true repentance.

3. Holding on to patterns of one's sinful nature or culture that are incompatible with biblical commands.

4. Inadequate ongoing relationship with active and growing believers.

These factors have plagued the church in a wide range of cultures and contexts. Many disciple makers easily overlook the ways one or more of these factors may have influenced churches in their own home context. Yet they see all too clearly ways that these factors impact some churches in the Majority World (the fruit of past missionary labors). In the vast majority of such cases, the rapid growth that led to shallow discipleship was not the fruit of rapid *reproduction*. It was not a situation of spiritual generations of disciples reproducing disciples and churches reproducing churches.

The cases cited of rapid growth resulting in shallow discipleship tend to be first generation believers and churches, reached in great numbers with inadequate discipleship (generally involving one or more of the problems named above). Biological reproduction then yields second and third generation biological Christians with average discipleship similar to or less than that of the first generation. In contrast, rapid growth in the context of a healthy movement (four or more generations of churches reproducing churches) consistently produces disciples with a very passionate and contagious faith. This may contrast somewhat with discipleship produced by the slow growth to which most of us are accustomed.

CPMs generally have values that tend to address each of the four factors mentioned above. Discipleship through inductive Bible study establishes a pattern of regular study of God's Word, obedience to God's Word, and growing together with others. It also brings faith commitment based on a substantial process of grappling with foundational biblical truths and the need to turn from one's old life to embrace the new.

CPMs normally have some pattern for follow-up and discipleship. Many have thorough curricula designed to equip believers with firm doctrinal foundations for their life in Christ. The rapid generational reproduction often seen in movements results naturally from healthy disciples reproducing healthy disciples. As already mentioned, shallow disciples tend to rarely reproduce (except biologically).

Third, "Targeting rapid growth may frustrate workers." Rapid growth is not and should not be a goal per se. As Craig Ott writes, "Our concern is not so much for speed as for locally reproducible methods that in the long run can launch a self-sustaining movement" (Ott and Wilson 2010, 99). The rapid multiplication seen in CPMs results naturally from God blessing the use of appropriate means for making disciples and planting churches. These usually include reaching groups (rather than individuals), abundant prayer, consistent evangelism by all believers, involvement of all believers in studying and applying God's Word, and empowering local leaders. The application of these means doesn't guarantee a resulting movement. God doesn't promise a direct cause and effect in these matters, and neither should we. But faithful use of appropriate means concretely welcomes God's Spirit to sovereignly do the work that only he can do, according to the Father's good pleasure.

Simple low-cost approaches can multiply much more quickly than approaches requiring a large investment of resources. Applying these and other CPM-oriented patterns often *naturally* results in rapid multiplication. In fact, though, the early stages of catalyzing a CPM *rarely* happen quickly. Things like learning a new language and culture, finding a person of peace, investing in leaders, then having a Discovery Group continue to the point of decision to follow Christ can take many years. CPM principles are far from a recipe for quick success.

CPMs multiply rapidly, but not because of focusing on rapidity. They focus on *immediacy*: immediately obeying the Lord's word, as did Jesus' first disciples when he called them, saying: "'Follow me, and I will make you become fishers of men.' And *immediately* they left their nets and followed him" (Mark 1:17–18 ESV). Disciples in CPMs frequently obey the Lord's word without delay or reservations. This results in rapid life transformation and rapid multiplication of believers and churches. In CPMs, such Christianity is normal.

One mission leader claimed that CPM trainers caused people to labor under "unrealistic expectations." However, CPM training normally encourages people to do their best to follow biblical patterns, while acknowledging that only God decides if and when a movement happens. As long as we don't *promise* rapid growth, we need not fear disappointing workers. Prayer and effort toward a large, aspirational vision inspires more progress than a small, easy-to-achieve vision. Jesus encourages faith that moves mountains, so even if a particular ministry does *not* end up yielding a rapidly multiplying movement, God is likely pleased with such faith, prayer, and effort.

Fourth, "Targeting rapid growth may ... tempt [workers] to exaggerate numbers." The temptation to exaggerate numbers exists among *all* workers around the world, no matter what approach they use in their ministry—CPM, traditional, or otherwise. This problem looms largest any time funding is connected with reported numbers. This would include arrangements by which donors in a Western nation send funds to support a "national" church planter (Zylstra 2019; Throckmorton 2020). Although there are exceptions, CPMs generally avoid using outside funds to pay church planters. And many CPMs aim to prevent reporting problems through the use of independent verifiers, asking when groups meet and then occasionally making surprise visits.

Objection 2. The CPM/DMM paradigm does not adequately include the biblical role of teaching by spiritually mature teachers.

To address this concern, we first need to ask how God would have us measure what constitutes "adequate" teaching by spiritually mature teachers. I suggest that the adequacy of biblical teaching can be measured by these five factors:

1. Are people coming to true saving faith?

2. Are people maturing as disciples, rooted and established in Christ?

3. Does the teaching lead people to obey everything Jesus commanded?

4. Does the teaching raise up leaders equipped to teach others, as a solid foundation for generational growth and multiplication?

5. Are the churches becoming healthy, biblical *ekklēsia*?

To the extent that trusted people have investigated the CPMs recognized by the 24:14 Coalition (www.2414now.net), I believe the answer to all five questions is yes. The teaching is adequate if the fruit is soundly biblical. Yet this leaves a few questions still remaining.

Do movements have a role for teaching by spiritually mature teachers? Yes, especially for teaching believers. Many CPMs have intensive teaching of new believers and leaders at all levels. For example, in answer to the question, "What is the role of teaching and preaching in the movement?" Bhojpuri movement leaders responded, "Teaching and preaching of the Word is a regular part of the believers' gatherings. Teaching also takes place every month in the advanced leadership training, which gets passed on through the generations of the movement. Conferences and seminars also include teaching and preaching" (John and Coles 2019, 189).

These leaders also described this consistent pattern of training: "We do teaching in different zones across North India. The training happens first in the zone office a few days a month, then the state office, then by areas, then by districts, then in subdistricts, then in villages. So everyone receives training" (2019, 163).

Is a human mediator always biblically required for people to be effectively taught by Scripture? Most Protestants, through the centuries, have agreed with the Westminster Confession of Faith (Chapter 1.7) concerning the perspicuity (clarity) of Scripture: "Those things which are necessary to be known, believed, and observed, for salvation, are so clearly propounded and opened in some place of Scripture or other, that not only the learned, but the unlearned, in a due use of the ordinary means, may attain unto a sufficient understanding of them."

We believe God's Spirit can speak directly to his people by illuminating Scripture (when appropriately translated from the original languages). Human teachers can be helpful, but a human priesthood of intermediaries *is not required*. The Reformers strongly asserted this biblical principle against the claims of the Roman Catholic Church. Yet, in some cases their modern followers have quietly established their own denominationally approved intermediaries.

Misapplication of biblical examples has exalted the use of ancient communication models and produced suspicion of more reproducible models of hearing from God's written Word. For example, when Ezra ascended his high wooden platform to instruct God's people in the Law (Neh 8:1–8), most people were illiterate and written biblical text was extremely rare. When the apostles did the teaching and preaching recorded in Acts, most people were still illiterate and most of the New Testament had not yet been written, much less compiled and made available to God's people individually. Mass printing of the Bible was 1,400 years in the future, and electronic distribution of Scripture was 1,900 years in the future. The most effective method available for conveying God's truth to a maximum number of people was one well-trained literate person speaking to an audience.

Preaching as structured monologue still has value in our day, but we now have incredibly reproducible means to put millions of people in direct personal contact with God's Word. Serious intent to proclaim God's message to *all* the world's peoples calls us to maximize "all possible means" (1 Cor 9:22) to make known the news of salvation. The goal of ongoing spiritual maturity also calls us to prefer approaches that do not encourage dependency on certain experts for spiritual feeding. The DBS approach used in many CPMs prioritizes learning from and applying the Word of God, which is living and active to accomplish his purposes.

The emphasis of Scripture points us toward maximizing all people's access to God's Word rather than worrying lest the message be insufficiently mediated through certain people. Our first priority should be Spirit-led application of

Scripture by as many people as possible. Interpretation by mature teachers has great value, but we should not turn mature teachers into a bottleneck, hindering the delivery of God's Word to those who need to hear it.

What is the biblical standard of spiritual maturity for teaching others? Because of space limitations, I suggest the two most foundational texts: the criteria for elders found in 1 Timothy 3:2–7 and Titus 1:5–9. Titus 1:5 and Acts 14:21–23 describe identifying local people who meet these criteria as a next stage after initial entrance of the gospel among a group, and as part of the process of establishing a mature church. The requirement: "He must not be a recent convert" (1 Tim 3:6) applies contextually within each local setting as the gospel enters new groups and places.

When *all* local believers are relatively recent converts, this criterion takes a back seat to others, as Philip Towner notes in Paul's instruction to Titus for the Cretans: "Titus's task of appointing elders from among recent converts (notice that in this case Paul cannot rule out recent converts …) must not have been easy" (2010, 229). In CPMs, the local believers showing most spiritual maturity are identified for spiritual leadership.

What do we mean by teaching? Some of this second objection might arise from CPM proponents' own use of the word *teach*. In explaining the importance of discovery in the DBS approach, trainers often say something like "outsiders facilitate rather than teach."[2] In that context, the intent is clearly to eschew the common approach of "authoritatively explaining the meaning of a text." However, facilitating a DBS also constitutes a form of nondirective biblical "teaching."

The Greek word *ginōskō*, used over two hundred times in the NT, involves *experiential* knowledge, not just accumulation of facts. Teaching means "to cause a person to know something…. Teach, instruct, and train mean to cause to gain knowledge or skill…. Teach can be used of any method of passing on information or skill so that others may learn" (Merriam-Webster 2020).

How does this process happen? Based on personal experience in classrooms and church, most of us tend to assume that "teach" means a one-way lecture: one person talks and everyone else listens quietly and absorbs more or less of what they hear. But people learn in many ways, and one-way lecture turns out to be among the least effective—both for retention and for life change. Much of the teaching described in the New Testament was interactive. We see this in Jesus' interaction with his disciples and in the thirteen New Testament uses of the word *dialegomai* ("discuss, dialogue"). We find ten of *dialegomai's* occurrences in Acts, describing Paul's approach to proclamation (Acts 17:2, 17; 18:4, 19; 19:8, 9).

CPMs employ a variety of teaching methods. Many movements use inductive Bible study patterns. Some use more directive teaching, but still in an interactive format. Most movements gather leaders in coaching groups for peer coaching and mutual learning. All have various levels of specific curricula they use in discipleship.

---

2   As, for example, in Watson and Watson, 73.

Is there no role for teachers in CPM? Yes, there is a role, but teachers need to be relationally grappling with everyday life, empowering local people from start to finish. Our criteria for choosing teacher's roles needs to be what most advances God's kingdom, not what most satisfies the desires of those who like to teach. We certainly see in Scripture numerous descriptions and examples of teachers and teaching. CPMs aim to apply this gift in the ways that will best produce mature, active, and reproducing disciples.

Objection 3. CPMs leave open a door for false teaching because of inadequate theological training for leaders.

This objection hangs on two key concepts. First, one's definition of adequate versus inadequate theological training. Second, the assumption that the primary or only prevention for false teaching is theological training.

What is our standard or criterion for adequate theological training? For some from an institutional church background, the obvious answer would be an official degree from a recognized and biblically sound seminary, or perhaps at least a diploma or certificate from a recognized and biblically sound Bible school. Yet these traditional answers fall short in at least three vital ways.

First, none of these criteria are mentioned anywhere in the Bible. That doesn't make them *wrong* answers, but it calls us to think well beyond our initial gut reaction if we intend to find God's answer. Adequate training in the New Testament took place in a variety of ways and contexts. Unlike the modern academic model of training, heavily dependent on voluminous books and resources, the apostle Paul described his training model as easily reproducible to multiple generations: "And the things you have heard me say in the presence of many witnesses entrust to reliable people who will also be qualified to teach others" (2 Tim 2:2).

The criteria Paul listed for church leaders in 1 Timothy 3 included "able to teach" along with over a dozen other criteria. And the characteristics given to Titus include, "He must hold firmly to the trustworthy message as it has been taught, so that he can encourage others by sound doctrine and refute those who oppose it" (Titus 1:9).

These abilities can be nurtured in numerous ways, through interaction with mature teachers and God's Word. The leaders of movements value biblical education. But they do not wait for disciples to complete a degree before equipping them to entrust God's truth to reliable people. And those reliable people in turn convey the trustworthy message of the gospel to others also.

For example, Victor John says: "We also teach through everyday life lessons. Deuteronomy 6:7 ... This teaching happens through being together in everyday life, not just sitting in a classroom" (John and Coles 2019, 161). He adds,

> *Many ministries do a lot of theoretical training, with Bible college and so on, but they don't give people a chance to practice what they learn. We teach one thing then say, "Go and do it." So whatever they learn, they immediately apply in their lives. That's why they learn more. We teach a little, then they do it and learn from their experience as well as from our teaching. That enables them to really work effectively. When they learn from us, that starts the process. When they start implementing what they learned, they learn many more things, because God is teaching them. (John and Coles, 165)*

CPMs aim for theology (knowledge of God's truth) to consistently lead to life application. Orthodoxy consistently links to orthopraxy. Ott notes, "Church multiplication occurs most rapidly where church planting does not require theologically trained and ordained pastors but is led by teams of lay or bivocational workers … this is the New Testament pattern" (Ott and Wilson 2010, 385).

Second, most CPMs have a "pattern of sound teaching" passed on to believers in the movement. Disciples' eagerness to study the Bible often leads to development of increasingly substantial organic theological training. For example, Shodankeh Johnson (2021) describes how the training process in their CPM in Sierra Leone developed into a four-year college. It started as a Bible study in 1998, which grew into a one-year certificate course. Within a few years the government approved the course curriculum for four-year degrees. The school now offers four-year degrees in theology and numerous other fields. Extended biblical training plays an important role in many CPMs.

Third, brief reflection demonstrates that theological education does not necessarily prevent false teaching. In the Protestant denomination in which I was raised, for example, I heard numerous sad stories of (and sermons from) pastors whose faith was, in my opinion, *less* biblically sound *after* seminary than before. An abundance of theological knowledge can be very useful, but it doesn't *guarantee* ability to stimulate healthy biblical faith in others. Many modern heresies come from theologians with doctorates from seminaries. Heretical movements often arise from a teacher so talented that his or her followers develop the habit of uncritically accepting and repeating whatever he or she says. Notable examples would include Jehovah's Witnesses, Christian Science, and Mormonism. Historically, many heretical groups have been named after the gifted teacher who effectively taught erroneous interpretations. Examples would include Apollinarism, Arianism, Sabellianism, Marcionism, Montanism, Henricians, and Pelagianism.

The leaders of movements nurture sound biblical faith through interactive study and application of God's Word. Every disciple is trained to grapple with Scripture and its application for themselves. They are also trained to ask one another, "Where do you see that in the Bible?" This constitutes one of the best preventions for heresy. Movement leaders also generally have some connection with the global and historical body of Christ. This provides points of comparison and safety in the broad interpretation and application of Scripture within the movement.

To avoid false teaching, disciples in CPMs also consistently apply the "one anothers" of Scripture, providing mutual accountability in the way of the Lord. They make a regular practice of living out verses such as, "Let the message of Christ dwell among you richly as you teach and admonish one another" (Col 3:16); "Therefore encourage one another and build each other up, just as in fact you are doing" (1 Thess 5:11); and "But encourage one another daily, as long as it is called 'Today,' so that none of you may be hardened by sin's deceitfulness" (Heb 3:13).

Many Christian leaders assume that correct preaching becomes correct theology of the listeners. Studies, however, show that to be false (Weber 2018). Listeners in the pew never have to confront their wrong theology. In CPMs, believers wrestle with God's Word at a deeper level than just hearing it. In small group discussion of the Bible, issues tend to rise to the surface more quickly. People either grow in sanctification or they leave. One research project concluded: "No significant patterns of heresy were found among those dozen movements" (Sergeant, Loc 2019, 2730–41).

We must acknowledge that in the fallen world of this age, God's people will always be subject to the temptation of false teaching. No amount or caliber of theological training can "error-proof" the people of God. We see in the New Testament that the very best of teaching didn't prevent all false teaching. Paul's approach included his "pattern of sound teaching" (2 Tim 1:13; cf. Rom 6:17). It also involved ongoing relationship—albeit from a distance (through letters)—to address various issues as they arose. And Paul depended heavily on local pastoral leaders guarding the flock (cf. Acts 20:28–31; Titus 1:9). Leaders of movements commonly apply similar preventative measures to guard against false teaching.

Objection 4. CPMs have inadequate ecclesiology. (Their "churches" may not be real churches.)

Interestingly, Ott and Wilson state that

> Many of the churches planted by Paul would not meet what many today might consider a minimal standard for being an established church. Nevertheless, he addressed even the most problematical congregations as "the church." This forces us to consider more carefully what genuinely constitutes a local church in the biblical sense. (2010, 4)

This objection that "Their 'churches' may not be real churches" reflects a shortage of accurate information about the realities of CPMs. In no case have I seen analysis of an actual CPM paired with criteria for a "real church" which yielded a negative conclusion. The objection appears to be based on one or more of three factors:

1. Lack of information about actual CPMs

2. Criteria for "church" inordinately dependent on Western church traditions

3. Confusion of CPMs with "Insider Movements," many of which *do*, in my opinion, have inadequate ecclesiology. See Waterman's critique of the Insider Movement paradigm's ecclesiology and characteristics of biblical *ekklēsia* (Waterman 2011, 460–67; Waterman 2016).

A pattern used by many movements has become known as "church circles" (Smith 2012, 22–26). This tool enables leaders to track the development and maturing of groups into churches, using the biblical descriptions in Acts 2:36–47 and other relevant New Testament texts. These circles commonly include baptism, God's Word, the Lord's Supper, fellowship, giving and ministry, prayer, praise, evangelism, and leadership.[3]

Throughout the NT and the first two hundred years of church history, Jesus' followers most commonly gathered for worship in homes. So although this gathering pattern is no longer the most common, hopefully no one (explicitly or implicitly) views house churches as "not real churches."

A survey of various criteria or marks of the church has yielded only one major "mark" that some could well argue as lacking in CPMs. For example, the Belgic Confession, drafted in 1561, lists the first of the "marks by which the true Church is known" as "If the pure doctrine of the gospel is preached therein" (Belgic Confession n.d.).

This could provide critics with a reason to exclude CPM ecclesiology from their reckoning as churches—if they interpret "preached" in the traditional sense of an ordained male pastor standing behind a pulpit, delivering a one-way message to a passive congregation of lay people. In its context, this would have been the intent of those who crafted the Belgic Confession. We do well to ask whether some modern leaders are (consciously or unconsciously) applying this criterion when then they accuse CPMs of inadequate ecclesiology. Some might say CPMs don't have "preaching" of the Word because there's no pulpit, no expert on a stage with a microphone giving a long monologue, and no passive listeners.

The presentation of God's Word in CPMs often follows a different pattern. On some occasions a leader may expound biblical truth to a mostly silent audience. However, deeper engagement with Scripture more often happens in an interactive fashion (as, for example, in DBS), with everyone actively involved in thinking, discussing, and applying the truths of Scripture. They likely don't have a pulpit, and they don't assume one person has all the right answers. They focus on applying God's Word, often with clear accountability to one another for obeying what they have received.

Movements prefer to have disciples who consistently *apply* God's Word rather than passive listeners to weekly polished monologues. But I suspect that the shortage of weekly Sunday "preaching" in many CPMs leads some, whether

---

3 Different movements might interpret the biblical elements in different ways, but each has commitment to biblical *ekklēsia* as they apply the NT texts in their various contexts.

implicitly or explicitly, to conclude that the weekly (or more frequent) gatherings in CPMs are not "real churches."

One version of this objection can be found in the article "9 Marks of a Healthy Church" (9Marks n.d.), the first mark of which is preaching. "An expositional sermon takes the main point of a passage of Scripture, makes it the main point of the sermon, and applies it to life today."

Although expository sermons are my own preferred preaching style, what if this definition of preaching was considered the only proper presentation of Scripture to God's people? Not only a great many CPMs, but the vast majority of traditional churches (including evangelical churches) worldwide might not meet the criteria of "healthy churches." I suggest we do better to focus on God's goal (his Word understood and applied in life) rather than just one specific and limited means to that goal.

One respondent to my survey in regard to these eight objections commented,

> Serious Bible students ... would probably ask if the attributes of early church evident in Acts 2 and Acts 4 and Paul's many one-another commands are occurring in a given movement. And undoubtedly the answer they would find is yes. Then they would ask if there were elders, and find the answer is yes. And they would ask about a good grasp on the truth, and the answer would be yes. Then they would ask if they are building unity with other segments of the body of Christ, and the answer would be yes—yes, that is, where sufficient time on each of these has allowed development of them, I would estimate one to two years sometimes.[4]

As noted by this respondent, the process of groups becoming churches takes some time. Yet each CPM has a concept of what they consider to be a church (*ekklēsia*), and they use criteria generally consistent with the characteristics found in the New Testament (Waterman 2011).

Objection 5. The "Person of Peace"[5] strategy is not really taught in the texts of Matthew, Luke, or Acts.

Granted, some advocates of CPM have claimed more clarity of *detail* for the "person of peace" strategy than is explicitly taught in the New Testament texts. Evidence for this may be seen in the slightly varying descriptions of (or criteria for) a person of peace given by various CPM trainers. However, a consideration of relevant biblical texts together does reveal a distinct pattern often used for apostolic entrance into new places. When Jesus sent out the Twelve, he commanded them: "Search there for some worthy person and stay at their house until you leave" (Matt 10:11).

---

4 Included with response to the survey, dated October 25, 2019.
5 According to Coles and Parks, "Luke 10 describes a person of peace. This is a person who receives the messenger and the message and opens their family/group/community to the message" (2019, 321).

New Testament scholar D. A. Carson, in his commentary on Matthew, remarks on this sending: "It is surely not unnatural for Jesus to treat this commission of the Twelve as both explicit short-term itinerary and a paradigm of the longer mission stretching into the years ahead. The Twelve become a paradigm for other disciples in their post-Pentecost witness" (1984, 242).

We see a very similar instruction in Jesus' sending of the seventy-two in Luke 10: "Whatever house you enter, first say, 'Peace be to this house!' And if a son of peace is there, your peace will rest upon him. But if not, it will return to you. And remain in the same house ... " (Luke 10:5–7 ESV). This pattern shows up again in many stories in Acts as well, for example, Cornelius (Acts 10), Lydia (Acts 16:14–15), and the Philippian jailer (Acts 16:31–32). Over and over, an openhearted person of influence opens the doors to bring their family into faith in Christ.

The New Testament does not present this as the *only* way to reach people in a new area, but it does portray this approach both in divine command and apostolic example. Throughout church history, God has used key people to open doors effectively for the gospel to those within their sphere of influence. Thousands of everyday examples are lost in the mists of history, but we have records of numerous high-level, key people whose conversions led their sphere of influence (in some fashion) to Christ. Among those could be mentioned Ezana of Axum (northern Ethiopia and parts of four other nations in the fourth century), Mirian III of Iberia, Sigeberht of East Anglia, Peada of Mercia, Olof Skötkonung (king of Sweden), Ranavalona II (queen of Madagascar), and Pōmare II (king of Tahiti).[6]

God is now using the growth of movements, especially in the Majority World, to remind individualistically oriented Westerners of a biblical truth. People from non-Christian backgrounds don't always come to faith as an isolated individual, standing against everyone else they know. People often come to faith along with family members or significant others who connect with their faith journey. We see this in New Testament descriptions (note the frequent use of the word *oikos*) as well as in Majority-World contexts of the twenty-first century. The most notable exception to this globally common pattern of faith journeys is Western culture in recent centuries.[7]

Sadly, this individualistic exception seems to have strongly flavored the experience and purview of most critics of CPM. I posit that we need not quibble about details of the description of a person of peace. Neither should we claim that

---

6 Many of these were mass conversions of pagans into nominal Christians. Yet the influence of a key person undoubtedly brought to those within their sphere of influence a greater *proximity* to the message of Christ. The point of commonality is God's use of a key person to open for others a door toward the gospel.

7 Note also that the modern Western pattern of individual conversion has happened primarily in contexts already nominally Christian, with individuals converting from nominal Christian faith to heartfelt Christian faith.

finding a person of peace constitutes the *only* right way to begin apostolic work in an unreached place or group. However, given Jesus' teaching and the examples in Acts, plus historical and contemporary evidence of the strategic importance of a "key person," it seems unhelpful and counterproductive to object to movement catalysts being trained and encouraged to look for a person of peace in pioneer locations.

Objection 6. "Obedience-based discipleship" is a dangerous paradigm, running the risk of bypassing grace and teaching legalism.

If "obedience-based discipleship" meant attempting to attain salvation through obedience, that would be deeply problematic. However, the phrase is intended to simply reflect one foundational element of Jesus' command to "make disciples"—namely, "teaching them to obey everything I have commanded you" (Matt 28:19–20). Warrick Farah comments:

> Much of contemporary forms of discipleship are based on a Western education model of church, where people were seen as lacking the right doctrine and theology. This is certainly important, but it is also incomplete. The focus of Jesus in Matthew 28 seems to put the emphasis on behavior. Learning to do all that Jesus 'has commanded' necessarily entails a biblical outlook on life, where word and deed, plus the spiritual and the social, are combined into one coherent unity. (2020, 6)

CPMs commonly lay a foundation for faith through chronological study of "Creation to Christ" passages.[8] This imitates (in abbreviated form) the pattern God used through thousands of years of Old Testament history. We know that "God ... announced the gospel in advance to Abraham" (Gal 3:8) and that God's grace received by faith undergirded the law (Gen 15:6; Ex 19:4–8). Also, "the law was our guardian until Christ came that we might be justified by faith" (Gal 3:24). New Testament proclamation of the gospel built solidly on centuries of calls for obedience. God spent thousands of years calling people to obedience before giving a *clear* revelation of salvation through Christ and a command to be baptized in his name.

Taking a few weeks (or months) for a brief chronological study through Creation to Christ passages lays a vital foundational understanding of the true nature of God, of sin, of the need for the blood sacrifice to forgive sin, etc. I hope we all agree that whenever *anyone* reads the Bible and seeks to obey God based on what they have read, that's a good thing. Granted, only the power of the indwelling Holy Spirit makes consistent God-pleasing obedience possible. An unbeliever's attempts at obedience can never bring or earn salvation.

---

8 Different groups use different lists of Creation to Christ Bible texts. For two good sample lists of texts, see "Creation to Christ" at http://www.accelerateteams.org/index.php/our-guidebook and page 2 of "The Discovery Bible Study Method (DBS)," at https://intent.org/wp-content/uploads/2017/04/DBS.pdf.

Yet from a biblical vantage point, it seems advantageous if people learn from the start that the appropriate response to God's Word is to *apply* its teaching. This stands in stark contrast to the too-common pattern suggesting that the proper response to God's Word is simply to analyze, explain, and intellectually comprehend it. Accurate comprehension is exceedingly valuable when it leads to obedience. But as an end in itself, it falls far short of the discipleship to which Jesus calls us.

The phrase "obedience-based discipleship" is never presented as a substitute for "grace-based discipleship" or "love-based discipleship." In fact, David and Paul Watson extensively expound Jesus' teaching on the essential connection between love and obedience (Watson and Watson 2014, 39–45). They note the clear relationship: "If you love me, you will obey what I command" (John 14:15), and interact with Jesus' exposition of this theme in John 14:16–25 and John's reiteration of it in 1 John 5:3–4). However, contrary to the Watsons' unhelpful phrasing:—"Jesus equated 'obedience' to 'love' in the Gospel of John" (Watson and Watson, 39)—I would clarify that Jesus presented obedience as a *result* of love (not equal to it). The Watsons themselves reflect this more accurate connection a few pages later when they explain: "Our motives for being obedient determine if we are doing so out of love or legalism" (Watson and Watson 2014, 45).

The phrase "obedience-based discipleship" is intended to underline a contrast between discipleship characterized by active obedience versus discipleship characterized by *mere knowledge* or cognitive assent. Christians too often treat religious knowledge as an end in itself rather than embracing the fact that greater knowledge of God's truth should consistently lead to greater obedience. Scripture gives a stark warning that simply adding knowledge runs the risk of *increasing* sin! "If anyone, then, knows the good they ought to do and doesn't do it, it is sin for them" (Jas 4:17). For this reason, DMMs stress the importance of obedience in discipleship, not mere knowledge.

Does obedience-based discipleship, despite good intentions, bypass grace and teach legalism? As nearly as I can discern, this concern does not stem from any research among DMMs, finding evidence of disciples trying to be justified by obeying laws. Neither does it seem to emerge from evidence that salvation by grace through faith is *not* being taught or applied in DMMs. In fact, the story sets chosen for DBS emphasize that we *cannot* please God by obeying the law, thus we need a Savior. One sample set of DBS stories includes studies such as the following—providing clear lessons on commitment and discipleship:

- Who is Jesus? John 1:1–18
- What does Jesus offer you and ask you? John 14:1–7, 23–27
- What is the result of faith in Jesus? John 3:3–21
- What is your response? Acts 2:36–41; Psalm 32:1–5; Romans 10:9–10
- What is baptism? Romans 6:1–4; Galatians 3:26–28; Acts 10:44–48

Objections seem to come primarily from two concerns. First, the truth that God's grace, rather than obedience, must be the basis (foundation) of discipleship (e.g., Pratt 2015, 9–10). For this reason, I would acknowledge that the wording "obedience-based discipleship" is less than ideal. In its attempts to convey one thing (obedience rather than mere knowledge) it has caused confusion by unintentionally giving the impression of implying something else never intended (obedience rather than grace or love as the foundation of discipleship). It appears the concern has arisen from ambiguous wording of the concept rather than lived reality among CPMs.

Second, objections have arisen from a concern about obedience being presented chronologically as an early step in discipleship, prior to presentation of the gospel of grace (e.g., Kocman 2019). This concern seems to have been exacerbated by use of the phrase "disciple people to conversion" (Trousdale, 43), based on the example of Jesus' years of interaction with his disciples before they realized his divine nature or knew of his atoning death for their sins. To speak of "discipling" unbelievers can cause misunderstanding, since a person cannot be Jesus' disciple until they know about Jesus, and commit themselves to *follow* him. For that reason, while I affirm DMM's Bible-based *process* leading toward commitment, I prefer to avoid the confusing phrase "disciple to conversion."

The essential point is that, for most people, coming to saving faith involves a process—more than just a momentary decision. The process is especially vital for those lacking prior biblical knowledge or background. We need to consider what essential ingredients that process must include to bring a person to saving faith. Certainly the work of God's Spirit drawing the person (John 6:44), and certainly God's Word: "Consequently, faith comes from hearing the message, and the message is heard through the word about Christ" (Romans 10:17).

So we ask, "Do we want unbelievers to hear and consider God's Word?" Yes! And when a not-yet-believer hears and considers God's Word, what response do we hope for? Do we hope for mere passive listening until God's Spirit completes the drawing process and the person makes a faith commitment? Or do we hope that God's Word inspires some life response, even during the process, however inadequate it may be?

A Creation to Christ DBS (for example) never offers or promises salvation based on applying God's Word prior to faith. The issue of justification, which comes only by faith in Christ, begins to be addressed (as noted above) when a chronological overview of salvation history arrives at that point. Especially for Westerners who came to faith from some type of Christian-context background, we need to recognize the *process* normally required for those from a non-Christian background to come to faith (however short or long it might be). To the extent we recognize the needed process, we become less worried about the non-salvific steps involved in a person or group's gradually growing grasp of the *foundations* of saving grace, prior to its full revelation in the person and work of Jesus Christ.

Since, for some, the wording "obedience-*based* discipleship" has become a stumbling block, I prefer the phrase "obedience-*normal* discipleship,"[9] highlighting this wonderful characteristic of CPMs. Believers consider obedience to be *normal*: it's just what people do (of course!) when they love and follow Jesus as their Lord. It's not obedience *rather than grace* as discipleship's foundation. It's obedience to God's Word *rather than mere knowledge* of God's Word as the normal pattern of discipleship.

Objection 7. Discovery Bible Study is not a biblical approach to evangelism. The biblical pattern is proclamation.

Quite a few respondents commented that this objection contains a false dichotomy. The leader of a movement in SE Asia commented,

> *The biblical pattern is proclamation, as understood in biblical context. Many of the examples we see in the Bible are not large groups (we tend to associate proclamation with large groups), but there are more discussions with small groups of people, some of which start as dialogs with individuals, than there are large-group proclamation.*

> *The fact that we stress DBS does not speak of the proclamation we do in large groups…. This is very common, but is a different strategic leg outside the DBS groups… .*

> *The fact that we stress DBS does not speak of the Transformation Dialogs we do preceding and ramping up to DBS groups. These may start with individuals, but we try to move them into dialogs in groupings about spiritual truth, and this leads to DBS gatherings.*[10]

In other words, the New Testament shows proclamation taking place in a variety of ways and contexts. And in modern-day movements, proclamation can and is happening in many ways. DBS is but one approach. If by "not biblical," one means "not explicitly mentioned in the Bible," the same accusation would apply to altar calls, tracts, Bible distribution, radio, TV, satellite broadcasts, the Jesus Film, and designated church buildings. The accusation would reach far wider than probably any objector intends.

If by "not biblical" one means *contrary* to biblical teaching, this objection becomes simply another way of stating the following concern.

---

9   Others have suggested "believing-obedience discipleship," "love and obey discipleship," and "love and obedience-based discipleship."

10   Included with response to the survey, dated October 25, 2019.

Objection 8. It is missiologically unwise, even dangerous, to have unbelievers studying the Bible without any mature Christian present to guide their study.

The first response to this concern must be to reference what has already been said about the perspicuity of Scripture. This point of view, which considers a human intermediary essential for accurate communication of God's message, seems based on the flawed assumption that God's Word and God's Spirit are insufficient to convey God's truth.

Jesus, by contrast, spoke favorably of people being taught directly by God as a doorway to saving faith. "It is written in the Prophets: 'They will all be taught by God.' Everyone who has heard the Father and learned from him comes to me" (John 6:45). A prime way the Father draws not-yet-believers to Jesus is for them to listen to and follow God's Word. Merrill Tenney comments, "Verse 45 indicates that God would do his drawing through Scriptures and that those who were obedient to God's will as revealed in the Scriptures would come to Jesus" (Tenney 1981, 76).

D. A. Carson comments on this verse: "Jesus in the Farewell Discourse promises the coming of the Holy Spirit—with a *teaching* role (14:26–27; 16:12–15)" (1991, 293). And the Pulpit Commentary offers this insight on the verse: "Direct teaching by God is the prime requisite of any spiritual apprehension, even of the mysteries of Christ the Revealer.... Divine teaching by the Spirit of the Father and Son is the preliminary ... to believing on Christ" (Exell and Spence 1950, 265).

This objection seems to reflect too little confidence in God's ability to speak by his Word and his Spirit. It seems, simultaneously, to reflect too *much* confidence in human teachers, and our accuracy in mediating God's truth. It also reflects a misunderstanding about the DBS process. Perhaps the normal role of a more mature believer in the DBS process has sometimes been insufficiently explained. Unbelievers are not left entirely on their own with no guidance whatsoever in their study of Scripture. Normally a more mature believer plays some role in the group's interaction with Scripture.

This is seen first in the choice of recommended texts to study (such as a Creation to Christ sequence or texts relevant to a specific felt need of the group). It is then normally seen in the regular mentoring (shadow pastoring) of one or two members of the group. In most cases, the believer meets on a regular basis with this person(s) to discuss the next text to be studied and hear any concerns or questions that have arisen from the previous study. In this way, the group's journey to faith is shepherded by someone more mature in the faith, yet in a way that allows the group to do their own contextualizing of biblical truths while trusting the Holy Spirit to "guide them into all truth."

Conclusions and Recommendations

Having discussed all eight of the most common types of objections to CPMs, I offer a few conclusions and recommendations.

1. Many problems *attributed* to CPMs have been based on hearsay or observation of ministry that actually does not fit the criteria of a CPM (consistent, multiple-stream, fourth-generation reproduction of indigenous churches). In some cases, accusations have been multiplied by inappropriately lumping CPM/DMM together with Insider Movements or other non-CPM approaches, as in this example: "The overemphasis on speed and pragmatism in the Church Planting Movement, Disciple-Making Movement, Insider Movement, Short-Cycle Church Planting, and their ilk is a dangerous result of bad theology" (Buser and Vegas 2020).

2. Many objections to the CPM paradigm arise from a shortage of information about what actually happens in CPMs. In many cases, those involved in CPMs have hesitated to share much information with the wider world, lest overzealous Christians or antagonistic non-Christians rush in and damage the ministry. Only in very recent years have security-sensitive reports made accurate information about movement dynamics more widely available. More study is needed, and we all do well to maintain a posture of openness to learn more of what actually is (or isn't) happening in CPMs.

3. Some objections arise from assumptions based on traditional church patterns in Christendom. We need not argue against or insult those patterns to observe a difference between what Scripture actually says and what we have previously *interpreted* it to say or chosen as contextual *Western applications*. CPMs invite us to see with fresh eyes the simplicity of the gospel message and the stunningly reproducible patterns that allowed it to flourish in early centuries and grow like yeast, and to allow the same kind of flourishing in many places today.

4. The wording of some CPM advocates and trainers has occasionally been less than careful. In some cases, weak exegesis and/or eisegesis has colored the justification of and training for CPMs. In other cases, overzealous advocacy for CPM has yielded statements inaccurately describing movement dynamics or reflecting unhelpful insult toward traditional church and church-planting models. However, an inaccurate or unhelpful statement by an advocate does not nullify this verified reality: millions of unbelievers becoming disciples of Christ, in over one thousand known CPMs globally.

God's kingdom is greatly advancing through Church Planting Movements and Disciple Making Movements in our day. We see this advance most notably among many least-reached groups: those who had remained mostly untouched by the past "great centuries" of mission outreach. In many places, the harvest field is becoming a harvest force, as obedient disciples reproduce disciples and indigenous churches reproduce indigenous churches. Movements are often misunderstood, but when we place the realities of modern CPMs next to the commands and examples of Scripture, we find great encouragement in these apparent works of God. We look forward to seeing how these movements will endure and manifest God's kingdom in the years to come.

References

9Marks. n.d. "9 Marks of a Healthy Church," 9Marks website, www.9marks.org/about/the-nine-marks.

Belgic Confession. n.d. "Belgic Confession." Christian Reformed Church website. https://www.crcna.org/welcome/beliefs/confessions/belgic-confession.

Buser, Brooks, and Chad Vegas. 2020. "Why Unreached People Groups Still Matter in Missions." In *The Gospel Coalition*, January 10, 2020, https://www.thegospelcoalition.org/article/why-unreached-people-groups-still-matter-in-missions/.

Carson, D. A. 1984. "Matthew," in *The Expositor's Bible Commentary, Vol. 8.* Grand Rapids: Zondervan.

———. 1991. *The Gospel According to John.* Grand Rapids: Eerdmans.

Coles, Dave, and Stan Parks. 2019. "Definitions of Key Terms," in *24:14—A Testimony to All Peoples.* Spring, TX: 24:14.

Exell, Joseph, and H. D. M. Spence, eds. 1950. *The Pulpit Commentary* (set of 23 volumes). https://biblehub.com/commentaries/pulpit/john/6.htm.

Farah, Warrick. 2020. "Motus Dei: Disciple-Making Movements and the Mission of God." In *Global Missiology*, 2:17.

John, Victor, with Dave Coles. 2019. *Bhojpuri Breakthrough: A Movement That Keeps Multiplying.* Monument, CO: WIGTake Resources.

Johnson, Shodankeh. Forthcoming. *Same God Here!* Chicago: Moody.

Kocman, Alex. 2019. "Is 'Obedience-Based Discipleship' Biblical?" https://www.abwe.org/blog/obedience-based-discipleship-biblical.

Merriam-Webster. "Teach." https://www.merriam-webster.com/dictionary/teach.

Ott, Craig, and Gene Wilson. 2010. *Global Church Planting.* Ada, MI: Baker.

Pratt, Zane. 2015. "Obedience-Based Discipleship." In *Global Missiology,* July 2015.

Sergeant, Curtis. 2019. *The Only One.* Pasadena, CA: William Carey Publishing.

Smith, Steve. 2012. "The Bare Essentials of Helping Groups Become Churches: Four Helps in CPM." In *Mission Frontiers,* September-October 2012.

Tenney, Merrill. 1981. "The Gospel of John," in *The Expositor's Bible Commentary, Vol. 9.* Grand Rapids: Zondervan.

Throckmorton, Warren. 2020. "Gospel for Asia Invades Africa." www.wthrockmorton.com/category/k-p-yohannan.

Towner, Philip, 2010. *1–2 Timothy and Titus*. Downers Grove, IL: IVP Academic.

Trousdale, Jerry. 2012. *Miraculous Movements*. Nashville: Thomas Nelson.

Waterman, L. D. 2011. "What Is Church? From Surveying Scripture to Applying in Culture," in *Evangelical Missions Quarterly*, 47:4.

———. 2016. "A Book Review of *Understanding Insider Movements*," at http://btdnetwork. org/a-book-review-of-understanding-insider-movements/ https://btdnetwork.org/wp-content/uploads/Blogs/2016/Review%20-%20 Understanding%20Insider%20Movements.pdf.

Watson, David, and Paul Watson. 2014. *Contagious Disciple Making*. Nashville: Thomas Nelson.

Weber, Jeremy. 2018. "Christian, What Do You Believe? Probably a Heresy About Jesus, Says Survey." In *Christianity Today*, October 16, 2018. https://www. christianitytoday.com/news/2018/october/what-do-christians-believe -ligonier-state-theology-heresy.html.

Westminster Confession of Faith. bpc.org/wp-content/uploads/2015/06/ D-ConfessionOfFaith.pdf.

Zylstra, Sarah. 2019. "Gospel for Asia Settles Lawsuit with $37 Million Refund to Donors." In *Christianity Today*, March 01, 2019. www.christianitytoday.com/ news/2019/march/gospel-for-asia-gfa-settles-class-action-refund-donors.html.

4

How Exactly Do We Know What We Know about Kingdom Movements?

Gene Daniels

The evangelical missions world seems to thrive on controversy. One recent example can be seen in the way we—in the widest collective sense—have responded to reports of the tremendous growth of the church among Muslim peoples.

One of the first books on the scene was Jerry Trousdale's *Miraculous Movements* (2012). Others soon appeared, including David Garrison's well-known *A Wind in the House of Islam* (2014). These authors used different approaches in their background research, but they painted similar pictures—pictures of large numbers of Muslims turning to Christ around the world. Today there are many reports, mostly unpublished, coming from the field, often containing some very large numbers. These reports argue that the trend is continuing and even accelerating.

At first the reports of rapidly expanding kingdom movements were well-received, but slowly there has been pushback. One respectful example comes from a review of Trousdale's book:

> [The book] ask[s] us to believe these marvelous events are taking place without providing a means for us to study these movements for ourselves. The end result of this is that miraculous events require miraculous faith on our part.... . Now, I don't doubt the author's veracity, but good scholarship requires some type of documentation; otherwise it becomes a matter of "he said" and "she said." (Morton 2012)

As the numbers have grown, so has the skepticism about the reports, particularly about the nature of the proof that is being offered. But before we discuss issues of proof, or lack thereof, this would be a good place to put some actual numbers into this contentious conversation.

Church Growth among Muslims

We would do well to consider the current reports of kingdom movements among Muslims within their historical context. Although the church has a long history of encounter with the Islamic world, the year 1850 serves as a good starting point for our purposes because it seems to be approximately when Protestants began reporting Muslim conversions as other than rare anomalies, based on David Garrison's work (2014, 12–14).

Figure 4.1 shows the number of Muslim Background Believers (MBBs), from 1850 to 1980.

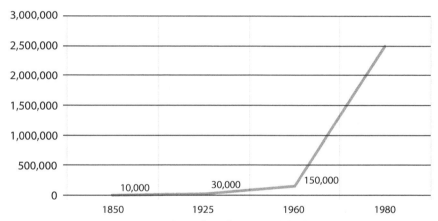

Figure 4.1 Estimated Number of MBBs Worldwide 1850–1980

A few comments are in order. First, throughout the nineteenth century there were scattered reports of converts, particularly when missionary activity was sponsored by colonial powers. This included, among others, Egypt (Sharkey 2009), North Africa (Motadel 2012), West Africa (Walls 1999), and Indonesia (Aritonang and Steenbrink 2008). However, in Indonesia and West Africa, which reported the most converts, it isn't always clear if these individuals were actually former Muslims or if they were converting from tribal religions. Therefore, we should use a very conservative estimate of the total number of Muslim Background Believers in 1850 to be roughly ten thousand.[1]

Second, Garrison's sources yield a number for circa 1925 of somewhere between eighteen thousand and twenty-eight thousand. He identified this growth taking place primarily in Ethiopia (Crummey 1972) and among the Kabyle in North Africa (Garrison 2014, 15).

---

1 It is unclear what research methods were used as the basis for these reports, although interviews with missionaries played a major role.

Third, we see an uptick immediately after 1960, due largely to the rapidly increasing numbers of MBBs in Indonesia (Garrison 2014, 13; Aritonang and Steenbrink 2008). The final source of data for 1960 and 1980 is drawn from the landmark study, "Believers in Christ from a Muslim Background: A Global Census" (Miller and Johnstone 2015).

Figure 4.2 takes us into the twenty-first century and includes data from the movements which are the primary concern of this chapter.

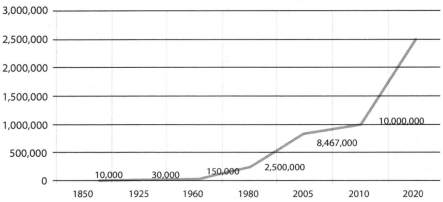

Figure 4.2 Estimated Number of MBBs Worldwide 1850–2020

The data for years 2005 and 2010 are drawn again from the study by Miller and Johnstone.[2] As a brief aside, of the estimated 10 million MBBs in 2010, approximately 7 million were in Indonesia alone! And finally, the estimate of MBBs for 2020 comes from a presentation by Justin Long on behalf of the 24:14 Network at the Vision 5:9 Network Assembly in Malta (Long 2019).

In his chapter in this volume, "How Movements Count," Justin Long explains the methods that movements use to count their members. This shows how most of the 2005–20 data was generated. However, the problem remains that this data is inaccessible to most people, due to very real security concerns. The data is embedded in a chain of trusted relationships, and unless someone is willing to invest years in developing their own part of that chain, they won't get anywhere close to the original field-data sources.

I have had the privilege of working with some of these movement leaders and reviewing some of the source data for their ministry reports. What I've seen affirms the picture being shared with the missions community. However, my personal opinion about the integrity of those specific reports does not change the fact that those with concerns have no way to verify the underlying empirical data.

---

2 Miller and Johnstone point out that the apparent change in the rate of growth between 2005 and 2010 is the result of a very cautious extrapolation of their data rather than a true decline in the rate of conversions. For 2010, they give a range of seven million to seventeen million MBBs worldwide. If the graph had been made using the middle of that range, the dip would disappear.

Groups of people coming to Christ in contexts hostile to that faith are a perfect example of what sociologists call a "hidden population," or more specifically, a kind of hidden population known as "social deviants." Muslim converts to Christ are a classic example of this since they deviated from acceptable social norms when they turned to Christ. And research among social deviants is always problematic because they are usually stigmatized, or even actively persecuted, and thus they prefer to remain hidden. Furthermore, formal verification of such data would require a known sample size, or at least a very close approximation, which is an impossible task due to the very nature of the converts' hiddenness (Salganik and Heckathorn 2004).

Although this may not satisfy those who have criticized the reports, it does remind us that the problem is not at all limited to research about movements in the Muslim world. Data "verification" or "confirmation" will never be satisfied when we are studying people who live outside of the social mainstream.

So what are we to do? By *we*, I mean the widest collective sense of the missions community: the researchers, field missionaries, funders, and other stakeholders. Are we forced into a binary choice—i.e., either to blindly believe or empirically reject these wonderful reports? I suggest the answer lies in using a different lens to evaluate what we are seeing.

The Impact of Epistemology

The matter at hand is a question of epistemology—i.e., the "area of philosophy that is concerned with the creation of knowledge, focusing on how knowledge is obtained and investigating the most valid way to reach the truth" (Truncellito n.d.). Epistemology directly addresses the fundamental issue tramping around our conversations like a circus elephant on the loose: How can we know if the reports of large kingdom movements in the Muslim world are true and believable?

Many people seem to make up their minds on this question based on whether or not verifiable empirical evidence is available to them personally. This is a form of deductive reasoning in which evidence is accumulated until we can prove, or disprove, something. However, it is also a very individualistic type of deduction, because it assumes that each individual is the arbitrator of truth.

Furthermore, this is a problematic way of generating knowledge about movements because of the security issues that I mentioned earlier. So rather than wrestling over the lack of data publicly available for individual deduction, I suggest we turn to a completely different way of thinking about these reports.

Inductive Reasoning

When faced with reports that are difficult to verify empirically, people often intuitively use something other than deductive logic—i.e., inductive reasoning. Deductive and inductive reasoning provide different grounds for belief. Deduction is a means by which we can prove, or disprove, a particular case from the study of the empirical evidence associated with it. However, juxtaposed to this is inductive reasoning, in which we attempt to draw a conclusion from facts or observations.

Many people default to deductive reasoning because it proposes to give "total support" for the conclusions drawn from it[3] (Hawthorne 2018). On the other hand, inductive reason does not purport to prove anything. Rather, induction is a means for deciding whether or not it is *reasonable* to believe something. This is done by considering any facts or observations available to us that have a bearing on the issue. These become the logical premise of our induction. Good inductive reasoning uses strong premises to provide good reasons to reach a conclusion—such as to believe, or disbelieve, a report (Hawthorne 2018). An illustration may be in order.

Suppose for a moment that a thirteen-foot-long great white shark was reported along the southeast coastline of the United States. This would catch your attention if you were planning your summer vacation in that area. You would probably read everything in the news about the sighting, and you might even read up on the probability of shark attacks. But you wouldn't likely feel the need to verify the reported size of the shark or where it was seen. Why? Because it is fairly common knowledge that great white sharks do indeed reach such great size, and because great whites have been spotted fairly often in those particular coastal waters in the past.

Therefore, using inductive reasoning, it seems quite *reasonable* to believe that a large shark was seen there again. Your induction would not prove the presence of the large predator, nor would it verify the shark's exact size if indeed the shark was present. But your induction would give you reasons to believe the report you heard.

This is what is known as "sample-based induction" (Parrish 2018). In this model of logic, the conclusion was not based on empirical evidence about a particular shark, which would be deduction; the conclusion, rather, was based on what is known about great white sharks, in general, from verified reports in the past.

This form of logic is as old as Socrates, and it is so ubiquitous in our thought patterns that we are seldom aware of when we shift from deduction to induction. We often don't feel a need to verify something (deductive reasoning) because we are already aware of facts or observations that give us a solid basis for forming a conclusion (inductive reasoning). Using this form of logic helps us decide whether or not it is *reasonable* to accept a particular report (Parrish 2018).

This, of course, begs this question: Are there any facts or observations from missions history that could help us form a conclusion about the reports from the Muslim world we are hearing now?

---

3   This is a very problematic assertion that ignores a myriad of practical and theoretical problems. But that is beyond the scope of this chapter.

Episodes of Growth in Frontier Missions

In order to justify the shift from empirical evidence to sample-based inductive reasoning as a means for generating what we know about movements, there would need to be episodes of growth in mission history that bear significant resemblance to the church growth currently being reported in the Muslim world. I believe there are at least two well-known cases we can turn to.

The first is the earliest expansion of the church throughout the Roman Empire (AD 40–250). If ever the church pursued its mission in a hostile environment, this would certainly be the exemplar.

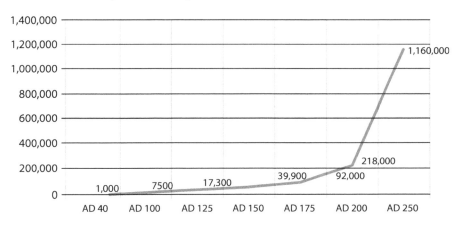

Figure 4.3 Early Church in the Roman Empire

This graph covers approximately two hundred years. It is, of course, based on estimations—in particular, those made famous by Rodney Stark in his book *The Rise of Christianity* (1997, 13). Also, I have chosen to use 250 AD as a cutoff point because it was before the Edict of Toleration issued by Galerius in 311 AD (Williams 1997, 899). As such, all the growth represented in the graph occurred while the church was still under various local restrictions and subject to various waves of persecution. This helps sharpen the comparison with growth in the Muslim world.

A second frontier-mission growth rate we can examine is that of the Protestant church in China. Below is a graph of that growth over approximately 140 years.

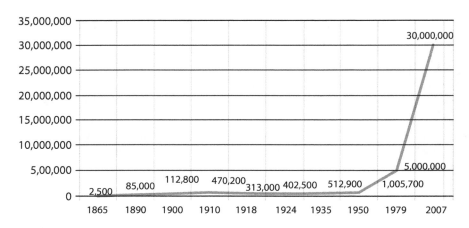

Figure 4.4 Protestant Churches in China

Several things should be noted about this graph. First, the nature of the underlying data for this graph is much closer to that informing the graph of church growth in the Muslim world. Whereas the data from the early Roman-era church was estimated based on historical retrospection, the majority of the data for China is actual. While it was assembled by Stark and Wang in their book *A Star in the East* (2015), the data for the years 1860 to 1950 was recorded by missionaries, for their agency reports, in real time.[4] Therefore, it was subject to the same questions and supposed problems concerning accuracy as we now hear about reports from the Muslim world. Yet in the case of the China data, we have the luxury of hindsight to see that it was, indeed, generally correct. The data for 1979 and 2007 are estimates made by Bays (2012) and Stark and Wang (2015), respectively.

Note also that the next-to-last year on this graph, 1979, was the year that many Chinese clergy were released from prisons around the country and there was a general easing of restrictions on Christian worship (Stark and Wang 2015, 69). Thus, we could consider this year to be a rough parallel to the Edict of Toleration in AD 311. Therefore, Figure 4.4 also visualizes growth that happened while the church was still facing significant persecution.

---

4 The reference information on the specific agency reports behind the data can be found on p. 127 of *A Star in the East*.

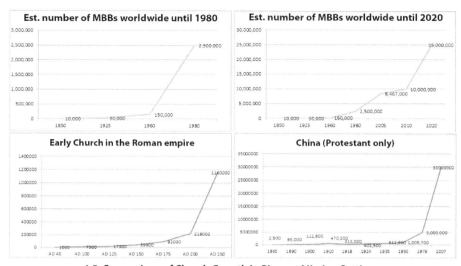

4.5 Comparison of Church Growth in Pioneer Mission Settings

The similarity of these charts is hard to miss. All of them graphically portray the principal of exponential growth—i.e., growth in which the rate of change is proportional with respect to the time. Charts of exponential growth start slowly, remaining nearly flat for significant periods of time, before turning up quickly (Chen 2020). In each scenario here, we see decades of slow growth followed by dramatic upturns.

Now let us apply the framework of inductive reasoning. First, all three graphs represent church growth in pioneer mission settings. Second, they all show growth during periods of reoccurring persecution against the new church. And third, we can have a high degree of confidence in using the two for comparison because history has verified them.

Therefore, these observations from missions history form a logical premise from which we may draw a conclusion. Although we have only examined two historical observations, their similarities to the current reports makes it *reasonable to* believe the overall pattern of growth being reported in the Muslim world is accurate.

There are two points in that last statement which should be unpacked. First, what we are saying is reasonable to believe is the overall picture emerging of exponential church growth in the Muslim world, not any particular report. And second, describing something as "reasonable" differs from claiming it to be "proven." The language of "proof" is rooted in the epistemology of empiricism, which I have argued is a poor fit for approaching the issue at hand.

Reason, on the other hand, simply means that a conclusion is based on solid logic, which in this case we have demonstrated from sample-based inductive reasoning. Therefore, when we shift to reasoning inductively, we find the patterns of church growth in the Muslim world not as hard to believe, even when we cannot personally verify them.

Summary

The goal of Motus Dei is to encourage robust academic dialogue concerning the gospel movements being reported around the world. One characteristic of robust academic discussion is that we carefully consider the epistemological frameworks which we have instinctively brought into our conversations.

We began with the issue of skepticism in the mission community concerning reports of large kingdom movements around the Muslim world. We also saw that a major point of contention is that the empirical data which supports these reports is largely unverifiable, due to legitimate security concerns. We noted that challenges like these are common in research dealing with social deviants. Then we charted about 170 years of church growth in the Muslim world so we could graphically represent the reported growth that is being contested.

We then explored one way people deal with data that they cannot verify empirically—i.e., the intuitive shift to evaluation based on inductive reasoning. Inductive logic does not prove any particular fact or incident, as empirical evidence purports to do; however, it can tell us if something is, or is not, reasonable.

We then looked at graphs of church growth from two other frontier mission situations: the Roman Empire and modern China. These bore a striking similarity to the pattern of growth being reported today in the Muslim world, because they all represent classic examples of exponential growth. Thus, we have argued that based on mission history, the overall picture presented by these reports is indeed reasonable, even if they are not currently "provable."

I realize that some people will find the shift from an epistemology of empirical proof to one of reasonableness difficult to accept. However, if we remember that we commonly use this form of logic in our daily lives, it might be easier to accept its validity regarding what God is doing in the Muslim world today.

References

Aritonang, Jan Sihar, and Karel Steenbrink. 2008. *A History of Christianity in Indonesia*. Leiden: Brill.

Bays, Daniel H. 2011. *A New History of Christianity in China*. Malden, MA: Wiley-Blackwell.

Chen, James. "2020. Exponential Growth." *Investopedia*. https://www.investopedia.com/terms/e/exponential-growth.asp.

Crummey, Donald. "Shaikh Zakaryas: An Ethiopian Prophet." *Journal of Ethiopian Studies*. Vol. 10, no. 1 (January 1972): 55–66.

Long, Justin. "Movements to Christ." 2019. Vision 5:9 Network Assembly, Malta, February 21.

Hawthorne, James. 2018. "Inductive Logic." *Stanford Encyclopedia of Philosophy*, https://plato.stanford.edu/entries/logic-inductive/.

Kreeft, Peter, and Trent Doughtery. 2010. *Socratic Logic*. Homer Glenn, IL: St Augustine's Press.

Miller, Duane Alexander, and Patrick Johnstone. 2015. "Believers in Christ from a Muslim Background: A Global Census." *Interdisciplinary Journal of Research on Religion*. Vol. 11, Article 10.

Morton, Jeffry. 2012. Book review of *Miraculous Movements*. *Journal of Biblical Missiology*, October 8, 2012. https://biblicalmissiology.org/2012/10/08/book-review-miraculous-movements-how-hundreds-of-thousands-of-muslims-are-falling-in-love-with-jesus/.

Motadel, David. 2012. "Islam and the European Empires." *The Historical Journal*. Vol. 55, no. 3: 832–56.

Parrish, Shane. 2018. "Deductive vs. Inductive Reasoning: Making Smarter Arguments, Better Decisions, and Stronger Conclusions." *Farnam Street Blog*, May 2018, https://fs.blog/2018/05/deductive-inductive-reasoning/.

Salganik, Matthew J., and Douglas D. Heckathorn. 2004. "Sampling and Estimation in Hidden Populations Using Respondent-Driven Sampling." *Sociological Methodology*. Vol. 34: 193–239. https://www.jstor.org/stable/3649374.

Sharkey, Heather J. 2009. "An Egyptian in China: Ahmed Fahmy and the Making of 'World Christianities.'" *Church History*. Vol. 78, no. 2: 309–26.

Stark, Rodney. 1997. *The Rise of Christianity*. San Francisco: HarperColins.

Stark, Rodney, and Xiuhua Wang. 2015. *A Star in the East*. West Conshohocken, PA: Templeton Press.

Truncellito, David. n.d. "Epistemology." *Internet Encyclopedia of Philosophy*, ISSN 2161-0002. https://iep.utm.edu/.

Walls, Andrew. 1999. "Africa as the Theatre of Christian Engagement with Islam." *Journal of Religion in Africa*. Vol. 29, Fasc. 2 (May 1999): 155–74.

Williams, Robert Lee. 1997. "Persecution." In *Encyclopedia of Early Christianity*, edited by Everett Ferguson. London: Routledge.

5

How Movements Count

Justin D. Long

Over 1,020 church planting movements (rapidly multiplying groups that have surpassed four generations of church planting in multiple streams) have been documented.[1] Together, they comprise over 73 million believers in over 4.3 million churches.

When people hear this fact, they often ask, How are they counted? One implication of this question is: Are they counted in a way that others can accept as credible? As a basis for an answer, let's begin with a broader question: How do Christian denominations, in general, count their members? How, for example, do denominations in America count?

How United States Denominations Count

Denominations, or groups of churches, in the US use various means to gather these statistics. These methods vary significantly with the size of each denomination.

Most denominations count one or both of two different types of numbers. *Attendees* is usually a broader and more complex number, encompassing seekers, children, and new believers who have not yet met the requirements for membership. This is usually counted as the number of people regularly in a worship service. *Members* is usually a smaller number of people who have reached some formal stage (such as baptism).

For example, the Albanian Orthodox Diocese of America counts attendees as the average number of people (including children) who attend liturgy

---

1 This chapter first appeared in *Accel* Volume 1, Issue 2, November 2019, pages 16–20 www.accelmag.org. It is reprinted by permission.

(the main weekly worship service) on a non-festival Sunday—that is, people who come to the main service on a day other than Christmas or Easter. The Allegheny Wesleyan Methodist Conference measures *attendees* as "average Sunday morning attendance," and *members* as "those whose name are on the attendance roll." Not every denomination counts both attendees and members.

Denominational statistics are usually gathered by means of some form of survey instrument—paper or electronic—which each church self-completes and returns to the denominational headquarters. Here are four examples ranging over various sizes and denominational flavors in the US.

The *Assemblies of God* (3.2 million members) asks churches to report the total each church considers members, regardless of age, as of December 31. As their researchers told me, "This definition provides a lot of leeway for the local church." *Adherents* includes all who "consider the church their home church, whether or not they are enrolled as members." Surveys are collected via both hardcopy and online options. Responses are checked if there appear to be significant discrepancies, usually by a phone call or by checking with district staff who have a closer working relationship with pastors.

Church of the Nazarene (0.8 million members) reports are self-filed by churches. No one attempts to audit; researchers make sure the numbers add up, starting with the membership number of each church from the previous year and adding the gains and subtracting the losses to make up the new total. If numbers don't add up, an email is sent or a phone call is made to clarify.

The *Southern Baptist Convention* (16 million members) uses the Annual Church Profile form to collect statistical data on all member churches. The form is returned via paper or online options. As with all denominations, not all churches fill it out every year. Returned data are compared against previous years to check for outliers; unclear data are usually referred back to state conventions for clarification.

The *United Methodist Church* (6 million members) groups churches into districts and annual conferences. Each church self-reports, typically using an online form. They submit their data to their district, who aggregates it for the conference, where it is aggregated for the national headquarters. A statistical team reviews the data, and if any major variances are identified, they ask the annual conference to clarify. This usually involves a phone call to the district or individual church.

In nearly every US denomination, either the church is small enough to have a specific list of all members (a "membership roll"), or it is large enough that churches report using the "honor system"—"we trust you to turn in accurate (if not necessarily precise) statistics using a fairly broad definition." Unclear data are clarified via phone or email. "We are not the IRS [Internal Revenue Service]," one denominational researcher told me. "We don't randomly select churches for an audit and send teams out to verify numbers. Besides, checking Sunday attendance isn't really enough [to determine total members]: you'd have to call every member to verify."

This highlights a complexity of denominational statistics. Attendance is a fairly easy number to estimate, even if it is not necessarily precise: just get a rough count of the number of people in a Sunday morning service. Membership, on the other hand, implies a commitment, and can introduce nuance. When does membership begin, and when does it end? If someone stops attending a church, and switches to a different church, they don't always announce this fact. How many absences should be allowed before they are "struck from the rolls"? Are people ever struck from the rolls? How long does it take after a death? What if people go to one church on Sunday morning and another church on Saturday night? (This happens when children, for example, attend another church's youth group.) These kinds of situations make statistical boxes difficult.

Moreover, *membership* usually introduces significant debates over who should be counted. One example of this is found in the article "Meaningless Membership".[2] The author compares attendance to membership and asks, "Convention-wide [in the Southern Baptist Convention], there are 16 million members. But only 6 million people show up on a typical Sunday. Where are the other 10 million Southern Baptists? Some are providentially hindered, but surely not 10 million."

How Movements Count

Movements, like US denominations, wish to count their members. There are several reasons for counting, but four seem to be common to most movements. First, movements emphasize growth, and they want to see if they are growing. Second, by counting members in various streams, problems (which can be identified in part by a correlation in lack of multigenerational growth) can be identified and addressed. Third, movements generally don't count to measure themselves in terms of their own growth, but rather to measure themselves against the surrounding non-Christian populations. The question they are trying to answer is, Are we making progress in reaching the lost? Fourth, some movements use this counting for reports to their partners in areas such as prayer, projects, and funding.

Three forms of "counting" are generally found.

1. Small Movements
Method 1—We know everyone in the movement, whether or not we document them on a membership roll.

---

2 Al Jackson, *9 Marks*, http://bit.ly/2MPDJ6u, April 28, 2011.

Some movements or premovements are small enough (under one thousand members, for example) that all the groups, leaders, and even members can be known. Perhaps the stories of the individual leaders can be recounted. (For example, "This man came to faith because that grandmother prayed for his healing and he was healed. Then he shared with his brother, and their whole family came to faith.") In their small numbers, they can easily be counted on a spreadsheet or a series of diagrams on papers. This is similar in practice to the "membership rolls" of smaller US denominations.

2. Moderately Large Movements

Method 2—Each of the various streams within a movement know their members very well, and their numbers are aggregated to count the whole.

Some movements or premovements are too large to easily have everyone listed on a spreadsheet. (This "too large" threshold is often reached when a movement grows to the size of thousands of members, and definitely reached at the ten-thousand-member level.) Particular streams or portions of the movement, however, can be small enough individually to be similar to small movements above. They can aggregate their own numbers, and then each stream's total can be counted together to come up with totals for the movement as a whole.

This process is similar to large US denominations that divide their churches into districts. Some streams might need to break their counts down further as they, in turn, get too large to count individually. However, when movements have thousands or tens of thousands of adherents, their individual streams are mostly "small-ish" and can be easily counted.

As movements become larger, they can encounter issues of security and technical logistics that make data collection risky or difficult. In a restricted-access area, a large data set of several thousand people can be very risky indeed. In places with very little technology or even very little literacy, the idea of gathering even sheets of paper might be challenging.

Because of these factors, a movement might decide to estimate their numbers based on data points like "the average number of people discipled by a leader" or "the average number of people in a group." These sorts of estimates are just as *accurate* as any American denominational count (such as, "We have ten churches, and each church has about two hundred people"), although they might be less *precise* (see discussion of accuracy and precision below).

For example, I helped one movement estimate its total membership at between 8 and 12 million people. The estimate was made on the basis of the number of leaders, the number each discipled on average, a survey of the number of "generations" of leaders in each stream, and the geographic spread of the movement, with an estimate of its saturation of individual districts. The estimate, with a range of millions, was a truthful and accurate statement, but obviously very imprecise.

3. Very Large Movements

Method 3—We are large enough to have the resources to invest in complex and regular counts.

Some movements are *very large*: organized in the millions, they are the equivalent of any national denomination in the United States or elsewhere (Southern Baptists, Assemblies of God, etc.). Because of their size, they have the resources to make a heavy investment in counting and doing a regular census of their members (which is something very few American denominations actually do).

To accomplish this, a research team physically visits most leaders and completes a survey to gather both quantitative and qualitative data. This can result in numbers that are both accurate and very precise and that are frequently updated. Such numbers are also, for obvious reasons, highly sensitive. Very large censuses are also complex processes that are difficult for smaller groups to implement.

Reliability

We know movements count their people in ways similar to how counts are made in other parts of the world. This similarity is natural: when adding up the number of people in a set and recording them, similar problems are encountered around the world and solved in similar ways. Are the counts reliable and credible? To answer that, we need to consider the various reasons why someone might look at a number and respond, "That's just got to be *wrong*."

Mistakes of Definition

Misunderstandings can happen when someone gives a number without explaining what that number is. For instance, is it *attendees* or *adherents*?

This can be especially true of movements that have both "churches" and "seeker groups." Such movements often bring "prebelievers" who are spiritually hungry together in groups to explore Scripture stories. Eventually these "seeker groups" (often named differently in different movements) will either disintegrate due to lack of interest, or their members will become believers and form a church.

"Seeker groups" are therefore closer to "attendees" in a Western church. Movements don't typically report those numbers. They are in constant flux.

Movements, when reporting, usually provide "churches" and "adherents," but the exact definition of "adherent" will vary from place to place. Generally, the majority of adherents are baptized believers. In some movements, however, believers might take a long time to be baptized, for a variety of reasons. Some movements report children, and some don't (as with some American denominations). Some count "adults" at a much lower age than the typical American denomination would.

As with all research, when examining or comparing numbers, it's important to know the definitions.

Accuracy, Precision, and Rounding

In the *World Christian Encyclopedia*, some denominations report their membership to the last digit; others round the number (usually to the nearest thousand). The difference between exact and rounded numbers is not *accuracy*, but rather *precision*. To say a denomination has 952 or 950 or 1,000 adherents is to make a true, accurate statement within the same order of magnitude, with varying levels of precision.

To use a different example: If my daughter asks me what time it is, and I reply "It's a quarter to ten," when the time is 9:43, I am not *lying*—I am being *imprecise*, but "close enough."

Variances in precision appear in all sorts of counts. The difference between 21 million and 20 million is less important than the difference between 20 million and 200,000. Similarly, if a given number is thought to be in the tens of millions, but precision is difficult, it might be enough to know whether it is on the low end (10 to 20 million) or on the high end (70 to 80 million).

Regardless of how denominations report their information, we need to keep in mind our own biases: A very precise number can give a false impression of precision. For many denominations—especially movements—the number of members is constantly changing. New people are joining, others are defecting; some are being born, some are dying. We need, therefore, to hold any single number loosely, and preferably to report in a rounded form (as I do, when I say there are over 73 million members of movements around the world).

Exaggeration

Occasionally, some have told me they believe the numbers in a movement are exaggerated. The primary motivation for movements to exaggerate their numbers would be financial: high numbers could be used in fundraising appeals. We have not seen any evidence for this in the movements we have documented. In fact, we have often seen movements intentionally *undercount*. Sometimes this means setting aside from the count portions of the movement which they feel aren't adequately researched, or for which the numbers aren't really certain. In some movements, counts are reduced by a percentage out of concern for error rates in the count method.

Further, our research has shown most movements fund the vast majority of their ministries internally. The percentage of outside money is minimal, especially when considered proportionally to the size of the larger movements. In other words, if their goal was to raise money by exaggerating their numbers, they would be doing a poor job.

For most movements, exaggeration isn't an issue due to their small size. The vast majority of individual movements are around the one-thousand-member level, and the members can be known, as we have highlighted above.

Finally, we have documented movements in five-year increments as they grew from 1990 to 2020. Movements have followed a variety of patterns of growth—plateauing and ending over those periods of time. Movements do not follow any lockstep patterns of growth that would indicate engineered numbers.

Deception

A final claim, occasionally leveled at movements, is that they are the fruit of outright deception. Either the accuser, or someone the accuser knows, "has been in the area," and "nothing is happening there."

When I have dug into such accusations, I have never found deception to be the case. In a few instances, when deception has been found in part of a movement, the movement leaders have publicly admitted it and corrected their reports. In my experience, movement leaders are highly motivated to find any deception.

Frequently, outside accusations of deception seem not to be based on any evidence other than that the accuser, or their colleagues, have been in the area without seeing similar results or evidence of the movement. They typically ignore that these movements are usually in extremely high-risk areas. If these budding plants are to survive, they have to become adept in hiding their existence from governments and religious leaders. Many movements have had leaders "stolen" by mainstream public churches, often through offering salaries. Some have had their groups labeled as "heretical" and reported to the government by other believers. Westerners have gotten "in the know," and then without discretion have shared what they know, sometimes with very detrimental consequences. And most of all, many of these movements are so contextual that outsiders often don't recognize them as Christian. Communities of people who dress in local fashions, gather and eat in local ways, and use local music do not look like what outsiders think of as "church." For all these reasons, movements are often invisible to outsiders.

The one thousand plus movements we have documented have each had multiple contacts with selected groups of trusted friends. This web of trust includes people from many different nations, mission organizations, denominations, and backgrounds. Our team has usually discovered them by being within reach of such a trusted relationship (otherwise we too would likely not know about them). In most of the larger movements, we have personally met with leaders at various levels who are working in very difficult situations, with significant security risks and very little money involved.

We have shared meals with earnest church planters who have shown us the scars of persecution. They have told us many stories, including their mistakes and failures, involving details that are too bizarre to make up. The similar patterns and details across unconnected movements add to the ring of authenticity.

Conclusion

Over one thousand movements have been identified in the world. Each of them falls into general-size categories of "small" (around one thousand members), "medium" (some thousands to tens of thousands), or "large" (over one hundred thousand to some millions).

All movements, in some way or another, with some regularity, attempt a count of their membership, for a variety of reasons. They use methods similar to Western denominations, with similar levels of accuracy. Precision falls off with increases in size, which is to be expected.

Movements are loath to share this kind of information with outsiders, because it can be misused and represents a significant security risk. Movements are often "hidden" from outsiders, and the security risks often make third-party vetting of the information challenging, if not impossible. Yet, at the same time note that outsiders do not usually see the need to vet or audit the information of Western denominations.

In general, the same methods applied to Western denominations are applied to movements and should be accorded similar assessments of their accuracy.

PART II
Missional Theology of Movements

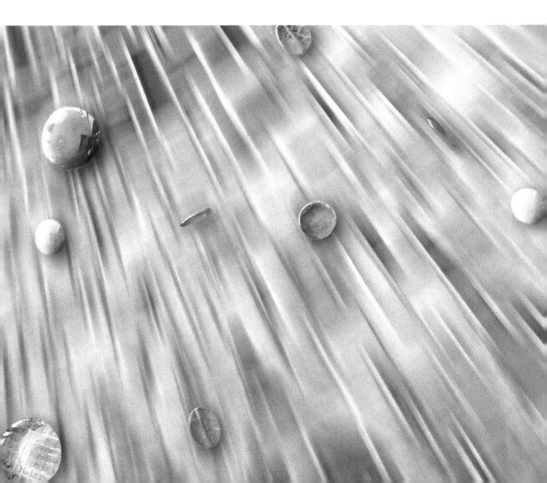

6

A Biblical Missiology of Kingdomization through Disciple Multiplication Movements of House Church Networks

David S. Lim

How should the global church understand and implement missio Dei to actualize the kingdom of God, so the will of God will be done on earth as it is in heaven (Matt 6:9–10)? What should our biblical vision and our mission strategy look like?

I believe the Bible reveals that God has a *simple* plan for world evangelization and transformation. The Scriptures clearly communicate that God desires all people to be saved (2 Pet 3:8–9) and to know the truth (1 Tim 2:3–5). I believe the all-loving and all-wise God has devised the *simplest* master plan to get the good news out to the whole world of fallen humanity. He did this by sending his Son Jesus not just to provide the way of redemption (cf. Gal 4:4), but also to model this strategic plan (Luke 7:20–23) and train his disciples how to implement this plan (Luke 9:1–6; 10:1–20) by the power of the Holy Spirit across the Roman Empire and the world (Acts 1:8; 8:4; 11:19–21; 19:1–10; Rom 15:18–20).

In this chapter, I will describe how I see *missio Dei*, as revealed in the Bible, in terms of its goal, structure, and strategy. I will attempt to show that instead of the predominant Christianization model, God's *simple* plan is "kingdomization." I share these as one of the indigenous leaders of a major house church network in Asia today.[1] Much of the missiology of movements has been written by Westerners, with a result that can tend to be dichotomistic and complex. I write as an Easterner, trying to harmonize different strategies and communicate them holistically and comprehensively. Movements don't have to be complicated, but it doesn't follow that they happen easily.

Simple Goal: Kingdomization, not Christianization

God desires to bless all peoples to inherit his eternal kingdom (reign) in heaven and experience his abundant life on earth, as they obey him as their Creator-King through their faith in His Son Jesus Christ. His goal is "kingdomization" or "societal transformation," by which individuals, families, communities, and institutions are enabled to relate with each other and with other communities with kingdom norms and values. In this age, this does not happen perfectly, but it does happen significantly. This involves building Christ-centered communities that grow in righteousness and justice, marked by self-giving love (*agape*), where every household (*oikos*)[2] will be blessed (cf. Gen 12:1–3). Righteousness refers to just (right) relationships, often summarized in one word: love—with God, with self, and with all people, especially those already in the kingdom (Gal 6:10). It also includes right relationship with creation. These relationships result from, and result in, God's peace (*shalom*).[3]

God clearly depicts his kingdom goal in Isaiah 65:17–25 (popularly called the "Isaiah 65 vision"), envisioning on earth a "new heavens and new earth." The first three verses describe the New Jerusalem as a "city of joy" where life is celebrated and God is delighted. Verse 20 sees people living long lives, presumably with healthy lifestyles, clean environments, and good governance, implying that the leaders are also godly and competent (cf. 1 Tim 2:1–2). Verses 21–22 show a society where social justice prevails, where each one's labor is rewarded accordingly, following the prophetic ideal of "each man sitting under his own vine and fig tree" with nothing to fear (Mic 4:4) and with the Mosaic laws of gleaning and the year of Jubilee enforced ("no poor people among you," Deut 15:4, cf. vv. 1–11; Lev 25). The next verse depicts prosperity passed on from one generation to the next, and the last verse describes harmony among animals, humans, and the whole creation. And verse 24 hints at a mature form of faith in the gracious God whose blessings do not need to be earned or pleaded for, religiously or otherwise (cf. Isa 58; Rev 21:22–27).

---

1 On HCNs in Asia, see Lim 2013, 2013b, and 2016; cf. Fukuda 2005, Choudhrie 2007, and Xin 2016.

2 *Oikos* is best translated as "household," for it is composed not just of the extended family but also of friends, tenants, and slaves, as seen in the instructions given in Eph 5:22–6:9 and Col 3:18–4:1 (cf. Lim 2017). This means that each *oikos* church crossed many cultural barriers, particularly gender, age, class, and ethnicity as they gathered and "broke bread" together around the same table as equals (cf. Gal 3:28).

3 On transformational mission, see Samuel and Sugden 1999.

However, historically, the church sadly pursued the "Christianization" vision, particularly in conceiving of its mission as a religious undertaking and its goal as building religious institutions (in short, to establish Christendom).[4] Rather than infiltrating and subverting the institutions and cultures, the Christian mainstream sought to establish its own institutions, thus maintaining subcultures separate from the pagan, religio-cultural and social orders in the world. This was based on three major shifts in their understanding of the kingdom of God, particularly in their concepts of holy people, holy places, and holy practices.

Holy People

First, God's kingdom is a royal priesthood of all believers (1 Pet 2:9–10, cf. Exod 19:5–6; Rev 5:10), but this was changed to the prevailing Christendom practice that only ordained clergy are "holy people" who can administer the sacraments, or ordinances. The New Testament (NT) church was a lay movement. They had no need for "ordained pastors."[5] The task of Spirit-gifted leaders is to equip "all the saints" to do the ministry, which is disciple-making or "spiritual reproduction/fruitfulness" (Eph 4:11–13). Each Christ-follower can be discipled to become an "elder of the city" who can be used by God to bless and transform their neighborhood and their workplace where Jesus can reign as Lord. And where Jesus reigns, God's kingdom (on earth) is realized.

This concept is important for effective kingdom expansion. Kingdomization should be realized simply by ordinary individuals and families who just do "zero-budget missions" (Luke 10:4a; Acts 3:6). The focus is on the glory of God (not any gifted human being) in the name of Jesus and by the power of the Holy Spirit (Acts 1:8; cf. Zech 4:6). Any Christ-follower can develop a simple (yet mature) faith with direct access to God and can represent him in whichever community, profession, and situation he places them in the world.

Holy Places

Secondly, all (secular) things on earth—including all natural (God-created) places, assets, and talents, and cultural (human-made) ideas, artifacts, gadgets, traditions, customs, worldviews, etc.—can be redeemed and sanctified through faith expressed in prayer to God in Jesus' name and obedience to his Word (1 Tim 4:4–5). Christ-followers rule with Christ in the heavenlies (Eph 2:6), yet grounded and rooted as salt and light (stars) in the socio-cultural structures of their times (Matt 5:13–16; Phil 2:14–16) without having to build physical structures related to their own gatherings. So there is no need to build religious facilities, for all properties of Christ-followers belong to (and can be used for) his

---

4 On the contrast between Christendom and "Servant Church," see Lim 1989.
5 On the historical development of ordination and clericalism in the post-apostolic church, see Lim 1987a.

kingdom (Acts 7:48; 17:24–28).[6] Worship can be done anytime and anywhere (John 4:21–24, cf. 1 Cor 10:31; Rom 12:1–8).

The goal is for all peoples to accept the kingdom's worldview and follow its lifestyle, which can be (and has been) contextually institutionalized into laws, policies, and structures. This can be achieved through the processes of evangelization and disciple-making—to form Christ-centered communities in any place, usually in residences (neighborhoods) and places of work or study (schools, factories, government offices, banks, stores, etc.). In all kinds of places, God's Word can be prayerfully discussed, applied, and lived out relevantly in people's daily lives. Any section or sector of creation can be sanctified and transformed into "holy ground" when people consciously and constantly live for his glory.

Holy Practices

The third distinctive kingdom feature is faith (worship) expressed in loving God through loving neighbors (Matt 22:37–39; 7:12), instead of doing religious rituals and ceremonies (Matt 6:1–18; 15:1–20; cf. Isa 58:1–12; Amos 5:21–24; Hos 6:6).[7] The proof of faith is love and good works (Heb 10:24; Eph 2:8–10; Jas 2:14–26), living the Micah 6:8 lifestyle: "act justly, love mercy and walk humbly with your God." In his inaugural address in Nazareth, Jesus taught that *missio Dei* was "to preach good news to the poor … and proclaim the year of the Lord's favor" (= Jubilee) (Luke 4:18–19). He had come to accomplish this mission so people could experience "everyday Jubilee" (cf. Lim 2019a). He performed good works as proof of his messianic identity to John the Baptist and his disciples (7:20–23).

Hence the visible expression of God's kingdom is to "love one another as I have loved you" (self-sacrificially) (John 13:34–35, cf. 1 John 3:16–18). In Matthew 25:31–46, Jesus taught that in the final judgment, God's standard for sheep to enter eternal life will be whether their faith worked out in love (Gal 5:6), particularly to the least of his family (the hungry, thirsty, strangers, naked, sick, prisoners). God's kingdom is a "bottom up" kingdom, where his blessings are generously shared and enjoyed, so no one is left behind poor (Matt 6:19–33; 19:21; Luke 6:20–26; cf. Acts 2:44–45; 4:34–37; 2 Cor 8:14–15).

Simple Structure: House Church Networks (HCNs)

What form, then, will God's kingdom take when it is manifested in any segment of the world? As the "second Adam," Jesus modeled not just a perfect person's character, but also a godly or righteous person's vocation for the kingdom (Acts 10:36–38). To work for the kingdom, he trained his disciples to form house church networks (HCNs) to transform the villages of Galilee by simply going forth without bringing outside resources into the community (Luke 10:4a).

6 Israel had only one temple, not one in each village, city, or region. On the multiple functions of the synagogues, see Lim 1987b.

7 On a biblical theology of "worship," see Lim 2008a.

He instructed them to find a "person of peace" (vv. 5–6) and disciple them in and through their home (vv. 4b–9). If they found no such household in a community, he told them to simply leave and go to another one (vv. 10–16).

Small (Oikos) Size

Jesus called twelve men to be his disciples, whom he turned into *apostles* ("missionaries" = disciple-makers; Mark 3:13–15)—to be sent out to make disciples—eventually to all nations. By this means the apostles and the early church extended the kingdom in and through house (*oikos*) churches across the Roman Empire and beyond. The formation of house churches (HCs) was the practical outcome of the priesthood of all believers. Each Christ-follower was empowered to use their homes to bless their neighbors where they lived (cf. 2 Tim 2:2).

Every believer was discipled to become "perfect/mature in Christ" (Col 1:28–29), with the confidence to serve as a priest (minister) of God in and through their home. (The Reformation recovered the doctrine of the priesthood of all believers, but failed to implement it.[8]) The New Testament describes disciples being made in small groups: each must grow in love, so they must practice and experience intimate relationships, as they teach, correct, love, and confess sins to one another.

Cellular System

How then is the kingdom organized as it is implanted as small groups in society? Jesus did not form a formal structure, but introduced a cellular system that consists of the constant reproduction of "new wineskins" (Mark 2:22) in the structures of society. The early church had a cellular order, in which the church existed whenever a group gathered for mutual edification (cf. 1 Cor 14:26–40) in order to scatter to share Christ's love through good works in the world (cf. Heb 10:24; Matt 5:13–16) (cf. Lim 1987; Stark 1996 and 2006). Each cell formed a part of a house church network (HCN), similar to the decentralized system of (zero-budget) volunteer leaders that Jethro advised Moses to form (Exod 18:21), where authority rests on the lowest units ("leaders of tens") which are assisted by the "higher" coordinating units. This outworking and structure of Christ's body on earth differs from the denominational hierarchies of local churches with episcopal, presbyterian, or congregationalist structure.[9]

---

8 Martin Luther, in his preface to the *German Mass*, wrote: "Those who really want to be Christians and to confess the gospel in deed and word would have to enroll by name and assemble themselves apart in some house to pray, to read, to baptize, to receive the sacrament, and to do similar Christian works. For in such a regime it would be possible to discover and punish and correct and exclude those who do not behave as Christians and to excommunicate them according to Christ's rule in Matthew 18. Here, too, a common collection of alms could be enjoined on Christians to be given voluntarily and distributed to the poor following Paul's example in 2 Corinthians 9… . Here, baptism and the sacrament could be administered in a brief and simple manner and everything directed to the word and prayer and love."

9 Perhaps best articulated in Simson 2001, chap. 5.

What about accountability? Each one is accountable directly to our King Jesus, who commissioned each of his followers to make disciples of the nations. Each believer's house (*oikos*) is a "house of prayer for the nations," used to love, serve, bless, and improve the homes of others. Each believer is also accountable to their disciplers and disciples in mutual accountability, including to confess sins to one another and forgive the sins of one another.

Network (Flat) Structure

The kingdom's organic structure is *decentralized* in the form of networks of friendships among the disciples and servant leaders. No hierarchy gives permission or controls the church, for only Jesus is the Lord and foundation of his church through the Holy Spirit. All leaders in HCNs see themselves as "servants of God" whose only job description is to "equip all the saints to do the ministry" of disciple-making (Eph 4:11–13; 2 Tim 2:2), each according to the spiritual gifts that the Holy Spirit sovereignly distributes to build up the one Body (1 Cor 12:1–13), one temple (1 Pet 4:10–11), one kingdom. It is a flat structure where leaders view themselves as "first among equals" and empower others to become better than themselves (Phil 2:3–4).

HCNs are lay movements, and their leaders ("tentmakers") serve in various sectors of society—not in the clergy-led structures of Christendom. Each Christ-follower is discipled to be self-supporting through a means of livelihood (Eph 4:28). HCN leaders in Christendom (and Buddhist) contexts will have to gradually phase out the need for the clerical (and monastic) order, as they learn about the "priesthood of all believers." Though they may continue to be supported by "tithes and offerings" at the start,[10] they will each transition to a livelihood or trade (to serve as models; 2 Thess 3:6–12), for many, most likely, as teachers of philosophy and ethics. Those who have leadership qualities will naturally rise into management and governance positions in the community and marketplace, literally as (righteous) "elders of the city."

Simple Mission: Disciple Multiplication Movements

What, then, is the mission strategy of HCNs to expand the kingdom to the whole world? What Jesus did was to equip and send his disciples (at first two by two) out into their world (Mark 3:13–15), and later to all nations, to catalyze disciple multiplication movements.[11] They needed to find a "person of peace" (Luke 10:5–6) and disciple them to disciple their family, kin, friends, and neighbors (vv. 4b–9) wherever they went. Every believer can be trained and empowered (given authority) to multiply disciples where they live and work. This is God's

---

10 Like Jesus, some may go "full-time" when they have well-to-do disciples in their HCN (Luke 8:1–3) who can take care of their needs.

11 On Jesus' disciple-making strategy, see Coleman 1964. The concept of a disciple multiplication movement was first popularized by Dawson Trotman and the Navigators in 1933.

simple plan to evangelize and transform the world speedily. Ideally, each disciple multiplication movement should have the following characteristics.

Disciple-Making Ministry

First, HCs are actually "disciple-making groups," which may also be called "simple (or organic) churches," "basic ecclesial communities" (cf. Boff 1986), "kingdom cells," "care groups," etc. Each must be a *small* (not more than ten families) Christ-worshiping and Scripture-honoring body of believers who have covenanted to meet regularly and are willing to be held accountable for their Christ-centered lives to one another. The objective is for each disciple to develop a kingdom lifestyle that loves God and all humans with Christlike, self-denying, and self-giving love—24/7/365.

Life is relationships; the rest is just details. To disciple means to equip Christ-followers with three main relational "habits of holiness": (a) hearing **God** through prayerful meditation to turn his Word (*logos*) into a word (*rhema*) to be obeyed (2 Tim 3:16–17); (b) making disciples through leading a HC in Bible-and-life sharing, so each one learns how to do personal devotions (or "quiet time") with *fellow believers* (Heb 10:24; 1 Cor 14:26); and (c) doing friendship evangelism to share what they learn of God and his will with their **nonbelieving** networks.

The HCs may be: (a) residential, where its members meet in homes, living out their faith in their neighborhood (Eph 5:21–6:4); or, particularly in urbanized and industrialized centers, (b) professional contexts, where its members meet to witness to their faith in their place of work or study (Eph 6:5–18), for the transformation of all socio-cultural structures.

Spiritual Multiplication

Second, "disciples" are those willing not just to be mentored to form a more Christlike character and equipped to discover and minister with their spiritual gift(s), but also to be equipped to do evangelism and lead their own HCs. They should become a "disciple-maker," empowered to lead their own HCs and HCNs. They will seek to turn their contacts into friends and into converts through "friendship evangelism," then also into disciple-makers by equipping them and sending them to form their own HCNs.

Early phases of disciple-making should be finished normally in less than a year, so that the discipler can leave and make more disciples and start more HCNs. This should happen intentionally, as HC members are encouraged to disciple new believers in new (their own!) HCs, or to pair up to start new HCs in other contexts as soon as possible. At the start of each HC (say, the first month), it is best that they meet as often as possible (if possible, daily). After several months (maximum of one year), HCs can meet less regularly, say, monthly and then quarterly, and later annually or even just through correspondence and social media, where possible.

Incarnational Approach

Third, how can spiritual multiplication actually begin, especially in multi-cultural and multi-religious contexts? Jesus trained his disciples to do his simple strategy effectively (Luke 9:1–6; 10:1–17). He also illustrated it cross-culturally among the Samaritans (John 4) and in the Gentile Decapolis (Mark 5:1–20; 7:31–8:10). When entering other cultures, Paul practiced "becoming all things to all people" (1 Cor 9:20–23), "making himself a slave (*doulos*) among them" (v. 19). Among local converts, his simple strategy could be called "incarnational movements," which included three dimensions: incarnational (1 Cor 7:11–17), contextual (vv. 18–20), and transformational (vv. 21–24).[12] Like Jesus, Paul and the early church did not train their disciples to establish a structure separate from the communities and contexts in which they lived and worked.

Kingdomization is an occupation plan, not an evacuation plan (1 Cor 15:24–25; Phil 2:9–11), because Christ is ruler over all things (Col 1:16–17) (Taylor 2015, 377). Christ-followers sanctify nonbelievers (1 Cor 7:14) and food offered to idols (10:20–26), because all things can be purified (Titus 1:15) by prayer and the Word (1 Tim 4:4–5). Jesus Christ entered European pagan cosmologies and transformed them Christ-ward. New Christ-followers can continue to join in many of the activities and festivities of their community with a clear conscience. When they are confronted and asked about their motivation, they can then explain and witness to Christ, even if it may result in persecution. Meanwhile, they should have already been trained to make disciples relationally and naturally before such conflict arises.

Incarnational movements contrast with the approaches of Christendom's "imperial missions" that has made Jesus look aggressive, foreign, and irrelevant, especially in Asia (Lim 2011). Perhaps worst is the heavy burden the Christendom pattern imposes on new believers and churches, especially among the poor. They come to think they must invest their very limited resources in supporting the salaries and theological studies of their clergymen—buying property, constructing cathedrals, and financing their religious activities. All these things make them look insensitively rich (and irrelevant) in relation to the houses and facilities in their poor(er) neighborhoods. Most of these projects have been highly subsidized from abroad, especially by denominational partners, up to this day. Most of them don't even have small budgets for community services, unless they partner with some Christian development organization.

In contrast, the rich harvest that Jesus expected from his disciples is being reaped nowadays through the simple incarnational approach of HCNs. By following the instructions of Jesus in his "zero-budget missions" (Luke 10:4a), every disciple leads someone (usually a relative or new friend, called a "person of peace") to trust and obey King Jesus in love and good works. As they serve one another, the people (especially community leaders) around them take notice of "how they love

12 Paul considers this to be a universal principle, since he teaches this in all the churches (v. 17b).

one another" (and the neighborhood) and soon also ask for their help. With proper mentorship in place, they then naturally rise to become leaders in the community.

Contextual Spirituality

Fourth, what about the cultural forms, especially religious rituals and festivals of their families and communities? Christ-followers should be allowed to develop contextualized religious practices, retaining many of them and redefining them as Christ-centered and Christ-ward customs, while finding "functional substitutes" for those beliefs and values that are idolatrous and occultic (cf. 1 Cor 7:18–20). For instance, most popular practices in karmic cultures, including ancestral and merit-making practices, can be simplified. Some may eventually be phased out as disciples live out the logic of non-samsaric and post-animistic worldviews, as they reflect prayerfully on the Word (Lim 2019; Fukuda 2012, 183–92).

Disciple multiplication movements sometime become more biblical and Christ-centered than the tradition-laden and liturgy-oriented denominations in today's uncontextualized and Westernized Christendom. They gradually learn how to get rid of anything sinful: idolatry, individualism, immorality, and injustice. Contextuality should also mark the HC meetings, with the free mixture of activities according to the needs and gifts of the participants, as set by the leader(s) in close consultation with all the members. Following the 1 Corinthians 14:26–40 pattern of meeting, all members come prepared to "spur one another to love and good works" (Heb 10:24) in their body-life together. In literate cultures, Christ-followers can go through any biblical text according to the needs and interests of the people present. In oral cultures, they can learn about Jesus and his teachings through storying, singing, and drama, which can more easily lead to worldview change (Evans 2008). Nowadays they can also download the Jesus Film and film clips from www.jesusfilm.org and www.indigitube.tv, with translations available in over 1,600 languages.

Concerning water baptism and the Eucharist, we prefer that disciples discover these commands as they read the Scriptures. We introduce these biblical practices sensitively (as in the New Testament), hoping not to cause extraction or expulsion from their family and community. Women and young converts need training in how to lead the head of their families to Christ.

Transformational Development

Fifth, what is the ultimate ideal of fulfilling Jesus' disciple multiplication movement to realize "everyday Jubilee"? The HCNs will ultimately help their societies have a simple yet profound religiosity marked by "loving one another" as members of one big family, as Christ loves us (John 13:34–35; 1 John 3:16–18). This may be most concretely expressed in the "common purse" of the earliest church's "caring and sharing economy" (Acts 2:42–47; 4:32–37; 6:1–7; cf. 2 Cor 8–9), for sustainability and socio-economic development where no one is left behind.

As each disciple grows in Christlikeness, they will be liberated from sin and selfishness to become more generous, more caring toward and sharing with their neighbors, which is the "agape" law of Christ (Gal 5:13–23; 6:1–2; Rom 13:8–10). They are discipled to do acts of kindness and justice locally and globally, which nowadays is called "transformational development," or "integral mission" (Lim 2019a).

This spirituality translates into discipling and transforming the global economic system too. Many HC leaders are involved in Christian development organizations that are already leading in building the third (other than capitalism and socialism) alternative economic order called the "solidarity economy." This equips and empowers the poor through social entrepreneurship and fair trade, so each person can have their own land (Lev 25) and their own "vine and fig tree" (Mic 4:4) to pass on to the next generations (Isa 65:21–23).

For instance, the HCNs that had "gospel explosion" in six big provinces in China spread from village to village through the witnessing lifestyles of ordinary Christ-followers who were known for their serving, caring, and hard work in their neighborhoods/communes. Even Communist cadres and leaders became "secret believers" in these HCNs (cf. Hattaway 2003).

Minimal Religiosity

Sixth and finally, disciple multiplication movements will result in HCNs whose spirituality requires minimal public religious practices. Following Christ does not require public displays of religiosity—in fact, Jesus discouraged such (Matt 6:1–18), which included alms-giving, praying, and fasting, which God rewards when done in secret. As each Christ-follower walks humbly and simply, 24/7, for God's glory (1 Cor 10:31; Mic 6:8), their community leaders will (ideally) establish *shalom*, in which their constituents enjoy life with love and justice (1 Tim 2:1–2). Their spirituality does not need to develop elaborate liturgies and hierarchies (cf. Amos 5:21–24; Ps 131). In my view, disciples simply need to maintain the three "habits of holiness" mentioned above.

As our world modernizes and globalizes, as science and technology advance rapidly, and as Christ-followers form HCNs organically, their inherited socio-religious traditions may be reduced and/or transformed into simpler forms—having overcome fears and guilt feelings, which have been the roots of superstitious practices, lucky charms, and elaborate rituals.

If a community already has good community services, HCs could aim to become part of the leadership and introduce devotions (prayer and the Word) in the existing structures. If the community lacks such ministries, disciples can start serving informally as volunteers and later help set up people's organizations or nongovernmental agencies to address particular needs with the blessing of the community leaders.

Conclusion

By God's grace, in the past twenty-five years most HCNs in all continents, especially Asia, North America, and Australia, have been catalyzing disciple multiplication movements. In China and the Philippines, HCNs have been sending multitudes of disciple-makers as "ants, bees, and (earth)worms"[13]: ordinary people using ordinary and organic ways to bless (develop and enrich) the lives of others. HCNs are spreading the gospel through nameless, faceless, and (apparently) powerless servants of God. Since 2005, the flagship mobilization program of the Philippine Missions Association (PMA) has focused on equipping and sending overseas Filipino workers (OFWs) to be tentmakers who catalyze disciple multiplication movements to bless the nations (Lim 2009 and 2013a).[14]

In parts of India, these workers are going from village to village to enrich farmers with organic farming technology. In Japan, businessmen are leading fellow businessmen and their employees to follow Jesus through business coaching. One top leader there is now pursuing a PhD in Urban Engineering in order to position himself to catalyze an incarnational movement among the Parliament (Diet) members in his district. In Thailand, the main leader has a satellite TV program that gives socio-cultural commentary on issues in various sectors of society.

These HCNs are catalyzing disciple multiplication movements to form transformational communities led by local Christ-followers who have not been extracted from their relational and religio-cultural communities. Such incarnational movements aim to form HCNs to simply multiply Christ-followers who can disciple and transform societies into Christ-following communities and workplaces. These contextualized, holistic, and transformational simple churches are truly indigenous: self-governing, self-supporting, self-propagating, and self-theologizing. They are planting HCs that can be copied by future generations of Christ-followers, so they intentionally avoid denominational churches and missions (= complex Christianity), which have too often been uncontextualized (= foreign-looking, if not actually foreign) and have almost always produced marginalized Christ-followers separated from their communities—despised and rejected by their family and friends, not because of the gospel but because of their extra-biblical forms.

So let us learn how to affirm our unity within the global body of Christ without forcing indigenous HCNs into the denominational structures of

---

13 On China's HCNs Back to Jerusalem movement, see Hattaway 2003. In the animal kingdom, these insects are "small yet terrible" in terms of enriching the harvests as they help in fertilizing the soil and the plants of the land where they subsist.

14 The main model used by PMA is the formation of "Company 3," in which Christ-followers are trained to just make two (local) disciples who will in turn be equipped to make two disciples; see Claro 2013. Another model is "Effective Tentmaking Made Simple"; see Lim 2012.

Christendom. Let us disciple all Christ-followers to "gossip Jesus" and multiply HCNs among their friends and kin in their neighborhoods and workplaces. Let us do this spiritual "network marketing" of the gospel from village to village, city to city, region to region, and nation to nation—till every home and workplace in the world has opportunity to know and obey Jesus as King. May God find us faithful in working together in and through disciple multiplication movements to actualize the kingdom of God effectively in all social structures among all peoples of the world in our generation—incarnationally, contextually, and transformationally!

References

Arterburn, Stephen, and Jack Felton. 2006. *More Jesus, Less Religion*. Colorado Springs: Waterbrook.

Banks, Robert. 1979. *Paul's Idea of Community*. Sydney: Anzea.

Banks, Robert, and Julia Banks. 1986. *The Church Comes Home*. Sutherland: Albatross.

Boff, Leonardo. 1986. *Ecclesiogenesis*. London: Collins; Maryknoll, NY: Orbis.

Chaojaroenrat, Sinchai. N.d. (in Thai) *House Network Church*. Bangkok: Christian Leadership Institute.

Choudhrie, Victor. 2007. *Greet the Ekklesia in Your House*. greettheekklesia@gmail.com.

———. 2010. *Mega Church to Meta Church*. Self published.

Claro, Robert. 2003. *A Higher Purpose for Your Overseas Job*. Makati City, Philippines: Church Strengthening Ministries.

Coleman, Robert. 1964. *The Master Plan of Evangelism*. Old Tappan, NJ: Revell.

Dyrness, William. 2016. *Insider Jesus*. Downers Grove, IL: IVP Academic.

Evans, Steven. 2008. "From the Biblical World to the Buddhist Worldview: Using Bible Narratives to Impact at the Heart Level." In *Communicating Christ through Story and Song: Orality in Buddhist Contexts*, edited by Paul De Neui, 128–50. Pasadena, CA: William Carey Library.

Fitts, Robert. 2001. *The Church in the Home: A Return to Simplicity*. Salem, OR: Preparing the Way Publishers.

Fukuda, Mitsuo. 2005. "Incarnational Approaches to the Japanese People Using House Church Strategies." In *Sharing Jesus Effectively in the Buddhist World*, edited by David Lim, Steve Spaulding, and Paul De Neui, 353–62. Pasadena, CA: William Carey Library.

———. 2010. *Upward, Outward, Inward: Passing the Baton of Discipleship*. Gloucester, UK: Wide Margin.

———. 2011. *Mentoring Like Barnabas*. Gloucester, UK: Wide Margin.

———. 2012. *Developing a Contextualized Church as a Bridge to Christianity in Japan*. Gloucester, UK: Wide Margin, 2012.

Garrison, David. 2013. *A Wind in the House of Islam*. Monument, CO: WIGTake Resources.

Hattaway, Paul, et al. 2003. *Back to Jerusalem*. Carlisle, UK: Piquant.

Higgins, Kevin. 2004. "The Key to Insider Movements: The 'Devoted's' of Acts." *International Journal of Frontier Missiology* 21 (4): 156–60.

Hoefer, Herbert. 2001. *Churchless Christianity*. Pasadena, CA: William Carey Library.

Kraft, Charles. 1979. *Christianity in Cultures*. Maryknoll, NY: Orbis.

Lim, David. 1987. "The Servant Nature of the Church in the Pauline Corpus." PhD diss., Fuller Theological Seminary. Ann Arbor, MI: University Microfilms International.

———. 1987a. "The Development of the Monepiscopate in the Early Church." *Studia Biblica et Theologia* 15 (2): 163–95.

———. 1987b. "The Origin, Nature and Organization of the Synagogue." *Studia Biblica et Theologia* 15 (1): 23–51.

———. 1989. "The Servant Church." *Evangelical Review of Theology* 13 (1): 87–90.

———. 2003. "Towards a Radical Contextualization Paradigm in Evangelizing Buddhists." In *Sharing Jesus in the Buddhist World*, edited by David Lim and Steve Spaulding, 71–94. Pasadena, CA: William Carey Library.

———. 2008. "Catalyzing 'Insider Movements' Among the Unreached." *Journal of Asian Mission* 10 (1–2): 125–45.

———. 2008a. "Biblical Worship Rediscovered: A Theology for Communicating Basic Christianity." In *Communicating Christ through Story and Song: Orality in Buddhist Contexts*, edited by Paul De Neui, 27–59. Pasadena, CA: William Carey Library.

———. 2011. "Towards Closure: Imperial or Incarnational Missions?" *Asian Missions Advance* 33: 20–22.

———. 2012. "Effective Tentmaking Made Simple." In *Blessing OFWs to Bless the Nations*, edited by Ana M. Gamez, 108–11. Makati, Philippines: Church Strengthening Ministry.

———. 2013. "Asian Mission Movements in Asia Today." *Asian Missions Advance* 41: 29–36.

———. 2013a. "History and Ministry of Philippine Missions Association: Leading the Global Shift to Tentmaker Missions." *Asian Missions Advance* 41: 2–6.

———. 2013b. "The House Church Movements in Asia." *Asian Missions Advance* 38: 3–7.

———. 2014. "Missiological Framework for the Contextualization of Christ-Centered Communities." *Asian Missions Advance* 44: 20–22.

———. 2016. "Asia's House Church Movements Today." *Asian Missions Advance* 52: 7–12. Also at www.asiamissions.net/asias-house-church-movements-today/.

———. 2017. "God's Kingdom as *Oikos* Church Networks: A Biblical Theology." *International Journal of Frontier Mission* 34 (1-4): 25–35.

———. 2019. "Appreciating Rituals and Festivals from within Buddhist Christward Movements." In *Sacred Moments: Reflections on Buddhist Rites and Christian Rituals*, edited by Paul de Neui, 105–21. New Delhi: Christian World Imprints.

———. 2020. "Jubilee Realized: The Integral Mission of Asian House Church Networks in Contexts of Religious Pluralism." In *Jubilee: God's Answer to Poverty?*, edited by Hannah Swithinbank, Emmanuel Murangira, and Caitlin Collins, 79–95. Oxford: Regnum.

Richard, H. L. 1999. *Following Jesus in the Hindu Context*. Pasadena, CA: William Carey Library.

Samuel, Vinay, and C. Sugden. 1999. *Mission as Transformation*. Oxford: Regnum.

Stark, Rodney. 1996. *The Rise of Christianity: How the Obscure, Marginal Jesus Movement Became the Dominant Religious Force in the Western World in a Few Centuries*. New York: HarperCollins Publishers.

———. 2006. *Cities of God: The Real Story of How Christianity Became an Urban Movement and Conquered Rome*. New York: HarperCollins Publishers.

Taylor, David. 2015. "Contextualization, Syncretism, and the Demonic in Indigenous Movements." In *Understanding Insider Movements*, edited by H. Talman and J. J. Travis, 375–83. Pasadena, CA: William Carey Library.

Walls, Andrew. 1996. *The Missionary Movement in Christian History*. Maryknoll, NY: Orbis.

Xin, Yalin. 2016. "The Role of the Host Families in the Missional Structure of a House Church Movement." In *Evangelism and Diakonia in Context*, edited by Rose Dowsett, et al, 315–24. Oxford: Regnum.

The Word Spread through the Whole Region: Acts and Church Planting Movements

Craig Ott

Protestants in general and evangelicals in particular are known as "people of the Book." It is thus right and natural for us to examine church and mission practices in light of Scripture. Church planting movements (CPMs) and related strategies have faced such scrutiny, and the verdicts have ranged from enthusiastic affirmation to harsh condemnation. These movements and the claims they make are dramatic and unapparelled to anything observed since the first century. They advocate simple, reproducible methods that mobilize new local believers to lead congregations with minimal dependency on expatriate missionaries, foreign funding, or formal theological training. In short, they are controversial and the responses to them—pro and con—have often been extreme. Here is the question before us in this chapter: What light does the Bible, in particular the book of Acts, shed upon these movements?

This chapter will attempt neither a biblical justification nor a critique of CPM strategies. Nor will it evaluate specific methods, such as Discovery Bible Study (DBS). Rather, the purpose is to study examples in the book of Acts where the gospel spread rapidly, churches were planted and grew, and whole regions were reached with the gospel. From these examples we will then ask what dynamics can be identified that should inform current CPM strategies and practices. We will begin with a word about reading and applying Acts today. Then we will briefly examine the specific cases described in Acts. We will conclude by reflecting upon these dynamics and how they might inform CPMs today.

Reading and Applying the Book of Acts

Missiologists have sometimes been accused of lacking theological justification for their strategies. It is argued that rather than proceeding from biblical teaching as the starting point, they have developed strategies or observed what God is doing in the world, and attempted to theologically "reverse engineer" what they observe to justify their methods. While shallow proof-texting can be rightly criticized, the task of theologically reflecting upon observed phenomenon is not so far from what we find in the book of Acts. The apostles did not initially grasp the full theological implications of how God was at work granting uncircumcised Gentiles the gift of the Holy Spirit and creating a new people—the church—which was not merely an extension of Israel.[1] This led to conflict in the early church that was only resolved seventeen years after Pentecost at the Jerusalem council (Acts 15). There the apostles and elders theologically reflected upon what God was already doing by examining anew the teaching of the Old Testament prophets and then drawing implications for the further development of the rapidly expanding Jesus movement. Only after observing the unanticipated yet unmistakable grace of God toward Gentiles were they compelled to reexamine Scripture to understand what God was doing and find direction for the future.[2]

It is a hermeneutically dubious undertaking to attempt to proof-text or find an explicit justification in the Bible for every contemporary mission strategy or method. However, it is in keeping with the example of the early church to theologically reflect on contemporary gospel movements. We do not ask if such movements today are identical to what we find in Acts, but rather if are they consistent with the trajectory and theology of what we find in Acts. Therefore, this chapter focusses less on the methods and more on the dynamics of evangelism, church planting, and the regional spread of the gospel as reported in Acts.

The Purpose of Acts

Understanding Luke's purpose for writing Acts must guide our interpretation of it. New Testament scholars have debated this question (see Strauss 2011). Of the various theories on the purpose of Acts, it seems most likely that Luke is writing primarily to Gentile believers to provide not merely a reliable historical recounting of developments in the early church, but especially to demonstrate dynamic spread of the gospel to the ends of the earth in the power of the Spirit. A concurrent theme is the legitimacy of Gentile inclusion in the new people of

---

1 For example, Peter would not even enter the house of a Gentile apart from the threefold vision he received from God (Acts 10). Leaders of the Jerusalem church are somewhat incredulous that a Roman soldier should receive the Spirit just as they had (11:1–8). Initially, the Jerusalem Christians who were scattered to Syrian Antioch did not even preach the gospel to Gentiles. When others preached and large numbers of Gentiles became followers of Jesus in that notoriously immoral city, Barnabas is sent there to investigate the situation (11:19–24).

2 For various views of the biblical hermeneutics exercised by the Jerusalem council, see Wiarda 2003.

God as fulfillment of his purpose for the nations. The repeated mention in Acts of the growth of the church underscores that God was fulfilling the messianic promise of bringing salvation, light, and blessing to the nations.[3]

Luke is relatively unconcerned with specific methods or strategies, and focuses more on the agency of the Holy Spirit in the progress of the gospel. Much of the narrative of Acts includes the dual elements of (1) travel narratives describing how the gospel was preached and embraced beyond Israel, and (2) the spread of the gospel despite various forms of opposition, particularly opposition by Jewish leaders. In this story, Paul becomes the paradigmatic apostle to the Gentiles and lightning rod for Jewish opposition. Acts, being the second of Luke's two-volume treatise, continues themes from the Gospel of Luke. One of the themes is Jesus' welcoming of the marginalized, a motif which then finds greater fulfillment in Acts as the Spirit moves to include the Gentiles in the church. Another theme continuing from Luke's Gospel is the growth of the kingdom as realized in the growth of the church.

Mode over Methods in Acts

By taking a more principled approach to the dynamics of Acts rather than looking for specific missionary methods, contemporary mission practice and strategy is freed from a rigid attempt to merely imitate what happened in Acts. We need not subject every innovation in mission to some kind of litmus test: "Do we find that in the Bible?" If Luke wanted to write a handbook on evangelism and church planting, he would have written something quite different than what he gave us in Acts. He left out too many critical details if that had been his intent. Luke focusses on the agency of the Holy Spirit, not human agency. That is no doubt good. Had he written such a methods primer, we would have attempted to slavishly follow it, and it would also have left us little freedom to contextualize our methods to various cultural and religious contexts.

Thus, biblical mission is less a matter of imitating what we find in Acts and more about continuing the story in the salvation-historical trajectory of Acts in the power of the Spirit. To attempt to merely mimic the ministry of the apostles would be to miss the extent to which they contextualized their method and message to the specific audiences they were reaching (Fleming 2005). Furthermore, much of Acts reports nonrepeatable salvation-historical developments unique to the birth of the church as the New Covenant people.

We should also note that Paul was at home in both the Hellenistic and Jewish cultural worlds.[4] Thus the cultural gaps he had to bridge were small

---

3   On the fulfillment motif in Acts, see Bock 1998; Peterson 2009, 29–32; Jipp 2018, 31–50.

4   Regarding Paul having grown up in Tarsus, Calvin Roetzel comments, "Thus as a young man his feet were firmly planted in two different worlds: the Hellenistic world with its rich cultural heritage, and the world of the people of Israel with its Scriptures, traditions, and law. So firmly comfortable in both was he that he was an ideal person for translating a gospel that was fundamentally Jewish for the Hellenistic environment of his converts" (2009, 475).

compared to the gap between, say, North America and Namibia, or Singapore and Suriname. It is also easy to forget that although Paul made frequent use of the Old Testament, he did not possess the New Testament as he was evangelizing and planting churches. The world in which we live today is obviously vastly different from the world of the first century. This opens up to us possibilities for the advancement of the gospel unimaginable in the first century: modern technology, travel, communications, and globalization. Therefore, when seeking to apply lessons from Acts to contemporary mission practice, we look less for specific methods to imitate and more for the spiritual dynamics and underlying principles that guided first-century mission—the mode, so to speak, more than the methods.

Church Planting Movements in Acts?

One additional concern must be addressed before moving forward. Critics of CPM strategies have argued that CPMs do not exist in the Bible (e.g., Wu 2014). It may well be that we have no explicit New Testament description of a movement that would meet the definition of a CPM resulting in hundreds or thousands of churches with tens of thousands of believers within a few years.[5] It might be thus protested that this inquiry asks something that Acts doesn't intend to answer. However, we need not find an exact description of a CPM in the New Testament in order to learn from the dynamics of rapidly growing, expansive movements that *are* described in Acts.

Numerous passages describe remarkable numerical growth of the church and the spread of the word (2:47; 5:13–14; 6:1, 7; 9:31; 11:21, 24, 26; 12:24; 13:49; 14:21; 16:5; 19:10, 20). The growth is emphasized with descriptors such as "daily" (2:47; 16:5), "rapidly," a "large number" (6:7), "flourishing" (12:24), "in power" (19:20), and increase in "great" numbers (11:21, 24, 26; 14:1). Benjamin Wilson comments in this regard, "The growth summaries are replete with constructions which in one way or another stress both the frequency and the extent of the numerical increase of the Christian movement." Furthermore, "Most often the [growth] summaries are presented in the imperfect tense, creating the impression of ongoing quantitative increase" (2017, 320). Geographic descriptions of "all" (9:31; 19:10) or "whole" (13:49) regions being reached not only underscore that the number of disciples increased, but also strongly imply that churches were being formed in the various localities.

This kind of remarkable growth and spread of the gospel can only be explained in that disciples were being reproduced, evangelists and leaders were being reproduced, and ultimately churches were being reproduced. Central to CPM strategy is the idea of church multiplication. I have argued at length elsewhere

---

5 Most examples of CPMs cited by Garrison (2004), Trousdale (2012), Smith and Kai (2011), and others have these kinds of numbers and usually talk of movements experiencing at least four generations of churches planting churches over a short time period.

that the concept of multiplication is not only present in the Acts narrative, but important to it (Ott 2019, 103–21). The language of "be fruitful and multiply and fill the earth" (Gen 1:22) is a repeated concept in the Old Testament relating to God's people (e.g., Jer 23:3)[6] and woven into the eschatological vision of filling the earth with God's glory (e.g., Isa 11:9). Jesus builds upon this idea in the kingdom parables. Growth of the kingdom in Luke's Gospel finds fulfillment in the growth of the church in Luke's second volume, Acts (Reinhardt 1995; Rosner 1998). Timothy is exhorted to develop leaders who will reproduce new leaders to multiple generations (cf. 2 Tim 2:2). Passages such as 1 Thessalonians 1:8 and Romans 15:19–23[7] further strengthen the view that churches once planted could be expected to evangelize their region and reproduce. We need not prove that this spiritual reproduction was mathematically exponential (2 becoming 4, becoming 8, 16, 32, etc.) to use the language of multiplication in a more general sense to describe what we see in Acts. The English Standard Version translates forms of the Greek *plēthunō* as "multiplied" in 6:7, 7:17, 9:31, and 12:24.[8] Therefore, it is not misguided to inquire into the dynamics of church growth and multiplication in Acts. Acts provides a sound biblical-theological lens through which we can reflect upon contemporary CPMs. With this in mind, we now turn to several case studies in the book of Acts.

The Jerusalem Church

The church in Jerusalem was birthed on the Day of Pentecost. With the outpouring of the Spirit a new era had dawned. Peter's Pentecost sermon resulted in the baptism of three thousand new believers that day (2:41), a dramatic increase from about 120 (1:15). Despite growing opposition, the church then grew to a total of five thousand (4:4),[9] the increase continued "more and more" (5:14; 6:1), grew "rapidly" (6:7), and later there were "many thousands," which

---

6 Wilson writes, "The usage of αὐξάνω and/or πληθύνω in several of the growth summaries of Acts may ring to some degree with notes of eschatological fulfillment, signifying that God's promise of growth to his people is finding its fulfillment in the progress of the Christian movement" (2017, 322).

7 Douglas J. Moo (1996, 895–96) cites John Knox's understanding of this text: "[Paul] could say that he had completed the preaching of the gospel from Jerusalem to Illyricum only because this statement would have meant for him that the message had been proclaimed and the church planted in each of the nations north and west across Asia Minor and the Greek peninsula—'proclaimed' widely enough and 'planted' firmly enough to assure that the name of Christ would soon be heard throughout Asia minor and the Greek penisula."

8 In favor of "multiply," see Kodell 1974; Reinhardt 1995, 52–54; and Wilson 2007.

9 There is debate whether the number five thousand is the cumulative number of believers in Jerusalem, or if this indicates five thousand in addition to the three thousand mentioned in 2:41. It is also unclear if in 4:4 only men are counted, or if the Greek *andrōn* should be taken to describe both men and women. Either way, the growth was remarkable. On the reliability of the numbers, see Keener 2010. There are very few places where Luke reports specific numbers, and in each case they are Jewish background believers. This may indicate Luke's desire to refute claims that there were only a few Jewish followers of Jesus (Wilson 2017, 325).

can be translated "tens of thousands" (21:20).[10] Although the example of the Jerusalem church is in some ways unique,[11] if nothing else, it demonstrates that dramatic, rapid, uncoerced "mass conversions" are not impossible. They're not necessarily a result of compromising the gospel message. On the contrary, they can be evidence of a remarkable work of the Spirit. The faith of these new believers was not superficial, as evidenced in 2:42–47 and later descriptions.

An additional detail is noteworthy. Luke states, "And the Lord added to their number daily those who were being saved" (2:47b). Peter did the preaching, but it was God who brought people to faith and enfolded them into the community of believers.[12] The new believer at the time of salvation[13] becomes associated with the new messianic community and participates in the life of that community. The Greek term translated "added" (*prostithēmi*) in 2:41, 2:47, 5:14, and 11:24 was used in early Jewish proselyte literature in a technical sense to describe people being gathered to or joining a fellowship, indicating a break with their former Gentile community and association with the people of God (Reinhardt 1995, 99–100). Because Acts 2 describes Jews becoming followers of Jesus as Messiah, they are, broadly speaking, not breaking with their Jewish heritage and beliefs, but fulfilling them.[14] Yet God does add them to the new messianic community to which they formerly did not belong. To become a follower of Jesus entails God's enfolding of that person into a local fellowship of Jesus-followers, with whom that person now identifies. Baptism is the mark of that enfolding which gives the believer a new identity in Christ (1 Cor 12:13). The Christian who does not associate with such a local fellowship is an anomaly. Acts reports that nearly everywhere the gospel was preached, communities of believers—churches—came into being.

Finally, in Acts 6:1–7 Luke links the continued growth of the Jerusalem church with the resolution of conflict in the church and the refocusing of the ministry of the apostles on "prayer and the ministry of the word." Verse 1 indicates that "the number of disciples was increasing" as the conflict regarding distribution of food between Greek-speaking and Hebrew-speaking widows erupted.

---

10 On interpreting the Greek *muriades* as tens of thousands and possibly as many as fifty thousand, see Keener 2010, 141–43, and Schnabel 2004, 732. This number probably includes not only believers in Jerusalem, but also in Judea.

11 Pentecost marked a salvation-historical turning point in the outpouring of the Spirit. Many would have been previously exposed to Jesus' teaching and miracles.

12 See Bruce Metzger's comments on the Greek phrase ἐπὶ τὸ αὐτό, translated "to their number," as having acquired a quasi-technical meaning that could be rendered "in church fellowship" (1971, 305).

13 This is indicated by the use of a present participle in the original Greek *tous sōzomenous*, "as they were being saved" (Longenecker 1981, 291–92; Petersen 2009, 164).

14 Later in Acts 21:20, we find in the Jerusalem church that "many thousands of Jews have believed, and all of them are zealous for the law." However, it was a break with the legalistic traditions of the scribes and Pharisees. Acts 15 had far-reaching implications for what it means to be the people of God, not strictly defined by adherence to the Law of Moses and including uncircumcised Gentiles as equal heirs of the promise.

This presented a serious threat to the unity and health of the emerging movement. Only after this conflict was resolved does Luke indicate the continued growth of the church in verse 7: "So the word of God spread. The number of disciples in Jerusalem increased rapidly, and a large number of priests became obedient to the faith." As Peterson concludes, "The satisfactory resolution of the conflict in the Jerusalem church made it possible for this ministry of the gospel to flourish and for church growth to take place even more *rapidly (sphodra)*" (2009, 236). Movements must attend to the unity of believers and address needs as they arise if they are to continue to grow healthy and strong.

Judea, Samaria, and Syria

Until chapter 8, Acts describes the spread of the gospel largely within the immediate environs of Jerusalem. When persecution in Jerusalem scatters the believers, the gospel enters Judea, Samaria, and Syria. Luke reports on their fruitful witness, "Then the church throughout Judea, Galilee and Samaria enjoyed a time of peace and was strengthened. Living in the fear of the Lord and encouraged by the Holy Spirit, it increased in numbers" (9:31). In Syrian Antioch, a "great number of people believed and turned to the Lord" (11:21, 24, 26). For our inquiry, several features of the story are significant.

First, at least initially, we know of no intentional sending of evangelists or missionaries to the outlying regions. This occurred only when Christians were driven by persecution from Jerusalem. This reminds us that the gospel often spreads apart from any formal ecclesial commissioning or mission strategy. Circumstances of persecution, famine, war, economic upheaval, and the like may be orchestrated by God to stimulate human migration, moving ordinary Christians to new places where they become witnesses for Christ.

Second, the scattered followers of Jesus spontaneously preached the gospel wherever they went (8:4). They "gossiped the gospel," so to speak. It was entirely natural for these relatively young believers[15] to share their faith with others who they encountered along the way. Philip, a deacon (6:5), later acquires the title of "the evangelist" (21:8), but at this point of the story this does not have the character of a formal office. He ends up in Samaria preaching and performing miracles, causing "great joy in that city" (8:4–8). Given the hostility between Jews and Samaritans, it is striking that any of the persecuted Jerusalem Christians would have settled there. But they did, they shared the gospel, and God worked through them. Only after God's hand was clearly already at work among the Samaritans did the apostles Peter and John travel to Samaria to investigate the situation and bestow the gift of the Holy Spirit (8:14–17). This visit might be viewed as apostolic sanction of the barrier-breaking work that God had

---

15 This persecution likely broke out within a few years of Christ's resurrection and Pentecost (Riesner 1998, 59–60; 118–24).

already begun among these ethnically mixed "half-pagan and half-Yahwistic" people (Samkutty 2006, 58). After this, Peter and John fully embrace mission to the Samaritans as they "returned to Jerusalem, preaching the gospel in many Samaritan villages" (8:25).

Third, these messengers were "ordinary" believers. The apostles remained in Jerusalem (8:1). When the gospel made its first major breakthrough among Gentiles in Syrian Antioch, it was not the Jerusalem Christians who evangelized them, but rather believers from Cyprus and Cyrene (11:19–21). As Schnabel comments, "[Luke] has not suppressed the historical fact that the initial impetus for a genuine missionary outreach among Gentiles came not from Peter (or Paul) but from Hellenistic Jewish Christians from Cyprus and Cyrene whose names we do not even know" (2004, 672). This further underscores the reality that ordinary believers, particularly those neither sent nor sanctioned by the Jerusalem church, were empowered by the Spirit and naturally shared the gospel. God blessed this beyond expectation.

This conversion of large numbers of uncircumcised, pork-eating, immoral Gentiles was a remarkable confirmation of God's acceptance of them apart from outward signs of Jewish piety. Luke reports twice in these few verses the significant growth of the number of believers in this predominantly Gentile city: "a great number of people believed and turned to the Lord" (11:21) and "a great number of people were brought to the Lord" (v. 24). Barnabas is sent by the leaders in Jerusalem to Antioch to examine this rather unexpected and unorthodox situation. There would have been good reason to doubt the legitimacy and sincerity of such a movement. But fortunately, Barnabas had eyes to see "what the grace of God had done," and he establishes the work by encouraging "them all to remain true to the Lord with all their hearts" (v. 23). His acceptance of this work of God is neither begrudging nor with scepticism; rather, Barnabas "was glad." He and Saul then "taught great numbers of people" (v. 26). Sound instruction was a critical need in the blossoming church of pagan-background believers.

Finally, it is not the Jerusalem church but this church in Syrian Antioch that reconfirms Paul's calling and sends Paul and Barnabas on the first *intentional* mission to the Gentiles reported in Acts (Acts 13:1–3). Indeed, it was the Holy Spirit sending them through the sending of this church, as indicated by the juxtaposition of "they placed their hands on them and sent them off" in verse 3 and "The two of them, sent on their way by the Holy Spirit" in verse 4. We see the vision for and commitment to missionary-sending in this young church.

Thus, we observe continuity and discontinuity in this landmark work of God in Syrian Antioch: discontinuity in its emergence apart from Jerusalem's direct involvement, continuity in its recognition by Barnabas on behalf of the Jerusalem church and the strengthening of the church through the authorized teaching of Barnabas and Saul. This linking of churches with one another was also demonstrated in the charitable collection the Antioch church gathered for the Jerusalem church (11:27–30). Later the doctrinal authority of the Jerusalem council is accepted (Acts 15). This networking of churches was a feature of Paul's mission, evidenced in other charitable collections (e.g., 2 Cor 8–9), the sending of greetings, and by the exchange of coworkers or representatives from the different churches (Ollrog 1979).

Pisidian Antioch

On the first missionary journey of Paul and Barnabas, we are told that from Pisidian Antioch, "The word of the Lord spread through the whole region" (13:49). The region under the jurisdiction of Antioch included over fifty villages (Schnabel 2004, 1107). This spread of the word did not likely depend upon Paul and Barnabas alone, but more likely occurred through the local believers. We can reasonably assume that Luke's language of the word spreading here is consistent with other occurrences of the word spreading and growing where conversion and church growth is indicated (e.g., 6:7; 12:24; 19:20). Thus, this indicates that others throughout the region became believers, and it would have been natural for them to gather in homes forming house churches, as was the case elsewhere. This spread of the Christian message and reception by large numbers incurred the opposition of the Jewish leaders, forcing Paul and Barnabas out of town (13:50–51). Yet, despite opposition, "the disciples were filled with joy and with the Holy Spirit" (v. 52).

A final note on this case is that not long afterwards Paul and Barnabas returned to encourage the believers and appoint elders in the churches (14:21–23). On later occasions, Paul revisited the churches in this region, again strengthening them (15:41–16:5; 18:23). Paul's letter to the Galatians was likely written to these churches. The appointment and ongoing encouragement of leaders was important to the continued flourishing and health of the churches. Those appointed as elders were presumably relatively new believers. Yet we later read that an overseer (or elder) must not be a recent convert (1 Tim 3:6; 5:22). These elders may have been from a Jewish background and thus not recently converted from paganism. But there is no clear evidence for that. Roger Gering, in his book *House Church and Mission*, argues that because churches met in private homes, the head of the household as homeowner and host of the church was likely the elder of that house church (2004, 205–210). "Together as a group such overseers could have formed the leadership team or council for the whole local church in that city" (206). Another commentator states, "For these early churches there was no professional clergy to assume their leadership. Consequently, the pattern of the Jewish synagogues seems to have been followed by appointing a group of lay elders to shepherd the flock" (Polhill 1992, 319).

In any case, they would have been relatively new believers. Paul and Barnabas evidenced faith in the Spirit's future equipping power as they "committed them to the Lord, in whom they had put their trust" (14:23). Only later, when more mature believers were available, did the qualifications of elders become more formalized with the higher standards that we find in the Pastoral Epistles. If this understanding is correct, we can conclude that in the early emergence of a movement relatively new believers can occupy positions of leadership.

Ephesus

Ephesus is the clearest case of church growth resulting in the saturation of an entire province with the gospel and the reproduction of churches. Paul writes to the Corinthians explaining the reason for delaying a visit to them, "But I will stay on at Ephesus until Pentecost, because a great door for effective work has opened to me, and there are many who oppose me" (1 Cor 16:8–9). In Acts 19 we discover the nature of that open door. Before describing that, we note that open doors for ministry and opposition often go hand in hand. Paul's preaching evoked an uproar and near riot (19:23–41), and he compared the fierce opposition there to fighting wild beasts (1 Cor 15:32). We may think that opposition is the sign of a closed door. But we have seen repeatedly that church growth often occurred in the midst of opposition.

The "effective work" in Ephesus had the result that "all the Jews and Greeks who lived in the province of Asia heard the word of the Lord" (v. 10).[16] This all occurred within a two-year period. Later, in verse 20, we read that "the word of the Lord spread widely and grew in power." Those last words indicate both breadth and depth of the movement—quantity *and* quality. Ephesus, with some two hundred thousand residents, was one of the largest cities in the Roman Empire and the most prominent commercial, travel, and religious center of the province of Asia (Schnabel 2004, 1206–11). Evidence of this spread of the gospel and the reproduction of churches is found in the existence of the so-called "seven churches of Asia Minor" described in Revelation 2–3 and the churches in Colossae[17] and Hierapolis (Col 4:13). There were likely other churches, but only these are explicitly identified. We also know that Paul did not plant all these churches himself. For example, he had not even met many, if any, of the Colossian and Laodicean believers (Col 2:1). Epaphras, himself from Colossae (Col. 4:12), brought the gospel to Colossae, and possibly also to Laodicea and Hierapolis (Col 1:7; 4:13). Luke's concern is not the identity of the evangelists, but rather the work of the Spirit in them causing the word of the Lord to grow and spread in power (Acts 19:20).

16 This should not be taken to mean that every individual person living in the province heard the gospel. Rather a region is considered evangelized when churches have been established in the key centers of the region (Reinhardt 1995, 264–65). This is the sense of Romans 15:19b, 23, where Paul indicates that he has completed his work in the entire eastern Mediterranean Roman Empire.

17 Colossae was located in the province of Phrygia, near the province of Asia.

Two interesting connections are explicitly mentioned in Acts 19 regarding the manner by which the gospel saturated the region. The first is found in verses 9–10: "[Paul] took the disciples with him and had discussions daily in the lecture hall of Tyrannus. This went on for two years, *so that* all the Jews and Greeks who lived in the province of Asia heard the word of the Lord." There is a direct connection between Paul's teaching in Ephesus and the spread of the word into the whole province. Paul's teaching there, in public, and from house to house (20:20), entailed at least in part, no doubt, equipping workers such as Epaphras to become evangelists in the wider region. Thus, Ephesus became the strategic hub from which the gospel spread into the entire region.[18]

The second feature is found in verse 19: "A number who had practiced sorcery brought their scrolls together and burned them publicly. When they calculated the value of the scrolls, the total came to fifty thousand drachmas." These believers made a break with their former beliefs at great personal expense.[19] This burning of the magic books is followed by the important words, "*In this way* the word of the Lord spread widely and grew in power" (vs. 20). The willingness to separate themselves from their former occult practices had two results: increased opposition and increased spread of the gospel. Wherever Paul preached the gospel, even in the face of persecution, he called his audience to turn away from serving idols to serve the living and true God alone (e.g., Acts 14:15; 17:29–31; 1 Thess 1:8–10). However, it must also be noted that this break with pagan practices (burning the magic books) did not come immediately following their conversion, but rather after having been gripped by the fear of the Lord (19:17–18).

In Acts 20:13–25 we read of Paul's parting address to the elders of the church of Ephesus. He charges them with the spiritual care of the church and warns of false teachers. His concern is clearly for the ongoing health and leadership of the church. Space does not allow us to consider the further development of the church in Ephesus and the movement in the province of Asia, other than to say that the exhortations of Revelation 2–3 remind us that the spiritual vitality even of such a remarkable movement is not guaranteed.[20]

Biblical Dynamics of Church Planting Movements

We have established that rapidly growing movements, which in some cases saturated whole regions with the gospel, were evident in the experience of early Christian mission as reported in Acts. *We should dismiss a fundamental skepticism that such*

---

18 Schnabel (2008, 284–85) rejects this view that there was a "radiation effect" from Ephesus into the surrounding region. However, numerous commentators affirm the view presented here (e.g., Bruce 1952, 356; Reinhardt 1995, 277; Witherington 1998, 576; Keener 2014, 2835–38).

19 The value was equivalent to 137 years of a laborer's wages (Schnabel 2004, 1221).

20 For a discussion of the church in Ephesus in missiological perspective, see Cooper 2020.

movements could occur today or that they are by nature superficial or unhealthy. The bigger question regards the implications of these biblical cases for CPMs today. As already noted, our purpose is not to attempt to imitate specific methods described in Acts. Rather we seek to identify the underlying dynamics that would guide contemporary CPMs and help us answer these questions: Is any given movement developing in the trajectory of what we find in Acts, and do our methods facilitate or hinder such? I propose seven dynamics.

1. Movements Are a Work of the Triune God

The Spirit empowers the messengers and the message of the crucified and resurrected Christ, and the Father adds to the church those who are being saved. The advance of the gospel and the launching of movements is entirely God-centered and God-empowered. As Joshua Jipp puts it, "Acts is about God.… . Luke-Acts is from beginning to end a narrative construal of God and God's activity" (2018, 14). Paul recognized this when he wrote, "I planted the seed, Apollos watered it, but *God* has been making it grow. So neither the one who plants nor the one who waters is anything, but only *God*, who makes things grow" (1 Cor 3:6–7).

This is not to suggest that methods are irrelevant, since God chooses to work through human means and workers are accountable for the quality of their work (1 Cor 3:12–15). But all human effort is in vain if God ultimately does not grant the growth. Jesus stated it this way: "Remain in me, as I also remain in you. No branch can bear fruit by itself; it must remain in the vine. Neither can you bear fruit unless you remain in me" (John 15:4). CPM practitioners must live and work in this awareness and in full dependence upon the only one who can produce true spiritual growth. Thus, prayer and dependency upon God must be the method behind all missionary methods. Movements cannot be produced by merely adopting a particular method or strategy.

Regarding the work of the Holy Spirit, a brief word must be said about the role of signs, wonders, exorcisms, and supernatural events, which are repeatedly mentioned in Acts as accompanying the spread of the gospel. Paul regards Spirit-empowered signs and wonders as a way by which Christ worked through him in reaching the nations (Rom 15:19). These miracles confirmed apostolic authority and the authenticity of the message (2 Cor 12:12; Heb 2:4). They also demonstrated the power of the inbreaking kingdom of God. In the words of Dirk Van der Merwe, they are demonstrations of "the immense power of the Gospel—how the proclamation of the gospel is victorious over the power of evil" (2010, 91). We should not be surprised at reports today of CPMs being accompanied by such remarkable signs of God's power.[21] However, Scripture cautions against a preoccupation with the miraculous (e.g., Mark 8:11–12; 13:22; John 4:48;

---

21 For accounts of signs and wonders throughout church history in various traditions, see Cooper and Gregory 2005. In the 1980s signs and wonders were promoted as *the* key to effective evangelism in what was called "power evangelism" and the "third wave" of the Holy Spirit (e.g., Wimber and Springer 1986; Wagner 1988). For a critique, see, for example, Sarles 1988, Carson 1992, and Rommen 1998.

2 Thess 2:9). Be it through visible signs or more subtle transformation, the gospel can only advance in the power of the Spirit.

2. Movements Are Fueled by the Word of God, the Gospel

The preaching and teaching of the gospel are so central to the Acts narrative that the growth of the church is equated with the growth or spread of the word of the Lord/God (e.g., 6:7; 12:24; 13:49; 19:20). Brian Rosner summarizes his study of this dynamic in Acts: "The theme of the progress of the word is widespread and central to the purpose of the book of Acts, being anticipated by elements in Luke's Gospel, set up by Acts 1:1–11 and confirmed throughout by the progress reports" (1998, 233). David Pao speaks of the "conquest of the word" in Acts (2000, 150–67). This reminds us of Romans 1:16: "For I am not ashamed of the gospel, because it is the power of God that brings salvation to everyone who believes: first to the Jew, then to the Gentile."

Space has not allowed an examination of ways in which the gospel message was contextualized in the speeches of Acts to communicate to the various audiences (see Flemming 2005, 56–88; Prince 2017, 72–144). The speeches make abundantly clear that there is no single way to explain the gospel, and that the presentation must take the audience into consideration. Suffice it to say that biblical contextualization will seek not to change the central message of the gospel but to establish common ground, to employ forms, rhetoric, arguments, and plausibility structures that will make the message of the gospel understandable to the audience. Gospel messengers should never attempt to remove the offense of the cross, but rather should seek to make the *meaning* of the cross clear. In the end, the gospel calls people to reject all forms of idolatry, renounce sin, and embrace the resurrected Christ as Lord and Savior. The salvific work of Christ, to be truly understood, must be placed in the larger biblical story of redemption and the kingdom of God.

Paul not only preached and taught in public, such as in synagogues and the hall of Tyrannus, but he also taught from house to house (Acts 20:20). At times he reasoned with his audience (17:2, 17; 18:4, 19; 19:8–9; 20:7, 9). The Bereans were considered of noble character because they evaluated Paul's message by examining Scripture (17:11). The gospel was communicated with the goal not only to evangelize unbelievers, but also to edify believers. Devotion to the apostles' teaching was a notable feature of the Jerusalem church (2:42; 4:2; 5:21, 42). Barnabas and Paul taught in Syrian Antioch for a year (11:26), and teaching was a key aspect of Paul's calling (2 Tim 1:11). Early in Paul's travels he did not remain long in most locations, often being forced to leave due to persecution. However, he taught for a year and a half in Corinth (18:11) and for three years in Ephesus (20:31).[22]

---

22 Philip Towner (1998) proposes that these longer stays marked a change in Paul's strategy, but Schnabel rejects this thesis as too speculative (2004, 1191–92). In any case, Paul's stays even in Corinth and Ephesus were extremely brief compared to most contemporary missionary practice.

Disciple making movements (DMM) have the Bible as the centerpiece of their method, with reliance on DBS, whereby participants themselves answer questions about the meaning of Bible stories. The impression is sometimes given that more didactic teaching and the spiritual gift of teaching is unimportant in DMM strategy. Here we must find a balance. On the one hand, people should be empowered to interpret and apply the Bible themselves. On the other hand, there is still a need for instruction to correct misunderstandings and false teaching. When the Levites reintroduced the Law of Moses to the people, "They read from the Book of the Law of God, making it clear and giving the meaning so that the people understood what was being read" (Neh 8:8).

People commonly interpret texts and even miracles through the lens of their worldview, as was the case in Lystra where the people identified Paul and Barnabas as Greek gods (Acts 14:8–18). Second Peter 3:16 indicates that "[Paul's] letters contain some things that are hard to understand, which ignorant and unstable people distort." Both in the first century and today, false teaching is an ever-present threat to the health of churches. Paul exhorts Timothy and Titus not to neglect the ministry of teaching. For CPMs to remain healthy, there must be a place for clear and ongoing instruction in the Word of God.

3. Movements Are the Result of Evangelism that Intentionally Plants Churches

As individuals embrace the gospel, they are added by God to a local fellowship of believers (Acts 2:41, 47). Nearly everywhere that the gospel was preached, communities of believers were formed that typically met in homes. Occasionally multiple house churches in a city came together in one larger location (1 Cor 11:18; 14:23). Although the church in Jerusalem met as a larger body in the temple area, they also met regularly in homes (Acts 2:46; 5:42). Thus, the smaller household-size fellowships were the social building block of the early church. It was expected that as individuals became followers of Jesus, they would become identified with and regularly participate in such a fellowship (Heb 10:25), baptism being the marker of enfolding into the church (1 Cor 12:13). Although the New Testament writers also speak of what we call the "invisible," or "universal," church—a description of the new people of God as a heavenly reality—they most often speak of the church as a local assembly of believers (Banks 1994, 29–46).

While there is a place for ministries focused exclusively on evangelism and other specialized work, they must have the larger goal in view that new believers become part of a local fellowship of Jesus-followers. Where such churches do not exist, they must be planted. Evangelism and church planting go hand in hand. The goal of DBS groups must be to develop into fellowships with the marks of New Testament churches, exercising the full functions of churches under recognized spiritual leaders. Such fellowships may not have the outward appearance of typical Western churches with buildings, budgets, professional clergy, and formal institutions or programs. They may well bear greater similarity to the churches described in Acts, meeting in private homes, and with leaders who are relatively young in the faith and lacking formal training.

4. Movements Empower Ordinary Believers to Share Their Faith

We see in Acts that God used gifted persons such as Peter, Philip, and Paul to establish the first churches in a region. But movements of multiplying churches only emerge when numerous "ordinary" Christians become the evangelists, church planters, and leaders. The spread of the gospel into Judea, Samaria, and Syria was the result of simple followers of Jesus bearing witness as they were scattered by the persecution in Jerusalem (8:4). Those who preached to Gentiles in Antioch did not come from Jerusalem (11:19–21). This movement did not depend upon the apostles or a few particularly gifted persons. In the other cases we've examined, it is highly unlikely that the growth of the churches and the saturation of whole regions with the gospel resulted from the ministry of Paul and just a few coworkers. Rather, local believers who had newly come to faith in Christ were the evangelists. We can reasonably assume they also established believing communities—house churches—in the various localities. An example of this was Epaphras.

Throughout the history of the expansion of Christianity, so-called "indigenous agency" has been the key to the evangelization of whole regions as local believers were empowered as witnesses for Christ and as church planters. Often such witness has been spontaneous, unplanned, and beyond the control of foreign missionaries. This is the case today in many CPMs. This should not surprise us, nor should we attempt to control it or slow it. Aberrations and unhealthy developments will no doubt arise along the way, as in the early church. That, however, does not negate the fact that the Spirit is at work. The appropriate response is found in the next point.

5. Movements Are Sustained By Developing Local Leaders

To argue that ordinary believers were responsible for evangelizing whole regions and planting churches does not suggest that well-equipped leaders were unimportant in the ongoing ministry of these churches. As the movement began to grow beyond Jerusalem, Peter and John were sent to Samaria (8:14), and Barnabas was sent to Antioch (11:22). Paul instructed and appointed elders in the churches he planted. In fact, he considered a work incomplete where elders had not been appointed (Titus 1:5). During the first missionary journey, leaders were appointed by Paul and Barnabas, although they were very young in their faith (Acts 14:23). Paul instructed the elders in Ephesus for three years and charged them to care for the flock of God and guard against false teachers (20:29–31). If Gering's argument that the first overseers were in fact the household heads in whose homes the churches met holds, this would provide a biblical precedent for the frequent CPM practice of a head of a household leading a house church. Just as in the early church where the standards for leadership were raised as the churches matured, so too movements today might increase the standards for leadership as the movement matures.

At this point we might ask, Were such rapidly growing movements able to remain healthy and strong? Wilson remarks that, at least initially, in Acts, "the growth summaries occur consistently in contexts which highlight the quality of the community life and visible actions of Christian congregations (cf. Acts 2:47; 6:7; 9:31; 11:24; 19:20)" (2017, 331). When we examine later reports of these churches in the New Testament, the answer is mixed. From Revelation 2–3 we learn that some churches in Asia Minor, such as Smyrna and Philadelphia, continued strong; others, such as Sardis and Laodicea, were in deep spiritual danger. The churches faced the challenges of false teaching, immorality, self-sufficiency, and spiritual lethargy.

Paul's warning to the Ephesian elders regarding false teachers is later repeated to Timothy, then serving in Ephesus (2 Tim 4:3, cf. 2 Pet 2:1–3), where he did, in fact, encounter them (1 Tim 1:6–7; 4:1–3; 2 Tim 3:8). Although the Ephesians ultimately rejected false teachers, they lost their first love (Rev 2:1–7). The churches of Galatia faced teachers of a false gospel (Gal 1:6–9), and the Colossians wrestled with syncretism (Col 2:8, 16–23). Thus, even movements described in Acts had no guarantee of ongoing spiritual health.

One key to the future health of a CPM is the equipping of local leaders who are able to care for the churches after the apostolic team departs. Paul underscores that leaders must be able to teach (1 Tim 3:2; 2 Tim 2:24), and the Pastoral Epistles are full of exhortations to teach sound doctrine (1 Tim 4:11, 13; 6:2; 2 Tim 2:2; Titus 2:2, 15). The ongoing health and sustenance of CPMs will depend much on the equipping of leaders who will not only shepherd the church, but instruct it, protect it from false teaching, promote its spiritual vitality, and continue its missional thrust.

6. Movements Can Expect to Face Opposition

In every case described above, the movement experienced some form of opposition. Wilson notes, "The references in 4:4, 13:48, 17:34, and 18:8 all describe the success of the Christian mission directly after the depiction of resistance to Christian spokespeople" (2017, 327). No attempt was made to alter the method or message in order to avoid opposition. In some cases, opposition came as overt persecution from religious leaders, government officials, or a popular uprising. At other times it was spiritual opposition in the form of harassment from demonized persons, divisive teaching, or syncretistic compromise.

When false gods are renounced, idolatry is abandoned, life priorities are rearranged, and the universal lordship of Christ is proclaimed, both seen and unseen powers will arise in opposition. Ultimately, the spread of the gospel represents the inbreaking of the kingdom of God and the overthrow of the powers of evil. Paul places the conflict in cosmic perspective: "For our struggle is not against flesh and blood, but against the rulers, against the authorities, against the powers of this dark world and against the spiritual forces of evil in the heavenly realms" (Eph 6:12). And yet in the midst of such opposition we see that the gospel progressed, churches were established, and effective ministry took place.

Not surprisingly, movements today often experience great opposition also. While wisdom should always be exercised, and contextualization of the message must be emphasized, attempts to avoid opposition by compromising the message would be a grave departure from apostolic practice and contrary to the very teaching of Jesus that opposition will be inevitable (e.g., Matt 5:11–12; John 15:20; cf. 2 Tim 3:12). Yet we can be encouraged that even severe opposition is subject to God's sovereign plan, and that the gospel can and will advance in his power and in his timing.

7. Movements Should Be Linked With the Larger Body of Christ

One can easily overlook that Paul connected the various churches with one another beyond their locality. Although local congregations were somewhat autonomous, they were not entirely independent. They were networked in various ways (Stenschke 2019). The churches were represented at the Jerusalem council, and they adopted the decision of the council (Acts 15; 16:4). Though this was a somewhat unique situation, it does point to accountability in the larger body of Christ.

Paul reported back to his sending church in Antioch (14:26–28) and to the Jerusalem church (21:17–19). He continually sent coworkers from one church to another, such as Apollos being sent from Ephesus to Corinth (18:27). These coworkers were to be received as representing his apostolic authority teaching and encouraging the churches (Mitchell 1992; Schnabel 2004, 1437–45). We also see such interaction in the many greetings at the end of Paul's letters, which were also circulated among the churches. It is noteworthy that Paul's thirty-eight coworkers named in the New Testament came from nearly every church Paul had planted and worked in locations other than their home (see Schnabel 2004, 1426). They served as coworkers, travel companions, delegates, or messengers, creating a bond among the churches (Ollrog 1979).

Various churches made charitable contributions for the Jerusalem church (e.g., 2 Cor 8–9) as a sign of solidarity. The practical advantages of such networking for mutual encouragement, teaching, accountability, and assistance are obvious. However, this practice also represents a deeper theological concern for the unity of the body of Christ (e.g., Eph 4:4–6). Every local church is spiritually linked with the universal church, bridging space and time. That unity needs to find practical expression.

Today we live in a complex world of Christian denominations, traditions, and affiliations unimaginable in the first century. This confusion, however, should not cause strategists and leaders of contemporary movements to neglect the importance of being connected with other churches and the wider body of Christ. CPMs today must find ways to be networked regionally and internationally with other likeminded churches, leading to mutual encouragement, accountability, and cooperation in world evangelization.

Conclusion

We should give our best efforts, exercise wisdom, learn from history, develop new methods, and follow biblical guidelines in reaching the nations with the gospel and launching CPMs. It is a matter of wise stewardship to invest our energies and efforts in approaches that have the most promise of bearing fruit. Not all methods are equally effective, and no one method will be effective everywhere. We can be grateful for ongoing research and resources to discern the best means. At the same time, we must remember that movements cannot be humanly manufactured by merely adopting a particular method or strategy. God must give the growth. Only by the grace of God and in his timing will CPMs emerge.

Biblical scholars have argued that Luke intentionally did not provide a proper conclusion to the book of Acts. His "rhetoric of silence" prompts the reader to enter the story and continue the ongoing mission of bringing the gospel to the ends of the earth (Marguerat 2002, 205–30; Troftgruben 2010). We, as followers of Jesus, have inherited this ongoing task today. Will we continue writing that story? Will the disciples we make, the churches we plant, and the movements that emerge be consistent with the salvation-historical trajectory that was launched in Acts? These are the questions that everyone engaged in CPMs must answer with great faith, commitment, and discernment.[23]

Reference List

Banks, Robert. 1994. *Paul's Idea of Community*, rev. ed. Peabody, MA: Hendrickson.

Bock, Darrell. 1998. "Scripture and the Realisation of God's Promises." In *Witness to the Gospel: The Theology of Acts*, edited by I. Howard Marshall and David Peterson, 41–62. Grand Rapids: Eerdmans.

Bruce, F. F. 1952. *The Acts of the Apostles*. Grand Rapids: Eerdmans.

Carson. D. A. 1992. "The Purpose of Signs and Wonders in the New Testament." In *Power Religion: The Selling Out of the Evangelical Religion?* edited by Michael Scott Horton, 89–118. Chicago: Moody.

Cooper, Kate, and Jeremy Gregory, eds. 2005. *Signs, Wonders, Miracles: Representations of Divine Power in the Life of the Church: Papers Read at the 2003 Summer Meeting and the 2004 Winter Meeting of the Ecclesiastical History Society*. Rochester, NY: Boydell.

23 I wish to thank John Cheong, members of the Deerfield Dialog Group (colleagues at Trinity Evangelical Divinity School), and the editors of this volume, who read this chapter and gave valuable feedback.

Cooper, Michael T. 2020. *Ephesiology: A Study of the Ephesian Movement.* Littleton, CO: William Carey Publishing.

Flemming, Dean. 2005. *Contextualization in the New Testament: Patterns for Theology and Mission.* Downers Grove, IL: InterVarsity.

Garrison, David. 2004. *Church Planting Movements: How God Is Redeeming a Lost World.* Midlothian, VA: WIGTake Resources.

Gehring, Roger W. 2004. *House Church and Mission: The Importance of Household Structures in Early Christianity.* Peabody, MA: Hendrickson.

Jipp, Joshua W. 2018. *Reading Acts.* Eugene, OR: Cascade.

Keener, Craig S. 2010. "The Plausibility of Luke's Growth Figures in Acts 2.41; 4.4; 21.20." *Journal of Greco-Roman Christianity and Judaism* 7: 140–63.

———. 2014. *Acts: An Exegetical Commentary*, vol. 3. Grand Rapids: Baker Academic.

Kodell, Jerome. 1974. "The Word of God Grew: the Ecclesial Tendency of Logos in Acts 6,7; 12,24; 19,20." *Biblica* 55, no. 4: 505–19.

Longenecker, Richard N. 1981. "Acts." In *The Expositors Bible Commentary*, vol. 9. Frank E. Gabelein, gen. ed. Grand Rapids: Zondervan.

Marguerat, Daniel. 2002. *The First Christian Historian: Writing the "Acts of the Apostles."* Cambridge: Cambridge University Press.

Metzger, Bruce M. 1971. *A Textual Commentary on the Greek New Testament.* London: United Bible Societies.

Mitchell, Margaret M (Margaret Mary). 1992. "New Testament Envoys in the Context of Greco-Roman Diplomatic and Epistolary Conventions: The Example of Timothy and Titus." *Journal of Biblical Literature* 111, no. 4: 641–62.

Moo, Douglas J. 1996. *The Epistle to the Romans.* Grand Rapids: Eerdmans.

Ollrog, Wolf-Henning. 1979. *Paulus und seine Mitarbeiter.* Neukirchen-Vluyn, Germany: Neukirchener Verlag.

Ott, Craig. 2019. *The Church on Mission: A Biblical Vision for Transformation among All People.* Grand Rapids: Baker Academic.

Pao, David W. 2000. *Acts and the Isaianic New Exodus.* Grand Rapids: Baker Academic.

Peterson, David G. 2009. *The Acts of the Apostles.* The Pillar New Testament Commentary. Grand Rapids, MI; Nottingham, England: William B. Eerdmans.

Polhill, John B. 1992. *Acts*, vol. 26, The New American Commentary. Nashville: Broadman & Holman.

Prince, Andrew J. 2017. *Contextualization of the Gospel: Towards an Evangelical Approach in Light of Scripture and the Church Fathers.* Eugene: OR: Wipf & Stock.

Reinhardt, Wolfgang. 1995. *Das Wachstum des Gottesvolkes: Biblische Theologie des Gemeindewachstums.* Göttingen, Germany: Vandenhoeck & Ruprecht.

Riesner, Rainer. 1998. *Paul's Early Years: Chronology, Mission Strategy, Theology.* Grand Rapids: Eerdmans.

Roetzel, Calvin J. 2009. "Tarsus." In *The New Interpreter's Dictionary of the Bible*, vol. 5, 474–76. Nashville: Abingdon.

Rommen, Edward, ed. 1995. *Spiritual Power and Missions: Raising the Issues*. Pasadena, CA: William. Carey.

Rosner, Brian S. 1998. "The Progress of the Word." In *Witness to the Gospel: The Theology of Acts*, edited by I. Howard Marshall and David Peterson, 215–33. Grand Rapids: Eerdmans.

Samkutty, V. J. 2006. *The Samaritan Mission in Acts*. New York: T&T Clark.

Sarles, Ken L. 1988. "An Appraisal of the Signs and Wonders Movement." *Bibliotheca Sacra* 145 (577): 57–82.

Schnabel, Eckhard. 2004. *Early Christian Mission*, 2 vols. Downers Grove, IL: InterVarsity.

———. 2008. *Paul the Missionary: Realities, Strategies, and Methods*. Downers Grove, IL: IVP Academic.

Smith, Steve, and Ying Kai. 2011. *T4T: A Discipleship Revolution*. Monument, CO: WIGTake Resources.

Stenschke, Christoph W. 2019. "Die Bedeutung der übergemeindlichen Verbindungen im Urchristentum für die neutestamentliche Wissenschaft." *Journal of Early Christian History* 9, no. 3: 1–47.

Strauss, Mark L. 2011. "The Purpose of Luke-Acts: Reaching a Consensus." In *New Testament Theology in Light of the Mission of the Church*, edited by Jon C. Laansma, Grant R. Osborne, and Ray F. Van Neste, 135–50. Eugene, OR: Wipf & Stock.

Towner, Philip H. 1998. "Mission Practice and Theology under Reconstruction (Acts 18-–20)." In *Witness to the Gospel: The Theology of Acts*, edited by I. Howard Marshall and David Peterson, 417–436. Grand Rapids: Eerdmans.

Troftgruben, Troy M. 2010. *A Conclusion Unhindered: a Study of the Ending of Acts Within Its Literary Environment*. WUNT 2.280. Tübingen, Germany: Mohr Siebeck.

Trousdale, Jerry. 2012. *Miraculous Movements*. Nashville: Thomas Nelson.

Van der Merwe, Dirk G. 2010. "The Power of the Gospel Victorious over the Power of Evil in Acts of the Apostles." *Scriptura* 103: 79–94.

Wagner, C. Peter. 1988. *The Third Wave of the Holy Spirit: Encountering the Power of Signs and Wonders Today*. Ann Arbor, MI: Servant.

Wiarda, Timothy. 2003. "The Jerusalem Council and the Theological Task." *Journal of the Evangelical Theological Society* 46, no. 2 (June): 233–48.

Wilson, Benjamin R. 2017. "The Depiction of Church Growth in Acts." *Journal of the Evangelical Theological Society* 60, no. 2 (June): 317–32.

Wimber, John, and Kevin Springer. 1986. *Power Evangelism*. San Francisco: Harper & Row.

Witherington, Ben III. 1998. *The Acts of the Apostles: A Socio-Theoretical Commentary*. Grand Rapids: Eerdmans.

Wu, Jackson. 2014. "There Are No Church Planting Movements in the Bible." *Global Missiology* 1, no. 12. http://ojs.globalmissiology.org/index.php/english/article/view/1711/3794.

8

God's Expanding Family: The Social Architecture of Ekklēsia Movements

Trevor Larsen

The number of movements to Christ around the world has multiplied dramatically since 2006.[1] As these young movements increase in size and maturity, they face the challenge of developing into *"ekklēsia* movements." I use the word *ekklēsia* (Greek for "church") to signify linked believer communities which follow patterns similar to those described in the New Testament period, not necessarily the patterns of conventional churches in the modern era.[2] Culturally fitted to their contexts, movements consist of disciples making disciples while linking them into communities of God's expanding family. This chapter focuses on movements among unreached people groups (UPGs), which must survive and thrive in adverse conditions.[3]

In this chapter, I will explore patterns of thriving ekklēsia movements consistent with those of New Testament movements. I will first investigate selected biblical patterns of ekklēsia movements during the New Testament era, then describe how some current movements among UPGs express those patterns.

---

1   I am using the definition of "movement" upon which many organizations have agreed: four or more generations of believer communities of more than one thousand believers, within a limited number of years.

2   "Many of the churches planted by Paul would not meet what many today might consider a minimal standard for being an established church. Nevertheless, he addressed even the most problematical congregations as 'the church.' This forces us to consider more carefully what genuinely constitutes a local church in the biblical sense" (Ott and Wilson 2010, 4).

3   See more resources at www.FocusOnFruit.org, where a book on "Ekklesia for Movements" will be available in 2021.

New Testament developmental phases of ekklēsia, such as the pre-Pentecost embryonic phase and the birth, childhood, young adult, and adult phases, offer rich lenses of reflection diachronically. As I hope to show, the phase-by-phase development of ekklēsia from embryo to adulthood is a critical issue in the global reality of emerging movements today.

Hermeneutical Lenses for New Testament Ekklēsia Movements

To study ekklēsia movements, we must address these questions: 1) What passages of the New Testament describe ekklēsia movements? 2) What are the contexts and developmental stages of ekklēsia in those passages? 3) What authority do these biblical descriptions have for development of ekklēsia movements today? To answer these questions, I will draw on three hermeneutical lenses.

The first lens for understanding ekklēsia in its embryonic phase is the **Jesus band**, described in narrative passages of the Gospels and in Jesus' teachings. Jesus' prototype believer community began with attachment to Jesus: "Follow me." Those who were attached to Jesus joined others who had responded to his call.

Second, Jesus' prototype of believer community was missional. Jesus presented to his disciples a model of missional believer community initiated by the Jesus band, in which missional pairs identified receptive households and attached to them to renew them as households of faith. This social pattern brought the gospel to receptive families and then to villages.

Third, Jesus redefined ekklēsia as the family of God (Matt 12:20). Renewed households which linked to each other as a redefined family were the social structure containing the fruit of gospel proclamation. Jesus trained his disciples to become brothers and sisters, known by their love and servanthood and by giving honor rather than seeking it. Jesus redefined patrons and leaders as servants who nurtured the family of God.

Fourth, Jesus taught about ekklēsia as representing the kingdom of God on earth. Jesus gave people with faith in Christ the authority of God's kingdom to overturn the kingdom of darkness and release mankind from its bonds (Matt 16:18–20). When people assemble in threes to pray for the renewal of a brother or sister (Matt 18:15–20), Christ the King is in their midst.

Fifth, Jesus described ekklēsia as a work under development, both as a building being built by him and as plants growing through their attachment to him. These were the fundamental characteristics of the Jesus band, the prototype believer community.

The second lens for understanding the birth and development of ekklēsia in different cultural contexts is the **disciples' communities of the Spirit**, as described in the narrative passages of Acts. The Holy Spirit plays the central role in forming ekklēsia in Acts, empowering apostolic agents to catalyze gospel expansion and renew social structures that support movements. The Spirit-formed fruit of the gospel is ekklēsia. God increases ekklēsia's geographic and ethnic diversity, as the disciples' communities advanced by phases from the Jerusalem community (Acts 1–7) to bridging communities (Acts 8–12) to Gentile-region communities (Acts 13–28). Repeating patterns in each phase and context reveal ekklēsia as an expanding system adjusting to each new context. The apostolic agents linked diverse regional churches together into a mosaic.

The third lens for understanding ekklēsia comes from the **social dynamics in movements**, as found in portions of the Epistles. These are rich in the social dimensions of the gospel, revealing not only the community's values and behaviors, but also the relational connections that framed ekklēsia.

A principle coloring all three of these hermeneutical lenses is "pattern imitation," one example of which is Paul's well-known statement in 1 Corinthians 11:1: "Follow my example, as I follow the example of Christ." In eleven passages, Paul encourages multiple churches and mission team members in pattern imitation. This is critical to the expansion of ekklēsia movements, for teaching alone would not have kept up with the pace of growth.[4] A hermeneutic of pattern imitation highlights selected aspects of the social structure of ekklēsia movements described in the biblical narratives and the nondidactic portions of the Epistles that are rich in social dynamics. In this chapter, I will not highlight a fourth lens for understanding embryonic ekklēsia—i.e., the epistolary teachings on ekklēsia.

Five Ekklēsia Movements in the New Testament

An overview of five movements in the New Testament reveals that the preaching of the gospel by apostolic agents produced at least five expanding ekklēsia movements. As movements expanded in geographic breadth, numbers of believer communities, and ethnic diversity, mobile apostles linked them into a family-like mosaic.

First, the Jerusalem movement multiplied to three thousand on the Day of Pentecost (Acts 2:41), then to five thousand men (Acts 4:4; this many heads of households indicates about twenty thousand believers) in just three years. By Acts 21:20, Jerusalem Jewish believers numbered "many thousands," who were "ardent observers of the Law." This amount of gospel fruit in Jerusalem was surprisingly large, considering that there had been a mass exodus of believers from Jerusalem due to persecution (Acts 8:1).

A second linked movement began seven years after the Jerusalem movement, through the witness and disciple-making of Greek-speaking Jews who had been driven from their homes after Stephen's martyrdom (Acts 11:19–21).

---

4 Paul uses the Greek words *mimetei* ("imitate") and *tupos* ("type" or "pattern") in several of these passages, and encourages pattern imitation in other ways—to the Thessalonians (1 Thess 1:5–10; 2:14; 2 Thess 3:7–9), Philippians (Phil 3:17; 4:8–9), Ephesians (Acts 20:18–35), Corinthians (1 Cor 4:14–17; 1 Cor 10:31–11:1), Timothy (1 Tim 4:11–12; 2 Tim 2:2; 3:10–14), and Titus (Titus 2:7).

This second movement expanded from Jerusalem to Jews in Judea, Samaria, Cypress, Phoenicia, Cyrene, and Antioch. Certain Jewish believers from Cypress and Cyrene bridged across culture to win many Gentiles in Antioch. Greek believers in Antioch signaled that ekklēsia was becoming something beyond a renewal movement within Judaism.

When the Jerusalem church heard the report, they gave the believer community in Antioch special attention by devoting Barnabas to its maturation for a full year. Barnabas invited Paul to help, and Antioch became a mission center from which this second movement expanded to other areas. Mission teams came to and went from Antioch on seven different occasions. Though we are not told the number of believers in this second movement, we are told of many unnamed believers spreading the gospel, resulting in a significant increase in breadth and ethnicity. Greek-speaking, bicultural Jews played a key role in this missional expansion.

A third linked movement multiplied in the region of Pisidian Antioch, Iconium, Lystra, and Syrian Antioch. We are not told the number of believers, but Acts 14:21 tells us there were many disciples in the city of Derbe. Acts 14:23 reports that within one year of the preaching of the gospel, a team of elders was appointed for each of many new churches, indicating a fast rate of multiplication and maturation. This ekklēsia movement started with Jews in the region, but soon grew strong among Gentiles.

A fourth linked movement took place in the province of Macedonia, with churches first established in Philippi, Thessalonica, and Berea. Three years later, Paul praised the new believers in Thessalonica for their influence throughout the provinces of Macedonia and Achaia and beyond (1 Thess 1:7–8), indicating that new believers had spread this movement widely. Paul praised this movement for their transformed lives, which were a strong witness (1 Thess 1:3–4, 9-10; 3:2–5), and for imitating the movement in Judea in enduring suffering for the gospel (1 Thess 2:14; 2 Thess 1:3–4).

A fifth linked movement occurred in the province of Asia Minor, centered in Ephesus. After the Jews rejected Paul's attempts to reach them, Paul spent two years intensively discipling a small number of disciples in a privately owned rental hall. These Ephesian disciples proclaimed the gospel widely during this time, "so that all who lived in the province of Asia, both Jews and Gentiles, heard the word of the Lord" (Acts 19:9–10). Based on the large value of the magic books burned in Ephesus during a renewal (Acts 19:19–20),[5] we estimate over ten thousand believers near Ephesus alone, after two years. Ekklēsia was established in ten cities in the province of Asia Minor.

---

5 The magic books burned in Ephesus were estimated to be worth fifty thousand drachmas, about fifty thousand day's wages. An average household's daily wage in the US in 2019 was two hundred dollars, so these books would be valued at ten million dollars in the US in 2019. We might picture each of ten thousand households today burning their magic books worth one thousand dollars to total ten million dollars. In any case, the report of magic books worth fifty thousand drachmas indicates a large number of believing households.

The Nature of Ekklēsia:
Spiritual Family and Expanding Organism

In the book of Acts, ekklēsia is created by the Spirit. The Holy Spirit is central in empowering apostolic agents and through them birthing ekklēsia movements. The Spirit empowers witnesses (Acts 1:8; 4:31) and uses miraculous signs to convince unbelievers (2:4ff). When the gift of the Spirit comes upon new believers (2:38), they are added to the believer community and actively participate in ekklēsia's practices (2:38–47). The Spirit guards the purity of ekklēsia (5:3, 9), empowers those to be selected as leaders (6:3), and guides apostolic agents to open the next area (8:29). The Spirit generates ekklēsia, fills it with power, and miraculously transforms it. Epistolary passages collaborate this theme; the Spirit distributes capacities to its members to build it, while unifying it (1 Cor 12). The Spirit bears witness with our spirit that we are children of God (Rom 8:16).

This community of the Spirit is also a social community, built on the primary social unit of renewed families. In the Gospels and Acts, the Spirit forms ekklēsia to fellowship with God and each other, as a distinctive mark of the church, using family terms. Believers are called "the household of faith" (Gal 6:10). Young leaders are to treat ekklēsia members as fathers, brothers, and sisters (1 Tim 5:1–2). Paul uses family terms with his disciples: he was like a father and mother to them, and he addressed them as his brothers and sisters (1 Thess 2:7–14).[6] The nature of ekklēsia as the household of God (Eph 2:18–19) influences the social structure of ekklēsia movements.[7]

What emerges in the biblical images is that ekklēsia by nature is a living, growing organism, in the process of being built up and expanding. Ekklēsia is expansive, not static, by nature because the gospel that produces it continuously adds more adherents, and this produces movements. Jesus promised he is building his ekklēsia (Matt 16:18).

Biotic images picture how ekklēsia grows, lives, sustains itself, bears fruit, reproduces, and moves into new areas and peoples (Eph 2:21–22; 4:15–16). It grows through repeating patterns: the social units replicate themselves as larger and larger units of the same kind. In the Bible, ekklēsia has no buildings and is not limited to any location; it has organic structure.

Social Structures in Ekklēsia
That Support and Sustain Its Multiplication

Three social structures have strong biblical support and are critical in ekklēsia movements today: 1) two interdependent wings of ekklēsia, 2) three levels of linked ekklēsia units, and 3) teams of leaders.

---

6   See also 1 Pet 2:17; 5:9; 1 John 3:1; John 1:12; Eph 2:19; Gal 6:10; Phlm 2; Rom 16:2, 13.

7   "Given the family character of the Christian community, the homes of its members provided the most conducive atmosphere in which they could give expression to the bond they had in common" (Banks 1994, 56).

The Two Interdependent Wings of the Body of Christ

Mission teams were the first wing that drove the expansion of the organic system (Acts 9:15; 13:1–3), complemented by local believer communities as the second wing that solidified the fruit of the gospel locally. These two wings working together developed ekklēsia movements.

Jesus provided the prototype of a mission team that birthed and then partnered with a local believer community as a two-winged organism. The mission of the Jesus band followed Jesus' holistic pattern: preaching the gospel, healing the sick, and freeing the demonized (Matt 10:1–6), which resulted in people becoming receptive to the gospel.

How was this fruit-bearing organized socially? In his three mission trainings of the Jesus band, Jesus taught repeated patterns he had already demonstrated in his ministry. He trained his disciples to rely on the hospitality of receptive households to provide an operational base for mission in a new area (Luke 10:4–7). After the first training, Jesus sent his inner circle of twelve on a mission to the Jews only (Matt 10:5–6), then sent them to Jews and Gentiles after a second training (Luke 9), and then sent the seventy-two on mission after his third mission training (Luke 10:1–11). Taken together, his mission trainees learned about gospel preaching, identifying receptive households, healing, and freeing the demonized by immediately after training doing what they had observed and heard Jesus doing.

The Jesus band's pattern in the first stage was "mission pairs to receptive households." This mission thrust expanded as each mission pair successfully connected to responsive hosts in the area. Jesus' mission team then followed the same pattern to expand from "receptive hosts to receptive villages" in the second stage. This household-based mission strategy fit well with the centrality of *oikos* in the society, which included nuclear family and others attached to them. Jesus' mission was financed when itinerate mission pairs placed themselves in a vulnerable position financially and socially by leaving their home base, then responsive hosts provided for their needs in a reciprocal relationship. The mission pair served responsive households and their relational networks. This extended family network provided credibility in the area and supplied mission teams' practical needs.

Sometimes their mission approach included a third phase: "mission pair to transformed witness." The Samaritan woman immediately shared about Messiah with her village, and they believed (John 4:39). The Gerasene demoniac immediately proclaimed the gospel in the Decapolis region (Mark 5:19–20), and Zacchaeus the tax collector immediately witnessed to his household and social circle (Luke 19:1–10). In each phase a missionary pair connected to a responsive household. This connection renewed the household spiritually and empowered it as a new center of ekklēsia expansion.[8]

---

8 For further discussion of how Jesus and the disciples used transformational dialog in the process of group formation, see chapter 1 of *Core Skills for Movement Leaders*, available at www.FocusOnFruit.org.

Mission teams in Acts repeated the Jesus band's pattern of birthing then partnering with the local believer community as a two-winged organism of mobile teams and local communities. Examples include Peter and his team with Cornelius' household (Acts 10:44–48), and Paul and his team with the households of Lydia and the Philippian jailor (Acts 16).

Most new areas were reached by apostolic mission teams, the driving force multiplying ekklēsia movements.[9] Mission teams' second role after birthing ekklēsia, was "appointing local elders in every church," a consistent pattern implemented within one year of the preaching of the gospel (Acts 14:23). The third role of trans-local apostolic agents was to build the scalable architecture of trans-regional ekklēsia movements. This included providing foundational teaching and encouragement based on feedback from Paul's representatives (1 Thess 3), problem solving (Acts 6 and 15; 3 John 9–12), training and mobilizing other apostolic agents, and helping local leaders mature (Acts 20:17–38). This process continued long after handing over leadership to teams of local elders. The fourth role of apostolic agents was to weave together ekklēsia from different regions into a trans-regionally linked family (Rom 16; Col 4; Phlm). They did this by making personal visits, writing letters, praying, sending emissaries, sending commendations, and sharing information about regions in financial need.

Local ekklēsia conserved and nurtured the fruit of the gospel and supported local and near-region expansion. Teams of local elders solidified ekklēsia. They identified selected believers to join mission teams for a time.[10] Some local believers played a stronger role in the bridging of the gospel to new social segments, especially bicultural mobile individuals such as Peter, Philip, Priscilla, and Aquila, as well as bicultural ekklēsia such as the Greek-speaking Jewish segment of Jerusalem's ekklēsia.

Apostolic agents, prophets, evangelists, and pastor-teachers equipped all believers to be priests, who then actively built ekklēsia (Eph 4:11–16). The sphere of the equipping of apostolic agents and prophets in the biblical narrative was trans-regional (Acts 9:15). Most believer-priests served their ekklēsia locally, though the mobile jobs of others widened their ministry, and some (such as Timothy) were recommended for mission teams.

Three Levels of Linked Family Networks

The term *ekklēsia* is used flexibly in the Bible of three social-unit sizes or levels; all were an expression of ekklēsia. Ekklēsia multiplied as many *house* ekklēsia which were linked as one *city* ekklēsia.[11] Multiple city ekklēsia shared identity with other

---

9   There are exceptions to the primary role of apostles in opening new areas. Unnamed believers driven from Jerusalem by persecution birthed ekklēsia in new areas (Acts 11:19).

10 Onesiphorus traveled from Ephesus to Rome to support Paul in prison, as he had done in Ephesus (2 Tim 1:16–17).

11 "Many NT scholars believe that both forms—small house churches and the whole church as a unit at that location—existed side by side in early Christianity" (Gehring 2004, 25).

cities as a regional ekklēsia. *House ekklēsia was the primary component of ekklēsia for the first two or three centuries.*

Jesus provided the prototype of house ekklēsia. Peter's house was the center of Jesus' ministry of teaching and healing, prayer and fellowship in Capernaum (Mark 1:29, 33; 2:1; 3:20; 9:23). Peter's house was the operational base for mission to Capernaum, Chorazin, and Bethsaida, around the Sea of Galilee. This home became available to him when he called Peter, the head of this household. With Peter, Jesus gained two disciples (Peter and Andrew) and Peter's extended family (including his mother-in-law). Through Peter's extended family, the Jesus band enjoyed access to their wide relational network. The home of Martha in Bethany similarly provided a household operational base for Jesus' mission in that area (Luke 10:38–39).

The early church movements were centered in households. "Households thus constituted the focus, locus, and nucleus of the ministry and mission of the Christian movement" (Elliot 1981, 188). Early house church gatherings included the word, bread breaking, prayer, koinonia fellowship, and shared funds (Acts 2:41–47; 4:32–37).

How many believers gathered? Weighing archeological research, Krautheimer (1965, 15–17) concluded that from 30 to 150 AD believers gathered only in houses, and their gatherings included a common meal.[12] Based on rabbinic text and archeological investigation, Gehring (2004, 45) describes the typical living room in rural Palestine at the time as five square meters, or fifty-four square feet. Ten people could gather if seated closely together. Common courtyards provided somewhat larger space during the warm season. In Corinth, Gehring (2004, 135–36) describes 3-meter by 4-meter workshops unearthed, the largest 4.5 meters by 6 meters, and posits gatherings of twenty people (2004, 135). Sometimes a room was added on flat rooftops of larger homes. A gathering of 120 (Acts 1:12–15) represented the upper seating limit (Gehring 2004, 65).

Acts 4:4 mentions five thousand men, which I view as heads of households. Gehring posits an average of ten to twenty people per household, including servants and extended family (2004, 87). This indicates an estimate of fifty thousand to one hundred thousand believers. If we use half of Gehring's smaller number—i.e., twenty-five thousand believers—and estimate that four households on average (twenty people) could gather in the largest rooms in the largest of their homes, there would have been approximately 1,250 house churches in Jerusalem by Acts 4:4, three years after Jesus' resurrection.

---

12 "Archaeology confirms that for the first three centuries, the meeting place of Christians was private homes, not distinctive church buildings" (Ladd 1974, 532).

Home-based meetings depended on patronage in the expansion of ekklēsia.[13] Patrons' larger houses became natural gathering points, and this often made the host the leader. The home of Mary, John Mark's mother and Barnabas' aunt, became a frequent gathering place. Mary was wealthy enough to have a house with a courtyard and a servant (Acts 12:12–13). Lydia, a dealer in luxury cloth, had both the wealth and the influence to host and legitimize new believers in Philippi (Acts 16:14–15, 40). Priscilla and Aquila's mobile business was successful enough to serve as a missional center for gatherings in Rome, Corinth, and Ephesus (Acts 18:18, 26; 1 Cor 16:19).

City ekklēsia was a collective of multiple house ekklēsia in the same city or small area. We have indications of eight house ekklēsia (or at least renewed households) in Rome who shared a joint identity as one city ekklēsia (Rom 16). From the descriptions, we can estimate that the larger of these house gatherings included twenty believers. Paul identified several people by name, though he had not been to Rome. Believers he knew elsewhere had moved to Rome, then these believers sent word of others. These eight house churches were treated as one spiritual family in Rome, though the number of house churches and the breadth of the city make it unlikely that they all met together.

Believers who gathered in six house ekklēsia in Corinth shared a joint identity as one city ekklēsia. Only in Corinth does the Bible report that the *whole church* of a city met together in one place. Meeting in one place, whether the whole church or a portion of it, provided an occasion to test whether the rich and the poor would demonstrate their unity in Christ by sharing their food during the Lord's Supper.

Judging from the large number of people who lived close enough to burn their magic books in Ephesus, the "church of Ephesus" was probably not limited to the city proper but also included believers in nearby areas. Fellowship would have been more frequent with those who lived closer. City ekklēsia could have had a double meaning, sometimes referring only to those house ekklēsia within the city and on other occasions adding the additional house churches near the city.

Larger city *ekklēsia* gatherings (more than twelve) occurred at Tyrannus' lecture hall in Ephesus, at Corinth, and at the upper room in Jerusalem (120 people). The church quickly outgrew the largest of these, for the "five thousand men" in Acts 4:4 were too many to have met together in the temple courts of Jerusalem. Clearly, gathering the whole church together in one place was not a necessary condition for the shared identity of each city ekklēsia.

We know for certain that there were at least second-generation churches during the period described in Acts. The lecture hall of Tyrannus functioned as a

---

13 "The ability to attract such individuals [patrons] in greater numbers was probably a significant factor in the social 'triumph' of Christianity. These individuals provided the network of social relationships and economic capabilities that made possible growth, expansion, acquisition, and adaptation" (White 2004, 57).

mission center training for first-generation Ephesian believers, then those trained intensively by Paul spread the gospel. The small number of believers Paul trained intensively could not have personally proclaimed the gospel to everyone in the province of Asia Minor in two years (Acts 19:10). Thus, at least third-generation churches are indicated.[14] The churches in Hierapolis, Laodicea, and Colossae were reached by Epaphras (Col 1:7; 4:12), one of their own, who may have been in the first-generation church Paul trained in Ephesus. Third-generation local leaders identified as "the brothers and sisters at Laodicea," Nympha, Archippus (Col 4:15–17), and Onesimus (Col 4:9) extended the ministry that Epaphras had initiated, and Epaphras remained influential throughout the Lycean valley. Local leaders, rather than Paul, were the primary church planters, for Paul had not met many of the believers in Colossae (Col 2:1).

Heterogeneity increased as numbers increased, as evidenced by differences in ethnicity (Acts 6:1), economics (Jas 2:1–7), and affiliation (1 Cor 1:11–15), which surfaced tensions. Differences within city ekklēsia tested unity and pushed believers to redefine oneness in Christ as inclusive of differences.

Regional ekklēsia was the shared identity of multiple city ekklēsia in a wider region. On some issues, all the house and city ekklēsia in a region acted with one joint identity. Believers in the province of Macedonia shared a joint identity as one ekklēsia that contributed to the needs of the poor in Jerusalem (Rom 15:26), though there were multiple city churches in Macedonia (2 Cor 8:1). Ekklēsia in Samaria, Judea, Achaia, and Galilee were described as each having a regional identity (Acts 9:31; Rom 15:26; 2 Cor 9:2) and each consisting of many city ekklēsia (the churches of Galatia: 1 Cor 16:19; the churches of Judea: Gal 1:22).

Differences of culture, ethnicity, religious background (e.g., god fearers; idol worshipers) and religious variant (e.g., believers from the circumcision party: Acts 11:2; 15:1) led to theological dispute within the Judean regional ekklēsia (Acts 10:1–11:18). Increasing diversity challenged the expanding ekklēsia movement and helped its theology and its problem-solving to mature.

Three levels of ekklēsia were linked in a family-like mosaic as they expanded. All three levels of ekklēsia operated as an expanding family network. Kinship terms were commonly used by trans-local apostolic agents as greetings, which helped believers strengthen and broaden their sense of redefined family. Deep relational ties bonded them together. Disputes were settled in a family way. Donations were carried by apostolic agents from one regional ekklēsia to share in the suffering of another regional ekklēsia (Acts 11:27–29), which helped strengthen family bonds.

Traveling apostolic agents from mission teams commonly used commendations to weave together believers in one area with believers in other

---

14 Paul's practice was to multiply disciples in three generations after himself, as evident in 2 Timothy 2:2. Readers often overlook that there is a *group* of believers in each of these three generations.

areas (cf. Rom 16). The organic social architecture built by apostolic agents framed expansion to other regions and people groups, such as Paul asking the Romans to help with his mission to Spain (Rom 15:22–24). This encouraged ekklēsia to bridge from one people group to the next and built unity between them. Ekklēsia became a multicultural mosaic at the regional ekklēsia level, and in certain multicultural cities, like Antioch.

Leadership Teams

A team of elders oversaw each city ekklēsia, though some likely included believer groups in the regions around their city.

If my estimate of 1,250 house churches in Jerusalem in Acts 4:4 is accurate, Jesus' twelve disciples were far too few to have led them all. Who led more than one thousand house churches in Jerusalem? From the renewed *oikos* household social structure, leaders emerged and were recognized by each small group of believers. The Twelve as a leadership team would have given oversight to more than a thousand house church leaders.

The mission team leader's first action, upon returning to a new brotherhood of believers they had birthed, was to select a team of leaders for every ekklēsia (Acts 14:23). Transferring leadership of a newly established city ekklēsia from the mission team to local elders within one year of people hearing the gospel was an established, repeating pattern of apostolic teams. Selecting teams of local elders ensures locally fitted leadership, supports leaders' growth and succession, and frees the mission team to bridge to the next area with the gospel. A team of leaders provides a visible model of transformation to a believer community. They model what should be imitated, give spiritual guidance, teach, and solve problems.

The Ephesian elders who were retrained in Acts 20 probably extended their reach beyond the borders of city ekklēsia to include the outlying areas, since the large number of magic books burned during a renewal indicate a large movement. This was likely a small region leadership team. James, John, and Peter were prominent in the leadership team over the small region of Jerusalem.[15] They arranged for the formation of a second-level leadership team over the feeding of widows (Acts 6:1–7), due to the increasing demands of expansion.

Mission leaders also operated in teams, making periodic mentoring visits to help teams of local elders mature. Senior members of mission teams trained junior members and gave them assignments. Paul selected a small number from each region to train while travelling together (Acts 20:4), some of whom were later sent to other regions.

---

15 For an extended discussion of how modeling, spiritual guidance, problem solving, and regional scaling work out in practice, see *Core Skills for Movement Leaders*, chapters 7–10.

Biblical and Social Features of Ekklēsia Movements in UPGs Today

Having described the ekklēsia movements in the New Testament, I now want to reflect on a network of movements in UPGs today that I have been serving. The New Testament's description of movements both legitimizes similar movements happening today and provides guidance for them. Over a period of sixteen years, ending in December 2014, a movement in Asia had grown to eighteen thousand believers in small groups in twenty-seven UPGs in one country and had multiplied in two other countries. Five years later, in December 2019, this network of movements had multiplied to three hundred thousand believers in small groups, in fifty-eight UPGs in one country and in eighteen UPGs in other countries.

Sixteen male movement catalysts who lead this network of movements have been in dialogue about ekklēsia for many years, and have been implementing these principles. Fourteen are Bible college graduates; four have doctorates in theology. One is a Bible college president; three others are seminary professors. The following discussion summarizes dialogues over two decades as they implemented in the field and reflected on Scripture. This is what they believe and what they practice. In a recent discussion, they asked me to emphasize two aspects of the nature of ekklēsia before discussing the three social structure elements of ekklēsia.

Movements as "Spirit Brotherhood"

In the past, one of the movement catalysts read the entirety of the book of Acts for the first time then gave me a summary of its essence. He used two Arabic words to summarize Acts to me. In English, these are "Spirit" (born of Spirit, and spiritual in nature) and "brotherhood" (family bonds between all those who have God as Father). I consider this an apt summary of Acts. In a recent dialogue, this movement catalyst emphasized that first and foremost, ekklēsia is "Spirit brotherhood." What does he mean?

Ekklēsia is spiritual at its core and not merely social. Ekklēsia movements are of God and belong to God; it is God's divine work. This brother emphasized that ekklēsia's central source is the Word of God, and that the gospel is the lens that guides us to integrate the Torah, Psalms, and Gospels and shapes our monotheism as Christocentric.[16] God revealed himself to humanity and initiated the formation of his renewed people as ekklēsia.

He stressed that we are only God's servants who participate in God's mission to build ekklēsia. Other catalysts listened to him during a joint Zoom call. They then added to this theme, highlighting the central role of the Spirit in ekklēsia in 1 Corinthians 12 and 14. The Spirit is the one who supplies divine capacity to build up the body of Christ, and the Spirit unites us in Christ.

---

16 Muslims believe God revealed three books prior to the Qur'an: the Torah, the Psalms, and the Gospel. Muslim-majority contexts, believers use these terms to denote the whole of the Old and New Testaments.

Ekklēsia is a spiritual family formed by its head. These movement catalysts voiced their shared conviction that the brotherhood bonds they experience in the ekklēsia movements they lead are much deeper and richer than any they have experienced in conventional churches they had previously served. They underlined that these brotherhood bonds, created by the Spirit, are what link ekklēsia movements in oneness. It is the spiritual-social structure of brotherhood that functionally replaces the organizational structure found in conventional churches to solidify a movement. Their field experience of shaping ekklēsia movements has expanded over the years. This has enabled them to experience the richness of their spiritual brotherhood and led them to much reflection on this biblical theme.

Movements as Organic Systems

In joint discussion, these movement catalysts emphasized that ekklēsia is an organism, not an organization. It is a system, but an organic system. They reported that in conventional churches they had previously led, only five percent of the members were active; but in ekklēsia movements they lead now, *most* members are active, and 20 percent of believer-priests are leading others. Describing why and how more believer-priests actively lead is a long discussion beyond the scope of this chapter. Put simply, in movements progress happens in smaller increments, making these roles more attainable for all believers.

In their experience in conventional churches, these catalysts reported that the focus was buildings, gatherings, and spiritual needs only. But in ekklēsia movements, they mobilize the capacity of believers into communities to meet social and emotional needs as well as spiritual needs. They describe ekklēsia as a living organism that grows and bears fruit. They experience the gatherings of ekklēsia to be organically self-reproducing, thus always expanding and not limited to certain buildings or to certain regions.

Ekklēsia's Social Structures Supporting Multiplication

1. Ekklēsia is a living organism with two interdependent wings: apostolic teams and multiple local ekklēsia.
2. Ekklēsia is an expanding network, linking God's family at three levels.
3. Both wings of ekklēsia are led by teams of leaders.

As mentioned previously, these principles are the consensus of sixteen movement catalysts—a consensus which emerged through much Bible discussion, field implementation, and evaluation together over many years. Each of these men have "apostle-like" gifting.[17] They open new fields and new UPGs for the gospel. Their apostle-like giftings had not been affirmed in conventional churches, but it is affirmed in their "brotherhood." The brotherhood these men share has sharpened their apostle-like giftings.

---

17 "Apostolic agents" differ from New Testament apostles in that they do not receive revelation from God. They are like the New Testament apostles in that they desire to proclaim the gospel where Christ is not known, in new UPGs. And like the apostles, they have influence trans-regionally as they build the linked mosaic of ekklēsia.

This mission team catalyzes the formation of many house churches, linking them so that each is joined to a "cluster church" of ten to fifteen home groups. Likewise, each cluster church is joined to a "small region church" of three or more linked clusters. And they work to connect each cluster church to a "wide region church" of three or more linked small region churches. Apostolic teams set multiplication of small groups into the DNA of movements: small groups that study the Bible inductively, pray, and serve one another and their community. They establish the fruit by linking house churches into clusters, under teams of local elders. They develop teams of leaders over each cluster church and over each regional church. The leadership teams they equip oversee increasingly larger sets of believer groups, as these movements multiply.

The first level of ekklēsia, the house church, is the prominent feature of kingdom expansion in these UPGs. Our review of the architecture of the New Testament period revealed that house ekklēsia was likely limited to ten to twenty in many homes, but in some cases forty or more believers could gather. Because of tight security, the average house church among UPGs in our country is five believers. Movements in non-UPG areas of other countries report larger gatherings. House churches in UPGs do not typically add more people to small groups, because social pressure and persecution slows progress. Instead, they evangelize and birth new small groups and help them grow. As a result, believer groups in UPGs are smaller, but the multiply into more generations of groups. This movement has tracked believer group multiplication to twenty-three generations and leaders' groups to seventeen generations. Growing leaders' groups as fast as the gospel transforms households is one of our constant and most urgent challenges and drives much of our leadership development.

The second level of ekklēsia is city ekklēsia. In Rome, we saw indications of eight house ekklēsia joined as one city ekklēsia, likely totaling about seventy-five believers, led by a team of elders for the city. Among UPGs, large gatherings very often suffer backlash and obstacles increase. A cluster church of ten or fifteen linked small groups totals fifty to seventy-five believers, led by a team of elders. The elders oversee the collection and use of a cluster purse, baptisms, the influence of the Word, and the Lord's Supper. They guide the cluster's community-development ministry, obedience-oriented Bible studies, and mentoring of new leaders. Cluster churches are thriving in many UPGs. A cluster church sometimes meets together when its elders consider it wise. They develop their unity face to face in a leaders' group for each cluster, through cross visitation, and through ministries together.

Groups birthed from the same mother group in the next two or three generations need equipping to function well as a cluster church. Influential local leaders invite group leaders to visit other group leaders, since relational trust must be built, because of deep suspicions in UPGs. After trust begins to develop through cross visitation, one or more leaders' groups are formed for the cluster.

A mentor guides their development as a leadership team. Each mentor uses a checklist of learning modules to equip each leaders' group, to help the leaders better support ekklēsia in their region.[18]

As ekklēsia grows to wider and wider regions, it is aggregated based on travel routes, language, religious variant, and relational trust. Wider than cluster church is small region church. Just as the Ephesus city leadership team likely influenced the house ekklēsia around Ephesus, a small region leadership team oversees all the cluster churches in an area, often within a one-hour driving range. Proximity allows them to do joint planning and problem-solving more frequently and build relationships of trust and love. This movement uses "coaching circles," in which three leaders help a peer leader find a solution for his challenge by asking questions and giving support. In Acts 6, the elders directed the small region ekklēsia in Jerusalem to resolve an economic and ethnic dispute over food for widows. Recently, one UPG movement catalyst was too ill to travel, so the small region's elders met and came to a consensus on what to do when a cluster leader had been beaten and hospitalized, conferring with their distant mentor by phone for his wisdom.

A wide region leadership team might oversee two adjacent provinces, or one province, or a portion of a province, depending on how much fruit local leaders have multiplied. Shortly after a major earthquake, though their movement catalyst was detained elsewhere, the leadership team over the wider region mobilized believers in the ekklēsia network in this UPG to help disaster victims. A sum equivalent to five months of a carpenter's wages had been donated by the time the catalyst arrived two days later. The wide region leadership team had performed their role as area leaders and had been linking the many house ekklēsia in the region together with the house ekklēsia who were disaster victims.

In Acts 15, the Jerusalem elders met with mission team leaders to jointly settle a dispute. In our UPG movements, a multi-region leadership team meets for three days each quarter to jointly tackle challenges, discuss the Bible, and mutually support one another in a strong brotherhood. This quarterly gathering has played a big role when we have experienced persecution and during the COVID-19 pandemic, during which we have lost many lives. Because the mission team is trans-regional, they link their network of small groups and leaders' groups to work together to distribute food to the hungry, restart jobs for the unemployed, help repair broken economic systems, and help people struggling with their children's education. The engagement of organic ekklēsia with community needs supports the movement's multiplication. The socially scalable architecture of ekklēsia described in this chapter allows its spiritual community to support its own maturation and expand as a family network into new areas and UPGs.

---

18 These checklists form much of chapters 9 and 10 of *Core Skills for Movement Leaders*.

A Final Word

The apostle Paul praised the ekklēsia in Thessalonica, who—though discipled by him for only three weeks—quickly replicated his pattern and became a model imitated by ekklēsia movements in several provinces. Paul heard how the Thessalonians imitated the patterns they had learned and affirmed their movement as part of God's expanding family. His prayer request is echoed by many movement leaders today: "Pray for us that the message of the Lord may spread rapidly and be honored, just as it was with you" (2 Thess 3:1b).

References

Banks, Robert. 1994. *Paul's Idea of Community: The Early House Churches in Their Cultural Setting*. Peabody, MA: Hendrikson.

Elliot, J. H. 1981. *A Home for the Homeless, A Sociological Exegesis of 1 Peter, Its Situation and Strategy*. Philadelphia: Fortress.

Gehring, Roger W. 2004. *House Church and Mission: The Importance of Household Structures in Early Christianity*. Peabody, MA: Hendrickson.

Krautheimer, R. 1965. *The Beginnings of Christian Architecture*. Baltimore: Penguin.

Ladd, George. *A Theology of the New Testament*. Grand Rapids: Eerdmans, 1974.

Larson, Trevor. 2019. *Core Skills for Movement Leaders*. Yogyakarta, Indonesia: Focus On Fruit.

Minear, Paul S. 1960. *Images of the Church in the New Testament*. Philadelphia: Westminster.

Ott, Craig, and Gene Wilson. 2010. *Global Church Planting*. Ada, MI: Baker.

Van Gelder, Craig. 2000. *The Essence of the Church: A Community Created by the Spirit*. Grand Rapids: Baker.

White, L. M. 1990. *Building God's House in the Roman World: Architectural Adaptation among Pagans, Jews, and Christians*. Baltimore: John Hopkins University.

John's Missiological Theology:
The Contribution of the Fourth Gospel to the
First-Century Movement in Roman Asia

Michael T. Cooper

Over the past three decades of my involvement in missions around the world, we have seen an explosion of gospel presentations largely focused on a message of salvation formulated in the Western cultural milieu. From the ubiquitous Four Spiritual Laws to the equally ubiquitous Three Circles, these presentations focus on the sinfulness of humanity, humanity's inability to overcome sin, the need for a Savior, and the need to make a personal decision to accept the Savior's death on a cross for salvation from hell. More recently, with the introduction of a chronological method of evangelism, beginning in Genesis and moving through the New Testament, presentations often termed something to the effect of Creation to Christ have been used as tools to disciple people into a saving relationship with God.

In the first- and second-century church, the stories about Jesus ultimately recorded in the Gospels were the primary instruments to share the good news of Christ's incarnation into the world to declare God's glorious pursuit of relationships with his creation. In various ways, the Gospels describe what it means to follow Christ in our actions, beliefs, and participation in community. While they most certainly convey the message of salvation and eternal life for those who believe, they go further in their insistence on identifying with the life of Jesus Christ. In other words, the Gospels portray a beautiful mosaic of what it means to be members of the household of God (Eph 2:19).

The Gospels are primarily evangelistic and missionary in nature and provide examples of how the stories of Jesus connected with the people they were intended to engage. The Synoptic Gospels—Matthew, Mark, and Luke—express three distinct examples of relating the good news to particular cultures. Matthew (c. early 60s), originally written in Aramaic, focuses on a Hebrew audience. Mark (c. 57–60), revealing a second-language writer's challenge with Greek, is written to a largely oral Gentile audience. Luke (c. 63–65), with perhaps the most clearly declared audience, writes to Theophilus and demonstrates an accurately researched portrait of the Savior. All three Gospels possess a high degree of similarity in their presentation of the life and ministry of Jesus Christ. For example, the Synoptics share a similar geographic sequence in tracing Jesus' ministry from Galilee to the wider northern part of Palestine, then a focus on Judea and Perea, and finally his ministry in Jerusalem.

This chapter focuses exclusively on John's Gospel as an example of connecting the stories about Jesus to the stories of a culture, or what is expressed as missiological theology. The Fourth Gospel is an evangelistic presentation focused on addressing specific cultural, religious, and philosophical systems observed by John in Asia Minor during his early ministry in Ephesus (c. 67–70).[1] Primarily concerned with challenging beliefs associated with the goddess Artemis and god Dionysus, as well as with the philosophy of Heraclitus, the Gospel's focus results in a missiological theology that effectively connects the story of Jesus with the stories of the cultures in Asia Minor (Cooper 2020, 87). After describing the term "missiological theology," in this chapter I will focus on the features of John's Gospel that make the apostle a missiological theologian. If the practice of missiological theology was indeed an impetus in the exponential growth of the early church, we might find implications for CPM/DMM today.

Defining Missiological Theology

Missiological theology is differentiated from biblical or systematic theologies in that missiological theology is concerned with the missionary nature of God in Scripture. In addition, missiological theology considers Scripture's grand narrative of God's relentless missionary pursuit of relationships with his creatures in his mission to unite all things in Christ as a key hermeneutic (Eph 1:10). David Bosch claimed, "God's very nature is missionary" (1991, 390), and missiological theology captures God's missionary nature as expressed throughout the sixty-six canonical books of the Bible. It sees a thread of God's self-revelation beginning at creation in Genesis and ending with the consummation in Revelation.

---

1 In *Ephesiology: The Study of the Ephesian Movement*, I argue that John most likely arrived in Ephesus during the Jewish Wars, after Paul's death in AD 67 and prior to the destruction of the second temple in AD 70 (Cooper 2020, 83–84). Salient points for an early date: 1) Polycarp's death in AD 69; 2) no mention of the temple's destruction in the Fourth Gospel; 3) Jewish Wars provide motive for seeking refuge in Ephesus; 4) Ephesus is a significant center of Christianity by AD 53; 5) Mary traditions place her in Ephesus with John (she would have been in her seventies).

Missiological theology is gospel-oriented and interested in the clear communication of Jesus in such a way that he naturally connects to culture. It produces that "ah-ha moment" in the life of a cultural actor and results in identifying with Jesus' life and work. Simply defined, missiological theology is the theologically, culturally, historically, and religiously informed communication of the message of the person, works, word, and will of God. Such communication is faithful to the unchanged, true stories about Jesus and is meaningful to people in their particular contexts. Missiological theology does not change, adapt, or contextualize Jesus' stories to make them relevant. It looks for the connecting points between Jesus' story and the story of culture.

Missiological theology is distinguished from contextualization. Bruce Nicholls defines contextualization as "the translation of the unchanging content of the Gospel of the kingdom into verbal form meaningful to the peoples in their separate culture and within their particular existential situations" (1975, 647). Missiological theology does not translate the message of the gospel as much as it understands the breadth of the message and connects the message where applicable to the culture it is engaging. For example, when Paul engaged with philosophers at the Areopagus, he did not translate Jesus and the resurrection so that the philosophers could understand. Rather, he made the meaning behind what the philosophers believed related to the altar and Zeus explicit to God, who will judge the world by Christ. This was not a redemptive analogy, as suggested by Don Richardson (1981). The references to the altar and Zeus were not analogous to the story of God; rather, they were equivocal to the story. For example, Paul's reference to Aratus' *Phenomena* (Acts 17:28) attributes YHWH (God), to Zeus.

Missiological theology begins with a proper missiological exegesis of culture. Briefly stated, missiological exegesis is the hard work of a missionary to understand the people of a culture. It includes a study of a people's history, beliefs, and cultural particularities with a view toward identifying God's activity among them in order to connect Jesus' stories to theirs. Missiological theology requires the missionary to become a missiological theologian. Such a theologian uniquely identifies God's work in the world in the lives of cultural actors and then properly connects stories about Jesus with stories of the culture. A missiological theologian is not interested in adapting these stories, but rather focuses on the unchanged, true stories about Jesus that a culture might identify with as a part of their story.

In this manner of theologizing, a missiological theology will be indigenously grounded, as it is rooted in the grand narrative of God's redemptive history, which includes the history of a people. Missiological theologians are able to observe and apply a missiological hermeneutic in their interpretation and application of Scripture. Shawn Redford defines such a hermeneutic as "an over-arching hermeneutic infused with both missional assumptions and spiritual vitality as they engage in the act of interpreting Scripture in their time" (2012, 1). As we consider the Fourth Gospel, then, we must recognize its missionary nature.

The Missionary Nature of the Gospels

While the details provided in all four Gospels testify to their accounts being documented close to the actual events, none of them identify the authorship by personal name. Although the authors of the third and fourth Gospels do use first personal single pronouns in reference to themselves (Luke 1:3; John 21:25), only the Fourth Gospel identifies the author as the "disciple who bears witness to these things" (John 21:24).

Justin Martyr (c. AD 155–57) first refers to the Gospels as the memoirs of the apostles in his defense for the practice of the Eucharist (*First Apology* 66). Irenaeus (c. AD 180) later reinforces apostolic authorship in his defense of Christianity against Celsus (*Against Heresies* 3.1.1). For the early church, apostolic attestation of the Gospels crystalized their reception and canonicity. Thus, Matthew and John were apostolic eyewitnesses of the events, Mark was an eyewitness (Mark 14:51), but also recorded his Gospel from the apostle Peter's perspective; while Luke, a colleague of the apostle Paul (Acts 16:10–11), conducted what we might think of as early historiographic research for his narrative account.

The oral nature of Greek and Roman learning in the first century points to the idea that written documents were more often heard than read. Paul certainly had this expectation for his letters (Col 4:16). Such emphasis on the oral nature of learning is highlighted in Papias' remarks, "I did not suppose that information from books would help me so much as the word of a living and surviving voice" (in Irenaeus, *Against Heresies* 3.39.3–4). The Gospels, carrying on an oral tradition that encouraged the transmission of Jesus' stories by word of mouth, were written with evangelistic purposes and served to codify the life and ministry of God incarnate. Indeed, Irenaeus relates this movement from the oral to written Gospels:

> We have learned from none others the plan of our salvation, than from those through whom the Gospel has come down to us, which they did at one time proclaim in public, and, at a later period, by the will of God, handed down to us the Scriptures, to be the ground and pillar of our faith. (*Against Heresies* 3.1.1)

He continues with the purpose of the Gospels: "These have all declared to us that there is one God, Creator of heaven and earth, announced by the law and the prophets; and one Christ, the Son of God" (*Against Heresies* 3.1.2). As Justin Martyr relates, the Gospels were intended to be heard and explicated.

> And on the day called Sunday, all who live in cities or in the country gather together to one place and the memoirs of the apostles or the writings of the prophets are read, as long as time permits; then when the reader has ceased, the president verbally instructs, and exhorts to the imitation of these good things. (*First Apology* 62)

The missionary purpose of the Gospels and their continued oral transmission helped catalyze the phenomenal growth of the early church. The formation of the

Gospels in general and John's ability to connect Jesus' stories to the stories of his audience in the Fourth Gospel offer two examples of ways missiological theology serves as a key tool to ensure an indigenous Christianity rooted in true stories that make sense to a culture's story.

The Purpose of John's Gospel

There are at least three reasons why John wrote a narrative account about the life and ministry of Jesus. First, Eusebius relates that John's Gospel filled the gaps left by the Synoptics. His source is often attributed to Papias, the disciple of John and second bishop of Hierapolis (Hill 1998; cf. Manor 2013). Eusebius writes,

> And when Mark and Luke had already written their own Gospels, it is said that John gave an unwritten proclamation all the time, and finally came to write for the following reason. The three Gospels already having been written and distributed to all, as well as that he welcomed them and testified to their truth, but the only thing missing in the writing was a narrative about the things done by Christ at the beginning of the proclamation. The record is certainly true. For it is seen that the three evangelists had written down only the deeds done by the Savior during one year after the imprisonment of John the Baptist, and they indicated precisely this element at the beginning of their historical accounts. (H.E. 3.24.5–8)

As Eusebius specifies, John sought to supply the stories lacking in the other three Gospels, and indeed his Gospel is unique compared to the Synoptics. John does not record any exorcisms or parables and reflects a meditative tone focusing on Jesus' life and teaching, something reminiscent of biographies of philosophers. Such a focus might be expected from John, who wrote to a predominately Greek-speaking, multiethnic audience familiar with, if not adherents of, the philosophy of Heraclitus of Ephesus (sixth century BC).[2] This view is indicated due in part to John's use of μαθητής (*mathetes*, disciple) seventy-five times, as well as to the philosophical nature of his prologue.

John desired the hearers of the narrative about Jesus to have not only a cognitive benefit, but also an example to imitate. In that sense, John stands in line with early Greek philosophical references to discipleship. For example, Seneca (c. AD 64) relates this notion succinctly regarding the disciples of Socrates: "Plato, Aristotle, and the whole throng of sages who were destined to go each his different way, derived more benefit from the character than from the words of Socrates" (Ep 6.5).

Second, not only did John desire to present the stories about Jesus that were absent from the Synoptics, he also wanted to connect those stories to his audience. Jerome relates the tradition passed down regarding John's purpose:

---

2 I appreciate the work Craig Keener has done on John's Gospel, but I disagree with him in regard to date and importance of the *Sitz Im Leben* for interpreting John. In my estimation, Keener views John as too Jewish and not enough as an apostle sent to clearly articulate a message about Jesus. So there is no surprise that Heraclitus is not prominent in Keener's assessment of John's prologue (see Keener 2010, 341–43).

When [John] was in Asia, at the time when the seeds of heresy were springing up … he was urged by almost all the bishops of Asia then living, and by deputations from many churches, to write more profoundly concerning the divinity of the Savior, and to break through all obstacles so as to attain to the very Word of God (if I may so speak) with a boldness as successful as it appears audacious. Ecclesiastical history relates that, when he was urged by the brethren to write, he replied that he would do so if a general fast were proclaimed and all would offer up prayer to God; and when the fast was over, the narrative goes on to say, being filled with revelation, he burst into the heaven-sent Preface: "In the beginning was the Word, and the Word was with God, and the Word was God: this was in the beginning with God." (Commentary on Matthew, Preface, 2)

Living in a cultural context where Artemis and Dionysus were objects of worship, the bishops of Asia sought a definitive answer to the nature and person of Jesus. Not only did John juxtapose Jesus to the Asian objects of worship, he also positioned Jesus as greater than the philosophers since he also taught in a temple. Most strikingly, in the Fourth Gospel Jesus is the fulfillment of Heraclitus' λόγος (*logos*, word) philosophy (John 1:1).

Finally, John communicated the arrival of the Word who came to save the world. This story did not reside solely in the Jewish narrative, but the story is for all people, as John makes utterly clear in his use of κόσμος (*kosmos*, world). More than all the other Gospels combined, John uses the word fifty-eight times to communicate that God's work was not merely a Jewish work, but a global work of cosmic proportion. Jesus is not simply the Jewish Messiah, but the Christ of the κόσμος. Consider the following table that illustrates John's emphasis on Jesus' ministry to all people.

Verses in John's Gospel	World Connection
1:9	The true light came into the world
1:10	He made the world
1:29	He takes away the sin of the world
3:16	God loves the world
4:42	He is the Savior of the world
6:14	He is the prophet who is to come into the world
6:33	He gives life to the world
8:12	He is the light of the world
8:26	He declares to the world what he has heard from the Father
12:19	He is the Son of God who came to the world
12:47	He came to save the world
14:31	His work demonstrated to the world his love for the Father

Table 9.1: John's Use of κόσμος (Cooper 2020, 64)

Foundational to understanding John's missiological theology is the occasion for the Fourth Gospel. That occasion can be summarized by three points: 1) gap-filling; 2) story-connecting; and 3) world-saving. Its primary focus on connecting the untold stories of Jesus to a Roman Asian audience who recognized the stories in their own culture propelled disciple making and church planting throughout the region. We now turn to those connecting stories.

John's Missiological Theology[3]

The Fourth Gospel is an evangelistic presentation addressing the religious and philosophical systems in Asia Minor, specifically those associated with the goddess Artemis and the god Dionysus, as well as with the philosopher Heraclitus. John was not concerned with embellishing the Synoptics with his personal eyewitness observations of being with Jesus. He desired rather to fill in a few gaps about Jesus' life and ministry, especially those gaps that connected with the culture of his audience. Nor was he concerned with the chronology of Jesus' ministry. It also seems unreasonable to suggest that the destruction of the Jewish temple or the Jewish War would have influenced his writing. If the Gospel is dated to the beginning of the Jewish War when John arrived in Ephesus, the temple's destruction has no bearing on the Gospel itself. In fact, the significance of John's references to the temple (John 2:14–21; 7:14–28; 8:2–59) should be juxtaposed to the importance of the temples of Artemis throughout the area of Asia Minor. If in fact John's audience comprised non-Christian Ephesians and Asians, they would have had no regard for the Jewish temple, if they had even known about it at all. It makes more sense that John's references to the temple in his Gospel positioned Jesus as the most high God who was greater than any god or goddess worshiped in temples made by human hands. Jesus superseded the worship and rituals occurring in a temple, no matter where the temple was located—Jerusalem or Ephesus.[4]

John's Gospel was a message that would have connected with a people who were proud to live in the city of a wonder of the ancient world where "all Asia and the world worship" Artemis (Acts 19:27).[5] His primary concern was connecting Jesus' story with the story of those in Asia Minor in such a way that they would clearly see the one true God as the creator and sustainer of the κόσμος (John 6:35–51; 8:12; 9:5; 10:9, 11–14; 11:25; 14:6). He alone gives the right to become children of God, rather than Artemis, who acted as the protector of childbearing (John 1:12). Jesus performed genuine signs, such as the wedding-feast miracle,

---

3 This section is largely borrowed from *Ephesiology: The Study of the Ephesian Movement* (Littleton, CO: William Carey, 2020). Used by permission.

4 See Andreas Kostenberger, "The Destruction of the Second Temple and the Composition of the Fourth Gospel, *Trinity Journal* 26 (2005): 205–42, for a discussion of the impact of the temple's destruction. I obviously disagree with Kostenberger's assessment.

5 Luke typically uses οἰκουμένη (inhabited earth) rather than κόσμος (world).

which would clearly demonstrate his primacy above Artemis, the goddess of matrimony (John 2:1–12). Jesus can respond to religious leaders and call them to be born again, in distinction from Dionysius who was twice born of Zeus (John 3:1–15). Jesus had special knowledge of people such as the woman at the well (John 4:1–45), who, like some women in Asia Minor, consorted with men in the antics of the symposium. Jesus' reference to being the living bread signifies his preeminence above other gods and goddesses, whose theophaginic rituals connected the practitioner with the deity. Only Jesus can take away the hunger of humanity (John 6:22–59).

Story of Jesus	Cultural Issue in Ephesus
Logos (1:1–3)	Philosophy of Heraclitus
Right to become children of God (1:12)	Artemis, who acted as the protector of childbearing
Wedding-feast miracle (2:1–12)	Artemis, the goddess of matrimony
Call to be born again (3:1–15)	Dionysius, who was twice born of Zeus
Samaritan woman (4:1–45)	Courtesans in Ephesus
Living bread (6:22–59)	Theophaginic rituals associated with gods and goddesses
Teaching in the temple (7:14, 28; 8:20)	Location of philosophical schools (Tyrannus?)
Light of the world (8:12)	Juxtaposed to Artemis' *phosphera*
Foot-washing (13:5)	Familiar custom in Ephesus and Asia Minor

Table 9.2: Connections between Jesus' Story and the Asian Story

John's superb missiological theology made Jesus real to those who had never heard of him. The fact that John was an eyewitness further testified to the authenticity of Jesus as "the true light, which gives light to everyone" (John 1:9), who came into the world to give abundant life (John 10:10). Jesus was rejected and despised by his own people (John 1:11). However, those from other nations (John was writing in a context where there were as many as fifty distinct ethnic groups) would find solace in a personal God who sacrificed himself and resurrected to new life so that they might also receive eternal life (John 4:39–42, 46–53; 10:16; 12:20–26; 16:8–9; 17:20–21). This was a message for the entire world, a message that John repeats in order to make clear that Jesus is the one true God and Lord, supreme over all others.

It is clear that John effectively connected the stories of Jesus appropriate for the culture of Roman Asia. It became an indigenous expression of Christianity that resulted in the continued growth of the churches throughout the region.

This resulted in mature disciples, New Testament leaders, and healthy churches. These were not without issues, as problems crept into Christianity. Nevertheless, Jesus' own testimony about the churches of Asia Minor provides a conspicuous understanding of some markers of healthy churches. Revelation 2–3 describes the following key characteristics of a healthy church:

1. Listens to the Holy Spirit (Rev 2:7, 11, 17, 29; 3:6, 13, 22)
2. Confronts false teaching (Rev 2:2)
3. Proclaims God's glory (Rev 2:4–5)—the works of their first love (missiologically theocentric passion to declare God's glory to the nations)
4. Stands up for the marginalized (Rev 2:6)
5. Stands firm in the faith (Rev 2:13)
6. Goes beyond the work of love, faith, service, endurance (Rev 2:19)
7. Endures hardship (Rev 3:11)
8. Maintains sound doctrine (Rev 3:3, 8, 10)

Historical reflection concerning the first-century church leads to a significant observation. The timeframe for the writing of the four Gospels (c. AD 60–80), and the oral nature of their transmission, corresponds to significant growth of Christianity (see Figure 9.1). For those involved in CPM/DMM today, such growth should encourage us to consider the implications of missiological theology in our contemporary methodologies.

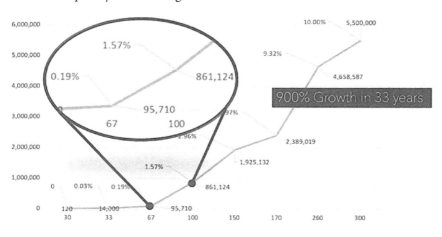

Figure 9.1: Growth of the Early Church

Implications for CPM/DMM

Missiologists and missionaries generally agree that "missions is the mother of theology." Theology is best developed out of an understanding of context. We can certainly observe this as much in the theology that emerged in the sixteenth century as in the theology that emerged in the first century. John's missiological theology provides an outstanding example of the way we can connect the unchanged stories of Jesus to culture. We can draw several implications for CPM/DMM from the practice of missiological theology as outlined above.

First, as we see in Jerome's account of John's writing of the Gospel, missionaries must pray and fast for God to reveal what he is doing and how he wants his story to connect with a culture. We are not seeking divine revelation. We are seeking to properly identify where God is at work and seeking wisdom in how we might join him in his work.

Second, in order to connect God's stories with culture effectively, missionaries—whether from inside or outside the culture—must practice missiological exegesis. Conducting field research in order to understand a culture's history, belief systems, and philosophy is critical to formulating an evangelistic engagement that will ensure an indigenous Christianity. Without such field research, the likelihood of Christianity being perceived as foreign increases, as does the likelihood of syncretism (Cooper 2021).

Third, connecting the stories about Jesus to culture is critical to the healthy growth of a movement. From the time John wrote his Gospel until the time he wrote Revelation, the church grew from an estimated 96,000 to 861,000, and it continued to grow (see Figure 9.1). Numbers and growth do not necessarily indicate health. However, in the case of the churches in Asia Minor, Jesus' warnings as well as his commendations contributed to a healthy trajectory of the early disciples.

Finally, proper missiological and theological education is obligatory for the ongoing health of a movement. Doing missiological theology does not happen in a vacuum. It assumes more than a cursory knowledge of missiology and theology. It requires a depth of study that digs profoundly into the missionary character of God and the missionary narrative of Scripture, then their proper application to context. Such a pursuit is not suited for every disciple. Nevertheless, a movement must include those who reach a competency of missiological and theological education that will ensure the transmission of sound teaching (1 Tim 4:6). This does not presume formal education, but it does require intentionality in equipping those who are gifted in such pursuits in order that they might equip the saints for works of ministry (Eph 4:11). Such depth is seen in John's study of the Asian culture, as well as in his application of theology to context.

Conclusion

The Fourth Gospel presents a unique perspective on the life of Jesus Christ. The manner in which the apostle John shares the narrative of the good news reveals a missiological theology connected to the story of the people of Roman Asia. Beginning with the remarkable λόγος prologue harkening to the Ephesian philosopher Heraclitus (c. 535–475 BC) to sundry references to cultural practices of the region—courtesans, theophagy, foot-washing, and more—John paints a portrait of Jesus that is not only relevant for the people but demonstrates that Jesus is as much the Messiah of the Jews as the Christ of the κόσμος. The significance of the Fourth Gospel's context is paramount for understanding John's message to the Asians. John's model of connecting stories about Jesus to the culture of the Roman Asians reveals the importance for movement leaders to understand the religion, ethnic particularities, and history of the people they engage in order to ensure an indigenous Christian expression.

This missiological theology properly exegetes culture, reflects on what God is doing in a culture, and connects God's narrative to that of the people in such a manner that there is one distinctly expressed story of God's relentless pursuit of his glory through more people worshiping him. The Fourth Gospel is not a contextualized message of good news, nor is it an example of redemptive analogy. Instead, the Fourth Gospel is a missiological theology accurately sharing the good news of Jesus Christ in real stories about him that relate to the stories of the culture. Therefore, the Fourth Gospel provides a movement leader with an example of effectively engaging culture with the narrative of the Savior.

The heart of the gospel is to tell the story of Jesus. John brilliantly portrayed Jesus in a way that made sense to those in Ephesus and Asia Minor. John connected with his audience on philosophical, religious, cultural, and ethnic levels to communicate Jesus' story in a way that it would become their story. It was no longer just the Jewish story of a Messiah. It was the story of the one true God who would restore the world, including the world of those in Asia Minor (Cooper 2020, 88).

References

Bosch, David. 1991. *Transforming Missions: Paradigm Shifts in Theology of Missions.* Maryknoll, NY: Orbis.

Carson, D. A., Douglas J. Moo, and Leon Morris. 1992. *An Introduction to the New Testament.* Grand Rapids: Zondervan.

Cooper, Michael T. 2020. *Ephesiology: The Study of the Ephesian Movement.* Littleton, CO: William Carey.

———. 2021. "The Potential Risk of Syncretism in Church Planting Movements." *Evangelical Missions Quarterly* 57 (1).

Keener, Craig. 2010. *The Gospel of John: Two Volumes*. Grand Rapids: Baker Academic.

Köstenberger, Andreas. 2005. "The Destruction of the Second Temple and the Composition of the Fourth Gospel." *Trinity Journal* 26: 205–42.

Manor, T. Scott. 2013. "Papias, Origen, and Eusebius: The Criticisms and Defense of the Gospel of John." *Vigiliae Christianae* 67: 1–21.

Nicholls, Bruce J. 1975. "Theological Education and Evangelization." In *Let the Earth Hear His Voice*, edited by J. D. Douglas. Minneapolis: World Wide.

Redford, Shawn B. 2012. *Missiological Hermeneutics: Biblical Interpretation for the Global Church*. Eugene, OR: Pickwick.

Richardson, Don. 1981. *Eternity in Their Hearts: Startling Evidence of Belief in the One True God in Hundreds of Cultures Throughout the World*. Grand Rapids: Baker.

Ancient Sources

Eusebius, *Church History*

Irenaeus, *Against Heresies*

Jerome, *Commentary of Matthew*

Justin Martyr, *First Apology*

10

Households of Peace: Relationships, Boundaries, and the Gospel

James Lucas

The Middle East has been our home for over a decade. During this time, I have helped develop Scripture resources for movements at different stages among oral-preference cultures. In these cultures, people primarily study the Bible by listening. These experiences have profoundly shaped the way I read, hear, and interpret the Bible myself.

In this chapter, I will bring some of these dimensions to the study of households of peace in Luke and Acts. This will add new insights to the discussion of "people of peace / households of peace" that can help our theology and praxis of movements. Luke describes how Jesus, his disciples, and Paul used homes to reach preexisting networks, both *oikos* and other networks. Luke also describes how preexisting networks both joined people together and also pulled them apart. Furthermore, Luke uses common compositional techniques, aimed at oral-preference learners, to develop and prescribe the boundary of the movement: those who have entrusted themselves to Jesus. Clarifying this boundary enabled the movement to expand to new peoples. In these ways, Luke's inspired stories may help us reach people in preexisting networks today.

Collectivism and People / Households of Peace in Movement Thinking

In the New Testament era, the Middle Eastern and Mediterranean region was comprised of collectivist cultures (Richards and James 2020). In these cultures, people thought of themselves as members of groups defined by certain foundational values which united them. As such, these foundations also served as boundaries. People did not think in terms of "I belong to you," focusing on belonging from an individualist perspective. They thought more in terms of "We belong to We."

They were bound as a collective group by values that centered them on one another.[1] These values defined who belonged together and thus helped preserve the group and their values.

These shared values formed many different social networks. Some collective groups were based in shared bloodlines (which they took to be a foundational value that united them). Others were based on mutual help, legal ties, or shared religious beliefs. People could belong to a number of groups, based on different values which connected multiple networks.

Much evangelical theology has focused on individual discipleship. Of course, this has a role. However, reproduction of churches and church-planting movements involves discipling groups of people. In this sense, church (*ekklēsia*) is a group or a network of groups.

Many have recognized the role that household (*oikos*) groups played in first-century collective life and church planting. In Matthew 10, Mark 6, and Luke 9–10, Jesus sent his followers to announce the kingdom among Jewish towns and villages. Jesus' instructions centered around homes and households. Luke 10:5–7 records his instruction that if his followers found "someone who promotes peace" in a home they entered, they were to stay with that household. Acts records stories of people coming to faith along with their oikos (Acts 10; 16:11–15, 27–34).

Given our desire to make disciples of groups of people and reach existing networks, much study and discussion has focused on these passages. Many have sought to identify shared characteristics among these "people of peace" (PoP) who come to faith along with their household in the Gospels and Acts. While various writers provide slightly different characteristics of a PoP, they basically define a PoP as someone yet to believe in Jesus, whom God has prepared to receive the good news about Jesus, who serves as a bridge to their existing network.[2] However, these approaches define an individual and so can still tend to be individualistic. More recently, people have begun to use the language "households of peace" (HoP) (Smith and Parks 2015) to highlight even more collective elements. These interpretations have led many to look for such PoPs and HoPs as a key strategy for catalyzing movements.

---

1 Through a more focused biblical-theological approach, I am engaging somewhat with the "bounded" and "centered" set theory of belonging, which first originated with Paul G. Hiebert (1994).

2 This description was shaped by the summary of the literature in Matthews 2019. See also Garrison 2004, 45, 213; Smith and Kai 2011, KL1131–37; Addison 2012, 209–21; Trousdale 2012, 89–97; Watson and Watson 2014, 123–29.

Hearing and Interpreting Luke and Acts in Their World

The overwhelming majority of first-century Mediterranean people were functionally illiterate. Only a small minority (perhaps 5 to 10 percent) could read. In that cultural context, people composed and read texts differently than we do today. Firstly, people normally read texts out loud, both to themselves and to groups who listened. For example, Revelation 1:3 blesses the reader (singular) of the book and those (plural) who hear the words written in it (cf. Luke 4:17–21; Acts 15:21). Both those who could read and those who could not *heard* written texts.

Secondly, first-century Mediterranean texts were composed to be received audibly, so they used many compositional devices which are designed to guide listeners to follow the text (Robbins 1991, 145; 1994, 80).

Thirdly, people in oral cultures were skilled at listening. They developed strong memory skills, which they used to make connections and interpret what they heard read to them.

Fourthly, in the first century, communities had access to fewer texts due to the high cost and low availability of long texts (Botha 2012, 97). Even if they didn't memorize them, many Jewish people would regularly hear the Scriptures read in synagogue gatherings; thus they were very familiar with them (Acts 15:21).

Finally, since people often listened to texts in groups, they could discuss what they heard with others present (e.g., Luke 4:22).

The New Testament was composed in this culture, so we do well to bear these dynamics in mind as we exegete Luke and Acts (Achtemeier 1990; Harvey 1988, 1–60). For example, Luke and Acts were composed to be heard aloud as sequential narratives (cf. Luke 1:1–4, Acts 1:1). They did not originally have chapter divisions, headings, or verses. They repeat terms, ideas, and events that hearers would remember and so recognize potential links and connections. Similar terms and stories in later parts of a Gospel often take up and build on what has been said previously. Themes develop as a result.

Luke and Acts clearly assume their hearers have a good familiarity with the Greek Jewish Bible (Darr 1992, 28). Sometimes Luke explicitly points out these references (e.g., Luke 4:17–19). Other times these references are more implicit or subtle (e.g., "leaping" in Acts 3:8 may echo Isa 35:6). Luke characteristically makes use of both explicit and implicit references to Scripture to create layers of meaning in his stories (Hays 2016, 229). Luke states his purpose: to provide a narrative account of "the things that have been *fulfilled* among us" (Luke 1:1–4; my emphasis), and so assumes that hearers will see the meaning of the events in the story and how they fulfill previous hopes and prophecies.

While many modern Westerners are low-context communicators who assume that everything should be said explicitly, Luke used high-context communication in Luke and Acts. He assumed that images, pictures, echoes, and repetition would be recognized by their hearers. Luke, for example, does not say "Jesus is God," but rather tells a series of stories demonstrating that Jesus is God. Hearers are to conclude from them who he is. The same holds true for many other themes. This is not a sign that Luke was a poor low-context communicator, but rather that he was a very effective communicator in his high-context world. As low-context communicators, we need to recalibrate to this style of composition used in first-century texts in order to interpret the New Testament more fully.

Part 1: Luke

Luke recounts many stories of Jesus in homes. This is no surprise in light of the foundational role households and homes played in that society. When Luke talks about homes and households in stories, he could assume his hearers, who lived in similar cultures, would understand the role they played.

Households and Homes in Palestine

Households (*oikos* in Greek) were the basic building blocks of society. An *oikos* included all the people under the legal authority of the head of the household, who was typically a man. The members of his oikos might include his wife, children, any slaves he owned, and perhaps some other blood relatives under his legal authority (Moxnes 1997, 20–21). While this might make it sound like households were huge, shorter life expectancy kept numbers low. Written records preserved from Roman Egypt around the time show that households in towns and cities ranged from two to ten people, averaging four to five (Bagnall and Frier 1994, 68). Architectural evidence from Pompeii suggests most homes held between four and eight people (Oakes 2009, 82).

The household normally lived together in the same home. Indeed, *oikos* was also the basic word for "home." This could include houses, apartments, or small living spaces in shops and workshops (Adams 2013, 7; Osiek and Balch 1997, 6). For example, Luke uses *oikō* for the people in Cornelius' household and the home where they lived (Acts 10:2, 30). To make these links clear, I will use the word *householder* for a head of household. This is because it maintains the focus on their role and their authority over their household and physical home.

Missiologists have recently begun to apply the word *oikos* to mean someone's relational network. When we read these stories in the New Testament, it is good to remember that *oikos* simply meant household, and not read this wider "social network" application anachronistically into the stories.

Homes were the center of much of social life. People hosted their neighbors, relatives, and friends for meals and celebrations (Luke 14:12). People would travel to stay with relatives and friends (Luke 1:39–56; Acts 10:5–6). Business associates would meet in homes (Luke 16:1–4). Palestinian homes usually had a central room, approximately five by five meters, or sixteen by sixteen feet, which served as the space where meals, discussions, cooking, and parties took place. Sitting on the floor was rare; guests reclined on benches or couches in these gatherings (Safrai 1976, 737).

Rabbis would also teach their disciples in homes. Householders would open their home for a rabbi to teach, and townspeople would attend. One saying from the time encouraged people, "Let your house be a meeting-house for the sages and sit amidst the dust of their feet" (*Aboth* 1:4; Safrai 1976, 965). Traveling rabbis would particularly rely upon people opening their homes to them.

As Jesus travelled around, he often relied on this practice. He often taught in a person's home, in settings in which many townsfolk attended (Luke 5:19; 7:36–50; 14:1–2). When Mary and Martha welcomed Jesus into their home, Luke tells us that Mary "sat at the Lord's feet listening to what he said" (Luke 10:39). They had hosted Jesus, and he was giving a lesson to his disciples in their home, which Mary joined.

Levi

Jesus announces his ministry by reading Isaiah 61:1–2, which is the center of the final section of Isaiah (chapters 56–66), describing the future coming of God's kingdom. God's servant would proclaim the Good News, freedom for prisoners, healing for the blind, and the year of the Lord's favor, when all debts were forgiven. Jesus claimed, "Today this scripture is fulfilled in your hearing" (Luke 4:16–21).

A series of stories then tell us about how Jesus lived out these prophetic hopes. As he traveled from town to town, he proclaimed the kingdom, healed the sick, freed people from spiritual affliction, and declared the forgiveness of sin. He also called people to follow him and discipled the Twelve as they accompanied him (Luke 5:11, 27; 8:1).

These themes come together when Jesus calls Levi the tax collector to become his disciple (Luke 5:27). Tax collectors were despised by most Jewish people, largely because they often overcharged and extorted people (Luke 3:12–13). Jesus called Levi to become his own disciple, and Levi "left everything and followed him" (Luke 5:27–28).

Levi would have been a relatively wealthy householder, possibly with a large home and oikos. He held a "large" celebratory banquet for Jesus in his home (Luke 5:29). Many people would be invited to such grand banquets. Luke says a "large crowd" of Levi's fellow tax collectors and others were reclining together with them eating (Luke 5:29). When the Pharisees and the teachers of the law saw this, their reaction was to grumble. They asked, "Why do you eat and drink with tax collectors and sinners?" (Luke 5:30).

For first-century Jews, following the food-purity laws prescribed in the Torah was an important value. It was linked with their collective identity as the covenant people of Yahweh. The Pharisees were more concerned with observing these food-purity laws than many other Jewish people. The Pharisees even avoided eating other Jewish peoples' food in case they had allowed impurity to contaminate it at some stage while it was prepared (Sanders 2016, 344). More widely, people tended to avoid eating with those who blatantly violated the law in various ways, because being drawn into relationship with these "sinners" could corrupt them. Sirach 12:13–14 highlights the weight of this feeling: "Who pities a snake charmer when he is bitten? … So no one pities a person who associates with a sinner and becomes involved in the other's sins."

Jesus answered these Pharisees, "It is not the healthy who need a doctor, but the sick. I have not come to call the righteous, but sinners to repentance" (Luke 5:31–32). The themes of forgiving and healing come together. Jesus is not being contaminated, nor is he condoning sin; he is making sinners healthy by forgiving them and calling them to be his disciples.

We also see a sense of divine reversal in this story. Luke tells us the Pharisees "grumbled," which may lead hearers to recall the stories of the Israelites who grumbled in the wilderness as God freed and formed his people (Gowler 2007, 199). Sinners are forgiven and accepted, while the Pharisees oppose this establishment of the kingdom.

The Twelve

After discipling the Twelve for some time as they observed him, Jesus then sent them out to extend what he had been doing. He sent them to proclaim the kingdom, heal diseases, and drive out demons (Luke 9:1–2, 6). Like Jesus, they went from town to town. They would have spoken and healed in the marketplaces, and some of those who heard them would have hosted them in their homes. There the disciples could speak to their hosts and other townsfolk who attended in their home. Jesus focused on how the Twelve were to treat those householders who hosted them in their home. He told them to stay there until they left the town (Luke 9:4).

The Seventy-Two

Soon after sending out the Twelve, Luke recounts that "the Lord appointed seventy-two others and sent them two by two ahead of him to every town and place where he was about to go" (Luke 10:1). The Septuagint retelling of Genesis 10 lists seventy-two nations of the world. Sending the Twelve and then seventy-two others as harvesters seems to foreshadow the bringing of Gentiles into the people and work of God (Nolland, 1993, 549).

As with the Twelve, Jesus sends the seventy-two to proclaim the good news of the kingdom and heal the sick (Luke 10:9). Jesus tells them what to do if a householder invites them into their home. They are to greet their household with "peace." During the ensuing discussions in their home, it would then become apparent whether or not the householder—i.e., the host—would receive their message. Jesus says, "If a son of peace (*huios eirēnēs*) is there, your peace will rest on them; if not, it will return to you" (Luke 10:6, author's translation). The expression "son of peace" carries a Semitic sense of being destined for something, like "sons of the resurrection" (Luke 20:34–36) (Marshall 1978, 420). If the host is a son of peace, they are instructed "Stay there (*menete*), eating and drinking whatever they give you, for the worker deserves his wages" (Luke 10:7).

Jesus probably isn't implying that the seventy-two might not like the hummus, but rather that they, or perhaps others (like the Pharisees), might be concerned that the host hadn't observed the food-purity laws. They might also not wish to become relationally connected by receiving hospitality from them and becoming dependent on them. Jesus told them to stay with any son of peace and eat and drink with him. This means accepting them and not drawing boundaries between themselves. They are also to remain in this home, even if someone else (perhaps a more important person in the village) invites them. It seems that Jesus did not want them to dishonor the first householder who hosted them.

Zacchaeus

Jesus meets a chief tax collector named Zacchaeus as he is leaving Jericho and tells him, "I must stay (*meinai*) at your house (*oikō*) today" (Luke 19:5). Similar to the story of Levi, when Zacchaeus welcomes Jesus, "All the people saw this and began to mutter, 'He has gone to be the guest of a sinner'" (Luke 19:7). In the midst of this scene, Jesus declares, "Today salvation has come to this house (*oikō*)," meaning the members of the household (Luke 19:9). Just as when Jesus ate with Levi, some who consider themselves more righteous than this sinner grumble and oppose this work of God. Sinners receive forgiveness, while some obstinate people reject it.

Luke Develops a "Type-Scene"

Authors sometimes tell similar stories, with similar settings, characters, and plot lines. Although some variation naturally occurs in the stories, a similar scene or story is recognizable. Literary scholars call this a "type-scene" (Matson 1996, 18).[3] Authors often repeat keywords to help to make connections between the type-scenes. The Hebrew Bible uses type-scenes often in the way it tells stories, as do Luke and Acts (Alter 1981, 47–62, Matson 1996, 18).

Luke tells the stories of Levi, the Twelve, the seventy-two, and Zacchaeus to develop a type-scene intertwined with the kingdom coming through Jesus in those who receive him. Luke's hearers would hear the gospel in sequence and would likely have noticed the echoes and retention of words, plot, and themes in the stories in the following ways:

---

3 I draw heavily on David Matson's work. However, I believe the type-scene begins with Levi and is refined further in Luke 9–10 and 19.

1. Luke repeats a number of plot elements and words in the stories which make them sound similar. People "enter" and then "stay" in the "home" of the recipient of the kingdom work of Jesus. Receiving their hospitality or specifically "eating and drinking" is mentioned. In two of the stories people grumble or mutter (Luke 5:30; 19:7).

2. The coming of the kingdom is fulfilled in people through Jesus and his representatives. Jesus enters into table fellowship with Levi and Zacchaeus. Likewise, when his disciples are invited into a home, if the host then shows himself to be a son of peace, they are to treat him similarly.

3. Table fellowship occurs despite opposition from some who feel that by associating with these people, they are not upholding existing boundaries relating to the Torah (potentially disregarding food-purity laws and associating with "sinners" who blatantly disregard the law). Jesus, of course, is not corrupted but restores these people. He instructs his disciples to follow his example and not hold back from eating with a son of peace and his household.

4. Jesus brings God's reign among his people in fulfillment of past promises. Yet some opposed this as it happened, believing they were upholding God's reign and the boundaries of inclusion in God's people, based on Torah observance.

Part 2: Acts

Acts continues to tell the story of the early Jesus movement, which had begun among Jewish believers, as it expands across cultural boundaries from Jerusalem to Judea and Samaria and on to the ends of the earth (following Acts 1:8). The expansion of the movement would raise issues of collective identity, values, and boundaries. The spiritual unity of followers of Christ from Jewish and Gentile backgrounds is central to Luke's purpose. Luke tells stories using the type-scene to address the issue of boundaries, and along with it how the movement is able to spread into existing networks and to incorporate all believers into the people of God.

Homes, Jewish-Gentile Networks, and Table Fellowship

Along with households and blood relations, gift-giving provided another chief way individuals and groups established and maintained networks across society. High-status people acted as benefactors to others who depended on them. Academics often call these dependents "clients," but benefactors often called them "friends" (Cairns 2006, 37). Benefactors helped their clients, who in return gave them loyalty, services, and respect.

These networks commonly centered around the benefactor's home, where his (or her) "friends" would meet them. Hospitality and meals were part of these benefaction relationships. Many benefactors had a reception room (an atrium) in their home for these purposes. The atrium in wealthy homes could usually hold around forty people (Murphy-O'Connor 2004, 132).

Jewish people made up perhaps 10 percent of the Greco-Roman world, and many cities in the Eastern Mediterranean had significant populations of Jewish people (Smallwood 2001, 120). High-status Gentiles acted as benefactors to Jewish communities around them (Cohen 1989, 17). The Torah food-purity boundaries, however, meant that Jewish people did not eat food served by Gentiles. Table fellowship, therefore, served to maintain the Jewish collective identity, even while Jews participated in networks with Gentiles on a very concrete daily basis (Barclay 1996, 437; Bock 2007, 390).

Cornelius

Some Gentiles revered the God of the Jews and attended synagogue gatherings in their cities. Luke describes these Gentiles using terms such as "a worshiper" and "God-fearing Greeks" (e.g., Acts 13:16; 17:4). Cornelius was such a person: a devout God-fearing Gentile (Acts 10:2). He was close to Judaism spiritually as well as geographically (Tannehill 1994, 133–34). Yet, as a Gentile, he remained outside the people of God.

God sends an angel to Cornelius and gives Peter a vision which centers on food-purity rules. Cornelius sends two servants and a soldier to invite Peter. They tell Peter that Cornelius is a God-fearing centurion who is "respected by all the Jewish people" (Acts 10:22). They highlight that Cornelius is a person of high social status and hint that he is a benefactor of Jewish people. This was intended to persuade Peter to come, but ultimately it was the vision that convinced Peter.

High(er)-status Greco-Roman people acted as benefactors to philosophers and teachers. They would host the teacher in their homes, which enabled the teacher to get a hearing from their social networks (Keener 2013, KL 27525).

Cornelius was part of multiple networks and had assembled members of them in his home to hear Peter. Cornelius lived with his oikos (Acts 10:2). He gathered his "relatives and close friends" (Acts 10:24). If Cornelius was from the region, these "relatives" could have been his blood relatives who lived nearby. If not, he may have married a local woman (as many soldiers did) and they could have been her blood relatives (Keener 2013, LK 19943). Cornelius' "close friends" most likely meant some of his client network.

This story echoes Luke's type-scene. Peter and his companions "enter" (eisēlthen) Cornelius' home. They find many gathered together there, most probably in his atrium (Acts 10:27). Peter begins to teach them, making many allusions to Scripture. His speech climaxes in Acts 10:36 with his proclamation of the "good news of peace through Jesus Christ" to them. Romans called Caesar the "Lord of all the world" (Pinter 2019, 260). Peter proclaims that Jesus "is the Lord of all" (v. 36), and concludes by saying that Jesus is the "judge of the living and the dead. All the prophets testify about him that everyone who believes in him receives forgiveness of sins through his name" (vv. 42–43).

Pistis ("faith") is the language used throughout Acts for conversion (Morgan 2015, 382). In Acts, the word is normally used in straightforward relational terms (Morgan 2015, 389). It carries the sense of individuals being persuaded to entrust themselves in complete confidence to someone else. Peter proclaims these truths about Jesus and calls his audience to entrust themselves to him. They receive forgiveness as they entrust themselves to Jesus.

"While Peter was still speaking these words, the Holy Spirit came on all who heard the message. The circumcised believers who had come with Peter were astonished that the gift of the Holy Spirit had been poured out even on Gentiles. For they heard them speaking in tongues and praising God" (vv. 44–46). The group (Cornelius and his household, relatives, and clients) have received the good news. Seeing this happen, Peter concludes, "Surely no one can stand in the way of their being baptized with water. They have received the Holy Spirit just as we have" (v. 47). They are baptized, and Peter and his companions then "stay" (*epimeinai*) with them (v. 48).

Initially the "circumcised believers"—i.e., Jewish Christians—in Jerusalem oppose this. They criticize Peter: "You went into the house of uncircumcised men and *ate* with them" (Acts 11:2–3; emphasis added). Peter then recounts the story and concludes, "So if God gave them the same gift he gave us who believed in the Lord Jesus Christ, who was I to think that I could stand in God's way?" (v. 17).

The language of gift and trust is tied in with benefaction. Both Jews and these Gentiles received salvation and the gift of the Holy Spirit as they believed/entrusted themselves to Jesus (e.g., Acts 4:4; 9:42). When the circumcised believers hear this, they stop objecting, praise God, and say, "So then, even to Gentiles God has granted repentance that leads to life" (Acts 11:18).

The Ends of the Earth

After the story of Cornelius, Luke tells how some unnamed believers, originally from Cyprus and Cyrene, left Jerusalem and went to Antioch. They shared the good news with Greeks there, and "a great number of people believed and turned to the Lord" (Acts 11:19–21). From there, Paul and Barnabas preached the good news more widely to Gentiles, and many came to faith. They returned to Antioch and reported how God had "opened a door of faith to the Gentiles" (Acts 14:27).

At this point, the issue of boundaries comes up again. "Certain people came down from Judea to Antioch and were teaching the believers: 'Unless you are circumcised, according to the custom taught by Moses, you cannot be saved'" (Acts 15:1). These collectively oriented people understand the importance of collective boundaries. The deeper issue is *which* boundaries united them as God's people.

The elders meet in Jerusalem, and Peter recounts the story of Cornelius, concluding: "God did not discriminate between us and them, for he purified their hearts *by faith*" (Acts 15:7–11; emphasis added). James explains that the words of the prophets agree with this, and the "whole church" (Acts 15:22) accepts their decision.

Lydia

The upper classes looked down on marketplace preaching. So once traveling teachers had gained a crowd, they would try to move to teaching at meals and gatherings in someone's home, a more respectable forum (Keener 2013, KL 27525). Paul was a well-educated Jewish teacher. He normally began in new cities by speaking at synagogue gatherings. In fact, Luke describes this as his normal custom (Acts 17:2). Eventually, this often transitioned to him being invited by higher-status people to teach in their homes, which would have opened up social networks, given the role of homes (Acts 13:5–7; 16:13, 15, 40; 18:4–7; 19:8–9: a private hall, cf. 20:20–21). Scholars often argue that this sequence reflects salvation-historical priority, but it also reflects pragmatic missiology and social networking (Keener 2013, KL 24701).

Philippi was a Roman colony (Acts 16:12). Colonies normally banned foreign religious cults inside the city, especially if there were not many followers there (Witherington 1998, 490). When the Sabbath came, Paul and his companions looked outside the city walls for a Jewish Sabbath gathering. They found a small group of women. They "sat down and began to speak to them," which indicates teaching in a discussion format (Acts 16:13). As Lydia, a Gentile "worshiper of God," listened, "The Lord opened her heart to respond to Paul's message" (Acts 16:14).

This story now proceeds to echo the type-scene once again. "When she and the members of her household (*oikos*) were baptized, she invited us to her home. 'If you consider me a believer (*pistēn*) in the Lord,' she said, 'come (*eiselthontes*) and stay (*menete*) at my house'" (Acts 16:15). They did so.

Paul would have been able to speak to Lydia's networks. Lydia was an immigrant trader from Thyatira, so she would not have been a member of the small aristocratic Roman political elite of the city. However, as an immigrant she was not in a marginal minority. Over half the city, especially the traders, craftworkers and shopkeepers, were non-Roman immigrants (Oakes 2001, 50).

Lydia was relatively wealthy. She was a "dealer in purple," a trade associated with wealth. She was also a householder and had a home large enough to host Paul and his companions and gatherings (Acts 16:40). She would have had clients who depended on her in different ways: patrons of her own, suppliers, customers, acquaintances, and probably fellow Thyatirans with whom she shared collective connections in the city (Ascough 2009, 56). Similar to Cornelius, who gathered friends in his home, Paul likely taught various members of Lydia's social networks in the atrium in her home, as he taught a gathering of believers there later in the story (Acts 16:40). He also continued to speak at the place of prayer each Sabbath (v. 16).

The Jailer

When an earthquake freed Paul and Silas from the Philippian jail, the Gentile jailer asked them, "Sirs, what must I do to be saved?" His question would remind those who would later listen to the reading of Acts of the decision reached in Jerusalem. It also provided a case study of the Jerusalem counsel's application to a non-God-fearing Gentile (Tannehill 1994, 165). Paul and Silas replied, "Believe (*pisteuson*) in the Lord Jesus, and you will be saved—you and your household" (Acts 16:31). They urged a collective response. They were to entrust themselves to "the Lord Jesus" and receive salvation. After hearing the word, the jailer and his household were baptized. He then brought Paul and Silas into his house (*oikon*) and "set a meal before them" (vv. 32–34).

The jailer's household did not become a base for the believing community in Philippi. Paul and Silas met with the "brothers and sisters" at Lydia's house, where they encouraged them (Acts 16:40). It seems the jailer's household (and any other believers) gathered in her home, which had become the base for the community there.

No opposition to the table fellowship appears in these two stories. Opposition still accompanies the spread of the movement to this new people, though, from Gentiles sensing a challenge to their collective Roman values (Acts 16:19–21).[4]

Acts ends with Paul in Rome under house arrest, explaining to the local Jewish leaders that "God's salvation has been sent to the Gentiles" and boldly proclaiming "the kingdom of God" to all who came to the house Paul was renting (Acts 28:17–31). Isaiah's vision is coming to fulfillment through Jesus in his followers who trusted in him (Luke 4). God is restoring his people through his servant and then gathering "the people of all nations" to see his glory.

Summary and Application Questions for Movement Practitioners

In Luke and Acts, Luke uses compositional devices aimed at hearers in oral-preference cultures. Exegeting, as a series, the stories about householders who entrusted themselves to Jesus in Luke and Acts helps us recognize some of the themes developed in these stories. This concrete story-based approach to

---

4 Luke says that in Corinth, "Paul left the synagogue and went next door to the house of Titius Justus" (Acts 18:7). The move symbolizes the centering of the mission in a Gentile home. After this, "Crispus, the synagogue leader, and his entire household (*oikō*) believed (*episteusen*) in the Lord." The type-scene echo connects with the reversal theme, and we see a Jewish leader and his household entrust themselves to the Lord after the move to a Gentile base.

teaching makes sense to many members of oral-preference cultures. Yet many highly literate learners struggle with this concrete, nonconceptual approach and tend to appreciate more explicit conceptual statements.

Luke's stories describe people belonging to various social networks, including households, benefaction networks, taxation networks, family relatives (by blood or marriage ties), and religious networks based around synagogues. These collective networks were based on different collective values which bound these people together into various forms of networks. The stories describe how Jesus, and his followers, reached these networks through homes (though this was not their only approach). In Palestine and the Greco-Roman cities, homes were a key space around which various networks revolved and where people taught others. These social networks spread the good news and formed groups of Christ-followers.

We do well to build into our missiology an understanding of a variety of collective allegiances and networks today. However, is the *oikos* a major network in your context today? Are homes a key space around which networks revolve? Could other networks and spaces serve more effectively for initially reaching people? We can learn more from these stories in Luke and Acts than simply that reaching key people can be a way of opening up their preexisting networks. Too often, the discussion of these passages has stopped there. Preexisting networks and boundaries also decided people. The stories address these aspects too.

The stories also describe how some of the values which underpinned groups prevented others from belonging fully to the group. For example, the value Pharisees and Jews in general gave to observing the food-purity laws meant they didn't eat with Gentiles. This was a constant that prevented social belonging at some levels. Cornelius, Lydia, and the jailer were Gentiles and so not ethnically Jewish; this caused Jews to question their inclusion in the people of God. The values which join social networks can also separate them from other networks. Are there collective values in your context today which separate people? Are they holding you back from reaching social networks? Boundaries built upon values not intrinsic to the gospel can hold us back from reaching those God is reaching and prevent people from being part of the movement. What are the cultural and/or social boundaries around belonging together in Christ that need to be removed?

Through his stories, Luke prescribes that the boundary (and value) which underpins who belongs to the movement is faith (*pistis*). Faith was a relational term. It relates to entrusting oneself to Jesus. The sense of following the rabbi Jesus, or putting trust in the news about his resurrection and lordship, carry aspects of benefaction. Believers are centered on Christ and have entrusted themselves to him, collectively. The boundary is a relationship centered on Jesus. This explains the boundary and the door (Acts 14:27) of how people join the Jesus movement. Paul tells the jailer and his household to "believe in the Lord and you will be saved." When Cornelius, Lydia, and the jailer believe in (entrust themselves to) Jesus, they receive his salvation and are now his people. This is collective rather than individualistic. We belong to Jesus and to those who belong to Jesus. Members are bound by having trusted in him, because that is the collective boundary. Like Peter, we are to accept those whom God has accepted. The deeper issues/questions for movement practitioners are these: Are we accepting those who have entrusted themselves to Jesus? Is our understanding of salvation relational? How can this help movements to grow in unity together? How can this help movements in your context to expand and embrace people across preexisting boundaries?

Given that faith in Jesus is the boundary, this raises practical (and theological) questions about how people come to entrust themselves to him. In Acts, we see different ways that people come to entrust themselves to Jesus, including seeing signs and wonders (Acts 5:12–15); hearing stories about things Jesus said and did (Acts 4:4; 10:37–43; 16:32); being taught what these events mean (fulfilling God's plan) (Luke 1:1–4); and through God opening peoples' hearts (Acts 16:14). How can you share the good news of Jesus with those in preexisting networks?

These stories of "people of peace" explore the very collective nature of salvation and belonging to Jesus. Luke's messages in these stories go beyond simply highlighting that reaching certain types of people can enable movements to reach their preexisting networks. Luke's point is much deeper and broader. He highlights that entrusting oneself to Jesus is both the boundary *and* the door for collective people to join and belong to discipleship movements, which are themselves collective in nature. Grasping this collective boundary helps us to navigate belonging and how movements can expand into preexisting networks (which both unite and divide people). As we work toward movements, this perspective helps us navigate issues of belonging and expansion among preexisting networks in our contexts today.

References

Achtemeier, Paul J. 1990. "Omne Verbum Sonat: The New Testament and the Oral Environment of Late Western Antiquity." *Journal of Biblical Literature* 109 (1):3–27.

Adams, Edward. 2013. *The Earliest Christian Meeting Places: Almost Exclusively Houses?* LNTS 450; London: T&T Clark.

Addison, Steve. 2012. *What Jesus Started: Joining the Movement, Changing the World.* Downers Grove, IL: InterVarsity.

Alter, Robert. 1981. *The Art of Biblical Narrative.* New York: Basic Books.

Ascough, Richard S. 2009. *Lydia: Paul's Cosmopolitan Hostess.* Collegeville, MN: Liturgical Press.

Bagnall, Roger S., and Bruce W. Frier. 1994. *The Demography of Roman Egypt.* Cambridge: Cambridge University Press.

Barclay, John M. G. 1996. *Jews in the Mediterranean Diaspora: From Alexander to Trajan (323 BCE to 117 CE).* Berkeley, CA: University of California Press.

Bock, Darrell L. 2007. *Acts.* Grand Rapids: Baker Academic.

Botha, Pieter J. 2012. *Orality and Literacy in Early Christianity* (Biblical Performance Criticism Book 5) Eugene, OR: Cascade Books.

Cairns, Francis. 2006. *Sextus Propertius: The Augustan Elegist.* Cambridge: Cambridge University Press.

Cohen, Shaye J. D. 1989. "Crossing the Boundary and Becoming a Jew." *The Harvard Theological Review* 82 (1): 13–33.

Darr, John A. 1992. *On Character Building: The Reader and the Rhetoric of Characterization in Luke-Acts.* Louisville, KY: Westminster/John Knox Press.

Garrison, David. 2004. *Church Planting Movements: How God Is Redeeming a Lost World.* Midlothian, VA: WIGTake Resources.

Gowler, David B. 2007. *Host, Guest, Enemy and Friend: Portraits of the Pharisees in Luke–Acts.* Eugene, OR: Wipf and Stock.

Harvey, John D. 1998. *Listening to the Text: Oral Patterning in Paul's Letters.* Grand Rapids: Baker Books.

Hays, Richard B. 2016. *Echoes of Scripture in the Gospels.* Waco, TX: Baylor University Press.

Hiebert, Paul G. 1994. *Anthropological Reflections on Missiological Issues.* Grand Rapids: Baker.

Keener, Craig S. 2009. *The Historical Jesus of the Gospels.* Grand Rapids: Eerdmans.

———. 2013. *Acts: An Exegetical Commentary,* vol. 2: 3:1–14:28. Grand Rapids: Baker Academic. Kindle Edition.

———. 2014. *Acts: An Exegetical Commentary,* vol. 3: 15:1–23:35. Grand Rapids: Baker Academic. Kindle Edition.

Marshall, I. Howard. 1978. *The Gospel of Luke: A Commentary on the Greek Text.* NIGTC. Grand Rapids: Eerdmans.

Matson, David. 1996. *Household Conversion Narratives in Acts: Pattern and Interpretation.* JSNT Supplement Series 123. Sheffield, UK: Sheffield Academic Press.

Matthews, A. 2019. "Person of Peace Methodology in Church Planting: A Critical Analysis." *Missiology* 47 (2): 187–99.

Morgan, Teresa. 2015. *Roman Faith and Christian Faith: Pistis and Fides in the Early Roman Empire and Early Churches.* Oxford: Oxford University Press.

Moxnes, Halvor. 1997. "What Is Family? Problems in Constructing Early Christian Families." In *Constructing Early Christian Families: Family as Social Reality and Metaphor,* edited by Halvor Moxnes, 20–21. New York: Routledge.

Murphy-O'Connor, J. 2004. "House-Churches and the Eucharist." In *Christianity at Corinth: The Quest for the Pauline Church,* edited by Edward Adams and David G. Horrell, 129–38. Louisville, KY: Westminster John Knox.

Nolland, John. 1993. *Luke 9:21–18:34*. Vol. 2. Word Biblical Commentary. Dallas: Word.

Oakes, Peter. 2001. *Philippians: From People to Letter*. SNTSM 110. Cambridge: Cambridge University Press.

———. 2009. *Reading Romans in Pompeii: Paul's Letter at Ground Level*. Minneapolis, MN: Fortress Press.

Osiek, Carolyn, and David L. Balch. 1997. *Families in the New Testament World: Households and House Churches*. Louisville, KY: Westminster John Knox Press.

Pinter, Dean. 2019. *Acts* (SoGBC). Grand Rapids: Zondervan.

Richards, E. Randolph, and Richard James. 2020. *Misreading Scripture with Individualist Eyes*. Downers Grove, IL: IVP Academic.

Robbins, Vernon K. 1991. "Writing as a Rhetorical Act in Plutarch and the Gospels." In *Persuasive Artistry: Studies in New Testament Rhetoric in Honor of George A. Kennedy*, edited by Duane F. Watson, 157–86. Sheffield, UK: JSOT.

———. 1994. "Oral, Rhetorical, and Literary Cultures? A Response." *Semeia* 65: 7591.

Safrai, Shmuel. 1976. "Education and the Study of Torah." In *The Jewish People in the First Century: Historical Geography, Political History, Social, Cultural, and Religious Life and Institutions*, vol. 2, edited by Shmuel Safrai and Menahem Stern, 945–70. Philadelphia: Fortress Press.

Sanders, E. P. 2016. *Jewish Law from Jesus to the Mishnah: Five Studies*. Minneapolis: Fortress Press, 183–354.

Smallwood, Edith, M. 2001. *The Jews Under Roman Rule, from Pompey to Diocletian: A Study in Political Relations*, 2nd ed. Leiden: Brill.

Smith, Steve, and Ying Kai. 2011. *T4T: A Discipleship Re-Revolution*. Monument, CO: WIGTake Resources.

Smith, Steve, and Stan Parks. 2015. "T4T or DMM (DBS)?—Only God Can Start a Church-Planting Movement (Part 1 of 2)." *Mission Frontiers*. https://www.missionfrontiers.org/issue/article/t4t-or-dmm-dbs-only-god-can-start-a-church-planting-movement-part-1-of-2.

Tannehill, Robert C. 1994. *The Narrative Unity of Luke-Acts: A Literary Interpretation*, Vol 2. Minneapolis: Fortress.

Trousdale, Jerry. 2012. *Miraculous Movements: How Hundreds of Thousands of Muslims Are Falling in Love with Jesus*. Nashville: Thomas Nelson.

Watson, David L., and Paul D. Watson. 2014. *Contagious Disciple Making*. Nashville: Thomas Nelson.

Witherington, Ben III. 1998. *The Acts of the Apostles: A Socio-Rhetorical Commentary*. Grand Rapids: Eerdmans.

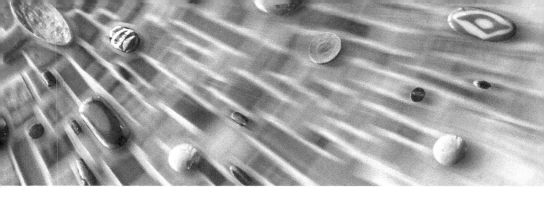

PART III
Movement Dynamics

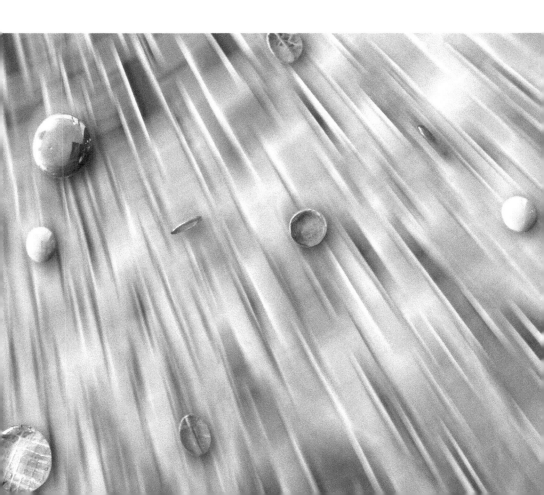

Why Movements Rise and Fall

Steve Addison

A movement is a group of people committed to a common cause. For good or for ill, movements are the driving force of history, and history is the story of the rise and fall of movements.

The mission of Jesus became a missionary movement. The church Jesus founded was a missionary church: its existence and activities were an expression of its missionary calling; its members were fearlessly determined to win others to faith in Jesus as the crucified and risen Messiah. Their mission field began at home in Jerusalem and Judea, and it extended to the ends of the earth. The goal and purpose of their missionary work was the making of disciples and the creation of communities of disciples—people who turned from their old way of life, put their trust in Jesus, and obeyed his teaching (Schnabel 2004, 95, 355–56).

If we are to understand how movements are born, why they rise and fall, and how they are reborn, we must return to the life and ministry of Jesus. Remaining in him is the key to the rise of movements and abandoning him is the reason movements fall.

Seven Characteristics of Movements

The pattern of Jesus' life and ministry reveal seven characteristics that are recurring patterns in movements, that multiply disciples and churches. These characteristics help us understand why movements rise and fall.

Figure 11.1 The Rise and Fall of Movements

Identity is at the heart of the rise and fall of movements. A movement is defined by its identity: strategy and methods are an expression of that identity. The baptism and testing of Jesus mark the boundary between his life in Nazareth and the birth of the new Israel. Jesus' baptism and wilderness experiences are foundational, revealing his identity as a movement founder. He was obedient to the living Word, dependent on the Holy Spirit, and faithful to God's mission.

1. Word—Obedient to the Word

At his baptism and in the wilderness, Jesus placed his life and ministry under the authority of God's living Word—he was the Son who expressed his love in complete obedience.

God's Word is God in action: he spoke, and his Word flung the universe into existence. Through speech, God creates, sustains, and shapes reality. When he speaks, he does so with authority as our Creator and Lord.

God created the first man and woman through his Word, blessing them and commanding them to fill the earth and subdue it. He also spoke to set a limit on their autonomy. They were not to eat of the fruit of the tree in the middle of the garden of Eden. God spoke with clarity and authority, and he expected them to obey, needing no other reason than his command. Obedience brings blessing, and disobedience brings judgment. Adam and Eve chose disobedience and placed themselves above God's Word. Humans have perpetuated this pattern of placing themselves above God's Word ever since.

In Jesus, the Word become flesh and lived among us (John 1:14), as both perfect God and perfect man. In his earthly ministry, Jesus spoke what his Father told him to say (John 8:28; 10:18; 12:49–50; 14:10; 15:15), and his words were God's words. He lived in surrender to the Father's will, obeying the Father's words (John 5:36; 8:42) and doing nothing in his own authority. Jesus obeyed both the Father's direct commands and the written words of God in the Old Testament.

Jesus expected his disciples to follow his example; he stated that to love God is to hear his Word and obey it (John 14:21). A disciple is simply someone who learns to obey everything Jesus commanded (Matt 28:20).

At the heart of God's mission in Acts is his powerful Word. The Word spreads, increases, multiplies, and grows in power—traveling to the ends of the earth and conquering the world, resulting in the multiplication of disciples and churches (Rosner 1998, 215–33).

Movements rise and fall depending on their obedience to the living Word of God.

2. Spirit—Dependent on the Holy Spirit

At Jesus' baptism, the Spirit descended on Jesus as he was praying (Luke 3:21), anointing him with power and authority to fulfill his mission. Jesus, filled with the Spirit, overcame Satan in the wilderness and returned in the power of the Spirit to launch his ministry.

The same Spirit who hovered over the waters at creation was the agent of Jesus' conception. From his conception to his ascension, the Holy Spirit was the key to the powerful ministry of Jesus of Nazareth.

Without the Spirit, there would be no missionary movement. Jesus told his disciples it was good he was going away (John 16:7), and that the Father would send the Holy Spirit so that every disciple would know the reality of the presence of God. The disciples were told that the Spirit would guide them into all truth, not speaking on his own but "speaking only what he hears" (John 16:13–14). As the Father sent him, Jesus sent his disciples, knowing that his presence through the Holy Spirit went with them (John 20:21–22).

Jesus' crucifixion, resurrection, and ascension opened the way for the universal outpouring of the Holy Spirit at Pentecost. When the Spirit came upon Jesus' disciples as they prayed, the church was born, and the mission began. The Spirit came to enable every believer to bear witness to Jesus (Acts 1:8), and gave wisdom, joy, faith, strength, and courage to the early disciples in the face of death. The Holy Spirit was at work in major breakthroughs; from Philip's encounter with the Ethiopian eunuch, to Peter's meeting with Cornelius, to Paul and Barnabas' first missionary journey—all were initiated by the Holy Spirit. "Restlessly the Spirit drives the church to witness, and continually churches rise out of the witness" (Boer 1961, 161).

God creates and redeems through his Word and the Holy Spirit. The rise and fall of movements is a reflection of their dependence on the leading and power of the Holy Spirit.

3. Mission—Faithful to the Core Missionary Task

At his baptism, Jesus identified with rebellious Israel and sinful humanity. In choosing to submit himself in baptism, he showed himself to be the Servant of God, prophesied by Isaiah, who would give his life as a ransom for many (Isa 40–55; Mark 10:45). What was revealed at his baptism was tested in the wilderness.

Each temptation struck at Jesus' identity and the nature of his mission. First, Satan goaded Jesus to satisfy his hunger by turning stones into bread. There would come a time when the crowds, satisfied with the bread that Jesus provided, would try to make Jesus king by force (John 6:15). Jesus walked away. Jesus provided hungry people with bread, but that was not the core missionary task, for he is the Bread of Life in whom we must believe (John 6:26–51).

The second temptation had Jesus perched high above the temple in Jerusalem. Satan dared Jesus to throw himself down and force God to rescue him. This was a temptation to use the power God had given Jesus for his own glory and as a shortcut to fulfilling his mission.

In the face of suffering, Jesus was moved with compassion and reached out his hand to heal the sick and cast out demons. Yet signs and wonders are not the core missionary task. Miracles are a sign that points to Jesus, but they do not compel belief. The towns of Chorazin, Bethsaida, and even Capernaum, where Jesus spent so much time, were in danger of God's judgment (Matt 11:21–24). Their inhabitants saw the miracles, yet they would not turn and repent.

Finally, Satan took Jesus to a high mountain and showed him the kingdoms of the world and all their splendor. Jesus could have it all if he would bow down before Satan and worship. Jesus could win the world through cultural and political power without the shame and horror of the cross.

Today we hear a lot about the transformation of society as the goal of mission. Jesus promised no such thing. The only towns and cities that were transformed by Jesus and his followers were transformed into riots. He promised his followers persecution and conflict, not influence. Social transformation can be a fruit of the gospel, but there is no guarantee it will come.

Bread, signs and wonders, cultural and political power—these are not the core missionary task. What did Jesus choose instead? He chose the cross. His mission was to save his people from their sins (Matt 1:21).

From the very start of his ministry, Jesus' intentions were clear. He founded a missionary movement and those who followed him became missionaries (Mark 1:17).

From his position of supreme authority, Jesus gave his followers a universal mission—make disciples of all peoples (Matt 28:16–20). This is the core missionary task. We are to make disciples of every nation, tribe, and tongue, by going, baptizing, and teaching them to obey everything Jesus has commanded.

Do this and the risen Lord promises we will never be without his presence. In the New Testament, missionaries establish contact with non-Christians, they proclaim the news of Jesus the Messiah and Savior, they lead people to faith in Jesus Christ, and they form new believers into local communities of disciples of Jesus (see Schnabel 2008, 29). Movements rise and fall in the degree to which they remain faithful to this core missionary task.

When Jesus walked out of the wilderness and returned to Galilee in the power of the Spirit, he knew who he was, and he knew what he had come to do. He expressed his identity in strategic action. Strategy is how a movement operates. Jesus' strategy had four recurring aspects: pioneering leaders, contagious relationships, rapid mobilization, and adaptive methods. Multiplying movements typically display these patterns.

4. Pioneering Leaders

Early on in his ministry, Jesus called disciples who would become the pioneering leaders of a missionary movement. He gave them a command: "Come follow me," and a promise:

> *"I will teach you to fish for people." He trained them by his example and by sending them out on missions that prefigured the eventual call to disciple the nations.*

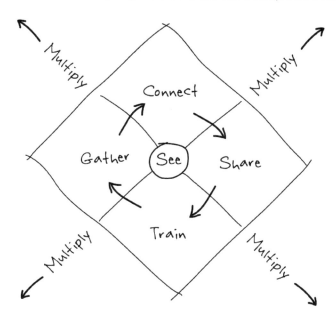

Figure 11.2 Movement Diamond

Pioneering leaders form missionary bands that become catalysts for evangelism in unreached fields, leading to initial discipleship, church formation, and church strengthening.

They see the end. Their identity is aligned with God's purposes. They submit to the leadership of Jesus through the Holy Spirit and the power of his living Word. They obey God's call to join his mission.

They connect with people. They cross boundaries (geographic, linguistic, cultural, social, and economic) to establish contact with people far from God.

They share the gospel. They communicate the truth about God and salvation through Christ. They equip new disciples to spread the good news throughout their communities.

They train disciples. They lead people to faith in Jesus Christ (conversion, baptism, gifts of the Holy Spirit) and teach them to obey all that Jesus commanded.

They gather communities. They form those who repent, believe, and are baptized into churches where they join together to study and obey God's Word, pray, celebrate the Lord's Supper, love one another, worship, give generously, and make disciples (Acts 2:42–47).

They multiply workers. They equip local church leaders to multiply disciples and churches. In partnership with the churches, movement pioneers form apostolic teams that launch into unreached fields.

5. Contagious Relationships

Jesus trained his disciples to go into unreached villages and look for responsive households that would become the entry point to the whole community. He led by example in his encounters with the Gerasene demoniac (Mark 5:1–18), Zacchaeus the tax collector (Luke 19:1–9), and the Samaritan woman (John 4:1–26). Through these individuals, the good news about Jesus reached entire communities.

The key to the rapid growth of any movement is face-to-face recruitment within preexisting social networks. The stronger the social network, the faster the movement spreads. But for a movement to grow, it must not only reach new people, it must keep them—and it must build them into a committed force for change. Movements made up of a collection of casual acquaintances will lack energy, commitment, and focus. A successful movement is both a tight and open social network. Jesus ministered to the crowds, but he didn't entrust himself to them unless they responded to his call to become disciples. He formed his disciples into a tight social network that maintained its openness to those outside.

6. Rapid Mobilization

Jesus bypassed religious professionals and went looking for ordinary people. He commanded fishermen to follow him and promised to teach them to fish for people (Mark 1:17; Matt 4:19). Jesus traveled not only with the Twelve but also with a wider group of disciples that included a number of influential and wealthy women who supported his ministry (Luke 8:1–3). Some disciples followed him throughout his itinerant ministry, but he sent others, such as the Gerasene demoniac and the Samaritan woman, home to share what God had done for them (Mark 5:18–20; John 4:1–42).

Christ gave the Great Commission to every disciple. Every disciple is charged with making disciples by going, baptizing, and teaching those who respond to obey everything Jesus has commanded. Every disciple has the Word, the Spirit, and the responsibility to fulfill the mission.

Paul followed Jesus' example. He rarely traveled alone. He had nine key team members who worked with him, many of whom came from the churches he started. As he moved on to unreached cities, he expected the churches to partner with him in the mission and to continue to reach their region in depth (Phil 1:4–5; 1 Thess 1:8) (Plummer 2006). He was confident he could move on as he committed the new churches to the Word and the Spirit (Acts 20:28, 32).

The church's missionary advance comes from the spontaneous, individual activity of its members, led by the Holy Spirit (Allen 1956).

7. Adaptive Methods

The most effective and sustained movements live in the tension between the chaos and creativity of spiritual enthusiasm and the stability provided by effective methods, strategies, and structures.

Jesus' methods were simple, yet powerful: he trained his followers to do what he did—enter an unreached community and form a base of operations. His teaching and his stories were memorized and passed on; he trained workers on the job; his movement required no central funding or control.

By the end of Jesus' ministry, the content of his message was imprinted on the disciples' minds and hearts. These profound but simple sayings and stories were easily transmitted as the missionary movement advanced from person to person, group to group, and culture to culture.

Adaptive methods are simple, reproducible, sustainable, and scalable. They are the scaffolding of a movement, not the building itself.

Movements that remain true to their identity (Word, Spirit, mission) will test the effectiveness of their methods and make changes that align with their identity. John Wesley, the founder of Methodism, had one mission—to disciple a nation. In pursuit of that mission he continually experimented, adapting his methods for spreading the gospel, making disciples, forming groups, and mobilizing workers.

Movements can suffer from "the failure of success." Convinced that what they are doing is right, they stop paying attention to the world around them. They stop learning and adapting. The informal methods that brought the initial success become formalized with inflexible procedures and structures. Creativity and innovation jump ship or must walk the plank. The solution is not to adopt the latest fad in methods, but to revisit how methods can best serve identity and strategy.

Identity Is Key

Identity—Word, Spirit, and mission—is the key that unlocks the rise and fall of movements. These are the heart and soul of a multiplying movement as a work of God. Identity leads to effective patterns of ministry—pioneering leaders, contagious relationships, rapid mobilization, and adaptive methods. Drifting from identity undermines movements. Life and renewal comes through a return to identity. The alternative is decline and decay.

Stages in the Rise and Fall of Movements

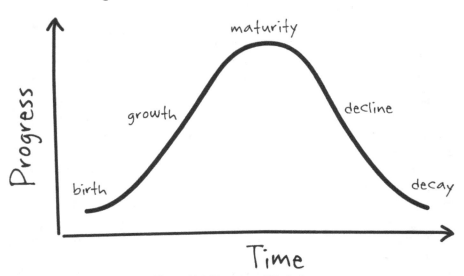

Figure 11.3 Movement Life Cycle

The life cycle of movements can be broken down into five stages—birth, growth, maturity, decline, and decay. This process is not inevitable. There is a sixth possibility—the hope of rebirth during maturity or decline. Rebirth interrupts the aging process and turns the movement back toward growth.

The movement life cycle is a pattern that shows up over long periods of time. The life cycle is a model. Models aren't perfect, but they do help us navigate complexity.

Stage 1. Birth: Commit to the cause

Whereas realists adapt themselves to the world, founders of movements want to change their world. Founders have five important tasks to complete.

1.1. Wrestle with God: Clear vision is a by-product of surrender.

The story begins for Jesus in the wilderness, where his identity is tested and proved. The apostle Paul received his call while lying face down on the road to Damascus. For the next three days he sat blinded, not knowing what would come next, completely dependent on God to rescue him (Acts 9). All his strength turned to weakness, and this dependence on God became the heart of the multiplying movement he helped birth.

A renewed awareness of God's authority frees a founder to question existing authorities and call God's people back to biblical realities and a new direction. In the struggle, founders learn obedience to the Word and to the Spirit and faithfulness to God's call.

1.2. Fuel discontent: Raise awareness of the gap between the ideal and reality.

Founders are unreasonable people, refusing to accept the world as it is. Movements are born because something needs to change. Founders help people see what is wrong and how to put things right. Movement founders raise the levels of discontent by pointing to the "ideal-real gap"—the gap between what is and what should be.

Founders refuse to accept the ideal-real gap, and in doing so they make everyone else feel uncomfortable. They are impatient and uncompromising. They see the deficiencies, but will not tolerate them. The old paradigm no longer fits reality, and the need for change becomes urgent.

1.3. Dare to dream: Know where you are going, even if you don't yet know how you'll get there.

A critique without a dream results in paralysis and cynicism. Founders are dreamers. They cast vision for a better future. They may not know how they will get there, but they know where they are going. Founders point the way because they can see the destination. They live their lives backward. The reality of the vision draws them into the future, despite the obstacles.

But what is the source of vision? When Jesus rose from the dead, he encountered a shattered band of disciples. If it had been up to their best efforts, the Christian movement would have been finished. Over forty days, Jesus opened their minds to understand God's purposes in the Scriptures. He made clear the core missionary task and promised them the power of the Holy Spirit.

1.4. Commit to action: Show how the vision can be turned into reality.

Discontent without vision leads to cynicism, but a dream without action is a fantasy. Founders dream, and then they enact those dreams. Ideas are only dangerous if they are turned into action.

Founders aren't interested in gradual improvement. They call for deep change, going outside existing structures to bring it about, and conflict often ensues. Jesus refused to be bound by the expectations of those around him. He committed to action. Nothing would stop Jesus from seeking and saving lost sheep.

1.5. Build a team: Call people who are willing to lay down their lives for the cause.

A committed founder is not a movement. Founders must attract committed followers. Because the movement is still in its infancy, founders don't have salaries, benefits, or positions of power to offer their recruits. Instead, they offer the reward of a cause worth living and dying for.

Each of the Gospels record how Jesus called his first disciples, who would form the nucleus of a missionary movement. Jesus' authority stands out. The disciples left everything to follow this Galilean carpenter who had no formal authority. The accounts of his baptism and wilderness testing reveal the true source of his authority.

From Birth to Growth

Nothing is more powerful than an idea whose time has come. But ideas don't make history—committed people do. A movement is born when someone commits to action.

Movements that make it through birth must face the challenge of growth, turning the idea into effective strategies and methods that get results.

Stage 2. Growth: Put the idea to work

Founders in growth face five essential challenges:

2.1. Put the idea to work: Ground the founding vision in effective action that produces the results for which the movement exists.

Growth is not the time for generating more ideas. It's the time to put ideas to work. Visionaries must become doers who turn dreams into reality by inspiring others to follow their example.

In the early stages of growth, founders are carried forward by conviction and intuition, not evidence. Like David standing before Goliath, they don't have all the answers but are willing to take a risk. They are willing to do something. They draw action-oriented people who likewise are motivated by conviction, not proof. Once there is action and progress, others will come on board, and the movement will pick up momentum.

2.2. Balance flexibility and control: Utilize effective methods and functional structures that enable the spread of the movement.

In the early stages of growth, it's too soon for the founder to release authority. If the leader steps back at this point, competing agendas will undermine a movement's identity. The founder must lead by example and keep everyone focused on getting the results for which the movement exists.

Movements don't live by passion alone. A movement must develop strategies and methods if it is to spread beyond the founding group. There's a dilemma: Systems reduce flexibility—yet flexibility without systems and structure results in chaos and fragmentation. In growth, the movement must remain flexible if it is to adapt to its environment. A dynamic movement is like a gymnast balancing flexibility and control, stability and change (Adizes 1979, 6).

2.3. Release authority and responsibility: Mobilize workers and leaders to consolidate and expand the movement.

To move from birth to growth, founders must mobilize leaders who multiply their impact. Great leaders give their people freedom and responsibility within a framework. A leader's greatest legacy is the cause they leave behind and the people aligned with that cause. Multiplication can take place when the founder releases authority and responsibility to people who know why the movement exists (identity), how to pursue its mission (strategy), and what to do (methods).

2.4. Let go: Avoid the "founder's trap" by empowering the movement to embody the cause.

In the early stages, the founder's commitment sustains a movement. Yet if that loving embrace lasts too long, it will end in suffocation. The movement will be caught in the "founder's trap" (Adizes 1999, 64–70). The founder's trap occurs when a founder remains in direct personal control and won't release authority and responsibility.

If the founder remains in control, the movement will stall. Founders overcome this challenge by focusing on the movement, not on themselves. They must develop action-oriented leaders who embrace the cause; they need to build a culture of discipline around identity; and they need strategies and methods that align the movement with identity.

The best antidote for the founder's trap is a mission that extends beyond the limitations of one individual.

2.5. Pursue prime: Put in place the people and systems to achieve the results for which the movement exists.

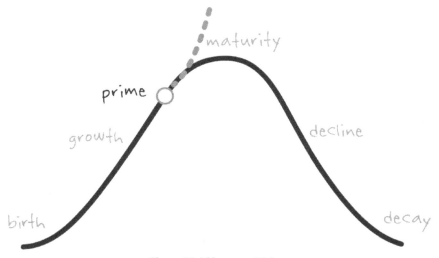

Figure 11.4 Movement Prime

Growth begins with the challenge of putting the idea to work. Once the idea is working, the movement is making tangible progress: it is attracting pioneering leaders and expanding its impact. It has both control and flexibility; its clear strategy and adaptive methods empower followers to achieve the movement's purpose. The movement embodies the founding ideal and is no longer dependent upon its founder.

Now it has a chance of reaching prime. In prime, an organization knows why it exists, where it is going, and how to get there. It is achieving the results for which it was created. Organizations in prime confront the brutal facts when they fall short, and adjust accordingly. The organization remains creative and flexible, ensuring long-term effectiveness (Adizes 1996, 27).

From Growth to Maturity

Approaching the peak of the movement life cycle, a movement must overcome the complacency that comes with success. Will it continue to renew itself or play it safe and protect its hard-earned gains? Maturity comes when a movement chooses security over identity.

Stage 3. Maturity: Enjoying the view

A movement in maturity has plateaued, reaching the pinnacle of its success and is content. The movement is still achieving significant results. But there is a loss of urgency, and with that loss, creativity and adaptability are diminished. The attitude is, "Let's keep doing what brought us success."

Formality, order, and predictability matter more than results. Movements mature when they choose to enjoy and protect their achievements. Momentum carries the movement forward, but at a declining rate.

3.1. Stumbling over success: Assuming past achievements will continue into the future. A movement that has succeeded in the growth phase is prone to arrogance. Hard lessons are forgotten. Progress is assumed.

Before Israel crossed the Jordan River to occupy the Promised Land, the Lord told them they were coming into a good land where they would prosper, but in their success they must be careful not to become proud and forget the Lord. Israel was told to remember and obey him and not pursue other gods—or they would be destroyed. Yet in their success they failed to remember (Deut 8).

3.2. Ignoring the ideal-real gap: Allowing reality to triumph over the ideal.

Movements emerge because something needs to change. New movements fuel discontent. Successful movements become content; they want to relieve the tension with the world as it is.

Movements stay young by maintaining the creative tension between what is (reality) and what should be (ideal). Movements grow old when they ignore the ideal-real gap, when they protect their accomplishments rather than risk adding to them.

3.3. Choosing extremes: Choosing between traditionalists (separation from the world) and progressives (peace with the world)—or allowing unresolved conflict between them.

In maturity, a split can open up between traditionalists and progressives. Progressives want to reduce the tension of the ideal-real gap by reducing the demands on members and making the movement more socially acceptable.

Traditionalists want to impose the stringency of the past, but without returning to the movement's original vitality. Progressives want the movement to be a loose social network open to society. Traditionalists want a tight social network closed to society. Both approaches fail because they are bereft of the inner reality that birthed the movement: they are adrift from their identity.

From Maturity Back to Growth

The story of Peter's encounter with Cornelius (Acts 10:1–11:15) is a case study of how God intervenes to unsettle a movement in danger of drifting into maturity. Here are the leadership lessons:

Confront reality: Restore the tension between the ideal and the real.

Seize the opportunity: Be attentive to God's intervention. Remember who you are: retrieve the past and make it serve the present. Align everything with the Word, the Spirit, and the mission. Apply the characteristics of strategy in an innovative way.

Raise descendants: Focus on generations of spiritual children, grandchildren, and great-grandchildren.

From Growth to Decline

Movements cannot stand still. If the warning signs are not heeded, the contentment of maturity will yield to the complacency of decline. Institutional survival replaces the founding cause as the reason for existence, and the movement becomes an inwardly focused institution.

Stage 4. Decline: Self-interest rules

Decline creeps up on its prey. Powerful institutions, living off the legacy of the past, assume they will continue forever. Movements become institutions when they abandon their cause and exist for themselves. Protected by dysfunctional bureaucracies, they are shielded from the surrounding world. Declining institutions no longer live for a cause beyond themselves; the thing that matters most is self-preservation. But when disaster strikes, the vulnerability of the institution is laid bare.

4.1. The world invades the church: Leaders adopt the values and behaviors of the surrounding culture.

Movements want to change the world; institutions fear a changing world. Hard decisions are avoided, and opportunities are lost. The momentum of the past continues to propel the movement forward, but only for a time. In decline there is nowhere to hide; it becomes obvious that this movement has become a failing institution. As decline takes hold, self-preservation becomes primary. As the institution loses touch with its reason for existence, survival is paramount.

4.2. *Centralized power and control: Leaders serve the institution and themselves, not the cause. Followers comply.*

Declining institutions reward leaders for serving the organization rather than the cause. Formality dominates. People are nice, but little gets done. Those with a financial or emotional attachment to the institution want to preserve it. The institution loses its moral and spiritual authority, and good people leave.

Declining institutions have lost their purpose. They stood for something once. That memory has now faded, and all that is left are the outward forms, not the inner reality. Institutions exist to perpetuate themselves—yet they don't remember why.

4.3. *Culpable blindness: Those in power regard themselves as invulnerable. They lose touch with the world around them.*

Like ancient emperors living behind the walls of a forbidden city, leaders of institutions are oblivious to the reality of the world around them. They were content. They were ignorant of their decline and insensitive to the rising tide of discontent. The system they preside over is corrupt, and they cannot change it because they are part of it, grew out of it, and depend on it (Tuchman 1984, 125).

From Decline to Decay

A movement in the latter stages of decline will rarely turn itself around. Decay follows decline, as the movement clings to existence while relying on external life support.

Stage 5. Decay: Existence on life support

These are the characteristics of decay:

5.1 From drift to denial

The declining institution has wandered from its identity. In decay the institution denies its identity as a missionary movement under the Word and the Spirit.

5.2 Breakdown and collapse

The institution experiences a rapid loss of membership, leaving a band of bureaucrats whose beliefs and behavior no longer reflect the movement's origins. The institution exists on artificial life support through asset sales, state support, and funds invested by past generations.

5.3. Bypassed

New movements arise on the fringe and are rejected by the declining institution; these new movements eventually replace the decaying one.

In Revelation, when the risen Lord writes to the seven churches, he calls each one to repentance. Renewal involves turning away from this world and turning back to God and his ways. But how can a church be renewed if it recognizes no authority higher than itself? What hope is possible if the church places its own word above God's Word or if it exchanges the spirit of the age for the Holy Spirit?

Stage 6. Rebirth: Dry bones can live

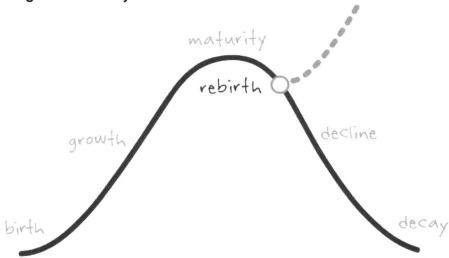

Figure 11.5: Movement Rebirth

Movements are not reborn through human creativity or design. Rebirth is more than improvement; it is a journey from death to life, and it is only achieved by returning to the Word, the Spirit, and the mission. It is a work of God.

Plateaued and declining institutions make the mistake of thinking all they need is some reimagining and restructuring. The valley of dry bones (Ezek 37) teaches us there is no life without the Word of God, no breath without the Spirit of God, and no direction without the mission of God.

6.1. Face God's discipline.

God's judgment prepares the way for rebirth. In Revelation, the church at Ephesus was in grave spiritual danger. Christ reminded the saints of their first love and then rebuked them, saying: "Consider how far you have fallen! Repent and do the things you did at first. If you do not repent, I will come to you and remove your lampstand from its place" (Rev 2:5). This is a church praised for its orthodoxy but condemned for its loss of passion.

"If Jesus was ready to come in this way to the Ephesian Church, He must have come repeatedly throughout history to various churches in similar judgment" (Beale 2015, 56). Rebirth begins with repentance: it begins with a return to identity in God's Word, Spirit, and mission.

6.2. Pursue deep change.

Rebirth requires a return to identity (Word, Spirit, mission). In John 13–17, Jesus prepares his disciples for his departure. Their relationship with him is about to change because he will no longer be physically present with them. How will they continue to relate to him? Jesus declares: "I am the true vine" and urges them to remain in him if they are to be fruitful.

Disciples remain in relationship with Jesus by obeying his teaching, and through the coming of the Spirit he remains in them. Then they will "go" and produce fruit that will remain, for love of the Father and the Son cannot be contained (John 15:16). This is the secret of rebirth: the life of Christ in us, the Gardener who prunes so that we will become even more fruitful.

6.3. *Realign everything.*

Rebirth requires a realignment of identity and a return to effective, realigned movement strategies—pioneering leaders, contagious relationships, rapid mobilization, and adaptive methods.

Nehemiah was a man of the Word, a man of the Spirit, and a man on a mission. When faced with dangers, he told his workers to pray and carry a weapon. Nehemiah aligned everything with God's purposes. He loved to make lists and delegate tasks; he mastered the important detail; he released authority and responsibility.

Rebirth is costly. It takes grace and determination, discipline and time to turn things around. But it can happen.

Conclusion

Movements are the driving force of history, and history is the story of the rise and fall of movements. At every stage of the movement life cycle, the way forward begins with returning to Jesus, the apostle and pioneer of our faith. His example is foundational. His leadership was centered on obedience to the living Word, dependence on the Holy Spirit, and faithfulness to his mission. The life of Christ in us is the key to leadership at every stage of the life cycle. Remaining in him is the key to the rise of movements. Abandoning him is the key to the fall of movements.

References

Adizes, Ichak. 1979. "Organizational Passages: Diagnosing and Treating Lifecycle Problems of Organization." *Organizational Dynamics* 8, no. 1: 3–25.

———. 1996. *The Pursuit of Prime: Maximize Your Company's Success with the Adizes Program*. Santa Monica, CA: Knowledge Exchange.

———. 1999. *Managing Corporate Lifecycles*. Revised. Paramus, NJ: Prentice Hall Press.

Allen, Roland. 1956. *The Spontaneous Expansion of the Church*. 3rd ed. London: World Dominion Press.

Beale, G. K. 2015. *Revelation: A Shorter Commentary*. Grand Rapids: Eerdmans.

Boer, Harry R. 1961. *Pentecost and Missions*. Grand Rapids: Eerdmans.

Plummer, Robert L. 2006. *Paul's Understanding of the Church's Mission: How Did the Apostle Paul Expect the Early Christian Communities to Evangelize?* Paternoster Biblical Monographs. Eugene, OR: Wipf & Stock Publishers.

Rosner, Brian. 1998. "The Progress of the Word." In *Witness to the Gospel: The Theology of Acts*, edited by I. Howard Marshall and David Peterson, 215–33. Grand Rapids: Eerdmans.

Schnabel, Eckhard J. 2004. *Early Christian Mission: Jesus and the Twelve*. Vol. 1. Downers Grove, IL: IVP Academic.

———. 2008. *Paul the Missionary: Realities, Strategies and Methods*. Downers Grove, IL: IVP Academic.

Tuchman, Barbara W. 1984. *The March of Folly: From Troy to Vietnam*. New York: Random House.

From Her Perspective: Women and Multiplication Movements

Pam Arlund and Regina Foard

Strategic-level meetings seem to have a lot more men than women in the room. Books on movements rarely mention women at all (and rarely include women authors). Although church planting has been looked at through various lenses, the study of gender has not yet been widely applied to movements. While all movement practitioners would seemingly agree that in Christ there is neither male nor female (cf. Gal 3:28), the default missiology seems to focus on the role of men. The reasons for this disproportionate representation are undoubtedly varied, but we must recognize that women are actively participating and even key figures in many multiplication movements. Additionally, very little research of any kind has focused on the role of women in these present global movements.[1]

Therefore, we must ask: "Is gender a factor in day-to-day activities of the movement? And if gender does play a part, what is that part? Are gender-defined roles in these movements bound and fixed, or are they fluid and changing? Does culture affect these gender-based roles?" We suggest that gender-based roles, and specifically the position of women in movements, should be examined considering both culture and role-specific categories.

---

1 We have chosen to make this chapter less academic and more anecdotal. The number of topics relating to movements, gender-based roles, sociological, psychological, and cultural anthropological disciplines would require greater in-depth research and academic rigor than permitted in this context. We therefore acknowledge the limitations in our approach. We hope that our work is recognized as an initial invitation to begin a deeper dialogue about women in movements.

In this chapter, we seek to highlight the fact that women also are thinking critically and strategically about church planting movements. We will also attempt to summarize and synthesize some of the diverse positions in which women serve in movements by presenting some of the case studies available to us. In these case studies, examples will show that women have catalytic roles, leadership roles, and participant roles in church planting movements. We make no claims that these case studies are either normative or indicative of all movements.[2] However, our experience indicates that they are not unusual. They are simply a beginning point for reflection.

An examination of the case studies included here indicates that women in movements do undergo a different spiritual formation process from the men in those same movements. This is due primarily to the cultural expectations for role-specific behaviors of women. These case studies show that when women engage in movements, they begin to take on new hybrid identities—retaining some of the characteristics of the traditional roles of women in society, but also growing, changing, and sometimes even being very obviously countercultural in their roles. In other words, they begin a spiritual formation process that all new believers go through—reevaluating cultural norms by considering the new role of Jesus in their lives, and by making decisions about who they are now, and who they are to become. However, because every society on earth has different expectations of men and women and different roles for men and women, the spiritual formation process is inherently gendered.

A well-known example of role-identity transformation is readily available to us in the story of the woman at the well in John 4. In this example of interaction between Jesus and the Samaritan woman, we see several boundary-crossing exchanges. Jesus himself crossed gender-role boundaries, cultural boundaries, religious boundaries, and language boundaries. Yet we must also recognize that the Samaritan woman also crossed several boundaries. She spoke to a Jewish man, and, more specifically, to a Jewish *rabbi*. This type of exchange would have been "unheard of" in their context. She had a rather long and argumentative dialogue with Jesus, and in doing so she ignored all the cultural norms of her day.

More importantly, however, than crossing these cultural barriers was the transformation that took place in her. Prior to the exchange with Jesus, she was an outcast in her own community. After the exchange with Jesus, she played an integral role in this movement that resulted in leading her entire village to Jesus. Jesus not only restores and transforms human dignity, but also raises up both men *and* women to participate with him in kingdom movements.

---

2 Pam Arlund produced the case study examples in this chapter. Through her role as Global Training and Research Leader with All Nations, she has studied and participated directly or indirectly with multiplication movements throughout the world. For the sake of this chapter, except in her own case study, we have chosen to use the formal "we" in our written communication on the subjects contained herein.

Gender Studies and Movement Missiology

Gender operates at individual, organizational, and interactional levels (Einwohner, Hollander, and Olson 2000). The very nature of movements means that something has changed in society. This suggests that there are very likely different ideas about women within the movement initially, and possibly these ideas would evolve as the movement develops. These changing roles for women may not be societal norms as seen in non-Christian society at large, nor are they likely to be valued or acknowledged within the traditional (older/legacy) Christian churches. Much has been written and a great deal of debate has already taken place on the role of women in the church. We will not address those arguments and debates here, but we acknowledge that the position one has in these debates seemingly influences, individually and collectively, the lens through which one views the role of women in movements.

Generally, gender roles are culturally defined, which means that they rely not only on individual interpretations of how those roles should be carried out but must also be negotiated in the public spaces (Williams 1995). Gender often establishes expectations for correct behavior, impacting everything from clothing to roles in society to ideals of beauty and moral character. Gender roles (and indeed all aspects of discipleship) can quickly become complex when one begins to examine the confluence of biblical values, non-Christian societal values, a specific multiplication movement's values, and other Christian values within a particular society.

Framing Schema (Individual/Thought Level)

Schemas were introduced into psycho-linguistic theory by Jean Piaget in the 1920s (Vinney 2019). Since their introduction to the world of social science, they have been applied to gender studies (Bem 1981), social movement studies (Snow and Benford 1988), and nearly all aspects of cognitive science. Schemas are simply mental constructs that individuals use to organize, analyze, and comprehend the world.

Since they have been so widely used, some scholars have very distinct definitions of schemas and their uses (McVee, Dusnmore, and Gavelek 2005). For our purposes, they are perceived as "thought units" or "groups of thoughts," as opposed to single, disjointed thoughts. Because they come in bundles, they are also sometimes called "scripts," as one item or event often assumes or requires the next part of the script for completion and thus is a "bundle."

It is important to note that schemas help organize the world, but they can also falsely or incorrectly organize. They can also grow and change over time. In the context of this study, analyzing schemas means understanding the perceived role of women in society, in traditional churches, and within movements.

Cultural Intelligence (Organizational Level)

Organizational culture is defined as the "pattern of shared values that define appropriate attitudes and behaviors and establish what is important for organizational members" (Zhou, Hu, Wu, and Gao 2018). Although multiplication movements may lack buildings, paid professional staff, or training institutions, we suggest that they are organized and operate as a kind of organization. We refer to these multiplication-movement organizations as MMOs. The MMOs, as well as organizations in general, have an organizational culture which includes leadership, values, patterns, beliefs, behaviors, goals, agenda, etc. Considering this, we suggest that multiplication movements are a *kind* of organization, not in the hierarchical-bound institutional form, but more in the collective-grouping working together for common goals and purpose form.

It is important to remember that, because organizations have a cultural environment, organizations can be culturally intelligent (or not) in ways similar to individuals (Yitmen 2013). Culturally intelligent (CQ) organizations are not only capable of crossing organizational boundaries but are also capable of engaging and interacting effectively across national, ethnic, gender, and other cultural borders (Zhou et al 2018). Further, we suggest that cultural intelligence facilitates understanding of these norms and practices of culture, including gender-specific roles (Brislin, Worthley, and Macnab 2006). Because cultural intelligence is not culture bound, culturally intelligent women are able to span cultural boundaries (Sharma and Hussain 2017, 97). Cultural intelligence is a key component in cross-cultural leadership capabilities (Deng and Gibson 2008, 182). No empirically validated study has determined that culture intelligence affects gender-bound roles differently. Women as well as men can develop cultural intelligence. Culturally intelligent women leaders are likely to be as effective as culturally intelligent male leaders (Ang et al 2007). We suggest that culturally intelligent women and men may have complementary roles and that neither women nor men are indispensable in God's movements. Roles constrain behavior, and therefore roles may affect the degree of trust between individuals and between MMOs (Perrone, Zaheer, and McEvily 2003). Cultural intelligence becomes a toolset that enhances individuals' abilities and capabilities to effectively engage across cultural boundaries, or in this case organizational boundaries (Ruth and Nester 2020).

When studying women in movements, we anticipate that cultural intelligence positively relates to women who are effectively engaging across cultural boundaries. Cultural intelligence increases the possibility that women will thrive, influences how they understand and thus communicate their role within the movement, and helps women relate more effectively to those with differing organizations, not in the movement.

Boundary-Spanning (Interactional Level)

Organizations are recognizing and increasingly demanding those individuals who can cross organizational boundaries, or "boundary-spanners" (Barner-Rasmussen et al 2014). One of the fundamental attributes of boundary-spanners is the "boundaryless mindset" (Zhou et al 2018). An individual with a boundaryless attitude toward cross-organizational relationships is interested in "creating and sustaining active relationships beyond organizational boundaries" (Briscoe, Hall, and Frautschy Demuth 2006, 31).

Boundary-spanners are thought to have several competencies which define their boundary-spanning capability. These competencies include "building sustainable relationships, managing under influence and negotiation, and managing complexity and interdependencies and managing roles, accountabilities and motivation" (Zhou el al 2018, 661). In effect, boundary-spanners are "cultural brokers" (2018, 661). Boundary-spanners are relied upon to effectively communicate, negotiate, cooperate, and build bridges and alliances (Faraj and Yan 2009). Women as boundary-spanners have a unique role in these more interactional facets of multiplication movements. In the context of this chapter, analyzing boundary-spanners means analyzing how women relate to, communicate, negotiate, and cooperate with other women, men, believers, non-believers, etc., and how others, in turn, relate to them.

In the case studies that follow, we will share examples that show participants in CPM's have boundary-spanning roles. Indeed, we suggest that the boundary-spanning ability becomes a critical capability for multiplication movements.

Uganda Case Study: Women "Empowered and Free"

Our first case study comes from Uganda. This specific movement includes about 1,400 churches that span many different people groups: Baganda, Basoga, and Acholi, to name a few. Within the movement, reportedly only 20 percent of the movement is female and only 5 percent of the movement leaders are female. This is "because of the beliefs and mindset of the people."[3]

Although there are differences in specific details within the cultures affected by the movement, the schema of the general non-Christian society, traditional churches (primarily Roman Catholic and Anglican), and women within the movement are presented in the following table.

---

3 The following quotes are from an open-ended questionnaire conducted in 2020 among movements that the authors were already familiar with. In all these cases, people preferred to remain anonymous for security reasons.

Table 12.1 Comparison of Schemas of Women's Roles in Uganda

Women's Roles Within:		
Non-Christian Society	**Traditional Churches**	**Movement Churches**
• Kneel before men • Leading is an abomination • Cannot make decisions • Cannot give advice to a man • Do domestic work without the help of the men • If they earn money, they give it to the men • Stay at home	• Women primarily carry out the same roles as general society, but within Roman Catholicism can also be nuns	• Lead at all levels • Run businesses, earn money, and keep their money • Are sent out as missionaries • Stand before men • Make decisions • Offer opinions • Often still do domestic work, but men sometimes help (but still do less)

Within the movement, it is normal for women to lead in prayer and worship. They can lead families. In contrast to women in general society, women in the movement earn their own money without giving it to anyone. They can also serve as pastors, apostles, evangelists, or teachers. Within the movement, women can speak without fear. Women in the movement churches now have a platform where they can stand bravely and sit and discuss or make decisions (lead).

The role of women within the movement has made women feel "empowered and free" due primarily to the way the movement was established. From the beginning, women were both allowed and encouraged to start new discovery Bible studies (DBS), to establish new churches, to pastor new churches, and to be involved in movement leadership. Although this has been a challenge, in that this is counter to the local cultural norms, the movement feels in general that this attitude has helped more than it has hurt. If some have refused to join the movement as a result of the role of women, they feel this has been made up for by the contributions of the women in labor, gifting, and reflecting the kingdom of God.

Although the male founder of this movement has clearly allowed women to lead, there is also still far more men in the movement than women. Although about a hundred churches within the movement consist of ex-prostitutes, women who were not in prostitution have proven harder to reach. Prostitutes are out in society, while most women are isolated in their homes. As such, prostitutes have been easier to access and reach, due at least in part because prostitutes are accessible in the public spaces. Some have felt that women are reluctant to step up and lead, as such roles are new to them and they appear uncomfortable in assuming these leadership roles. Accepting these newly defined roles for women who have come out of this movement is a process of spiritual formation. The transformational mindset, which recognizes the freedom that the Lord has brought and accepts the roles and opportunities available within this movement, is slowly occurring.

At the organizational level, the male leadership exhibited "cultural intelligence" by allowing women to lead in the movement, but also recognizing that shepherding these women through the process takes time. Establishing relationships and engaging other women have been difficult because women rarely attend meetings and generally stay at home. In addition, although women may be able to lead in the movement, they generally have domestic duties that keep them at home nearly all the time. These limitations present ongoing challenges for the role of women in this movement. The women's ability to overcome these barriers, cultural or otherwise, is essential for contacting and connecting with other women. Although this movement has accepted women for who they are, movement leaders have not yet developed a systematic outreach strategy that spans the boundaries between the women who stay at home and the women in the movement.

The male leadership in this movement (and other movements) could create greater opportunities for participation of the women by inviting women into the decision-making processes. The movement has not created even a few gender-specific outreaches or trainings that might find creative ways to meet, or creative ways or times to interact to simply make it possible for women to participate, given the demands of their domestic roles. In addition, they have not created any special topics within the trainings that might help women understand their biblical role. Those in the movement essentially are crossing boundaries primarily by reaching women who can come to meetings and trainings (although these are often within their villages already), through modelling, and by allowing women to lead. Given the role of women in society, this is significant. However, given the numbers, it's still not enough. More deliberate boundary-spanning efforts will need to happen to increase the numbers of women in the movement.

India Case Study: Women as Leaders in Rural Spaces

Our second case study comes from India. This particular people group is Hindu or animistic. They are a rural people whose primary focus in life is to control evil spirits and to bring the blessings of gods into their lives. This people group is low caste, as fishing and raising other animals to eat is their primary form of subsistence. This makes them "unclean" and "dirty" to the Hindu and Jain society around them, which is very strongly vegetarian.

This emerging movement includes about two thousand people, in four different people groups, who are close in proximity to one another and sometimes share the same villages. Within the movement, about 60 percent of the believers are women and about 80–90 percent of the leaders are women. None of the people in the movement categorize themselves as Christian. To them, Christians are "people paid by foreigners to worship a foreign god." Since the foreigners have never offered money, the locals decided that they were not Christians. They choose to call themselves "followers of Jesus."

The schemas of the role of women in this part of Indian society can be seen in Table 12.2.

Table 12.2 Comparison of Schemas of Women's Roles in India

Women's Roles Within:			
Non-Christian Society Rural	**Non-Christian Society Urban**	**Traditional Churches**	**Movement Churches**
• Subservient • Care for children and be homemakers • Carry the religious traditions • Cover their husbands with their good acts • Intermingle with other families, speak aloud in social gatherings, and have spiritual authority • Hide their faces from male relatives who are older • Should always sit lower than a male • Can joke with male friends and even pat each other in a brother-sister way	• Do not intermingle with other men (unless with their husband) • Do not speak in social gatherings • Women sit separate from men • Eat after men finish • Never touch a man	• Sit apart in Sunday gatherings • Have their own groups, separate from the men	• Work and construct homes, plow fields, and help out with businesses • Can lead at all levels • Lead almost everything • Visit the sick • Go out on evangelistic trips

Within the context of these village churches, the role of women sometimes seem odd to Christian outsiders who have come to "take a look" and see what God has been doing. This is because of the separation of men and women that is normal in the cities. It looks strange to most Christians that a woman would be the spiritual leader or lead prayer when men are present, etc.

Overall, however, the group outsiders (a husband/wife team who were always together) who ignited this movement feel that the way women are treated has helped the movement to expand. Within the traditional village context, women can be paid to offer prayers to the gods, and some women have had this as their primary job before following Jesus. One of the main gods is a goddess. The movement has enabled women to continue leading in ways familiar to the leadership roles that had already existed for women in the village context, such as offering prayers for people, even though some aspects of this have changed. For example, now prayers are offered without need of payment and are only offered to Jesus.

In general, the outsiders involved feel (through anecdotal observation) that the CQ of this group and its leaders are quite low. They are aware of the groups around them in their rural context. However, they have little concrete notion of life in the cities just a few hours away. They also receive relatively little news from the outside. The foreign workers also tried to involve traditional Indian believers in the movement. However, their CQ was also deemed too low to make them helpful. It seemed that they simply wanted to invite those in the movement to have churches like their churches in the cities. So the expatriate movement catalysts opted simply to try their best to keep all traditional Indian believers away from those villages. Since the villages were remote to begin with, this has not been very difficult. So in one sense we can see that the foreign workers (some of the expat missionaries) were more "bounded" and less willing to collaborate with other expat missionaries. In the case where the expat movement catalysts worked, we see an example of boundary-spanning. Here the movement is crossing geographical boundaries, however small, so that we see neighboring villages being reached from the origin-center of the movement. Boundary-spanning in this context is crossing boundaries or obstacles that separate and divide.

In addition, the group has very little overt thought as to how to encourage more men to follow Jesus or to raise up male leaders. The expatriate women communicated that they wished that the men and the youth would lead more and are now working to try to bridge that span and raise up more male leaders. So far, they have not been very successful in doing so. Cultural barriers may inhibit or limit the degree of boundary-spanning for women, even those with an "elevated" status, as in the case of the expatriate women. Still, we see women leading in a culture that predominantly restricts role-schema for women.

Chinese Muslims Case Study:
Expat Women as a "Third Gender"

In this case study, the main informant is one of the authors, Pam. I was involved in this movement directly for many years. The movement is among Muslims of western China. It is a small people group and therefore a small movement. In 2006, there were forty verified churches among them, but the political situation there has prevented verification of numbers in recent years. The schemas of women's roles in this part of China can be seen in Table 12.3.

Table 12.3 Comparison of Schemas of Women's Roles in China

Women's Roles Within:		
Rural Muslim Minority of China	**Non-Christian (Han) Chinese**	**Movement Churches**
• Typically work at home (as do men) • Go to school • Can get jobs outside of the home • Become head of their extended house once the husband dies • Women are leaders of villages (i.e., mayors) • Spiritual knowledge belongs to men. • Must marry	• Women work outside the home • Staying home to raise children or care for the home is not an option • Can be leaders in all spheres • Strong women leaders are active in many spheres of society • Almost everyone marries	• Women and men participate together • Women can lead churches, but would usually only do so if they were also head of their family

There was some concern at the beginning of this movement that I and another single female could not effectively share the gospel among a Muslim people group (i.e., we could not be adequate boundary-spanners due to our status as single females). However, it soon became clear that this would not be a prohibiting factor. Even on initial visits, men were comfortable to interact with us in ways that would likely not have happened if we were local women.

Our experience as foreign women was very similar to what foreign women in Afghanistan have often talked about: we seemed to be treated as neither men nor as women but as an entirely altogether different category that NGO employees in Afghanistan have come to refer to as "third gender" (Partis-Jennings 2019). As single foreign women with no domestic duties, we could interact with men or with women. We sociologically occupied a different role in society that was not identical to gender roles for local people. We tentatively suggest that this is often the case for societies unaccustomed to outsiders. Neither foreign men nor women are treated quite like the locals, but are treated as simply "foreign." These outsiders can still be accepted and find a role to play, but it is not identical to local roles. Belonging does not necessarily mean becoming identical; this is true for gender roles as well as other roles in society.

It is also true that women were teachers in both their local minority society and within the larger Chinese society. So perhaps the understood role of teacher opened the other doors to be able to do DBS with men. However, local women consistently told us that we were not treated the same as local women.

This fluid gender-role made it possible for us to raise up both male and female leaders within the local churches. It was never questioned within the movement whether women could be spiritual leaders or pastors. However, most of the churches in this movement were family or village based and church leadership did generally mirror household leadership. In other words, if the family was headed by a man, he generally led the family spiritually as well. However, this was not always the case, as some men did recognize the gifting and knowledge of their daughters and wives. In addition, we modeled from the beginning that women could be spiritual, learn spiritual things, and lead.

In this case, the foreign women became the boundary-spanners, bridging cultural gaps in more ways than one. Not only did we learn the language and try to adapt ourselves to the culture, but our role in society seemed to create a hybrid space that was easily interpreted by the locals. This led to church roles that were mimicries of general roles in society that already existed.

Admittedly, we gave this question a lot of thought and attempted to have high CQ, but at the end of the day our adaptation was constrained by who we were: single women who had never married. We felt we were called by God and cried out to him to give us favor and acceptance. Perhaps raising CQ also created a sense of inadequacy to the task, but also led to increased prayer for God to do the boundary-spanning for us that we could not do ourselves. We recognized, though, that boundary-spanning is a culturally intelligent competency and that in all cases of intercultural interaction, crossing language, cultural, and gender barriers are indeed an indication of culturally intelligent movement participants.

Conclusion

Women are igniting multiplication movements and leading in those movements all over the world. God is bringing together women, both expatriates and locals, and creating new roles for women in these movements. In each of these cases, the traditional schema for women is being transformed. This change has been produced through a process of spiritual formation and cultural adaptation. In most cases, leadership within each of these movements demonstrated a high level of cultural intelligence and had to improvise new roles for women in the movements. Their motivation for this adaptation was their deep desire to reflect

God's kingdom as they best understood it. Even when male-dominated leadership acknowledged this value for women and opened a way to include women, each movement struggled with different aspects of gender-based roles in the movement and leadership of women specifically. Further, this chapter does not cover the enormously valuable role of women in God's movements historically. We point to the many metanarratives just within the biblical narrative that included God's involvement of women in his story.

We also found that women do assume the same participant roles and leadership roles as men, but they also have limitations that men may not have. In some cases, women may not be able to cross gender boundaries because of cultural norms. However, within gender-based roles, women are capable of leading, training, and equipping as well as men. In our Ugandan and Chinese Muslim case studies, we see that women can cross gender barriers, as well as other cultural barriers that previously defined gender-based roles. In the case of our Chinese-Muslim case study, the expatriate women were given an even higher status in society than most women. This permitted these expatriate women to cross gender-based boundaries, cultural and language boundaries, and effectively engage across those boundaries.

We continue to be perplexed that there is not a greater sense of curiosity and deliberation within movement missiology about capturing the voice of the women in these movements. Why does there appear to be a dominance of homogeneity of male leadership speaking into and affecting movement leadership? If the roles of men and women are complementary, how can we increasingly invite women into the conversation on movements? We propose that greater intentionality should be given to inviting women (and local leaders from movements) into the conversation. Indeed, the suggestion of inviting women into the conversation presumes there has previously been a devaluation of the voice of women, or at least it has been overlooked.

In some of the case studies in this chapter, we have seen that women have parallel roles to their male counterparts, but are limited to gender-based leading. But we have also seen that women cross gender-based boundaries and can influence and lead movements. Cultural intelligence and boundary-spanning capabilities (including a boundaryless mindset) are key competencies for women in movements. In our case studies, women who possessed higher degrees of cultural intelligence and boundary-spanning capabilities not only participated in movements, but also led most effectively in these movements. We therefore suggest that cultural intelligence and boundary-spanning capabilities are critical competencies for crossing cultural boundaries for women.

We understand that varying factors, many of which are not addressed in this work, affect women in movements. The scope of this project did not permit a more in-depth approach that might have captured some of these other factors, including the correlation between gender and movement. The limitations of our work also did not permit a more in-depth study on the underlying disciplines that affect social movements and women. Future research should also highlight movements that women "ignited" and the gender-based roles between men and women in those movements. We encourage future research to expand the focus beyond the role of women within *existing* movements ignited by men, as we have presented here. We hope, however, we have initiated dialogue that constitutes a necessary first step in inviting women into the missiological discourse on movements.

References

Ang, S., and Linn Van Dyne, Christine Koh, K. Yee Ng, Klaus J. Templer, Cheryl Tay, and N. Anand Chandrasekar. 2007. "Cultural Intelligence: Its Measurement and Effects on Cultural Judgment and Decision Making, Cultural Adaptation and Task Performance." *Management and Organization Review* 3 (3): 335–71.

Barner-Rasmussen, Wilhelm, Mats Ehrnrooth, Alexei Koveshnikov, and Kristiina Mäkelä. 2014. "Cultural and Language Skills as Resources for Boundary Spanning Within the MNC." *Journal of International Business Studies* 45 (7): 886–905.

Bem, Sandra L. 1981. "Gender Schema Theory: A Cognitive Account of Sex Typing." *Psychological Review* 88 (4): 354–64.

Briscoe, Jon P., Douglas T. Hall, and Rachel L. Frautschy Demuth. 2006. "Protean and Boundaryless Careers: An Empirical Exploration." *Journal of Vocational Behavior* 69 (1): 30–47.

Brislin, Richard, Reginald Worthley, and Brent Macnab. 2006. "Cultural Intelligence: Understanding Behaviors That Serve People's Goals." *Group & Organization Management* 31 (1): 40–55.

Deng, Ling, and Paul Stephen Gibson. 2008. "A Qualitative Evaluation of the Role of Cultural Intelligence in Cross-Cultural Leadership Effectiveness." *International Journal of Leadership Studies* 3 (2): 181–97.

Einwohner, Rachel L., Jocelyn A. Hollander, and Toska Olson. 2000. "Engendering Social Movements: Cultural Images and Movement Dynamics." *Gender & Society* 14 (5): 679–99.

Faraj, Samer, and Aimin Yan. 2009. "Boundary Work in Knowledge Teams." *Journal of Applied Psychology* 94 (3): 604–17.

Mcvee, Mary B., Kailonnie Dunsmore, and James R. Gavelek. 2005. "Schema Theory Revisited." *Review of Educational Research* 75 (4): 531–566.

Partis-Jennings, Hannah. 2019. The 'Third Gender' in Afghanistan: A Feminist Account of Hybridity as a Gendered Experience." *Peacebuilding* 7 (2): 178–93.

Perrone, Vicenzo, Akbar Zaheer, and Bill Mcevily. 2003. "Free to Be Trusted? Organizational Constraints on Trust in Boundary Spanners." *Organization Science* 14 (4): 422–39.

Ruth, Rene, and Torsten Netzer. 2019. "The Key Elements of Cultural Intelligence as a Driver for Digital Leadership Success." *Leadership, Education, Personality: An Interdisciplinary Journal* 2: 3–8.

Sharma, Namrata, and Dilwar Hussain. 2017. "Current Status and Future Directions for Cultural Intelligence." *Journal of Intercultural Communication Research* 46 (1): 96–110.

Snow, D. A., and R. D. Benford. 1988. "Ideology, Frame Resonance, and Participant Mobilization." *International Social Movement Research* 1: 197–217.

Vinney, C. 2019. "What Is a Schema in Psychology? Definitions and Examples." Academic. Thought co.

Williams, Rhys H. 1995. "Constructing the Public Good: Social Movements and Cultural Resources." *Social Problems* 42 (1): 124–44.

Yitmen, Ibrahim. 2013. "Organizational Cultural Intelligence: A Competitive Capability for Strategic Alliances in the International Construction Industry." *Project Management Journal* 44 (4): 5–25.

Zhou, Nan Hu, Jianlin Wu, and Jibao Gu. 2018. "A New Scale to Measure Cross-Organizational Cultural Intelligence: Initial Development and Validation." *Chinese Management Studies* 12 (3): 658–79.

How Ethnodoxology Drives Movements

Paul Kuivinen

Ethnodoxology is the practice and study of ethnic worship by people groups or nations. It offers powerful movement dividends. This introductory chapter will review a brief history of ethnodoxology, explore unique features of music and why it is particularly beneficial to movements, and share firsthand examples and opinions from a number of movement leaders. Over the course of the chapter, you will see a number of ways in which ethnodoxology can help form more robust movements.

History

From biblical heroes to good-willed yet colonial missionaries to contemporary movement leaders, God's kingdom servants live lives filled with singing. Through those who have gone before us, we have inspiring examples, instructive experiences, and valuable scholarship. We can build effective ethnodoxology within today's church planting movements from these examples.

Movement Leaders Sing, and Get Their Disciples to Sing

Consider this hypothetical dialogue between Paul and Silas in Acts 16: "Praise God for a key person like Lydia," exclaimed Silas. "Her whole *oikos* came to faith and we baptized them all together. Then, in this very same town, the authorities arrested us. These shackles hurt. What do we do now?"

"Sing!" replied Paul. "I've been singing ever since the day Matthew told me that on the very evening Jesus knew he was going to get beaten worse than we just got beaten, he had all the guys sing with him after dinner. And it works. King David did it too! When he was being hunted in his own house, he sang:

'I will sing of your strength, in the morning I will sing of your love' (Ps 59:16). One day soon I'm planning to write these new believers to 'Let the message of Christ dwell among you richly as you teach and admonish one another with all wisdom through psalms, hymns and songs from the Spirit, singing to God with gratitude in your hearts (Col 3:16).'"

"All right, Paul!" said Silas. "Let's sing right now in this jail and see what God does!"

In his home in Sierra Leone, Shodankeh Johnson, leader of multiple movements across West Africa, leaned across his plate of chicken and french fries and told my wife and me, "I sing a lot. I sing at night. I sing in the morning. I sing in the shower. One of my problems when I first started visiting the Western world and I stayed in the homes of people, I totally forgot—I was singing in the house. One day I just realized: 'God help me, I'm not in Africa.' So all the homes where I stayed—everybody knows me for that. … Most every morning, after my devotions, I try to write a song. Even this morning I was just doing a song when somebody interrupted me, and so all day I have been trying to bring this song back to mind."

Shalom (pseudonym), a movement leader in Africa involved in cross-cultural work since 1995, shared with me, "I have written many songs—about fifty. I do this in my times of questions with God. I write them for my children."

Aila Tasse, a leader of disciple-making movements in multiple East African countries, told me, "When I pray, I sing."

Benny (pseudonym), a movement leader on the island of Java, said: "In our context, my wife writes music and songs. She wrote a song from Genesis 1 for the children, so they could understand it and repeat the story of creation easily."

Ethnodoxology: A Phenomenon and a Science

Many movement leaders are singers, and many healthy movements are full of singing. However, we have neither systematic data collections nor dedicated literature on the role of indigenous music in movements. Movement-related books sometimes mention music or singing in the course of anecdotes. Seldom, if ever, do they pause to examine the role of local music in the movement. This is not a criticism of these works, but highlights the gap summed up by Jerry Trousdale, "We collect fifteen pure data points from every New Generations affiliated people or urban affinity group each quarter. Ethnodoxology data collection is not part of this. That would require relatively expensive grounded research."

The word *ethnodoxology* was first seen in print in 1997.[1] Similar to "doxology," it is the expression of praise to God, yet specifically done through local ethnic cultural artistic forms. In the twenty-first century, the term *ethnodoxology* has also come to

1 The term *ethnodoxology* was coined by Dave Hall, founder of Worship from the Nations, a ministry of Pioneers. The earliest appearance of the term in print was a 1997 issue of the *journal EM News* (vol. 6, no. 3), by the editor, Brian Schrag.

refer to a science, namely, "the interdisciplinary study of how Christians in every culture engage with God and the world through their own artistic expressions."[2]

In this chapter, I use the word *ethnodoxology* as both "the expression of" as well as "the study of" ethnic Scripture-based songs and other art forms. Since 2000, forums dedicated to ethnodoxology have included Global Consultation on Music and Missions (GCoMM) and Global Ethnodoxology Network (GEN). Schools, including Fuller Seminary, Liberty University, Dallas International University, and Payap University, in Thailand, now have degree and certificate programs. Excellent publications on ethnodoxology include *Worship and Mission for the Global Church: An Ethnodoxology Handbook* (Krabill 2013) and *Creating Local Arts Together: A Manual to Help Communities Reach Their Kingdom Goals* (Schrag 2013).

Though most ethnodoxology work is being done with less-reached people groups in mind, the bulk of it is set within the traditional church paradigm. With this chapter, we embark on the first scholarly discussion of "How Ethnodoxology Drives Movements," namely, the phenomenon and study of indigenous Scripture-based songs among non-Christian unreached people groups (UPGs) within a discipleship movement framework.

Music in Modern Missions

Music systems and their instruments are regional. Melody types, rhythmic styles, polyphonic preferences, and musical instruments have similarities between geographically proximate people groups. This would have been true for the Acts 1:8 peoples of Jerusalem, Judea, and Samaria. For "ends of the earth" peoples, Paul would have embraced regional music systems wherever he went (e.g., 1 Cor 9:19ff). Global missionary travel has enabled larger leaps to non-proximate socio-cultural contexts possessing categorically different music systems.

Music systems are like codes made up of sounds to which cultural insiders are privy and literate. Insiders intuitively know the intended meanings of their particular sounds and feel the intended associated emotions when they hear them. This is because, starting at a very early age, they are the ones regularly attending the community events (private or public) where the meanings are being transmitted and the associated emotions are being born.

Missionaries, however, have often held the naïve assumption that their culture's music is a universal language with universal meanings and universal associated emotions. They, therefore, frequently chosen to "bless" unreached people groups with their imported music. These hymns and songs have great meaning and associated emotions to the missionary, but are void of either to the people to whom they have traveled. In many cases, this causes theological confusion, community ostracism, and even persecution. The following are a few examples.

In the 1951 movie The African Queen, we see a common twentieth-century example illustrated. A Methodist missionary couple has come to the village of Kundu in 1914 German East Africa. They are leading their congregation in worship with their European church organ and hymnals. From outside their Western-styled church building, we hear cacophony. As the camera pans into a pew-filled sanctuary, we see hundreds of tribal Africans vocalizing in monotone with expressionless faces, while the white missionary, dressed in his English garb, waves his arms in 4/4 time, energetically singing, "Bread of heaven, bread of heaven, feed me till I want no more. ..." These African parishioners are visibly not privy to the deep meaning nor the intended emotions these missionaries associate with their song.

Tonal language communities are particularly vulnerable to theological confusion, as their words can change completely when sung to a rising or falling Western melody. Dr. Mary Beth Saurman, an ethnomusicologist in Southeast Asia, chronicled the following examples of Western hymns and songs translated into Eastern tonal languages:

Thai: *"Nearer my God to Thee" becomes "Farther my God from Thee"*
Cantonese: *"Yes, Jesus loves me," in some lines becomes "Yes, Jesus loves pigs,"*
 and in other lines becomes "Yes, Jesus loves diarrhea"
Burmese: *"He leadeth me" becomes "He exposes himself sexually to me"*

Dr. Saurman personally shared with me a situation on the border of two Southeast Asian countries illustrating ostracism and persecution due to the use of foreign hymnody. On one side of the border, Jesus-followers would hide ostracized in their houses in order to sing their imported translated hymns. On the other side, consequences were even worse. Outright persecution was taking place as local police would often line up the believers from this same socio-linguistic community and shoot them.

Saurman's five years of research unveiled that unity is the highest cultural value in this cross-border community. So one Easter the believers decided to create and sing new local-sounding Easter songs with local gongs, while walking in a culturally appropriate circle. Many people, including leaders, came from four surrounding villages. Having seen and heard this demonstration of desire for unity, they divulged, "Today is the first day that we can see that we don't have to give up our culture to be Christian." Because of this watershed moment, there are now churches in each of these four villages, and persecution and ostracism on both sides of the border has significantly subsided.

In efforts to undo the effects of last century's general missiological approach to ecclesiological music, much of the current work of skilled ethnodoxologists is being invested in churches that adhere to the traditional Western church paradigm. Now that discipleship church planting movements have been occurring for the past three decades, it is time for robust dialogue, research, and action related specifically to ethnodoxology in movements. Where necessary, we who can articulate "how" and "why" arts function in culture, must come alongside movement leaders and their disciples, helping them understand the influential roles of their music in their contexts. We who are skilled song-creation workshop leaders need to contribute our expertise developing and empowering them to create their very own Scripture-based, movement-augmenting song repertoire. Their new songs must use their own sound codes, which their socio-cultural-linguistic community understands plainly and feels intuitively.

Science and Practice

Social sciences and disciple-making experience both provide us with insights into why songs are particularly helpful in movements.

Ethnomusicology Universals and Movement DNA

The social science of ethnomusicology has uncovered universal roles of music in cultures, one being unification. Music, along with all the arts (drama, dance, oral-verbal, and visual) are powerful ways, outside of normal speech, that societies transmit their deepest values. These heightened means of communication indelibly cement in the next generation the meanings embodied in their artistic sounds, behaviors, and visuals. Mutually sharing these associated meanings causes a community to feel unity.

Bruno Nettl, a formative scholar in North American ethnomusicology, concluded that one of the universal roles of music in culture is to unify subcultures within a greater society (Nettl 2005: 253, 255).[3] We can easily see in North America, for example, how country and western music or rap music serve to help unify their respective subcultures. This same phenomenon is at work among rural tribes and majority-world mega-urban subcultures.

In 2020, during an indigenous song creation workshop I led among the Limba people of Sierra Leone, Karim, a disciple making movement (DMM) area leader said, "When we sing our own mother-tongue music, we feel like we belong to our community." This is at the heart of movement DNA: keeping a preexisting social community together, led by their influential "person of peace," rather than extracting individuals out to a whole new community full of undecipherable coded messages.

In 2000, I guided three Central Asian musicians to produce their first album of twelve profoundly local-sounding Scripture-based songs. After the recording was completed, the vocalist exclaimed, "Last night my fiancé listened to our pre-published album. When she was done, with a serious look on her face she asked me, 'Does this mean we can worship God in our own language with our own style of music?' 'Yes,' I told her, 'that is exactly what this means.'"

3 Nettl also concluded that music universally serves to mediate the relationship between the human and the divine.

Local music keeps communities together. The music used to carry the lyrics *is* the message that community members hear when considering questions like, "If I follow Jesus, will my parents feel I'm abandoning them or staying close to them?" "Will my neighbor think it's weird, or think it's acceptable?" "Will our community leaders and authorities perceive it as threatening or unifying?" A Jesus-following community's arts and music contribute to defining that community. These markers highly influence, positively or negatively, that community's ability to multiply as a movement of Jesus-followers within their society like "yeast through dough."

God created music to have a number of unique qualities. These are especially suited to enhance multigenerational group disciple making among non-Christian frontier unreached peoples. Some of these qualities particularly benefit the disciple maker, and some the discipled.

Benefits to the Disciple Maker

1. Songs are sticky: easy to remember. A disciple maker can hang onto, immediately access, and pass on countless Bible passages and disciple-making principles when contained in a song. Even Alzheimer's and other dementia sufferers can often clearly recall songs from their childhood. Remembering a truth to share comes easily when embedded in a song.

2. Song lyrics do not change. Meter, rhythm, and rhyme stabilize song lyrics such that if the lyrics are changed, the song will not work. This internal fidelity-preserving mechanism causes the song message to stay the same through generations, as disciplers transfer songs to disciples and churches transfer songs to churches within a movement.

3. In John Blacking's book, *How Musical Is Man?* (1973), he concluded that all humans are musical by nature. Revealing an intuitive understanding of this, Shodankeh Johnson told me while we sat in his home, "When I come back to this place I just begin to sing some nice songs [and] people will begin to come. The songs begin to draw them, and once the songs draw them, I can now engage them. I can even find a person of peace through that. Some people will just hang around because they also love songs. Then they want me to teach them and train them and that creates the relationship. And out of that relationship you can start the Discovery Bible Studies."

4. Songs from within the culture affirm "I love this community." As mentioned earlier, songs created with the community's sounds that they can decipher will affirm the identity and value of the community. When introducing one's network of relationships to Jesus, the stabilizing element of that community's music affirms love and good will for that community.

Benefits to the Discipled

- People don't argue with a song. Dr. Daud Rahbar,[4] a Pakistani Muslim convert and scholar, told missiologist Don McCurry, "You can say anything you want to a Muslim in poetry or music and he will receive it; but if you preach it in prose, he will probably try to kill you." God made music a creative and emotional right-brain activity relatively free from the analytical, argumentative cerebral left hemisphere. This can help the person being discipled to give a hearing to the message in a way otherwise not possible.

- Songs are sometimes self-validating. Some genres have internal clues, known to the cultural insiders, which validate its content. This can affirm the Scripture message in the heart of the hearer. In 2014, I led a Scripture-song creation workshop for a people group native to the Central Asian Pamiri Mountains. One participant created a song from Genesis 22 in their genre called Mado—a slow-tempo religious genre used to communicate historically true stories about prophets. Two months later, I received a letter from the Christian who organized the workshop. He wrote, "I want to write you a story of how the songs have been received. I was visiting a [Muslim] friend [and] he was telling me the story of Abraham. At that point I played him the [Genesis 22] song. After listening he said, 'Do you see? Did you hear what that said?' He was in perfect agreement that it came from his people and that he needed to get me on the right side, the same side as the Pamiri singer who wrote the Mado." To this Pamiri Muslim man, the Genesis 22 content in the song was true because he understood the cultural clue that when a story is communicated with this particular genre, it is true.

- Songs play over and over in a person's subconscious. Shodankeh Johnson relayed another story: "People who are not even saved sing [Christian songs]. We've got some people who got saved and said, 'I dreamed and I was singing in my dreams. I was singing songs—Christian songs. What does that mean?' I said, 'I don't know. Ask God to tell you why you are singing. I know you are not a Christian, but why are you singing Christian songs? God is trying to tell you something.'" God uses songs to draw people to himself, even in the absence of a discipler.

- Songs often communicate better than prose. In 2019, at a song creation workshop among the Kono people of Sierra Leone, the group created a song in their style from Psalm 139:14–16. Elizabeth, a nonliterate participant and mother of four shared in our group debrief at the end of the day: "Not until now, when I sang Psalm 139 in my own language and in our own musical style, have I ever really understood that 'God has known me from when I was in my mother's womb.'" God often uses a song as a powerful teacher.

---

4 Dr. Rahbar (1926–2013) was a Cambridge University graduate and professor at the Kennedy School of Missions at the Hartford Seminary Foundation.

Now we will consider what movement leaders have seen in their own experiences. In 2019 and 2020, I had the privilege of sitting in different contexts with several multi-movement leaders. Let's allow these eight men, like a panel of experts, to speak to us from their majority-world perspective about ethnodoxology in their church planting movements.

- Dr. Shodankeh Johnson: leader of New Harvest Ministries based in Sierra Leone, and African Director of New Generations. NHM has sent long-term workers to fourteen countries in Africa.

- Boureima: lead facilitator of Fulnet (Fulani Network), based in Burkina Faso, a DMM initiative among the Fulani in twenty-four primarily African countries.

- Dr. Aila Tasse: founder and director of Lifeway Mission International, based in Kenya. He is the New Generations Regional Coordinator for East Africa and part of the East Africa Church Planting Movement (CPM) Network in eleven countries.

- Shalom (pseudonym): movement leader in a Muslim-dominated region with 344 spoken languages.

- Sasha Karbunar: movement leader in Eurasia with eighteen regional teams in his home country of Ukraine.

- Mrityunjay Kumar: CEO of Agape Bihar Charitable Foundation and CPM leader in India. He and his wife help lead over fifty thousand people.

- Victor John: movement leader in India; founder and president of Asian Sahyogi Sanstha India (ASSI). Victor's contributions are by way of his book *Bhojpuri Breakthrough: A Movement that Keeps Multiplying* (2019).

- Benny (pseudonym): movement leader on the island of Java, Indonesia.

What Role Does Music (And Other Arts) Play in Your CPM Context?

Aila: "Africans just make music. Africans express everything through songs—birth, death, rain, drought, working, grinding, and so on. Expressing through songs is how Africans connect to something or to someone. When Africans sing their mother-tongue songs, it connects meaning and emotion to their life.

"In our movement, they have put the DBS Scripture-set passages to song to help recall the details of the text for the DBS. In DMM level 2 trainings, they have been using songs to teach the lessons. They write songs to the foundational Scripture passages upon which the leadership principles are based.

"Among the Muslim communities in North Kenya, they even make dramas of the DBS passages, acting out the Scripture portion. They present these dramas in the markets with full dress. The people in the market watch and laugh and enjoy."

Benny: "The majority folk-traditional Muslims already use music and dance for their religious worship. So music is impactful because people always want to use songs to express themselves to God. People receive [concepts] easily in songs and can then easily share it with others. It is easy-to-remember Scriptures like Ephesians, John, or the Psalms with a song. People can teach the Bible to their families this way."

Victor: "As the number of fellowships multiplied, we launched the first Bhojpuri Song Book in 1998. It contained songs of worship and instructions on baptism, child dedication, marriage, and funerals, including appropriate Bible verses for use with each occasion. This was received with much enthusiasm and greatly strengthened the local worshiping communities. It facilitated use of a wider variety of worship songs, since people no longer had to depend entirely on memory of songs in Hindi translated from other languages. It also built a broader sense of unity, as all Bhojpuri fellowships could sing similar songs in their worship times" (John 2019, 12).

Shodankeh: "Music is really the bloodline for small groups and for the thing to move, even to maybe ten to fifteen generations. Without music this whole process would easily come to a stop—it would be boring and grow weak. Music is the central piece to the DNA of movements as far as Africa is concerned. Even in our intercession … we mix songs through [it] that will keep the people praying for ten hours. As long as we are praying and singing, praying and singing, they will keep going. It sustains prayer so much. I call music and prayer "the weapon of mass destruction." When you worship and sing and then pray, it has the power to break strongholds. So in the movement, we take it very seriously. It is critical. If you remove the song piece from the church planting and DBSs, within the African context, I'm telling you, the movement will come to a standstill. Definitely."

Mrityunjay: "Songs validate our message. In our Indian context, the mere form of a 'song' with rhyme validates its message. First, he who has a song in his heart is genuine because a song takes time to make. A person would not spend time out of his life to create a song about a lie. Second, a song cannot come from ages past through just one person. It must come through many people. Therefore, it must have the wisdom and truth of the ages and the authentication of the community."

What themes and topics in songs have you seen that are important to have in a church planting movement?

Shodankeh: "Thanksgiving, songs of hope, faith, encouragement, power—songs of power and authority; songs that glorify God—that describe God and all the power of God; and love—songs of love. [Shodankeh starts singing …]

Gewe longa, kba kba go tima
I nema pa te, tuva panda

Na yeno he nimu, ye si go bue-e
Gewe longa, kba kba go tima

I've built my house on the solid rock
I've made up my mind to build my house on the solid rock
I will sit with Jesus even when the wind blows
I've built my house on the solid rock

"Those things lift people up—songs of encouragement. It doesn't matter what you are going through, you know that God sees, God cares, he's coming for you."

Victor: "An audiotape was ... released in 2001 with eighteen Bhojpuri worship songs—the first ever of its kind. The songs focused on salvation, worshiping God, and rejoicing in salvation. These songs were not translations from other languages; all were written by Bhojpuri people in their own language" (John 2019, 13).

Is there anything you are doing, or want to do, to encourage new song creation in your movements?

Boureima: "The majority of Fulani are nonliterate oral people. Songs are so important in our movement that we have made it our goal to create five hundred new Scripture-based songs in 2020, with many coming from Jesus' parables."

Shodankeh: "Every church planter knows a lot of songs in the local language of the tribe he is going to. So once he gets there by the leading of the Holy Spirit, he will have the songs that he will begin to sing and people will begin to flow with the songs. That's how things start. The people will learn the songs and there will be a time when they begin to develop their own songs.... . And most of the songs are really songs coming directly from the Bible. Most times, somebody will just look up and say, 'I did this song yesterday from the DBS passage that we had.' And they will sing it and the others will hear. Then they will kind of correct the song, and the next day they will sing it."

"Right now we have a competition going on. It ends tomorrow. They are looking for the best songs—songs that line up with Scripture. Then they will have a gift—they are going to give the winner about two million leones [about $200]. Some people are praying the whole night for new songs. They are praying together, saying, 'God, give us a new song.' They practice as a team. So we encourage things like that in the movement. It happens every quarter, or maybe twice a year. In fact, in December we're going to do an even bigger one. We call it 'Songs and Festival.' They have to be new songs [and] you can make it in any language—all the languages that are within the movement. That [event] will be packed completely full. [There will be] dancing with the songs, traditional costumes ... and a judges' panel. It will last for three days. Every night there will be eliminations, and on the last day will be the grand finals."

Shalom: "I want to begin a music recording project called 'Let's Sing Scripture with Local Melodies,' because our people are oral communicators."

What advice would you give a CPM initiative regarding music?

Sasha: "Asking questions is very helpful. One of the most significant outcomes of your ethnodoxology analysis with our core team is that simply asking questions has gotten us to start thinking for the first time about our use of music and arts in our movement."

Shodankeh: "I say it should be intentional, making sure that music is part of what they are doing. And also that you pray that God will give them new songs within every tribe and group they are going to. Once God gives them the songs, they should really encourage people to develop their own songs as they get saved from their Discovery Bible Studies. And when people develop their songs, leaders should show appreciation. Once that is happening, it becomes viral. They want to keep on doing it and coaching other people. By the time you realize it, you have so many song-makers in the movement. That's why, in the movement, we build in a lot of motivation and encouragement."

Victor: "Working in the Bhojpuri language drew upon not only language but also culture, history, and everything these people represented—through songs, music, and drama. This approach had been missed in the past" (John 2019, 12).

Toward Robust Ethnodoxology in Movements

We have seen throughout this chapter that ethnodoxology helps drive the process of making disciples who multiply forward in the following movement-specific ways:

1. *Prayer*—Songs aid in prayer encouragement, sustainment, and content.

2. *Access*—Songs are ready-made *shema* statements: winsome, spiritual, relationship-building access into lost communities and to their people of peace.

3. *Assuring and unifying communities*—Songs say, "We can follow God with our language and within our culture."

4. *Discovery Bible Study*—Scripture songs allow real-time access to a Scripture passage in order to lead a group in discovery, even when a printed or audio Bible is not available.

5. *Bible understanding*—Songs aid in understanding the meaning of a passage.

6. *Obedience*—Songs connect truth with life, facilitating the question: "What will obedience to this passage look like for us?"

7. *Passing on God's truth*—A newly discovered truth is easy to share in a song.

8. *Developing leaders*—Having Bible passages about leadership in song form aids church leadership trainings.

9. *Church generations*—Songs hold their Scripture-based content purely and consistently through generations of retransmission.

10. *Longitudinal growth*—Songs stay within a person even to their last days, allowing a lifetime of maturation, building one's house upon the rock of God's Word.

11. *Strength in trial*—Songs allow the Word of God to dwell in us richly day and night, in peace and in persecution.

12. *Cross-fellowship unity*—Similar song repertoire forms a bloodline running through generations of churches within a movement, and a bond that spans geographic distance.

Music is incredibly important for the qualitative and quantitative health of discipleship movements. This serves as a call for us as movement researchers, practitioners, coaches, and leaders to raise the importance of ethnodoxology in movements. So how do we discover and share helpful principles and best practices? How do we provide training, so that every movement initiative across the globe has access to guidance on how to catalyze its own indigenous Scripture-based songs? How do movement leaders encourage the gifts within grassroots song creators? The following are a few starting ideas.

Ideas for Researchers

1. *Qualitative interviews and data collection*—These provide two significant outcomes. First, they provide a wealth of case studies and practical examples useful for new ideas and encouragement in other movement contexts. Second, the mere process of asking about the use of music and other arts in a movement causes leaders to ponder it, sometimes for the very first time.

2. *Quantitative analysis*—Quantitative conclusions, though admittedly challenging to obtain in social sciences with multiple variables, would be particularly persuasive for two purposes. First, for recruiting music and arts specialists. Second, for persuading funding sources to invest resources toward catalyzing sustainable Scripture-based song creation in movement initiatives.[5]

Ideas for Practitioners and Coaches

- Resources for catalyzing ethnodoxology

- Publications

  » *Worship and Mission for the Global Church: An Ethnodoxology Handbook*, James Krabill, ed. (2013)

  » *Creating Local Arts Together: A Manual to Help Communities Reach Their Kingdom Goals*, Brian Schrag (2013)

---

5 In 2019 I created a research tool intended to quantitatively identify correlations between increased use of indigenous arts in the CPM process and decreased time to begin the next generation of churches. To date, I have administered the assessment in seven African and two Eurasian movement contexts.

- Non-degree training opportunities
  - » Payap University—EthnoArts certification classes[6]
  - » Arts for a Better Future—a one-week EthnoArts training[7]
  - » Eurasia Media and Distribution Consultation (EMDC) offers an EthnoArts track[8]
- I believe that movements need their own global network with CPM DNA for developing local song creators and catalyzers. The process of song catalyzing can be done by guiding cultural insiders through a series of activities to discover together the unique characteristics of their poetry and music. DBS provides the Scripture-based song content. Groups then create their own new Scripture-based songs in styles appropriate for their movement.[9] The Motus Dei Network can be a place to catalyze this global network.

Ideas for Movement Leaders

Intentionally and concretely encourage songwriters in your movement. These people are gifted leaders in their own right, with capacity for powerful positive influence.

- Give words of encouragement, especially for first attempts at creating a song.
- Offer and deliver help to improve the quality of new songs.
- Organize competitions and festivals. If possible, include audiences, judges, and prizes.
- Set movement-wide goals for creating new songs.
- Gather and facilitate roundtable discussions for your movement song creators to share their best practices, dream, and pray together.
- Regularly ask your area leaders about who is creating new songs in their area.

"Sing to the Lord a new song; sing to the Lord all the earth" (Ps 96:1) is God's mandate and helps expand his kingdom. Researchers and coaches of movements can augment their contributions if they understand the history of music in missions and the roles of songs in society. Local leaders and practitioners can increase their movement's capacity to create their own Scripture-based songs through gleaning best practices from other movements and through having access to training opportunities for new-song development.

---

6 li.payap.ac.th ⇒ Training ⇒ EthnoArts

7 worldofworship.org/artsforabetterfuture

8 For security reasons, EMDC does not have a website. For more information, write to: info@emdcon.org.

9 I have led workshops among nineteen UPGs in the above approach and have presented the process to multiple audiences.

References

Blacking, John. 1973. *How Musical Is Man?* Seattle and London: University of Washington Press.

John, Victor. 2019. *Bhopuri Breakthrough: A Movement that Keeps Multiplying.* Monument, CO: WIGTake Resources.

Krabill, James, ed. 2013. *Worship and Mission for the Global Church: An Ethnodoxology Handbook.* Pasadena, CA: William Carey Library.

Nettl, Bruno. 2005. *The Study of Ethnomusicology: Thirty-one Issues and Concepts.* Urbana and Chicago: University of Illinois Press.

Schrag, Brian, and James Krabill, eds. 2013. *Creating Local Arts Together: A Manual to Help Communities Reach Their Kingdom Goals.* Pasadena, CA: William Carey Library.

Media to Movements: A Church Planting Fusion

Frank Preston

This chapter discusses two strands of biblical mission that have been interwoven since Luke's recording of the Acts of the Apostles: media and church planting.

What Is Media to Movements?

"Media to Movements" is a strategy that uses specific media content tailored for select audiences in order to *identify* seekers from unreached people groups and then invite those seekers into a seeker-to-conversion process. The operative word is to *identify*, not to persuade, with the ultimate goal of seeing seekers become reproducing disciples.

Scholars note two general approaches to using media. One approach is called "push media," in which media products are used to persuade the media consumer to adopt an idea put forth by the media provider. The second approach is called "pull media," in which media products are used to identify people who have a proclivity toward the message provided by the provider (Chipp and Chakravorty 2016). Media to Movements employs a "pull strategy"—communicating to people who are already open to religious change. The strategy is comprehensive, with church planting movements as the long-term outcome. It is grounded in a model reflected in Luke 10:2: praying that God will identify people from within the unreached group (persons of peace) who will carry the gospel to others within the unreached group.

Media in Church Planting

I have long enjoyed asking small groups to provide ideas of how media was used in the initial stages of the expansion of the gospel in the early church. Most often I hear things like "the writing of the books of the New Testament." This isn't surprising since we have a literate bias—an affinity for words on paper.

It is generally agreed that James was one of the first—if not the first—New Testament book to be written. James was likely written about AD 50, although perhaps several years earlier, followed by Paul's epistles, beginning in about AD 52. But the day of Pentecost (Acts 2) occurred around AD 30, some twenty years before the letter to James. So, more precisely, the first use of media in the early church was the public forum with Peter in Acts 2:14–41, then later Stephen in Acts 6:8–7:60, and as illustrated in Acts 17:1–4 when Paul spoke in synagogues and in 17:16–34 when he joined meetings of Gentiles in various places.

Scholars note that Paul's missionary efforts followed the main Roman roads to start the first churches and then spread to other nearby regions. Acts 19 provides another example of this, starting with Ephesus and then radiating out from there. Public speaking was the most noted media in outreach until the advent of the printing press in the mid-1400s (Eisenstein 1980). The Protestant reformation owes a debt to "unsung heroes" who operated the printing presses to make pamphlets and other written material (Cole 1984). Viggo Søgaard and James Engel (Engel 1979; Sogaard 1993) document the expansion of broadcast media of radio and television in the twentieth century as a new mode of communication. But as Søgaard notes, the broadcast media approaches were oriented to proclamation: one-way communication (Søgaard 2008, 61).

The rise of "new media" ushered in a revised approach to media consumption. Marshall McLuhan, Dale Eickelman, and Elihu Katz (Palmgreen, Wenner, and Rosengren 1985) were among many scholars who identified a shift that occurred in communications from strictly persuasion media approaches to what is commonly called a "use and gratifications" model of media consumption. Generally, this "use and gratifications" model subsumes the idea that people use media for their purposes, and not the other way around. By nature, new media is a two-way communication process that involves interaction and dialogue. But people only have a limited amount of cognitive resources to allocate to new ideas, so most people only consume media that fits their needs. If media producers' ideas don't immediately fit a consumer need, the message is tuned out.

The upside to this phenomenon is that if a person consumes a media message different from their normal media habits, it means they are interested in something different than they normally consume. This may seem simple, but this profound observation adds complexity to developing media strategies. Instead of simply making proclamational content, media producers need to discover a seeker's needs, then *identify* those consuming the message, and then provide the seeker with a process that meets the seeker's need.

For this reason, a media response system is as important as the message itself. This can be seen in Paul's ministry in Acts 17:2. Paul was called by God to proclaim the gospel to the Gentiles, yet this passage notes that it "was his custom" to go to synagogues. The genius of this approach can be seen in 17:4, where a large number of "God-fearing" Greeks and prominent women followed Paul for additional discussions and discipleship. Paul, speaking through their public forum, *identified* which kind of Greeks were more open to the gospel message, and he spoke to their need. He could have chosen to speak at bath houses where far more Greeks would be assembled, but Greeks who were "open for conversion" were more likely to be in the synagogue. This illustrates the principle that targeting smaller yet specific audiences, who are interested in the message, is more effective than broadcasting to the masses. These can become part of a response follow-up system, as those in Acts 17 who followed Paul outside the synagogue (Preston 2017).

John Wesley, leader of the revival resulting in the movement called Methodism in mid-1700s England, followed a similar approach. Instead of preaching in church buildings, he chose to speak to smaller crowds in the street, where he could also offer an opportunity to respond immediately following the message. Later, in his work in America, he produced a plethora of pamphlets for the purpose of "Identify[ing] Receptive People" (Hunter 2000, 5).

As Hunter argues, Wesley had two other foundational components to his church planting strategy. One was an "indigenous" approach to ministry. What Wesley meant by this was to keep words and forms as common to the target population as possible. Hunter quotes Wesley:

> *The most obvious, easy, common words, wherein our meaning can be conveyed, we prefer before others, both on ordinary occasions, and when we speak of the things of God. We never, therefore, willingly or designedly, deviate from the most usual way of speaking; unless when we express scripture truths in scripture words, which, we presume, no Christian will condemn.* (Hunter 2000, 6)

Another foundational component was "Multiply Recruiting Units." Nearly all the leaders of the early Methodist societies were lay people, some recent converts themselves. Hunter notes:

> *He [Wesley] was instrumental in the spawning of many hundreds of classes, bands, societies, and other groups with their distinct agendas, and he labored to develop the indigenous lay leadership this growing vast network of groups would need. He was driven most to multiplying "classes," for these served best as recruiting groups, ports of entry for new people, and for involving awakened people with the gospel and its power.* (Hunter 2000, 7)

Key to this concept was lay leadership of small groups that were encouraged to multiply. Many of these leaders had low literacy in both literature and the Bible. Wesley and his leaders developed weekly meetings for leaders and emerging leaders that followed a method of teaching that would encourage self-discovery in a group setting. Since Methodism was widely dispersed outside of major population centers, the classes needed to be self-regulated by following rules and guidelines set by Wesley and his team.

This is important, as a media strategy needs to consider issues beyond messaging; media is just one component in establishing a church planting strategy. Each component must naturally and smoothly guide seekers into a self-replicating, Christ-following fellowship.

Media to Movements in the Current Era

As noted earlier, media in the broadcast era migrated toward proclamational approaches: one-way communication. The Søgaard model (Søgaard 1993) and the Engel model of communication (Engel 1979) both flowed from secular business models that Engel used when he taught Consumer Behavior at Ohio State University. At each stage of the consumer decision-making process, media messages would persuade the consumer toward the end desire of the marketer. The right message at the right time would lead to a positive outcome for the marketer.

Though Christian media scholars are deeply indebted to Søgaard and Engel, their theories were enshrined in one-way communication philosophies. With the advent of New Media/Social Media, cracks in persuasion theories became pronounced. Google and Facebook are grounded in "use and gratifications" theories, defined as "people using media to meet their needs." This new era of media forces Christian media providers to retool media to fit the current era of communications. Yet in many ways we already have historical Christian examples in Acts 17 and in Wesley, where using media to identify seekers and then assisting them in their spiritual journey serve as adequate theoretical guides (Preston 2017). These are not new concepts for Christian media. Use and gratifications models guided early developers of Media to Movements strategies.

In 2010, two groups, equipped with these new insights, launched Media to Movements approaches in their respective areas: a North Africa Team with Gospel Ambition (pseudonym) and a Pioneers/Mission to Unreached Peoples (now "Beyond")/Mitra Asia collaboration in Southeast Asia. Both teams tried separate strategies, shared information, and began building best practices. Other individuals and organizations, such as Frontiers, Arab World Media, Visual Story, Mobile Ministry Forum, and a host of other like-minded coworkers, joined in the development of the concepts: some doing training and others experimenting.

In 2020, a survey was sent to over six hundred field workers who had taken one or more of the Media to Movements trainings (Preston 2020a). Sixty-two percent who took a training did so because they desired to see more fruitfulness in their work. The research noted that of those who implemented a Media to Movements approach after their training, "86% of the trainees reported mid-range-or-greater impact on their ministry practice, with 24% reporting *very significant* changes to our ministry practice." The group in North Africa experienced more conversions and disciples-who-make-disciples than had previously been seen in the history of the work there. The Southeast Asia team was initially identifying less than twenty potential persons of peace (PPOPS) per month. Currently the team reports in excess of 115 PPOPS per month. On average, 38 percent of the PPOPS show long-term growth as disciples, up from 17 percent in the early days.

In 2018, an ad hoc team of Media to Movements practitioners was established to coordinate best practices among multi-organization, multinational practitioners. Though training was a known need, the team felt they wanted to understand what other pressing needs were being felt by emerging practitioners. One identified need was coaching and consultation. Frontiers had an internal consultant from within their organization, and Arab World Media/Pioneers supported their teams in the Arab world, but the greater body of field workers were not being serviced. The Gospel Ambition team had developed software to support Media to Movements practitioners and had provided implementation materials, but felt they did not have capacity to service the greater mission body. Arab World Media/Pioneers and the Media to Movements ad hoc coalition are currently seeking to fill that need. Arab World Media has expanded its coaching team. With the help of Gospel Ambition, they have codified training and coaching for all field workers—national or expatriate—who want assistance in practice and technical implementation of a Media to Movements strategy.

Lesson Learned in Media to Movements

This section will offer a few notable observations, a more comprehensive version of which can be found in the Global Survey Report (Preston 2020a).

Dwight McGuire claimed that 2.5 percent of any population is open for religious change at any time (2010). This was first based on statistical theory and research on movements by scholars like Everett Rogers (Rogers 1995), and consistent evaluation of data supplied by Media to Movements practitioners to Kavanah Media empirically seems to confirm McGuire's assertion. This supports the idea that there are no closed fields, but unreached peoples remain unreached because of the lack of workers.

Wesley and others put forth a principle, drawing from Luke 10:2: not so much that the laborers are few, but that "from the harvest will come the harvesters" if field workers empower local lay leaders. One characteristic of disciple making movement (DMM) strategy is identifying potential persons of peace and then empowering them to grow as leaders in church planting within their context. This clear observation arose from the study on Scripture engagement in DMMs (Preston 2020b).

A second observation is that push media (persuasion media) strategies are no longer effective. Significant numbers of secular scholars have empirically demonstrated this through qualitative and quantitative research (Kruglanski and Webster 1996; McLeod, Kosicki, and Pan 1991; Petty and Priester 2002). Pull media that *identifies* potential consumers has a stronger theoretical and practical foundation. One only has to look as far as Amazon, Google, and Facebook to see pull media in action. Media to Movements strategies use pull media principles.

A third and less discussed observation is what social marketing researchers call "low identity" conversion, as compared to "high identity" conversion. In its simplest terms, low identity relates to social and cognitive costs as being low in the conversion process. In locations where Christianity is an accepted norm, a person can generally convert to become a "real Christian" without suffering significant loss. In a sense, becoming a new Christian adds to their identity structure. They still usually function as a member of their society and social group, work their same job, and remain in the same social status.

High-identity conversion brings significant costs to one's identity structure. Waardenburg describes Islam as a "signification system," where conversion to another religion would be paramount to social treason (Waardenburg 1974). In a high-identity conversion, seekers need to follow "stages, steps and processes" in the conversion process (Andreasen 1995, 142; Hassan 2005a). The strategy of reading a gospel presentation online and then praying to receive Jesus online was developed generally for Western populations but does not transfer to seekers in areas with another religious majority. Different strategies and response mechanisms need to be deployed. This core principle is taught in the Media to Movements training programs, particularly around persona development lessons.

Persona development is involved in the funnel model used by the Media to Movements practitioners. The funnel model has seen several iterations, all adapted from Quintan Wiktorowicz's model of recruiting jihadis, a high-identity conversion activity for a Muslim converting to high-risk religious practice among moderate Muslims (Beutel 2007, 12; Wiktorowicz 2005).

In the model developed by Gospel Ambition and Arab World Media/ Pioneers, following Wiktorowicz's categories, a high-identity convert passes through six stages: *belief disruption, cognitive opening, religious seeking, frame alignment, socialization,* and finally *joining.*[1]

---

1 See "The Funnel," article by Frank Preston, Media to Movements website: https://www.MediatoMovements.org/articles/the-funnel.

In the *belief disruption* stage, which Wiktorowicz called *exogenous conditions*, the seeker has an experience that disrupts their previously held beliefs. This disruption could come from a myriad of possibilities, but essentially something causes doubt in the seeker's belief structure. Normally these disruptions occur outside of any activity of an activist, not so much from the influence of a religious worker or religious organization.

This fits closely with John 6:44, where Jesus describes God using some means to prompt a seeker to initiate a journey that leads the person to the gospel. This journey could be slow or immediate, but the second stage of *cognitive opening* will then be activated and allows a person to consider that there may be life options other than their previous belief system. Wesley described this in terms of open flowers, and he knew this phase would be temporary (Hunter 2000, 5). At this stage the media producer both fosters faith and attracts seekers who are in their seeking process. It is important to encourage the seeker to move to the next stage of *spiritual seeking* by making sure there is content to connect cognitive openness to spiritual conversations. Openness is important, but the person needs to be guided toward spiritual content. When speaking with the Samaritan woman in John 4, Jesus directed the cognitive openness of a thirsty soul to the spiritual seeker stage: for "such people the Father seeks" (John 4:23).

Wiktorowicz notes that seekers at this stage are fairly passive, and in the funnel model the media producer offers products that are likewise passive—not calling for a commitment. But the ministry activity aims to foster movement toward the next stage. The seekers need more trust and information before they can make a religious change commitment, and the media counselor can guide that conversation. The media technology functions to identify and provide enough information to keep the seeker engaged. The media follow-up team must foster trust as the seeker is on his journey. In the absence of trust, pushing for a "conversion" or a "decision" may be too early at this stage.

Belief change in high-identity conversion will take time for most seekers. In my research on jihadi conversion, about half of those in a high-identify conversion process took an average of three months of back and forth conversation before conversion to jihadism took place. Those from Muslim backgrounds who were in the Christian conversion process had a similar experience of three to six months. The less a person knows of Christian culture or is entwined in Waardenburg's description of a signification system discussed earlier, the more time this transition stage will normally take.

In the *spiritual seeking* stage, seekers will need time and guidance to see a connection between their previously held religion and their emerging belief in a new religion. Rogers defines this process as making the message *homophilous* (Rogers 1995, 18–19). The new belief system has to find some connection with their previous belief system. The idea of contextualization may be similar, but the homophilous construct is far more robust because it relates to the construct that is essentially internal to the social network. A message being contextualized means it is external to the context but is made to look and feel internal to the context.

Frame alignment, or message alignment, occurs from homophilous messaging because it helps the message to be deemed credible, related to the issue that prompted the seeker's journey. This is often the case because the previous beliefs help "make sense" of the new belief system. In Jesus' conversation with the Samaritan woman (John 4), he constantly referred to the woman's need and related it to her previous belief structure. Paul did the same at Mars Hill in Acts 17, where he aligned the gospel with their pursuit of the "Unknown God."

The last two stages of *socialization* and *joining* allow the seeker to go deeper in firming up the foundations of an emerging belief system. As described in Matthew 13, seed sown "in context" of other growing seed is essential at this stage. This can also be seen in Acts where, of the twenty-one conversion stories, nineteen are group conversions. Seeds need other growing seeds to create a healthy environment. Media to Movements has adopted DMM approaches in employing a media strategy to accommodate a group conversion approach. Getting involved with Discovery Bible Studies with friends and relatives—people from their own social network—serves as *socialization* and then, as the group becomes a church, facilitates *joining*.

In the funnel model in figure 1, note the processes in ministry *activity* and *technology function*. In the ministry activity, engagement will vary from stage to stage. As discussed earlier, fostering in the early stages allows the seeker to be passive. My friend Rahmad makes this point in his testimony.

Rahmad reports that when he began "seeking" the claims of Christ, he took a public bus to a place where someone could explain the Christ to him. He got off the bus, stood across the street for a few minutes, and then caught another bus home. The next week he took the bus, got off at the same location, crossed the street, and stood by the gate for a few minutes, then retraced his steps to return home. The third week, he repeated the process, except this time he entered the gate. At this point, someone invited him in and introduced him to a man from his own ethnic group who was a follower of Isa Al Masih, the qur'anic term for Jesus Christ. This man shared his testimony of faith in Isa. Over many weeks, they developed a friendship, and later Rahmad joined a Bible study of other Muslim background believers (MBBs) from his ethnic group. Each step of his pathway was an increasing degree from being passive to becoming active in his spiritual search. *Fostering* is matching people's comfort of being passive to eventually becoming active. From a fostering posture, Rahmad's friend became a spiritual guide, to later discipling him in conversion and then growing in Christ.

In the technology function, media ads attract persona-based information seekers. Later, technology is aligned passively by only providing information and then increasing toward active engagement by asking for identifiers, such as name, contact, etc. But in the early stages, technology processes just attract the seeker with an option to connect them with someone willing to answer the seeker's questions. We do not recommend that the first landing page contain a button, "Pray to receive Jesus." The ministry in Southeast Asia never asks a person to make a faith decision in the media domain. They have found that in the later stages of *socialization* and *joining*, a person who makes a faith decision with an on-the-ground worker will have a high "sticking" rate of 38 percent (staying with biblical faith). Data analysis has shown that decisions made online, in the media domain, have a sticking rate of less than 3 percent, with some data sets reporting less than 1 percent. Jesus already warned about the reality of attrition in the parable of the sower (Matthew 13).

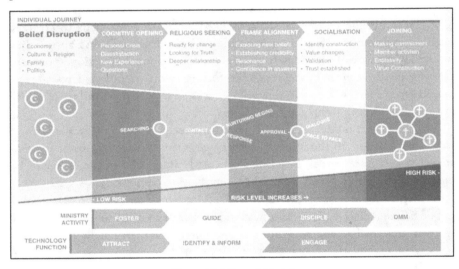

Figure 14.1 Funnel Model

Related to high-identity conversion are those in the conversion process who in some way involve their social network. In high-identity situations, group conversion is more normal, whereas in low-identity conversion, individual conversions are more normal. As already mentioned, nineteen of the twenty-one conversion stories in Acts are group conversions. Media to Movements seeks to engage reference groups of seekers so they can become believers, and house churches are started by people who know and trust each other.

Another observation arises around the question of whether discipleship can occur online or whether discipleship must be an off-line activity. Online discipleship programs can be effective if they are administered by local leadership.

I discuss this in "Scripture Engagement" (Preston 2020b). If online organizations bypass local workers, either church planters or churches themselves, to "disciple" seekers directly, the outcome will follow the descriptions in Matthew 13:18–22. Seed sown *in context* (in the field) with other seeds will flourish, whereas seeds sown by themselves (individualistically) will likely become victims of the elements.

Online discipleship programs often ignore the power of the reference group and the local context. Media organizations offering online discipleship generally do not work in concert with local leaders. They may have many good reasons for this, nevertheless the result is less than the best. Local leaders can use media organizations' products, but rarely are local leaders integrated into the product development and the launch of the media products. Sometimes local leaders are seen as *distribution channels*, but not as collaborative partners in the truest sense. In contrast, media organizations who work in tandem with local leaders can be a great asset for resource-lean areas.

The key question is "Who is driving the agenda of online discipleship?" If it is outside organizations, the individualistic descriptions of Matthew 13 will apply. It the "field" drives the agenda, then Matthew 13:23 multiplication applies. Media to Movements aligns itself with DMM teaching of empowering local leaders to be the disciple-making cadre.

Locally driven discipleship processes can use a wide variety of tools, including apps, websites, the Bible on cell phones, and the plethora of other tools developed by media organizations. But media providers need to follow Wesley's advice noted above and use the simplest and most normal mode of communication that the "indigenous" population uses (Hunter 2000).

Short Testimonies

In this chapter, I have focused on Southeast Asia and North Africa projects. But the research study conducted by the MTDMM (Media to Disciple Making Movements) Ad Hoc Coalition noted quite a few other testimonies. In one testimony the interviewee stated:

> In the first ten years (of ministry) we saw very little fruit. We had one baptism in the first eight years. [Now that we are using MTDMM strategy] the number of contacts, the number of people we were making contact with, was really high. And even the [number of] baptisms we were seeing was really high and that was super exciting (Preston 2020a).

This coworker had been ready to terminate his ministry, thinking the population was "too hard." The problem was that this person was working with the converse of the 2.5 percent principle—the 97.5 percent of unreceptive people. Media to Movements strategy directed the team to a more responsive population among the unreached group.

In a West Asian country, a team was launched to reach out to Syrian refugees. But the refugee population was diffused among the local population. How could a church planting team find Arab-speaking Syrian refugees among another majority group? For fear of reprisals, the refugees were unwilling to self-identify in one-on-one situations. But the team launched a Media to Movements strategy using Facebook before the team arrived. On their explore trip, they met face-to-face with all the Syrians who self-identified as seekers (from the campaign), and the team had significant spiritual conversations with these seekers. On day one of the team's arrival in country, they were able to start several discovery Bible studies with Syrian seekers.

Pandemic and Media to Movements

The COVID-19 pandemic has put on hold many incarnational church planting ministries. In the Southeast Asia work discussed above, the team began working from home during the country's lockdown phases. They reconfigured their team to be virtual and were able to carry on as before. Prior to February 2020, the number of PPOPS per month hovered around fifty. Once the pandemic hit and the team became virtual, the number of respondents increased, and the team was able to identify over 110 PPOPS per month. The field multipliers had to engage with seekers while distancing themselves in follow-up approaches. They used more text messages, then empowered stay-at-home families to start discovery studies using processes similar to those employed by Wesley and Methodism. In many ways, the COVID-19 pandemic played into the hands of the Media to Movements strategy. The systems of advertising, contacting, dispatching, and follow-up functioned quite well in non-pandemic and pandemic scenarios.

What Is Missing?

The Global Survey Report (Preston 2020b) highlighted the need for improved coaching processes, which groups like Arab World Media and the MTDMM Ad Hoc Coalition are addressing. But a glaring need remains for better training and coaching in the field for DMM practitioners. Many field workers are still measuring converts and baptisms but fail to grasp the core of DMM, which is training and empowering local leaders. To return again to Wesley, part of Methodism's success was lay leadership development. In Wesley's case, tasks done by lay leaders were not overwhelming. The emerging leader made sure everyone attended the meeting, then followed the course outline. Itinerate "circuit riders" were engaged in next-level leadership development of local leaders. This corresponds to the leadership development in the "Scripture Engagement" case study (Preston 2020b).

Conclusion

In this chapter, we have considered the essence of a Media to Movements approach focusing on identifying seekers, then maturing them toward becoming disciples who make disciples. Both biblical foundations and communications theory provide an impetus to deploy such a strategy. Those who have included this approach in their ministry have seen significant fruit. We believe the difference is identifying the "responsive 2.5 percent" people rather than the unresponsive. But beyond conversion, setting a standard to see "disciples who make disciples" alters metrics and leads to an end-to-end church planting strategy. The Ad Hoc Coalition has training, tools, and coaching for any field team wanting to consider employing this approach. Feel free to contact the team at https://media2movements.org.

References

Andreasen, A. R. 1995. *Marketing Social Change: Changing Behavior to Promote Health, Social Development, and the Environment.* San Francisco: Jossey-Bass.

Beutel, A. 2007. "Radicalization and Homegrown Terrorism in Western Muslim Communities: Lessons Learned for America." *Minaret of Freedom Institute.*

Chipp, Kerry Fiona, and Devarpan Chakravorty. 2016. "Producer push to consumer pull: Who curates new media content? Developing strategies for new media environments." *Journal of Product & Brand Management.*

Cole, Richard G. 1984. "Reformation printers: Unsung heroes." *The Sixteenth Century Journal*: 327–39.

Eisenstein, E. L. 1980. *The Printing Press as an Agent of Change: Communications and Cultural Transformations in Early-Modern Europe.* Cambridge: Cambridge University Press.

Engel, James F. 1979. *Contemporary Christian Communications, Its Theory and Practice.* T. Nelson.

Hassan, Riaz. 2005a. "On being religious: Patterns of religious commitment in Muslim societies." Institude of Defence and Strategic Studies Singapore.

Hunter, George. 2000. *John Wesley as Church Growth Strategist.* Northwest Nazarene University Wesley Center for Applied Theology.

Kruglanski, A. W., and D. M. Webster. 1996. "Motivated closing of the mind: Seizing and freezing." *Psychological Review* 103 (2): 263–83.

McGuire, Dwight. 2010. "2 1/2 percent: Church planting movements from the periphery to the center." *Evangelical Missions Quarterly* 46 (1): 24–31.

McLeod, J. M., G. M. Kosicki, and Z. Pan. 1991. "On Understanding and Misunderstanding Media Effects." In *Mass Media and Society*, edited by J. Curren and M. Gurevitch, 235–66. London: Edward Arnold.

Palmgreen, Philip, Lawrence Wenner, and Karl Erik Rosengren. 1985. "Uses and Gratifications Research: The Past Ten Years." In *Media Gratifications Research*, edited by Karl Erik Rosengren, Lawrence Wenner, and Philip Palmgreen. Beverly Hills, CA: Sage Publications.

Petty, R. E., and J. R. Priester. 2002. "Mass Media Attitude Change: Implications of the Elaboration Likelihood Model of Persuasion." In *Media Effects: Advances in Theory and Research*, edited by J. Bryant and D. Zillmann, 155–98. Mahwah, NJ: Lawrence Erlbaum Associates.

Preston, Frank. 2017. "Using media to accelerate church planting." *Seedbed* 31 (1): 5–12.

———. 2020a. *MediatoMovements global survey report*. MTDMM Ad Hoc Coalition. https://www.mediatomovements.org/article-tags/report

———. 2020b. "A Study on Scripture Engagement in Disciple Making Movements." *Evangelical Missions Quarterly* 56 (2): 37–40. https://missionexus.org/emq/.

Rogers, E. M. 1995. Diffusion of Innovations. 4th ed. New York: Free Press.

Søgaard, V. 1993. *Media in Church and Mission: Communicating the Gospel*. Pasadena, CA William Carey Library.

———. 2008. "Go and communicate good news." *Paradigm shifts in Christian witness*. Maryknoll, NY: Orbis. 57–65.

Waardenburg, Jacques. 1974. "Islam Studied as a Symbol and Signification System." *Humaniora Islamica* II: 267–85.

Wiktorowicz, Q. 2005. *Radical Islam Rising: Muslim Extremism in the West*. Lanham, MD: Rowman & Littlefield Publishers.

15

Terra Nova: Opportunities and Challenges of Movement Work in Diaspora Contexts

Bradley Cocanower and João Mordomo

Bakary,[1] my son, and I (Bradley) made s'mores (a dessert made of chocolate and roasted marshmallows), told stories, and laughed in front of the crackling fire. This was a new experience for Bakary, who had arrived in Italy as one of 183,682 asylum seekers to come to the country in 2017.

I asked my son to share his favorite Bible story with Bakary, a devout Muslim who had a sincere respect for the biblical prophets mentioned in the Qur'an. We had just celebrated Easter, so my son naturally thought of the story of the resurrection, and, much to my surprise, he did a fantastic job of articulating the gospel to Bakary, who looked on with a big smile and affirmative nods. My five-year-old son was the first person ever to share the good news of Jesus with Bakary. As I reflected on that experience—particularly the way two people with drastically different backgrounds had managed to come together and respectfully share stories of differing faiths—I couldn't help but thank God for allowing me to be a part of Bakary's "terra nova" story.

Terra nova, which is Latin (and Portuguese) for "new land," describes the fundamentally new reality that marks daily life for refugees and other members of diaspora communities around the globe. Bakary's "terra nova" story doesn't merely illustrate a convergence of different cultures; it also reveals elements of two phenomena that are changing the landscape of global missions in significant ways. First, many missiologists are reporting unprecedented numbers of churches being planted and Muslims and Hindus (and Buddhists, to a lesser extent) being

---

1   For the security of the individual, this is a pseudonym that is common in his country of origin.

baptized throughout the Global South. Second, more people are displaced today than at any other point in recorded history. The UN reported that 82.4 million people were forcibly displaced at the end of 2020, with about 34 million of those having fled to other countries as refugees or asylum seekers (UNHCR 2020). Global diaspora will increasingly not just call for, but also impact and shape, kingdom movements in the coming decades.

In this chapter we will consider insights and best practices gleaned from movement practitioners in diaspora contexts in the Global North and informed by our research focused on kingdom movements among asylum seekers in Southern Italy. We will discuss how kingdom movements seen around the world (primarily in the Global South) could be replicated in the Global North as a means of reaching refugees and migrants from the Global South. For the purpose of this study, we describe a kingdom movement as occurring when followers of Christ are empowered to take ownership of ministry and mission in a way that results in exponential multiplication of disciples and churches. A kingdom movement includes an intentional catalytic process (such as CPM, DMM, or T4T) of helping believers foster a heart for obedience, a love for Jesus, and a vision to reach the lost, as well as equipping them with the skills and tools necessary to do so effectively. It should be noted that our study falls within the emerging discipline of diaspora missiology, which focuses on ministry to the millions of people around the world who reside somewhere other than in their place of origin, whether by choice or by force.[2]

"From everywhere to everywhere" has become a diaspora ministry catchphrase, and with good reason. Diaspora groups are coming from and going to a wide variety of places. This chapter will primarily involve groups of people originally from the Global South who have made their way to countries in the Global North. By studying them, this chapter will reveal a number of significant advantages—and challenges—compared to movement work with similar people groups in their countries of origin. We will also make recommendations for practitioners and scholars who wish to catalyze kingdom movements among diaspora communities in the Global North.

Advantages of Movement Methodologies in Diaspora Contexts

Diaspora groups provide some of the greatest missions opportunities in the twenty-first century. Sam George suggests that "current refugee displacements will reshape the future of Christianity in many ways" (George and Adeney 2018, xx).

---

2 For further study, we recommend *Diaspora Missiology: Theory, Methodology, and Practice* (edited by Enoch Wan, 2014); *Diaspora Missiology: Reflections on Reaching the Scattered Peoples of the World* (edited by Michael Pocock and Enoch Wan, 2015); and *Scattered and Gathered: A Global Compendium of Diaspora Missiology* (edited by Sadiri Tira and Tetsanao Yamamori, 2020).

Daniel Zeidan asserts that "Europe's refugee crisis had created a historically unprecedented window of opportunity for sharing the saving message of the gospel with some of the least-reached people on earth—a segment of the world's population that would otherwise be in 'closed' or 'restricted access' countries hostile to the gospel and Christian mission" (Zeidan 2018, 89).

Leaders and practitioners involved in organizing efforts to engage diaspora communities—and bring spiritual, social, economic, and other types of transformation—have a variety of models and tools at their disposal. In this section, I will describe and evaluate some of the advantages characteristic of movement-oriented ministries focused on reaching individuals from the Global South who have now settled in the Global North. These advantages include heightened openness, distinctive felt needs, and spiritual revitalization in diaspora regions.

Heightened Openness

Much psychological, sociological, and missiological research in recent years suggests that immigrants—particularly refugees and asylum seekers—often have a heightened sense of openness toward new ideologies in their *terra nova*. Supported by evidence, social identity theory posits that diaspora members are motivated by a desire to enhance their own self-esteem by way of their social identity. This is generally achieved through group membership (Hogg 2006, 111), which can come in the form of "belonging" to a group of fellow sojourners or to a group from the host culture. Either way, this openness is multifaceted and can be very advantageous for kingdom work. Large numbers of refugees have come to Christ in short periods of time in several European countries in recent years. "One church in Germany," for example, "had baptized over a thousand Syrian and Kurdish believers during the last six months of 2016" (George and Adeney 2018, xvi).

Diaspora peoples often have a higher tolerance and receptivity toward new cultural practices, relational networks, and even religious doctrines than they otherwise would have had in their home context.

> Many refugees who have come to Europe are keen to leave behind their old way of life. They are open to the gospel and are attracted by the love they see expressed by Christians they come across in Europe. Many have expressed genuine interest in the Christian faith and, above everything else, show deep curiosity and admiration for the person and power of Jesus Christ and his message of love. (Zeidan 2018, 93)

This points to potential for explosive movement growth if practitioners do two things. First, understand the universal elements pertaining to displacedness. Second, find ways to leverage the advantages and overcome the obstacles unique to their specific contexts. Though certain elements of openness may not be universal, some sense of openness is virtually automatic for individuals looking to establish themselves in a foreign context. For example, refugees necessarily show greater tolerance for different cultural practices and norms in their new contexts than they would need to have in their home context. Survival, of course, requires this, but cultural and relational openness likely correlate to an individual's ability to thrive in a new culture as well.

Movement catalysts must carefully consider and leverage this in order to see movements started and sustained in diaspora communities. They must also keep in mind the need for speed (due to transience) and that potential movements will be based primarily on relationship, not geography.

Distinctive Needs

Diaspora communities tend to have very distinctive needs. In many cases these needs are neither typical of those most prevalent in the Global South nor those common in the Global North. They result from the individuals' radical transition from one place and one culture to another. For example, their need for friendship is pronounced, both for existential reasons (identity and belonging) and practical ones. In their new location they need, but often do not have, friends to help them in their transition. This serves as an opportunity for those seeking to reach them and catalyze kingdom movements. These agents of transformation understand that it takes time to build trusting relationships, and yet they may not have much time. They must therefore develop effective yet genuine strategies for accelerating the friendship process. This calls for prayerful consideration of, and insight into, the friendship needs of the diaspora community.

Personal recreation, adventure, and leisure are other important examples of distinctive needs. This may meet a plethora of deep, often unseen, existential needs, but this generally only comes by way of friendships. Another example of friendship need is that of childcare, which may be a vital lifeline for migrants who have no means of surviving unless they work. Language acquisition is also significant, since it contributes directly to the migrants' ability to survive and thrive in a new culture. It can be a difficult, painful process, particularly for shy individuals or those who aren't forced to communicate for work, and kingdom movement catalysts can position themselves to meet this need. Additionally, friendship needs include help with legal assistance, opening a bank account, finding a job, or even simply preparing a résumé. While seemingly trivial, "friendship help" with these things could make a significant difference to people in diaspora communities, and toward establishing kingdom movements among them.

The importance of meeting the distinctive needs of diaspora populations may bring to mind Maslow's hierarchy of needs. Regardless of one's views about Maslow and his hierarchy, those in the early stages of immigration often find themselves facing very distinct physiological needs (food and, sometimes, even water), security needs (safety and shelter), and belongingness needs. Movement practitioners can, have, and should place themselves strategically to help meet these needs if they wish to catalyze kingdom movements among diaspora communities in the Global North.

Spiritual Revitalization (by way of Diaspora Communities)

Twenty years ago, when I (João) was on a ministry trip to London, my cab driver was a Christian migrant from Nigeria. Near the same time, my taxi driver in Vancouver was a Christian from Pakistan. I found this pattern repeating itself in numerous cities in the Global North. Neither of these brothers moved to those places as missionaries, yet they both were on mission. (In fact, I honestly don't remember if I tried to share Christ with them or if they tried to share Christ with me! Or both!)

On ministry trips to London during the past two decades, we became increasingly aware that if it were possible to take a "spiritual X-ray" of the city, a huge number of spiritual hotspots would show up all around the M25 motorway, and many, if not the majority, of them would be the result of churches started by or for diaspora communities. This is true of many cities in the Global North. Jaume Llenas, a key evangelical leader in Spain, estimated that 70 percent of churchgoers in Madrid and 60 percent in Barcelona are foreigners (Llenas 2020). Large concentrations of Christian migrants bring with them the greatest gift possible to the largely post-Christian West: "Refugees are blessings in disguise sent by the Father to revitalize our churches" (Wightman 2018, 61).

But what about those migrants who are not Christians? What about the Muslim and Hindu and Buddhist migrants? The unfolding reality of their heightened openness (mentioned above) seems to be an Abrahamic "blessed to be a blessing" dynamic. Sam George points out that "in the face of a post-Christian, agnostic/atheistic worldview in Western Europe, the spiritual and religious fervor of the refugees is reigniting a spiritual quest on the part of Europeans for their own heritage" (George and Adeney 2018, xx). Kingdom movement practitioners among non-Christian migrants in the Global North have the distinct benefit of mobilizing Christian migrants to participate in catalyzing movements among non-Christian migrants, as well as blessing the host nation's cultural Christians by awakening them by way of "spiritual envy" (see figure 15.1 on the next page). While no single church planting or kingdom movement strategy serves as a silver bullet among diaspora communities in the Global North, astute practitioners are becoming increasingly aware of the power of "blessed to be a blessing" as a catalyzing agent for movements (Downes 2015).

Figure 15.1 Adapted from Mordomo

Challenges of Movements in Diaspora Contexts

Brazilian novelist Paulo Coelho has said that when we least expect it, life sets us a challenge to test our courage and willingness to change. This seems strikingly appropriate in the context of this discussion. Catalyzing kingdom movements in any context presents many challenges, but doing so among diaspora communities presents different and distinctive challenges, sure to test many practitioners' courage and willingness to change.

Transience

A frequent challenge to kingdom movement work in the context of diaspora is the transience of asylum seekers and migrants. We have a growing number of examples of migrants coming to Christ in their host contexts, then returning to their own people with a ministry mindset. Yet the evidence is anecdotal. And to date, research has suggested transience to be much more of a challenge than an asset to kingdom movement development (Cocanower and Mordomo 2020). In some contexts, transience has proven to be a limiting factor in fostering depth of relationships with asylum seekers and migrants. Relational depth is essential for effective discipleship; therefore, high levels of transience impact the discipleship process and force immigrants to build new relationships each time they move.

Immigrants often leave on a whim, or refugees are transferred to a different location with little notice. This results in limited time to react and has, in many cases, restricted the amount of closure in those relationships prior to departure. Even anticipated departure does not guarantee enough time to disciple someone well. This challenge has been faced and documented by practitioners in Greece, Italy, and elsewhere. If not anticipated and overcome, the issue of transience can serve as a major hindrance to seeing movement progress among diaspora communities.

In Europe, people commonly think of countries on the "migration highway" in terms of two primary categories: entry locations and destination locations.[3] Sicily and Athens are examples of entry points for many migrants en route to a different European country. Destination locations are typically countries or cities with more economic stability and opportunity, a favorable stance toward migrants, and/or a language commonly spoken by immigrants. Movement practitioners in highly transient contexts need to prepare for quick transitions and next steps. Many kingdom movement oriented ministries in Europe are leveraging basic technology, such as WhatsApp, to engage with and/or equip migrants who are leaving prior to the completion of an effective discipleship relationship.

Another valuable strategy is networking with other ministries positioned along the migration highway. Those doing similar ministry in nearby cities or countries can prove to be a tremendous lifeline when a spiritually hungry person ends up moving on and can connect with other ministries to support them in their faith journey. As Paul Keller, a practitioner in Sicily, stresses, "There is a need—because these guys are transient—to get to the gospel quicker" (Keller 2018). Ongoing exploration and development of new strategies and ideas such as these is urgently needed, to overcome the challenges of transience in kingdom movement ministry.

Weak Relational Networks

"The gospel still flies best on the wings of relationship" (Trousdale and Sunshine 2018, 265), because everyone has a personal network of friends, family, coworkers, and others with whom they come in contact on a regular basis. However, migrants resettle in new and unfamiliar environments without relationships and thus, in a sense, the gospel has lost its wings (or at least a few feathers!). Separated from their families and friends, they may begin to form new relationships, but depth and trust usually come very slowly. For example, some contexts such as Sicily have a competitive environment among refugees that tends to restrict community. Refugees often perceive each other as competitors for the same jobs, clients, or even legal documents.

Many have suffered betrayal of some sort, presenting a further challenge. Many immigrants have been lied to about opportunities in Europe and elsewhere, pressured into making a perilous journey, or even sold by their families. Along the journey, they experience all sorts of trauma. Many suffer from Post-traumatic Stress Syndrome (PTSD), which can present emotional and psychological barriers for migrants seeking new relationships in a difficult environment. The transient mentality complicates this further because asylum seekers observe the transience and know that those around them may leave at any given moment.

---

3 Asia also has "migrant-receiving" countries (such as Japan, Singapore, South Korea, and Taiwan), as well as numerous "migrant-sending" countries (such as Bangladesh, Burma, Cambodia, Indonesia, Laos, Nepal, Pakistan, Philippines, and Sri Lanka); however, there is not a "migration highway," per se.

Dylia Sasso, who has worked with refugees in Southern Europe for the past three years, observed that while most migrants become part of some form of community, they do not "trust deeply, and they are people who are willing to leave quickly" (2018). Her team of practitioners began a movement-oriented ministry in Sicily, expecting to see the gospel move through networks of deep relationships among refugees. This was not an unrealistic expectation since, as Garrison and others demonstrate, this is a key feature that enables kingdom movements (Garrison 2004, 209). However, this feature has been demonstrated mainly among movements in the Global South among peoples in their lands of birth, not among migrants in host cultures. In Sicily, for example, it became clear that relational networks are not so much a *resource* for movement practitioners as they are a *need* for most immigrants.

In seeking to catalyze kingdom movements in the Global North, one of the most significant tasks for practitioners might be the facilitation not just of friendships, but of social networks. Social network theory affirms the importance of social relationships in transmitting information and channeling influence, in such a way that change is enabled (Liu et al. 2017). Thus we should not underestimate the role of cultural outsiders as agents of gospel influence and change. They can do this in part by helping individuals connect with others who can encourage them, grow with them, and relate to their stories. As foreigners working hard to adjust to life in a new country, missionaries and movement practitioners can often find common ground on things important to refugees and other immigrants. They can work from that common ground to seek to catalyze kingdom movements in the Global North.

Unmet Needs

Many issues hinder asylum seekers from embracing the vision of giving their life to Christ and consequently making disciples. Just as distinctive needs offer opportunities for movement practitioners, unmet needs offer challenges. Some practitioners have pointed to unmet needs as a major obstacle. A team of practitioners in Sicily, for example, has found that unmet needs in diaspora communities, particularly among asylum seekers or irregular migrants, significantly hindered the momentum of a kingdom movement there. This dynamic often does not exist among people in their homelands—or, if it does, it is not to the same degree—because even in the face of harsh realities they have social networks to rely upon. But asylum seekers do not. They need documents and economic provisions and many other tangible, material things in order to have a sustainable future in their new context. Yet they usually have very little assistance in getting them. Because these things can be challenging to come by, migrants often hesitate to commit to anything that may hinder them from meeting their immediate, physical needs. For example, in Italy it has prevented potentially open non-Christians from participating in Discovery Bible Study groups or similar activities.

Among those baptized, the need for physical provision often results in their taking highly demanding and low-paying jobs. This makes it nearly impossible for them to be highly involved in discipleship relationships or church groups. Josh Ballard, a practitioner in Italy, illustrated this point: "The challenge [is] getting people to grab a hold of the responsibility to carry the message" (Ballard 2018). Ryan Hale, a teammate, similarly asserted: "The number one obstacle is finding people that are willing to be the priesthood of believers and carry the work" (Hale 2018).

During a visit to a kingdom movement implementation in southern Europe, several practitioners observed a ministry that provided employment for leaders who would work full-time in a catalytic role for kingdom movement work in the region. This is one potential solution to the challenge of unmet needs, but it has yielded varying levels of success in other similar contexts where it has been utilized.

Recommendations for Practitioners

In order for movement work and growth throughout diaspora communities in the Global North to realize its full promise and potential, the challenges above—and many others—will need to be overcome. The following recommendations are based on current research (Cocanower and Mordomo 2020). They serve as a starting point for practitioners and scholars to understand proven strategies that will be key to unleashing future sustainable movements among diaspora communities in the Global North. The following recommendations are equally applicable among different religious backgrounds, though our experience has been mostly with Muslim-background migrants and refugees.

Patience Needed For Fostering Spiritual Growth among Individuals from Non-Christian Background

Ministry to individuals in diaspora settings is often paradoxical: It requires patience even when time is of the essence, and nurture even in shallow relationships. Many practitioners working with refugees or migrants affirm patterns of spiritual openness and receptivity, notably among those from predominantly Muslim countries. Yet they recognize that for many Muslims, the journey of changing their spiritual identity to a new faith can be a long and complicated process. While support is essential in this nurturing process, pressure can be extremely harmful. Patience is truly a virtue (or at least a best practice!) in this case.

Pressure in a ministry context can consist of a persistent attempt to convince a person to believe or do something as soon as possible. In the discovery process, pressure can happen at various milestones. A practitioner might pressure someone who seems spiritually open to read the Scriptures. When a group has completed the DBS cycle, the facilitator may feel compelled to pressure them to make a decision for Christ. Once a decision for Christ is made, pressure may arise to "come out" to family, to be baptized, begin evangelizing, etc. Don Little addresses this tension, writing, "It is not the role of the discipler to tell the BMBs [believers from a Muslim background] when to come out. … It is always wrong to pressure a BMB to declare his or her faith to the family" (Little 2015, 199).

The same applies to pressuring someone to submit to the lordship of Christ. Such pressure takes away from genuine, voluntary decisions to move forward in their spiritual journey. The non-Muslim background practitioner should generally assume a posture of invitation and encouragement, even in the highly transient context of the Global North.

Many Muslim Migrants Are Open to Reading the Christian Scriptures

Many diaspora Muslims are open to reading the Bible, particularly the Taurat (Torah), Zabur (Psalms), and Injil (Gospels). This may result from a variety of factors. First, some individuals may be questioning Islam or curious about Christianity. Second, they may not perceive reading the Christian Scriptures as a threat to their faith, but rather as a compatible way to grow in understanding of Allah and how to live a life that honors God. Third, some Muslims want to demonstrate their difference from what the media has portrayed; they are open to relationships with members of other faiths.

We should not underestimate one complicating factor—and opportunity: many have never before had the opportunity to read the Christian Scriptures. This seems much more common than we might imagine, even in the open countries of the Global North. As globalization continues, increasing numbers of Muslims are settling in, or traveling to, the Global North. This potential openness to the Christian Scriptures can assist evangelism and discipleship relationships with a view toward catalyzing new movements.

Muslims and Christians Often Face the Same Challenges in Secular Societies

Dylia Sasso found herself uniquely positioned to connect with an imam's wife on a variety of deeply important issues. The imam's wife had voiced frustration to Sasso in a personal conversation about her perception that Italians assume she is forced to cover her head, and that she is mistreated in her home (Sasso 2018). Moreover, she confessed that she feels looked down upon, and said that Italians assume she is less educated because she is African. Once again, these challenges can and should be intentionally overcome by the cultural outsider desiring to represent Christ to these communities. Being misunderstood, misrepresented, and frowned upon also happens to Christ-followers. Movement practitioners can tap into their pools of empathy and minister to Muslims by exposing pejorative stereotypes and by acting in a way that assumes the best of Muslims, rather than the worst.

A second important consideration is the increasingly secular post-Christian culture that accompanies the cultural shifts common throughout the Global North. Rick Kronk states, "Muslim immigrants are often highly religious and find themselves immediately in conflict with liberal, and now largely secular, cultures of formerly Christian European nations" (Kronk 2010, loc. 474). The secularization of Europe proves challenging for both conservative Muslims and faithful Christians.

A clear example of a life centered around Christ and lived in submission and service to him shines brightly in the context of Europe. Muslims are often drawn to such a life. Sasso insightfully noted: "Despite the fact that I don't share all of her [the imam's wife] beliefs, she saw our belief in God and how that is played out in our life as more important than the differences we have" (Sasso 2018). Practitioners working with Muslims in the Global North should note such opportunities and leverage them for developing genuine relationships and sharing the good news of Jesus Christ with Muslims.

Holistic Mission and Service is Vital in Refuee Ministry

Those working with asylum seekers and refugees often feel overwhelmed: hearing their stories … seeing their pain … observing their struggle to get a foothold in a new place and a new language. Where does a minister of the gospel even start? Each person and organization needs to make that decision for themselves, but many options exist. Some may start with physical needs, others with psychological trauma, while others may focus on evangelism and discipleship. But in the end, addressing only one aspect of their needs will not suffice. Christians working with asylum seekers must find a way to meet the needs of the whole person.

Paradoxically, the needs are often so deep and so complex that we must acknowledge our limitations. We do best to focus on certain areas within the scope of our expertise and seek to invest in networking with others, to guide people toward a holistic solution. The limitations we experience on a personal level point us toward our need for community. We cannot overestimate the importance of working in teams and partnerships and creating ecosystems capable of demonstrating the fully orbed transformational power of the gospel.

Note that the Bible contains promises of hope for fulfillment and peace when we align ourselves with God's guidelines and creative design. Yet some question the Bible's value as a tool for humanitarian aid, particularly in a context where it could cause tension or offense. Because of this, few efforts are being made to build bridges between Muslims and Christians in Europe by way of the Bible. Yet the Global North generally offers liberty to use the Bible as a source of encouragement, hope, peace, and admonition. This also applies to the masses of desperate refugees arriving illegally by sea, who often find themselves caught in a vicious cycle of bureaucracy, corruption, and frustration.

The Bible can be used effectively to produce positive results, though it has the potential for division and harm if used imprudently. A secular study of Iraqi refugees in Australia suggested bridging "the gap between Western mental health services and traditional cultural and religious practices" (Slewa-Younen et al. 2014). This has implications for a wide variety of practitioners and humanitarian workers. It shows that religious practices play a vital role in providing holistic care to vulnerable people as they navigate a complicated transition.

Some migrants may not be looking for spiritual help or an opportunity to build bridges with Western culture, but that shouldn't negate an invitation to those who are. Slewa-Younen et al's research and accounts of practitioners in Europe have led to the same conclusion. The spiritual needs of migrants are the most overlooked and underestimated need in this humanitarian crisis. Because Muslims affirm the Taurat, Zabur, and Injil, the Bible can serve as a powerful tool for facilitating spiritual conversation and religious integration—for Muslims as well as Christians. Discovery studies are a very powerful tool for respectfully engaging refugees' needs—both spiritual and practical.

Jay Moon observes that "While poverty is typically identified as a deficit in the economics/technology sector (e.g., lack of clothing, food, shelter) it can also exist in the … ideology/belief sector … and social relationships sector" (2017, 210–11). He goes on to point out that poverty in one sector can lead to problems in other areas and thus hinder the process of discipleship. We need to recognize and remember that all areas of a person's life play a role in that individual's well-being and capacity for personal growth. Moon's call to holistic discipleship is timely, considering that many refugees struggle in all three sectors he describes. They struggle to survive economically; they lack caring, trusting relationships; and they are navigating uncharted territory in a country with totally different ideologies and beliefs.

Recommendations for Researchers

Scholars interested in researching kingdom movements in diaspora contexts, especially in the Global North, will find a paucity of research published on this topic, and thus a plethora of opportunities. This area deserves significantly more attention as the prevalence of kingdom movements continues to grow. To date, researchers have tended to focus on either kingdom movements or diaspora missions, but not on the convergence of the two. The proportion of movements occurring in the Global North remains surprisingly low, but this provides an opportunity for researchers. Pioneering research could provide vital information and help guide the growth of biblically grounded, impactful movements among individuals from the Global South who are living in the Global North.

Answers to the following questions would prove invaluable to current understanding of movement work in diaspora contexts:

- What movement approaches or ministries have been most effective in providing holistic blessing to refugees? As one example, how might business development serve as a disciple-making tool within diaspora communities (Mordomo 2016)?

- How do transient peoples differ from non-transient peoples psychologically, sociologically, and spiritually? How do these differences impact kingdom-movement approaches?

- What challenges are common for kingdom-movement implementation among a broad array of diaspora communities?

- What insights can be gleaned from critical evaluation of kingdom movements at the different stages of movement maturation in diaspora contexts?[4]

- What have been the long-term results, both positive (numbers of baptisms and churches planted) and negative (attrition rates, etc.) of movements in diaspora contexts? How does this differ from non-diaspora movement results? Qualitative and quantitative approaches are necessary.

Conclusion

Zeidan estimates that "more than two million Muslim refugees in Europe have never heard the good news of the gospel" (2018, 97). Similar staggering numbers apply to Hindus and other unreached peoples. These ring true throughout the Global North, not just in Europe. We can also take into consideration the unreached diaspora communities in major cities throughout Africa and Asia and, to a lesser degree, Central and South America. When we do so, we face the powerful realization that while we can prefer kingdom movements catalyzed in the geographic homelands of unreached peoples, we cannot consider those the only valid option. Nor should they be. We currently have unprecedented gospel opportunities in the contexts of the Global North.

Throughout the Global North, movement practitioners (and their children!) increasingly have—or can create—opportunities to share the gospel with people like Bakary, due to their heightened openness and distinctive needs. Growing evidence shows that many diaspora community members are open to becoming Christ-followers and can help bring spiritual awakening to their host cultures when they do. Movement practitioners must be aware of these opportunities, as well as the challenges of kingdom-movement work among diaspora peoples.

Jesus had very little time with his disciples—only about a year and half (Jones 2020, 6). Yet, during that time he patiently but urgently transformed lives and created a movement lasting until today. Such is the calling of disciple-makers among refugees and all sorts of migrants in the Global North. The harvest is

---

4   This question is particularly important if ministries repeatedly become stuck in the early stages of movement work, unable to gain enough traction to see a movement reach maturity.

plentiful, but the kingdom-movement workers are few. May the Lord of the harvest send his workers to the Global North to make disciples of all unreached diaspora communities in their terra nova.

References

Addison, Steve. 2015. *Pioneering Movements: Leadership That Multiplies Disciples and Churches*. Downers Grove, IL: InterVarsity.

Ballard, Josh. 2018. Interview with author.

Cocanower, Bradley, and João Mordomo. 2020. *Terranova: A Phenomenological Study of Kingdom Movement Work Among Asylum Seekers in the Global North*. Amazon Books.

Downes, Stan. 2015. "Mission by and Beyond the Diaspora: Partnering with Diaspora Believers to Reach Other Immigrants and the Local People. In *Diaspora Missiology*, edited by Michael Pocock and Enoch Wan, 78–88. Pasadena, CA: William Carey Library.

Garrison, David. 2004. *Church Planting Movements: How God Is Redeeming a Lost World*. Bangalore, India: WIGTake Resources.

George, Sam, and Miriam Adeney, eds. 2018. *Refugee Diaspora: Missions amid the Greatest Humanitarian Crisis of Our Times*. Pasadena, CA: William Carey Publishing.

Hale, Ryan. 2018. Interview with author.

Hogg, M. A. 2006. "Social Identity Theory." In *Contemporary Social Psychological Theories*, edited by P. J. Burke, 111–36. Stanford, CA: Stanford University Press.

Jones, Bill. 2020. *The Ministry Multiplication Cycle*. Eugene, OR: Wipf & Stock.

Keller, Paul. 2018. Interview with author.

Kronk, Rick. 2010. *Dreams and Visions: Muslims' Miraculous Journey to Jesus*. San Giovanni Teatino, Italy: Destiny Image Europe.

Little, Don. 2015. *Effective Discipling in Muslim Communities: Scripture, History and Seasoned Practices*. Downers Grove, IL: InterVarsity.

Liu, W., A. Sidhu, A. Beacom, and T. Valente. 2017. "Social Network Theory". In *The International Encyclopedia of Media Effects*. Edited by Patrick Rossler, Cynthia A. Hoffner, and Liesbet van Zoonen. Wiley & Sons. DOI: 10.1002/9781118783764. wbieme0092.

Llenas, Jaume. 2020. Personal conversation with author.

Moon, Jay. 2017. *Intercultural Discipleship: Learning from Global Approaches to Spiritual Formation*. Grand Rapids: Baker Academic.

Mordomo, João. 2016. "Business as Mission (BAM) to, in, and through Diaspora." In *Scattered and Gathered: A Global Compendium of Diaspora Missiology*, edited by Sadiri Joy Tira and Tetsunao Yamamori, 242–55. Oxford: Regnum Books International.

Pocock, Michael, and Enoch Wan, eds. 2015. *Diaspora Missiology: Reflections on Reaching the Scattered Peoples of the World*. Pasadena, CA: William Carey Library.

Prado, José R. M. 2018. "Brazilian Ministries to Middle Eastern Refugees." In *Refugee Diaspora: Missions amid the Greatest Humanitarian Crisis of Our Times*, edited by Sam George and Miriam Adeney, 55–61. Pasadena, CA: William Carey Publishing.

Sasso, Dylia. 2018. Interview with author.

Slewa-Younan, Shameran, Jonathan Mond, Elise Bussion, Yasser Mohammad, Maria Gabriela Uribe Guajardo, Mitchell Smith, Diana Milosevic, Sanja Lujic, and Anthony Francis Jorm. 2014. "Mental Health Literacy of Resettled Iraqi Refugees in Australia: Knowledge about Posttraumatic Stress Disorder and Beliefs about Helpfulness of Interventions." *BMC Psychiatry* 14 (1): 1–8.

Tira, Sadiri J., and T. Yamamori, eds. 2020. *Scattered and Gathered: A Global Compendium of Diaspora Missiology Revised and Updated*. Carlisle, UK: Langham Global Library.

Trousdale, Jerry, and Glenn Sunshine. 2018. *The Kingdom Unleashed*. Murfreesboro, TN: DMM Library.

UNHCR. 2020. United Nations High Commissioner for Refugees website, "Figures at a Glance." https://www.unhcr.org/figures-at-a-glance.html.[5]

Wan, Enoch, ed. 2014. *Diaspora Missiology: Theory, Methodology, and Practice*. Portland, OR: Institute for Diaspora Studies.

Wightman, Martin. 2018. "Standing in Solidarity: Canada's Welcoming Consensus." In *Refugee Diaspora: Missions amid the Greatest Humanitarian Crisis of Our Times*, edited by Sam George and Miriam Adeney, 73–79. Pasadena, CA: William Carey Publishing.

Zeidan, Daniel. 2018. "Ministry to Refugees Arriving in Europe." In *Refugee Diaspora: Missions amid the Greatest Humanitarian Crisis of Our Times*, edited by Sam George and Miriam Adeney, 89–97. Pasadena, CA: William Carey Publishing.

---

5 Note from the editors: This page is updated annually, typically in June.

PART IV
CASE STUDIES

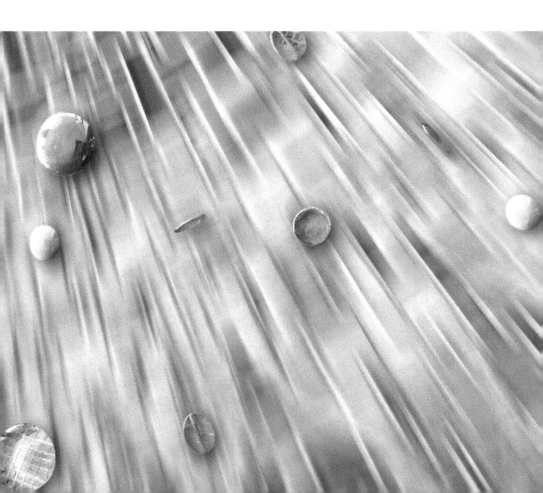

16

The Way of Life: Transference of Spiritual DNA within Movements in East Africa

Aila Tasse and L Michael Corley

Aila traveled into Kenya's savannah, fasting and praying, "Tell me which way to go." He felt God's presence draw near so powerfully that he was afraid to even open his eyes. In a vision, he saw what seemed like a slide show. In the first slide, he saw his hometown imam. Although a former mentor, after Aila became a Christian, the imam was responsible for driving him from his family. When Aila saw his image, he thought: "I hate him." Nevertheless, God challenged Aila to pray for him and bless him.

Next, he saw a slide of his hated brothers and father. Slides of other groups followed. Aila released pent-up bitterness as memories of persecution passed through his mind. He poured out his heart, and "A burden lifted off my chest."

In a second vision, he saw the Chalbi Desert. There had never been gardens there, especially not any cabbages. However, he saw "cabbages not only sprouting, but flourishing." Isaiah 43:18–19 came to mind: "Forget the former things; do not dwell on the past. See, I am doing a new thing…. I am making a way in the wilderness and streams in the wasteland." These visions of a harvest that replicates and flourishes were Aila's burning bush. Yahweh called this former Muslim to reach his people, as well as all his neighboring tribes.

For Aila, the cabbages symbolized a call to reach all people regardless of religion or culture. After reading Francis Omondi's book, *A Call to Share: The Unevangelised Peoples of Kenya*, Aila was shocked to learn that seventeen of Kenya's unreached people groups (UPGs) lived near him (Omondi 1995). He discovered, as John Piper writes, "The ultimate goal of God in all of history is to uphold and display his glory for the enjoyment of the redeemed from every tribe and tongue and people and nation" (1993, 228). Aila's call to disciple all twenty-six of the unreached *ethnē* in his country was confirmed.

The initiative became an interdenominational effort named Lifeway.[1] The name comes from John 10:10b: "I came that they may have life and have it abundantly." If people ask this former Muslim whether he is a Christian, Aila says, "I am a person of the way. If you are a person on the way, you will receive life." This is significant because faithful Muslims pray many times a day, "Show us the straight way (or path)." For Aila, abundant life is about mission, not self-fulfillment. During its first ten years, Lifeway mobilized believers to plant over 2,600 churches.

A Difficult Decision

The vision to see the unreached discover Jesus' abundant life motivated Aila to surrender everything. He was already a successful pastor with a church of one thousand people. And he had successfully mobilized disciples to reach other tribes. Why would he risk losing something successful? He realized traditional methods to multiply churches take too long, cost too much, and bring about minimal cultural transformation. But ultimately, it was because he wanted to obey Jesus.

How could Aila and his team see the spiritual DNA of a true Jesus-follower replicated from one generation to the next? Could DNA spread to all these groups in his lifetime? He struggled to find an answer. He now believes we can see the Great Commission fulfilled in our lifetime if ordinary disciples are coached to transfer the spiritual DNA to the next generation of disciples.

For years, discipleship experts and missiologists have advocated for multiplicative discipleship. But strategies were limited by individualism, superficial spirituality, and the clergy-laity divide. When we analyze transference of movement DNA, we emphasize the difference between replication and multiplication. Something that replicates has the same essence, whereas something that multiplies could produce genetic defects.

Unfortunately, too many churches produce converts with spiritual defects, rather than obedient followers of Jesus. Many of these "converts" never obey Jesus by making new disciples. As a result, they resemble seedless grapes. The fruit is real, but it doesn't reproduce. The potential of reproduction is a key difference as they stay connected to the source.

Lifeway leaders have a passion to mobilize kingdom-minded disciples of Jesus (people of the Way) who make disciples, which results in churches that

1   Dr. Aila Tasse founded Lifeway Mission International twenty-five years ago. Aila trains and coaches DMM leaders in Africa and around the world. He also serves as New Generation's Regional Coordinator for East Africa. Learn more about Lifeway at https://www.Lifewaymi.org/mission-2.

plant churches. They consider this "normal" and expected. Like Jesus' parable of the seed falling on good soil, each individual seed has potential: not just to become another grape, but to become a vineyard. And each vineyard has the potential to become countless generations of new vineyards through replication.

The Fruitful Way

In 2005, Lifeway formed a partnership with New Generations (NG). Together they began launching, strengthening, and multiplying movements. Together the team coined the phrase Disciple Making Movements (DMM) to emphasize the importance of transferring the qualities of a obedient follower of Jesus in a holistic approach to groups of people. The collaboration and relationships with these leaders provides a structure, similar to a trellis, that supports and encourages Lifeway, and other movement-generating vineyards, to maximize their fruitfulness through transference of the Jesus way.

LEGEND	LEVEL I	LEVEL II	LEVEL III	LEVEL IV
MOVEMENT STAGE		100+ churches and 4 generations	100+ churches and 5–6 generations	100+ churches and 7+ generations
TIPPING POINT STAGE	67–99 churches and 1–2 generations	67–99 churches and 3–4 generations	67–99 churches and 5–6 generations	67–99 churches and 7+ generations
MIDWAY TO MOVEMENT STAGE	34–66 churches and 1–2 generations	34–66 churches and 3–4 generations	34–66 churches and 5–6 generations	34–66 churches and 7+ generations
PIONEERING STAGE	1–33 churches and 1–2 generations	1–33 churches and 3–4 generations	1–33 churches and 5–6 generations	1–33 churches and 7+ generations

Table 16.1 Engagement Status

Lifeway faced several barriers to multiplying movements. These included a diversity of cultures and religions, challenging locations, and the gravitational pull of the traditional Western model of ministry. Aila led his team to overcome these barriers because he apprenticed himself to Jesus as a lifelong learner of the Way. By midway through 2020, the partners had mobilized others to engage 113 people groups (including urban and affinity groups) in ten East African countries.

To date, thirty-six of those engagements have reached "movement" status (a hundred churches and four generations of multiplication). Another seven are at the "tipping point" (see table 16.1–How we identify the progress of an engagement on its way to becoming a movement. Stages represent the number of churches; levels represent the number of generations). They need a few more churches or another generation to reach movement status.

Eleven engagements are "midway to movement," with over thirty-four churches. Forty-five engagements are in the "pioneering stage," with fewer than thirty-four churches. The engagement-status grid empowers leaders to evaluate and plot each engagement on the grid so their team can then identify needs and goals for prayer, training, resources, etc. in order to see each engagement reach movement. This is a central tool in our 3D evaluation, visualizing all three markers in one location: qualitative, quantitative, and sustainability.

In fifteen short years, seventeen of the thirty-six East Africa region's DMMs are in Kenya. Their team has seen 12,555 churches planted and 271,695 disciples reached in the region of East Africa. In many of New Generations' ten regions, like in East Africa, we see Unengaged Unreached People Groups (UUPG) engaged for the first time.

A Way for All People Groups

Scholars note certain social factors usually present when most movements happen. These include insulation from outsiders, a climate of uncertainty in society, and worship in the heart language (Garrison 2004, 221–22). However, according to Aila's experience, thirty-six people groups in East Africa have reached movement status, regardless of diverse social factors. The new Christ-followers in these movements come from diverse cultures, religious backgrounds, and socio-economic situations, and not all have access to Scripture in their heart language. The point is not that the barriers to the gospel traveling freely are inconsequential, but that they have found compelling lifestyles (strategies) which overcome such barriers more readily. Disciples are being replicated and churches are being formed, with similar DNA, in all these previously unreached groups in East Africa. This is happening simultaneously, not sequentially, and not because of expertise in contextualization.

Lifeway avoided the conflicts some other organizations faced about contextualization, in part by not emphasizing it. David Watson, one of Aila's mentors, recommends that disciple-makers "deculturalize, not contextualize, the gospel" (2014, 9). He elaborates, "The best way to do this is to use only Scripture for curricula, and allow local people to answer questions about Scripture, not listen to our answers" (2014, 15).

Aila's team points people to the authority of Scripture. This empowers each new group to listen to God's Word to discover what God is saying to them directly. "Contextualization, then, should be done by those coming to faith within a culture, as they ask themselves and one another, 'What must we change in our lives and culture in order to be obedient to all the commands of Christ?'" (2014, 17). This has resulted in activating the priesthood of believers.

Jerry Trousdale also introduced a proximate strategy in which indigenous disciples, close in geography, culture, and/or language focus on reaching hard-to-reach UPGs. "Outsiders can suggest relevant passages for study and provide outside mentoring for the group facilitator. But the onus of application is on the cultural insiders" (Waterman 2017). Existing leaders think about relevant cultures and how they can raise up leaders inside the new group to reach movement status.

Another barrier for movements exists in societies heavily influenced by Christianity. Some leaders were discouraged from focusing on training denominations or church associations because they would struggle to understand and adopt DMM, as well as to resist the gravitational pull of tradition (Tasse 2017, 17). Nonetheless, some, including Aila, did train them. As a result, over five-hundred partnering organizations and denominations work together in Sub-Saharan Africa with New Generations. Many of the over twelve thousand churches were started in Kenya, one of the most Christianized countries in Africa. Lifeway has seen all twenty-six of Kenya's unreached groups engaged, as well as some of the country's least-reached groups. Aila's team has made a commitment to see them experience a movement through mentoring, training, and loving them enough to allow them to hear directly from God about seeing transformation in their context.

Transference of the Spiritual DNA of Movements

The most significant barrier to overcome has been centuries of an individualistic and informational-based Western approach to discipleship. This limits effective replication. Movement thinking has captured the attention of practitioners worldwide. After twenty-five years, it should no longer be labeled a fad or a "new" way of thinking. In fact, some trainers love to describe it as an ancient and biblical way to approach discipleship.

DMM proponents advocate returning to the way Jesus did ministry rather than imitating just the apostles, as seen through Western lenses. "What Jesus did … his disciples still do" (Trousdale 2018, 161). We contend that we should imitate Jesus' pattern of ministry. The New Testament describes a rapid expansion into multiple contexts simultaneously. The world was "turned upside down" as his disciples replicated the kingdom DNA (Acts 17:6). This explosive growth in many directions was messy, far from perfect, but was nurtured to maturity through personal coaching and the Epistles.

Evaluation of Movements

As a good shepherd counts his flock entering the fold, he also inspects each for injury or sickness. Good shepherds understand the importance of both quantitative and qualitative indicators. Our leaders prioritize improving the evaluation of the spiritual DNA of movements. This includes three facets of evaluation: quantitative, qualitative, and sustainability indicators.

The quantitative factors for a discipleship movement can help evaluate impact. A key metric is the number of new churches started. The threshold to determine a movement is a hundred churches. This one data point represents quarterly reports with fourteen quantitative data points over fifteen years. The quantitative data empowers leaders of an engagement *close* to becoming a movement, so they can adjust through coaching, training, and allocation of resources. The shift in what we measure fosters movement. Rather than measuring how many come to an event, or how much is given to a church, the focus shifts to how many live on mission to pray, serve compassionately, and intentionally disciple the lost. New Generations defines a movement as at least a hundred new churches with at least four generations of replication. Identifying something as a movement implies the gospel has gone viral.

Movement metrics are simple guides to determine if a chain reaction of disciples making disciples has resulted in a cascade of churches planting churches. These indicate the priesthood of believers has been activated to make disciples who make disciples. By the grace of God, 128 of the 651 New Generations global engagements have reached movement status.

Qualitative factors are also crucial in evaluating movements. Without them, it is impossible to know if the work has a genetic defect. A key element to assess the health of replication is the number of generations from the base unit (usually either churches or disciples). Our threshold metric is four generations. This can indicate the DNA is healthy and replicating. But that number represents other dynamics that can indicate a need for shepherding intervention.

In 2 Timothy 2:2, we see a vision of at least four generations of multiplication. Paul challenged Timothy to empower "reliable leaders" and entrust them with the good news so they in turn would train others. Rather than an individual like Timothy reaching another individual, who would then reach another individual, the context indicates Timothy's team was charged as a group to empower groups of leaders—to reach, develop, and deploy others. A Western approach generally focuses on reaching individuals, and occasionally reaches groups (such as families). Movement-oriented practice generally focuses on reaching whole families, tribes, and people groups, and sometimes reaches individuals.

This leads us to the third category evaluation: measuring a group's ability to continue replicating without external assistance. The sustainability (or durability) threshold we use is seven generations of multiplication. When a movement exceeds seven generations of replication, we encourage teams like Lifeway to take steps back from the levels of engagement financially and allocation of time to partnering with an organization or denomination. This is because the partner has seen enough generations of replication to continue with reduced outside assistance. The role changes from hands-on coaching to mentoring and coaching from a distance.

Additional factors help make these decisions: leadership development, worship in the heart language, and local funding of training and compassion ministries. The 24:14 Coalition use "streams" as another metric to measure health (Long 2020). Streams also indicate the viral nature of a movement, especially if it jumps to a new location with the same people group or skips to a different group while continuing to bear fruit. A stream is a generational chain of churches, sufficiently unique in affinity or location to warrant separate strategy, nurturing, and tracking toward movement (Brown 2020).

We continue to pursue what we call a three-dimensional (3D) approach to evaluation by measuring: 1) magnitude; 2) depth; and 3) sustainability. We believe employing 3D evaluation sets the stage for the central issue of transference. The heart of transference consists of leaders understanding what must always be present in disciples to ensure faithful transference. The numbers and categories used for evaluation are not of primary importance. Most critical are skilled workers who listen to what the Lord says about how to shepherd the flock in obeying all of Jesus' commands.

We further believe these evaluative factors are best included in training. When ordinary disciples live it out because they were trained for it, coached into it, and evaluated upon it, the process empowers leaders to course-correct the movement accordingly.

Transference creates a new generation and ensures it has the same level of quality. As the DNA is passed on, it needs to be nurtured. If a vineyard has good DNA, it still needs to be pruned and cultivated to produce fruit that can reproduce. We have all seen the negative results of the "Telephone Game"—where a message is corrupted during transmission from one person to the next. Similarly, we all know how a copy of a copy of a copy results in eroding quality. This problem occurs when people do not go back each time to the original source: God and his Word. It occurs if a middle-man prevents disciples from owning the process of hearing from God directly, obeying him, and sharing with others. The challenge is to confirm that what is being transmitted is faithful to the biblical model.

Research Methodology

While local leaders continue to measure the magnitude, depth, and sustainability of movements, it was decided to conduct what we call an Internal Qualitative Assessment (IQA) to research (and ultimately improve) the quality of transference. The IQA was designed to be indigenously led, highly relational, and useful for direct application of shepherding decisions.

A grounded theory approach was chosen to discover the core features of spiritual DNA in movements. Grounded theory emphasizes what is studied over the methods (Charmaz 2001). Everything becomes data, including the impressions and thoughts of the interviewer, as recorded in their memos.

With this approach, one seeks to come without preconceived notions to discern what can be discovered from interviewing ordinary people.

Researchers sought answers to these three questions:

- What are the attributes of spiritual DNA that mark a DMM in individuals, churches, leaders, and movements?

- How is spiritual DNA effectively transferred from one generation to the next?

- Which external and internal factors help or hinder the transference of DNA in a DMM? [2]

Out of seventeen Kenyan movements, the IQA pilot was conducted among two of them. The first was "People Group A," in the northwest along the borders of Uganda and Ethiopia. People in Group A are Nilotic pastoralists, known as fierce warriors, and related to people in Uganda. Their population is estimated at over one million. The majority followed ethnic religions but also had 5 percent mainline Christians. Lifeway's work among Group A started in the fourth quarter of 2010. At the end of the first quarter of 2020, 404 churches had been planted to the seventh generation. These churches include 24,038 Christ-followers.

"Group B" is a Muslim people group (97 percent Muslim when engaged). Also living in northern Kenya and connected with an extensive cluster people group in southern Ethiopia, their population (in Kenya) is well over one hundred thousand. Lifeway partners first engaged them in 2010's third quarter. By the end of 2020's first quarter, 503 churches had been planted to the eighth generation, involving 15,090 Christ-followers.

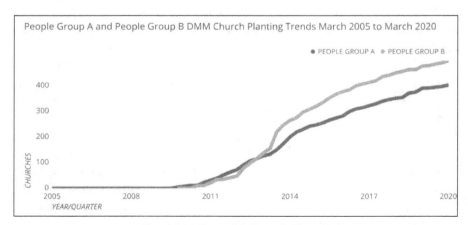

Figure 16.1 Group A & Group B Charted

<hr>

2 To answer these questions, we used semi-structured interviews using the following seven open-ended questions: 1) Please tell us what your life was like before you became a part of this group. 2) Please tell us about your experience of how you decided to follow Jesus. 3) Please tell us what it means to you to be a follower of Jesus. And please tell us what it means for you to influence others to follow Jesus. 4) Please describe your group and what it means to you to be a part of it? 5) As a follower of Jesus, what gives you direction and guidance in life? 6) Please tell us about the roles of leaders in your group and how they serve your group. 7) How does someone become a leader?

In each of the two movements, five churches were evaluated, beginning with six individual interviews. Additionally, a focus group of six to eight people from that church was interviewed to discuss their gatherings' DNA. Finally, a gathering of each of the churches was researched through participant observation. Thus, each pilot included seventy interviews (sixty individuals plus ten focus groups) and ten observations of gatherings.[3]

In the future, our "Global Analytics Team" will code the entirety of the interviews from the multiple movements in the region of East Africa. This information will be included with interviews from the other two regions to complete an organizational evaluation of six movements. This will help inform our grounded theory of the transference of spiritual DNA in movements.

While our analysis of the six movements is ongoing, we present the findings from the first two movements. Some of these initial findings (from new disciples in two very different types of movements) show uniqueness in disciples' perception of Jesus, themselves, and the mission Jesus gave us. These observations from the focus groups of the ten churches give us insight into the transference of the DNA of movements. The result is a communal approach to their spiritual journey on "The Way."

Initial Observations from the Internal Qualitative Assessment

As we studied how the new believers in these two movements described themselves, we discovered some unique ways they conceptualize transference of movement DNA. We also discovered some ways movement leaders can strengthen their shepherding roles.

The Way Is a Person

While Christians around the world believe Jesus is the "life," these churches in Kenya more often spoke of Jesus as "the Way." A common refrain observed from the research was, "Jesus is the way and the source of eternal life" (Galgalo 2020, Church A4). The verse most often quoted by the interviewees was John 14:6: "I am the Way, the Truth, and the Life." They worship Jesus as Savior and Lord since there is "no other way." This commonality is notable when ordinary people from diverse backgrounds—men, women, children, Muslims, animists, literate, and illiterate—connect with Jesus.

As we evaluated the DNA of disciples in fourth-, fifth-, and sixth-generation churches, another finding emerged: the primacy of thinking and speaking of God in their daily lives. More than any other, God was their most important topic of conversation. More meaningful than the frequency of their mentioning him

---

3 This resulted in 180 individual and thirty focus group interviews. Each session was recorded, transcribed, translated, and coded for analysis in the field. Leadership in each region is analyzing their data to course-correct.

is their confidence in him. "God is great. He is love, Savior, and I followed him" (Shedo 2020, Church B1). Believers in each church spoke of God's love. It was his love prompting them "to believe and get baptized." One Muslim background believer said, "I understand good things from him: the example of Jesus Christ, the love of Jesus Christ and the mercy he has for us" (Shedo 2020, Church B3). "Jesus Christ showed love to our community because God, who called us, is a loving God" (Galgalo 2020, Church A5). This is not an abstract list of facts, but illustrates that "the gospel is to declare something about a Person, about God in his revelation in Jesus Christ and about what God has done for us in Jesus Christ" (McKnight 2011, 93).

The Way Is a Lifestyle

Following Jesus on the Way is not a decision about doctrinal preference but a lifestyle of discovery and discipling others. For both movements, "Following Jesus means doing good deeds." Their sacrificial love and good deeds impact people and are essential elements in DNA transference. As Kierkegaard famously noted, "Christ did not appoint professors, but followers. If Christianity … is not reduplicated in the life of the person … then he does not expound Christianity, for Christianity is a message about living and can only be expounded by being realized in men's lives" (quoted in Rhode 1988, 117). These churches do not have official programs of evangelism or benevolence, but a lifestyle of loving God and people.

The gospel is good news. Interviewees equate accepting Jesus with following his ways, which fills them with joy and inspiration. "The righteous way is full of joy" (Shedo 2020, Church B3). Evangelicals typically call the Christian method of transference "evangelism" (Warren, 1995; Schwartz 1996; IMB 2016). However, those involved in DMM are taught to live their faith out loud, while being compassionate servants and praying for healing. As they intercede for a breakthrough, God leads them to a person of peace being drawn to God (John 6:44). This path bears fruit when disciples surrender everything to follow Jesus, while introducing others to him.

The Way Is a Communal Journey

An unexpected discovery of our initial research is that following Jesus as the Way is a communal journey of learning from one another while simultaneously sharing with others. Both movements focused on their shared experience of loving God in focusing on a relationship with Jesus, not just information about him. As a result, they emphasize staying connected with the Way while joyfully inviting others to join them.

A strength of DMM is inviting people on a journey by asking the *Golden Question*: "Would you like to gather with your family and friends to study God's Word?" They start discovery studies within their social networks. These believers understand their approach is unique and not traditional, like other churches:

"We don't have other groups, like the rest, but we come together because of DBS, so to discover together and do fellowship together from house to house" (Shedo 2020, Church B3).

As people explore faith in Jesus, their concept of the Way overlaps with using the term "disciple." That collective journey consists of an individual arriving at a destination and apprenticing themselves to the Master. This contrasts with an approach seemingly common in the West: "When we peel back the layers, we find that many Christians are using the way of Jesus to pursue the way of self … a majority of churchgoing Christians have embraced corrupt, me-centered theology" (Barna 2016). And even when focused on Jesus, most Americans consider discipleship a private matter (Barna 2015). In contrast, both discipleship movements focused on loving God by making disciples. These Kenyans view the Spirit's power as given primarily for reaching the lost together as a group (Galgalo 2020, Church A1).

The Way Brings Transformation and Crosses Barriers

Another theme discovered from the research is the way the gospel's transformative nature overcomes barriers. Jesus said our identifying mark is our love for others (John 13:35). These followers do not show compassion merely to win a convert. Their kindness demonstrates Jesus' love without conditions—what Aila refers to as "practical love." One woman intentionally moved to a different village, using her business skills as a hair stylist, in order to start discovery groups. She lowered her prices in order to serve the poor. Such actions enable people to "see the gospel" (Galgalo 2020, Church A3). Ordinary disciples help others discover Jesus' way through love, especially when those people are not like them culturally. People take notice when a person of peace no longer beats his wife, or when tribal tensions end with one group serving the other. Changes like these make people curious to know why.

All the churches in pilot number 1 also shared a miracle, even though the questions did not mention miracles. A broad category was the demonized set free (Shedo 2020, Church B1 and B4). They depended on Jesus' authority over demons. One testified, "We used to trust witchdoctors, then … told us to leave witchdoctors and come to Christ because … he will wash us with his blood." Another shared, "Before I knew Jesus, it's like I was in darkness, for I used to worship whatever … , including stones and trees, but since I believed in Jesus as my Savior, I … [have learned] that God can do even more than witches" (Shedo 2020, Church B2).

Another factor was healings. In one church, a deaf girl's hearing was restored (Shedo 2020, Church B2). In another, a blind woman could see after the church prayed for her (Shedo 2020, Church B1). God moved in each community in miraculous ways. They often looked back at the healing as a *kairos* moment for their people. The DNA of DMM transfers powerfully within a social network when miracles happen and confirm that the message is not of human origin. Miracles flowing from a lifestyle of caring have unique confirming power.

However, the greatest miracle seems to be the empowerment of ordinary disciples. Rejecting the tradition that only clergy can teach, all disciples are challenged to launch a Discovery Bible Study (DBS). Working within social networks enables the gospel to transfer readily. "The Bridges of God ... was the summons for missionaries to utilize the 'bridges' of family and kinship within each people group prompting 'people movements'" (McGavran 1981, 137). This unleashing of God's people brings the great miracle of a life-giving Way in the desert. The result is disciples from all walks of life embracing Jesus.

The Way Involves Groups Discovering and Obeying Together

Another finding in our research is the importance of group discovery and group obedience. The church reflects God's kingdom through a gathering of believers. "The Kingdom is about restoring the rightful reign of the King" (Trousdale 2018, 11). When groups study the Word together and manifest the reign of King Jesus, this transforms their community more powerfully than individualistic methods of evangelism.

"Learning" in these movements focuses more on discovery—which allows people to find the truth by answering questions as they directly interact with God's Word. Jesus regularly asked questions. In fact, the Gospels portray him asking far more questions than he was asked (Copenhaver 2014, xviii). Jesus also spoke to crowds in parables, where those who were curious had to think about the spiritual parallels. Jesus' teaching was also more interactive than modern approaches. Like Jesus, the discovery group facilitators reply to questions with questions and encourage participants to retell the stories of Scripture in their own words. As a result, people focus on the text and what they learn about God directly from his Word.

In this way, the Kenyan churches "disciple people toward belief." They allow people to interact and discover together how God revealed himself over time to his people. As followers are empowered to interact directly with God's Word,[4] a disciple-making revolution begins.

God desires all people to worship, love, and obey him. We work with him toward that end by launching disciple-making movements. The real game-changers are not those who merely believe in Jesus, but those who obey him. The way we will accomplish the Great Commission is through ordinary disciples being equipped and empowered to hear from God directly and obey him to make

---

4   Often the unreached, and especially many of the unengaged, are illiterate; so even if the Bible is translated into their language, they can't read it. But thanks to audio Bibles, more ordinary disciples can gain access to God's Word and interact by listening to it and then answering questions about how God is speaking to them.

disciples who plant churches. These believers depart their gatherings with a lifestyle of helping others obey Jesus, leading to community transformation.

> *DMM leaders worldwide train followers that God is the one who teaches everyone (John 6:43–45). If the ultimate authority is the word and not the opinion of a pastor or facilitator, then believers can hold one another accountable to God's way. During the Reformation, we got the priesthood of the believer half right…. The half we got right is that we do not need a priest to talk to God. The half we are still working on is that we also do not need a priest for God to speak to us. (Forlines 2017)*

When disciples hear from God and then live it out, they set an example for others to follow.

These disciples understand the adage that "Most truth is caught, not taught." "If we show unity in our work and show love, they will learn good things from us and get transformation" (Shedo 2020, Church B3). Even their fellowship and unity have a missional focus. They shared that they often ask the question, "How can we obey this together?" When you have a community of people loving a family far from God, people respond. These group dynamics increase ownership, long-term memory, and a more profound impact among those they serve. When people imitate Jesus' life, pass it on in their relationships, and do life-on-life as a group—people are affected deeply.

Conclusion

In December of 2019, Aila and team members went into the mountains to host a DMM training with the final unreached people group from his country. While they were there, violence spilled over from a neighboring country to where they were meeting. One of Aila's Lifeway friends and a co-trainer died in the cross fire.

Achieving the vision of cabbages growing in the desert has come at a significant price. But Jesus' love compels disciples to discover his joy while walking this path of reconciliation. It may be narrow, and it may lead through the shadow of the valley of death, but it is the Way of Jesus—life to life.

By equipping shepherds to evaluate, we create a pattern describing a movement's common essence, while allowing for custom expression. Leaders of movements can then guard the pattern and empower the pattern's transfer by teaching the next generation. Failure to safeguard and inspire proper transference of the DNA results in either a compromise of the gospel or a decline of the mission. Holding these in tension is a crucial factor to generational fruitfulness. As Harry Brown, president of New Generations, often says, "Our legacy is not what we can accomplish ourselves, but what the generations of disciples will believe and do when we are long gone."

References

Barna Group. May 25, 2016. "The End of Absolutes: America's New Moral Code." www.barna.com/research/the-end-of-absolutes-americas-new-moral-code/.

Barna Group. December 11, 2019. "What Do Young Adults Really Mean When They Say They Are Christians?" www.barna.com/research/resilient-discipleship/.

Barna Group. December 1, 2015. "New Research on the State of Discipleship." https://www.barna.com/research/new-research-on-the-state-of-discipleship/.

Charmaz, Kathy. 2001. "Grounded Theory: Methodology and Theory Construction." *International Encyclopedia of the Social & Behavioral Sciences.*

Copenhaver, Martin B. 2014. *Jesus Is the Question: The 307 Questions Jesus Asked and the 3 He Answered.* Nashville: United Methodist Publishing House.

Forlines, James. 2017. "When Disciple Making Movements Are Misunderstood." *Mission Frontiers* (November–December). www.missionfrontiers.org/issue/article/when-disciple-making-movements-are-misunderstood.

Galgalo, Joshua. 2020. January. Focus group interviews, Group A, Lifeway [Digital recording]. NG IQA project.

Garrison, David, 1999. *Church Planting Movements* (booklet). Richmond: International Mission Board.

———. 2004. *Church Planting Movements.* Arkadelphia, AR: WIGTake Resources.

———. 2014a. *A Wind in the House of Islam: How God Is Drawing Muslims around the World to Faith in Jesus Christ.* WIGTake Resources.

IMB, Editorial Staff. August 31, 2016. "Twelve Characteristics of a Healthy Church." www.imb.org/2016/08/31/2016083112-characteristics-healthy-church/.

Long, Justin. 2020. "How Movements Count." *Mission Frontiers* (May–June). www.missionfrontiers.org/issue/article/how-movements-count1.

McGavran, Donald A. 1981. *The Bridges of God.*

McKnight, Scot. 2011. *The King Jesus Gospel: The Original Good News Revisited.* Grand Rapids: Zondervan.

Omondi, Francis. 1995. *A Call to Share: The Unevangelised Peoples of Kenya.* Nairobi: Daystar University.

Piper, John, 1993. *Let the Nations Be Glad! The Supremacy of God in Missions.* Grand Rapids: Baker.

Rohde, Peter P., ed. 1960, 1988. *The Diary of Soren Kierkegaard.* New York: Kensington Publishing Corp.

Shedo, Ado. 2020. January. Focus group interviews, Group B, Lifeway [Digital recording]. NG IQA project.

Smith, Steve, and Stan Parks. 2015. "T4T or DMM (DBS)? Only God Can Start a Church Planting Movement!" *Mission Frontiers* (May–June). www.missionfrontiers.org/issue/article/t4t-or-dmm-dbs- only-god-can-start-a-church-planting-movement-part-1-of-2.

Tasse, Aila, 2017. "Disciple Making Movements in East Africa." *Mission Frontiers* (November–December), 12–15. www.missionfrontiers.org/pdfs/12_Tasse_39.6_1112-2017-3.pdf.

Trousdale, Jerry, and Glenn Sunshine. 2018. *The Kingdom Unleashed: How Jesus' 1st-Century Kingdom Values Are Transforming Thousands of Cultures and Awakening His Church*. Murfreesboro, TN: DMM Library.

Warren, Rick. 1995. *The Purpose-Driven Church*. Grand Rapids: Zondervan.

Waterman, L. D. 2017. "Different Pools, Different Fish: The Mistake of 'One Size Fits All' Solutions to the Challenge of Effective Outreach Among Muslims." Fuller Seminary. *Global Reflections* website. https://sparks.fuller.edu/global-reflections/2017/01/18/different-pools-different-fish-the-mistake-of-one-size-fits-all-solutions-to-the-challenge-of-effective-outreach-among-muslims/

Watson, David, and Paul Watson. 2014. *Contagious Disciple Making: Leading Others on a Journey of Discovery*. Nashville: Thomas Nelson.

Winter, Ralph D., and Steven C. Hawthorne. 1981. *Perspectives on the World Christian Movement: A Reader*. Pasadena, CA: William Carey Library.

Bhojpuri Case Study

Victor John, with Dave Coles _____

A book-length description of the Bhojpuri Church Planting Movement (CPM) can be found in *Bhojpuri Breakthrough* (John and Coles 2019), and all the following references refer to this book. In this chapter, we will highlight just two aspects of the movement:

> *What in the Bhojpuri context was unique and how did the movement deal with it?*
> *What leadership features of the movement are counter-cultural?*

What in the Bhojpuri Context Was Unique and How Did the Movement Deal With It?

A number of factors distinguish the Bhojpuri movement from many others among the 1,369 CPMs listed (at the time of this writing) by the 24:14 Coalition.[1] Some of these factors also appear in other movements. But many of them are not found in most current movements. Thus, the confluence of these factors contributes to the Bhojpuri movement's uniqueness.

The movement began in the 1990s before the term CPM was common— before any definition of the term or description of such movements had been published. Some key ideas for how to begin came out of a strategy-coordinator training in 1994. "The idea behind the Bhojpuri vision was to eliminate the territorialism of the old-fashioned approach to evangelism and church planting. … We didn't start with a blueprint for how the ministry would unfold; everything has been evolving through the years" (11, 12).

---

1 See "Global Movement Overview and the 24:14 Vision" on the page www.2414now.net/get-involved/movement-catalysts/our-task/.

The movement has flourished in an area that had been known as the graveyard of missions. "In the past, this region was very, very hostile to the gospel, which was viewed as foreign. It was known as 'the graveyard of missions.' When the foreignness was removed, people started accepting the good news" (3).

> *I had heard about the missionaries who had previously served in the Bhojpuri area—the stories of their hard work and their failures and successes. I thought: "If all this work can produce such small results, what's the answer? What's hindering the missionaries from seeing a plentiful harvest?" Obviously all the significant resources, high levels of training and well-developed partnerships weren't reaching the goal. This made me wonder about my own attempts: "Am I asking the right questions? Or am I actually causing offense to the non-Christians around me?" (6)*

Out of this wrestling came a fresh approach to gospel work among the Bhojpuri.

The movement began and has continued as a movement in an area where some legacy churches already existed.[2] As more movements have begun in decades since the 1990s, we have observed that movements often flourish best in contexts where Christianity has previously been little known.

It seems that in areas having a significant number of legacy churches, emerging movements have difficulty sustaining movement dynamics and multiplying to four or more generations. New believers may feel (or be told by members of existing churches), "To be a *real* Christian, you should worship every Sunday in a church building, as part of a larger congregation, led by a pastor ordained in a recognized denomination." When the standard for Christian life becomes weekly attendance (mostly passive) at a church building more than active daily obedience to Jesus' commands, spiritual passion tends to dissipate and rapid multiplication disintegrates into occasional addition. Kingdom breakthrough fades toward traditional maintenance.

In the Bhojpuri area, legacy churches primarily consisted of and were led by people from the lower rungs of the social order. In the caste-driven society of India, this meant lower-caste people. As a result, many church leaders had no background, encouragement, or model for effective leadership. Many of the missionaries only reached people with little influence in their communities—not decision-makers. These people became nice Christians, but they didn't have leadership qualities; nothing in their life or their caste background had given them the confidence to exercise leadership.

---

2 "Legacy churches" have already existed for a significant length of time. They are usually characterized by ownership of a designated church building, leadership by an ordained person, a significant element of biological and/or transfer growth in its membership, and patterns of worship and ministry following norms common in long-established Western churches. In some CPM literature, these have been described as "elephant churches," compared (mostly unfavorably) with "rabbit churches." For example, in Dale, Dale, and Barna, 2009.

On the positive side, missionaries brought the good news and brought hope for the lowest people in society, and they tried to sow the good news in abundance. They established a Christian identity, but one marred by foreign dependence and lack of indigenous leadership. Indians who became Christians remained very dependent on foreign personnel and resources. Their mindset prevented them from functioning without outside assistance... . Indian Christians thought only Western missionaries could evangelize or lead a church. (4–5)

In Northern India, the few Christians were especially weak and dependent: a tiny minority in a vast sea of Hindus and Muslims. The mindset was "us vs. them." "Us" meant a small minority lacking resources and adequate leadership. Hence they focused entirely on surviving as Christians rather than going out to share with others. Suspicion reigned toward non-Christians who came to the churches. Their deep suspicion overrode any motivation for outreach.

The church in India was also very westernized in language, culture, and style of worship. They didn't connect with the vast majority of the people around them. Instead of using the local Hindi word for God they used the English word for God. This kind of Christianity, the only Christian message available up through the early 1990s, offered no real hope for reaching the Bhojpuri or other groups in Northern India. (5–6)

All these factors contributed to a context in which legacy churches did not effectively reach the majority. However, in many cases, we have been able to help and encourage pastors of these churches. At the beginning of our vision-casting process, we invited all nearby pastors and church leaders to the first Bhojpuri Consultation, held in Varanasi in 1994. Since then,

Over the past twenty plus years, countless ... pastors have experienced a ... shift: from frustration to fruitfulness. Many formerly frustrated and depressed leaders now have abundant ministries reaching the lost. The movement includes some pastors previously confined to one location with just a few believers in a small church. Through a simple change of approach and some mentoring, they have grown amazingly and now minister in two or three different districts, mentoring many other leaders. (157)

"We mentor not only field people but also traditional pastors. The Lord has allowed us to influence them toward simpler, more reproducible church patterns" (172). We have found, time and again, that our holistic approach has greatly helped pastors who had previously experienced persecution and protests when using a direct, evangelistic approach.

The movement has primarily reached Hindus, yet has not been confined to primarily one caste or another. "In India's social context as a whole, caste still plays an important role. It underlies social tensions and feeds Hindu fundamentalism" (22). Yet, "Among the Bhojpuri, God is now moving among every caste, even with lower-caste people reaching upper-caste people. Believers from different castes may not socialize a lot with each other, but they have worship meetings together and pray together" (25).

The Bhojpuri movement has made a great difference in this caste-driven context. The population of the Bhojpuri area consists of 20 percent high-caste people and 80 percent low-caste or outcast Dalits and *adivasi*. The good news has tended to more quickly enter the low-caste 80 percent of the population, so the church reflects that social reality. This means we have had to address real issues related to caste (23).

> We focus on reaching persons based upon their language, geography, and economic status, rather than caste, because that helps the good news to take root throughout the region, and spread. Caste divides groups but language unites people, so we have intentionally chosen not to focus on caste. (24)

The movement employs a very adaptable access structure, called Community Learning Centers (CLCs), to provide credibility for workers entering new areas. God has called us to pioneer planting fellowships among whole communities. CLCs have opened countless doors for accomplishing this goal. A CLC enables leaders to focus on lost people and effectively connect with them. Through the CLC, we reach out and "incarnate" Christ's love to people who would otherwise never hear the good news or see it lived out in their context.

Our first CLCs opened in 2008, and these have changed the playing field for leadership development. We train local leaders: (1) to act as change agents; (2) to use the CLC programs to do good to all people (Gal 6:10); and (3) to locate the "person of peace" (Luke 10:5; Matt 10:11) within their local communities. By meeting needs in the community and solving local problems, CLC leaders build strong relationships in the community, always with the objective of advancing God's kingdom.

> CLCs embody a holistic approach to serving. Each CLC aims to provide access to the community, discover the person of peace, provide resources, implement locally relevant holistic service, and meet the needs of people where they live. When needs are being met, the good news of the Kingdom finds fertile soil, and CLC leaders can begin the process of disciple making and multiplication. Using the CLC approach, the good news has been planted in places that were previously barren ground. (33)

For example, during the COVID-19 pandemic of 2020, numerous CLC leaders were able to leverage goodwill gained through their CLC to aid people in need. Even during lockdown, they worked with police and government officials to distribute food, masks, and hygiene kits. Many conducted awareness programs and increased awareness with a variety of creative methods. In some cases, this opened doors to new contacts. Some also assisted needy people in opening a bank account, so they could receive benefits from the government's relief program. In a challenging social-political context during an especially difficult time, all these activities brought significant goodwill within communities and appreciation of the ministry by Jesus' followers.

The movement has experienced many miraculous healings, including some people being raised from the dead. Many movements have been blessed to experience miraculous healings and deliverances, but not many have seen people raised from the dead. Yet miraculous signs have never been a focal point in the movement. "Signs and wonders also play a significant role in this movement, yet they function as simply part of the fabric of God's great work" (xvi). "In our context, signs and wonders always follow wherever the gospel is preached. Miracles happen quite commonly in the movement, but we don't focus on those. We focus on obeying God and doing what he commands, to show his glory on earth" (198).

The movement makes wide use of Discovery Bible Studies (DBS) for the nurture and spiritual growth of believers. However, **DBS is not used with unbelievers.** This is unique in that the most commonly mentioned use of DBS in other movements has been with *unbelievers*, continuing after they come to faith (Coles and Parks 2019, 315). In the Bhojpuri movement, finding a person of peace in each location plays an important role (as mentioned above with CLCs and below in urban work), but that person does not normally start a DBS among unbelievers. They open the door to relationships with their family, friends, and/or community, through which the gospel is shared and manifested.

The movement began in rural areas, then has also successfully spread to urban areas. The majority of CPMs in the world today have spread primarily in rural areas. India has a huge unreached population in both rural and urban areas. "As God blessed the movement among the Bhojpuri and we shared with others about that work, some people gave us this challenge: 'All your ideas work in the village but they won't work in the city'" (103–4).

Urban work differs from rural work in many ways. Rural work is community based, with more socially homogeneous groups, so in one way it's much easier. Urban work tends to be fragmented and disconnected. Most people aren't local; they have arrived from villages or other states, so the community has many layers to consider.

In rural areas, you often meet the same people in the same places, and change occurs slowly. Even when people move away, their families remain. Cities are more transient. In urban work, when someone moves, they disappear; the whole family relocates. We had to overcome this major challenge (105).

The movement's entrance into urban ministry "began with prayer and research, which worked together. Prayer guides the research and gives wisdom to interpret and apply the results of the research. Each group and area is unique. Research reveals vital information about people's main issues of concern and corresponding points of potential access" (106).

Our research showed that the fast-paced lifestyle and rapid development of the city had fostered a number of serious social problems, including depression, suicides, rapes, divorce, juvenile crimes, murders, broken families, and immoral relationships… . Our research found huge numbers of young people migrating to Delhi for study and other reasons. Many faced loneliness, isolation, stress, identity crisis, and culture shock (108).

In response to the needs that had been discovered through prayer and research, "We opened a counseling center at a nearby mall, where over seventeen hundred young people have visited annually since it opened" (109).

This provides access to the youth and allows us to find persons of peace (Luke 10). This [person of peace] strategy had already proven effective among the Bhojpuri. Since people in urban areas often have little free time, we have found small gatherings (non-conventional worshiping communities) very effective because of increased flexibility (109).

More recently, we have decentralized our urban ministry, increasing the numbers of young people being reached. We currently have over twenty-five different centers where leaders are working in different urban areas.

> *The urban work became very successful for the following reasons. First, because we had a proven model working among the Bhojpuri. We applied CPM principles and used access to bless people and look for a person of peace, who then became the key to reaching their network of relationships. Second, God helped us do research and prayer and move in the right direction to learn effective means for access. Urban access approaches clearly needed to be different than rural ones. Third, we didn't wait for people to come to us. We actively reached out to people. Through the counseling work we went to schools and colleges. We gave awareness programs there on relevant subjects like child abuse, sexual abuse, and career options. These programs found a warm reception among the young people. (111–12)*

One additional comment on what has borne fruit in the urban context:

> *Both the group and individual approach have borne great fruit in Delhi. In both cases finding a person of peace is key. If I find one person who's open, I want to help them view their workplace or school as their harvest field. So that person of peace begins reaching a group of their contacts. These urban "communities" are completely different from rural communities, yet the good news is spreading among them. (113)*

India has a unique social problem of children abandoned (or runaways) at railway stations. "Abandoned children by the tens of thousands live at railway stations across India. They usually sleep only 2–3 hours a day due to fear of robbery, rape, and beatings" (Foreword, xii). As we minister to them, we aim to reunite them with their families whenever we can. "From the very beginning our foremost guiding principle has been: 'When we deal with children, whether orphaned or semi-orphaned or street children, we don't want to create a warehouse of children'" (88). "In our service to railway children, we focus primarily on restoration to their families. We engage with them to find out where they came from, who they are and how they ended up in this place. Then we work together with the government and the police and do what we can to restore them to their families" (89).

The Indian context has incredible and widespread social diversity. "When you travel even five to ten miles in India, you often find differences in dialect and culture" (165). One response of our ministry to that unique patchwork of diversity consists of very reproducible training that can easily be personalized.

Given that dynamic, it's better that the leaders use their own examples rather than repeating exactly what we said. Our teaching doesn't push information on them; it involves discussion and discovery together. We use a group learning process, so we as trainers also learn. Everybody puts together their experience and what they have learned, and new results come as the Lord directs (165).

We teach a little, then they do it and learn from their experience as well as from our teaching. That enables them to really work effectively. When they learn from us, that starts the process. When they start implementing what they learned, they learn many more things, because God is teaching them. What they learn from God, they learn much better. When they teach others, they pass on what we taught plus what God taught them (165).

This approach facilitates very reproducible yet contextualized training throughout the movement.

Contextual use of Bhojpuri language and culture has played a key role in the movement's fruitfulness. "It's not that attempts to reach the Bhojpuri suddenly started in the 1990s. But those doing the outreach hadn't used the Bhojpuri language in their approach... . When we talk now about the Bhojpuri language, it's a key element of our strategy—a very different mindset" (6). Contextual music and life rituals have also strengthened believers' gatherings and opened doors to share the gospel. "The Bhojpuri songbook contains written guidelines for what to do for events like marriage, childbirth, death, Holy Communion, child dedication, a child's birthday, an anniversary, baptism, and so on" (185). Here is one specific example of effective contextual outreach:

> Some groups have a ceremony a certain number of days after a person's death. This ceremony is done in a Christian way with prayer, not with the previous rituals. We don't necessarily eliminate the traditional gathering, but instead of mourning, we celebrate. People invite all their relatives to the ceremony and share the good news with them. ... People attending these ceremonies generally respond positively. It becomes a door opener for unbelievers, since they have never seen anything like it (185–86).

The movement has inspired and assisted the launching of CPMs among other unreached groups. Of the 1,371 currently-known CPMs, only about 10 percent have reached what the 24:14 Coalition describes as Level 7: Multiplying CPMs—"Catalyzing new CPMs in other unreached peoples and places." The Bhojpuri movement has reached that level, and we have highlighted that expansion to other groups in North India in chapters of the book entitled "Breakthrough Beyond the Bhojpuri" and "Breakthrough among Muslims" (121–55). This movement's impact on other groups has also been described in other publications (Coles and Parks 2019, 185–88). As of mid-2019, "About eight different language groups across Northern India have been impacted and those language groups have different sub-groups within them. The work in at least one of those has already reached the point where it can be classified as its own Church Planting Movement" (Coles 2019, 18).

The movement has felt the Lord's release to allow many of its stories to be told. Although the Indian context presents the movement with significant persecution, the movement's approach is both sufficiently open and sufficiently contextual that we felt it was time to publish key stories and principles from the movement. This contrasts with most movements which, in light of security concerns, do not allow their stories to be shared publicly. A case study of the Bhojpuri movement was first published in *Perspectives on the World Christian Movement* (Winter and Hawthorne 2009, 697–700). Descriptions of the movement have brought some criticism—often reacting to a second-hand oral report rather than the written descriptions. We shared a response to some criticism in an interview published in *Mission Frontiers*:

> *Dave: Sometimes people travel through an area where a movement has been reported and they don't see evidence of it, so they conclude there's not really a movement happening there. How would you respond to that?*
>
> *Victor: (laughs) You can walk in a jungle and never see any animals. That doesn't mean there are no animals in the jungle. Some people have a certain image in their minds of what a Church Planting Movement will look like. They think they'll see people crying in the streets, or shouting at the top of their voice that they're saved. They expect to see crosses on top of the houses, and no more temples or mosques or idols. They have this fantasy that when a movement happens the area will look very Christian… . We don't have people streaming to church buildings on Sunday morning. Bhojpuri believers live, dress and eat like other Bhojpuri people. They gather to worship in relatively inconspicuous ways. (Coles 2019, 18)*

The willingness to make public the dynamics at work in the Bhojpuri movement has helped many to better understand what is actually happening in this movement. This, in turn, has diminished some misunderstandings about CPMs in general.

What Leadership Features of the Movement Are Counter-Cultural?

Power dynamics. In Indian culture, as in many cultures of the world (and many churches throughout church history), those in power often prefer a structure that maintains their power and limits the power of those being led by them. The Bhojpuri movement has taken a counter-cultural approach by focusing on empowering others rather than holding onto power.

> The movement avoids honorific religious titles, and empowers all believers to become leaders in their context, using their unique gifts. This paradigm of leadership constitutes one of the keys to the ongoing reproduction taking place. Everyone in the movement knows their leaders and knows who they lead, but leadership truly functions as a means of serving rather than as a rank or a title. (xvii-xviii)

"Empowerment is a key element of our leadership training. We aim to empower leaders from day one" (164).

> The culture of empowerment impacts numerous aspects of the movement. First, in addition to encouraging new believers to share the good news, we model for them how to start new worshiping communities. And we empower them to start new groups immediately. We watch over and release these new disciples to lead the new groups they start... . Second, we empower grassroots leadership at the local level and we assist local leaders in starting new worshiping communities. We don't establish work dependent on outsiders, which would leave the work vulnerable. We empower local leaders. This brings local ownership, resulting in long-term viability and multiplication. Third, we empower and equip all believers to do ministry in Jesus' name." (176–77)

"The movement thrives because all of God's people are empowered to serve the Lord" (187). "Multiplication happens naturally when everyone takes ownership, everyone feels empowered and everyone obeys God's commands" (199).

Kavilash, one of the long-time workers with the movement, testifies:

> If I compare the early days with the present, many things are different, but some things have remained the same. The work is now much bigger, but one thing didn't change: since the very beginning there has never been pressure to bring results. The work is not numbers-oriented, so we can work freely without any pressure. We serve because of motivation from the heart. (14)

Women in leadership. Indian society has traditionally (and up to the present in many ways) held women in low esteem. The Bhojpuri movement, in radical contrast, holds women in high esteem and involves them in leadership.

> Gender issues are a huge problem in north Indian society. Men and women treat each other very differently after accepting Christ than they did before. They now exhibit love and caring that defies all previous customs and traditions. Men and women share equal

responsibility in sharing the good news and carrying it forward. They also share equal responsibility in multiplying disciples, leaders and churches. (45)

We view women and treat women as equal partners in the good news and in the ministry. This is counter cultural and intentional on our part. Our stand from the very beginning has been that men and women are equal. Just as God calls men, he calls women as well. If men can make disciples, women can make disciples. So we have many women who are leaders and church planters in the movement. They have discipled people and won whole households. We have no problem with appointing women as leaders in the church. The head of our organization is a woman, a wonderful servant leader. (196–97)

Absence of religious titles. The movement does not use honorific religious titles. "This movement is built on non-traditional but very biblical patterns of leadership and leadership development. We don't use special ecclesiastical titles for leaders (Matt 23:8–11), and we equip and encourage all believers to minister, using the gifts God has given them (1 Pet 4:10–11)" (173). "We empower and equip all believers to do ministry in Jesus' name. This means no clergy/laity distinction. We avoid the mindset of positional leadership and don't call our staff 'Reverend' or 'Pastor'" (177). "Our avoidance of titles intimidates some people, but it works. It's both radical and biblical" (158). "We just avoid the traditional Christian assumption that substantial ministry should have a direct connection with payment and a title" (177).

Overcoming challenges of caste. Contrary to the cultural pattern and the expectations of many who know Indian society, caste has not played a determinative role in the fruit being borne through the movement. In fact, the movement has some low-caste people ministering among (leading) high-caste people.

We have one low-caste woman who leads a worshiping community on the low-caste side of the village, then goes to the high-caste side of the village and leads another worshiping community there. Although she comes from a low caste and is female (which makes her an unusual leader in any village), God is using her effectively in both the high-caste and low-caste contexts. (25)

"Other Indians visiting with us were shocked she could do that. We learned that after she had prayed for healing for some high-caste people and God had healed them, they didn't care what caste she came from. God's truth and power can break down any walls" (xii).

Literacy not a prerequisite for leadership. "We believe that leadership should not depend on education or status. Our movement includes some leaders who are not literate at all" (172). "Leaders also need to make sure the entire church planting process is … *doable.* … If the process is simple, educated people can do it as well as illiterate people. But if it's complicated, only a few experts can do it" (118).

Learning Christian leadership is traditionally a very academic process. Looking at the Bhojpuri leaders' academic background in the early days, it would have been disastrous to try traditional Christian leadership training. The majority of them are oral learners. Although some of them have a few years of schooling, their aptitude for learning is basically oral and thus quite different than literate aptitude.

To approach things in a Western way, a person has to be literate to be trained as a disciple, leader, mentor, or church planter. … We aimed to keep it simple: focus on prayer and witnessing and simple learning of Scripture, applied in daily life (160–61).

Kavilash testifies:

When I first got involved with the Bhojpuri work I was not very educated. I had only finished second grade. As I got involved in the movement, I began to get more educated—mostly not in regular school subjects, but in biblical education. Then I became eager to learn and I completed up to eighth grade in just a couple of years. I was most excited about the trainings we did, because they enabled me to learn the Bible and go much deeper in understanding it. (14)

We worked with an illiterate woman who gained recognition in her community through her involvement in the child literacy program, the sewing program and the health awareness program. She takes ownership in doing these things and shares, "I used to be a nobody, but because of this work I have become a somebody." (55)

Plurality in leadership. Contrary to Indian cultural norms and the pattern of many churches globally, church leadership within the movement is usually plural. "Churches normally have multiple elders and multiple levels of leadership, not just one leader. When the church reproduces or when a leader is away, things work better with multi-layer leadership" (184). This attempt to follow the New Testament pattern has provided durability, stability, and reproducibility in the Bhojpuri movement.

Conclusion

God's Spirit delights to work in unique ways, and his work in the Bhojpuri movement has been unique in a variety of ways. Both in its leadership and in the dynamics of its growth, the Bhojpuri CPM has paved a unique path by the grace of God.

References

Coles, Dave. 2019. "A Still Thriving Middle-Aged Movement: An Interview with Victor John." *Mission Frontiers* (May/June).

Coles, Dave, and Stan Parks. 2019. "DMM – Disciple Making Movement." In *24:14 – A Testimony to All Peoples*. Spring, TX: 24:14.

Dale, Tony, Dale Felicity, and George Barna. 2009. *The Rabbit and the Elephant: Why Small Is the New Big for Today's Church*. Carol Stream, IL: BarnaBooks.

John, Victor, with Dave Coles. 2019. *Bhojpuri Breakthrough: A Movement that Keeps Multiplying*. Monument, CO: WIGTake Resources.

Narayan, Deepa. 2018. "India is the Most Dangerous Country for Women." *The Guardian*, July 2. www.theguardian.com/commentisfree/2018/jul/02/india-most-dangerous-country-women-survey.

Winter, Ralph, and Steven Hawthorne. 2009. *Perspectives on the World Christian Movement: A Reader* (Fourth Edition). Pasadena, CA: William Carey Library.

A Thai Multiplication Movement

Stephen Bailey, with Dwight Martin and Pastor Somsak _____

If you know the history of Christian missions among Southeast Asian Buddhists, you have learned to have low expectations for the expansion of Christian faith there. To speak of a multiplication movement in this region suggests the miraculous. After roughly 350 years of Christian missions in Thailand, less than 1 percent of the population is Christian, and many of these Christians come from ethnic minority groups, not the Buddhist Thai majority. Not surprisingly, when I heard that thousands of Thai Buddhists were becoming followers of Jesus, I was skeptical. Yet, the Free in Jesus Christ Church Association (FJCCA) reports that 17,206 Thai Buddhists became "followers of Jesus" between 2017 and September 14, 2020 (Martin September 14, 2020).

Such claims motivated me to go to Phetchabun Province in north central Thailand to see for myself. Pastor Somsak, the lay founder and director of the FJCCA, hosted me for three intense days of field observation.[1] In late 2016, God gave him a vision for 10,000 new believers. His church quickly met that goal. Of the 17,206 converts, 46 percent have been baptized and 58 percent attend a house church or mother church on a regular basis.

The movement has seen 770 house churches started, and twenty new mother churches have been built to support the network of house churches (Martin 2020). Recently, the FJCCA revised its goal from ten thousand new believers to ten thousand baptized believers by the end of 2020 (Martin August 2019). On one day, October 6, 2019, they baptized 630 new believers (Martin October

---

1 I was with the FJCCA team and Dwight Martin from August 31 to September 3, 2019.

2019). Two hundred others intended to be baptized that day but were unable to reach the venue. Then, on September 6, 2020, they baptized 1,435 new believers (Martin September 14, 2020).[2]

The center of the FJCCA movement is located at Pastor Somsak's business in Chon Daen town in Phetchabun Province. There he runs an oil change and car-wash business, which also provides office space for the FJCCA movement. Earlier in his life, Pastor Somsak successfully sold life insurance. Thirty years ago, God gave him a vision to plant what is now Chon Daen Church. Between 1987 and 2016, Pastor Somsak helped plant thirteen churches in Central and Northeast Thailand.

During my three days with FJCCA, I observed and participated in eight events that consisted of worship, evangelism, and discipleship teaching. Each of these took place in a different village. I observed at each place a steady flow of Buddhist-background Thai deciding to follow Jesus. Just as important, however, were the local lay Christians I saw doing effective evangelism and discipleship. Their teams are strictly volunteer, and typically consist of three to ten trained, young-to-middle-age adults. About 70 percent of the volunteers are women. Pastor Somsak has a commonsense business mind and sensitivity to Thai identity, values, and relational style. These, combined with digital metrics that track, measure, and guide the movement, make an effective and indigenous strategy for communicating the gospel to Thai Buddhists.

Thesis

I believe this case study demonstrates that social realities often play a more important role than cultural factors in Christian movements. If true, this might explain why the FJCCA movement focuses on organizational strategy, metric measurements, technology, networking, media, and helping new believers successfully move from their Buddhist community to the church. Like many Protestant churches in Thailand, the FJCCA preaches a quite-Western evangelical message, sings typical Thai Protestant songs that are mostly imported from the West, and builds buildings that look like Western Protestant churches. While they do make some important contextual adjustments, I have seen other Thai churches that are far more contextualized than FJCCA.[3]

This case study suggests that while contextualizing forms is important, when a movement effectively addresses local social realities (and even learns to ride the wave of global social forces), it can thrive. The FJCCA movement is successfully making disciples of Jesus in ways that help local, marginalized Thai (mostly

---

2 See the video of this event at https://youtu.be/UcXkeQxA-5Y.

3 For example, visit the *Prakun Muang Udon* Church which is connected to the Center for Applied Ministry Church Association. There one can observe highly contextualized worship and preaching, but it is a long way from a movement, even after several decades of ministry.

women) expand and empower their identities by affirming and expanding their identity by connecting them to the worldwide Christian community in ways similar to the global Pentecostal movement.[4]

In this article, contextualization refers to the intentional adaptation of Christian beliefs, values, and liturgical practices into local symbolic cultural categories. This adaptation creatively emerges in the tension between form and meaning as Christians attempt to faithfully communicate and practice the gospel in culturally relevant and understandable forms. By social realities, I refer to the empirical realities of the social and physical environment in which people live. In these environments, humans exercise their agency to pursue cultural goals and aspirations. Their success depends upon their opportunity and capability in engaging social and natural environmental obstacles. In more practical terms, social realities are things like local infrastructure, economics, technology, mobility, urbanization, social media, political movements, projections of cultural identity in society, and the way all these intersect with global forces that bring constant change and exchange.

Culture (a symbolic mental pattern) and social realities (generated by social systems in a natural environment in which people act) are interrelated. Culture is both a mirror of and for social action (Geertz 1973, 94). There is always some disconnect between cultural values and social realities, but this disconnect is acute in globalization, causing constant tension in nearly all local communities. As Sherry Ortner says, "… social actors, through their living, on-the-ground, variable practices, reproduce or transform—and usually some of each—the culture that made them" (Ortner 2006, 129).

In this case study, FJCCA Thai Buddhist converts can be seen using their agency to engage their social realities in ways that both affirm and expand their cultural identities. Obviously, some are more successful than others, but all live in the tension between preserving cultural identities and making necessary adjustments to them in pursuit of cultural goals as they navigate the demands of their social circumstances.

In what follows, I first describe how the FJCCA contextualizes the gospel into Thai cultural categories. I then describe multiple social realities which the FJCCA works with to allow their converts to remain rooted in their Thai cultural identity while reconfiguring and expanding them as part of a new Christian social and spiritual network. This, I argue, constitutes the important key to the success of the movement. These new Christians find Jesus to be a dependable Lord who rids them of bad karma and who answers prayer, but in the church they

---

4 Peter Berger, agreeing with David Martin, sees global Pentecostalism as a successful navigation of social forces by combining supernaturalism with the opportunity for "social mobility into a modernizing society" (Berger 2013). Martin has described Pentecostalism as the transnational mobile expression of pluralism, fission, choice, and voluntary association (Martin 2006).

find a new freedom that transcends their local social and spiritual obligations. Through the church they become connected to a diverse social community, where faith is exercised in freedom, empowering everyone. In the church they now belong to the God of the universe and to people in other provinces and nations. In this way they transcend their previous spiritual and social marginalization.[5]

Contextualization for Cultural Categories

This section explains the efforts of the FJCCA to contextualize the gospel for Thai culture in terms of three symbolic categories. These efforts relate to finding the appropriate Thai word for God, understanding the nature of God, and dealing with the idea of being "filled" with the Spirit in a society where spirit possession is quite common.

Language for "God"

The Thai word for God used in Thai churches is *Prachao*. But in reality, Thai does not offer an indigenous term that translates well the idea of a single, personal God of Creation. Although Thai Christians widely use *Prachao*, the term confuses local Buddhists because of its wide range of possible meanings. In Thai, *Prachao* can refer to a king, any number of Hindu deities, local spirits, or angels. Its meaning is not far from that of the old English meaning of "lord."[6] Upon hearing the gospel and that *Prachao* loves them and sent his son to die on their behalf, Buddhists silently wonder which *Prachao* (Lord) Christians are referring to. To avoid this confusion, the FJCCA has chosen to only speak of *Phra Yesu* or Jesus. This is not a trivial change of nomenclature. This change dramatically clarifies the gospel for Thai Buddhists, who can now understand that the message describes the God named Jesus who was incarnated as a man, and who died on behalf of the world to take away our bad karma. They can now be saved from the consequences of their bad karma.[7] The God, Jesus, stands ready to help and live with us today in our hearts and is ready to hear our concerns in prayer.

Father, Son, and Holy Spirit

A second issue relates to the doctrine of the Trinity. While the FJCCA acknowledges the Father, the Son, and the Spirit as they are presented in Scripture, they do not teach the doctrine of the Trinity using the language of

---

5 Evaluating the teaching of the FJCCA theologically is a fair and responsible task, but it is not my purpose here. It is also not my purpose to analyze the movement spiritually, although it seems clear to me that God is at work in the FJCCA. My purpose is social analysis. I urge the reader to focus on the description of what the FJCCA is doing in order to understand the potential social causes of this movement.

6 This problem is also present in the Lao, Burmese, and Khmer translations of the Bible.

7 In Thailand, "bad karma" refers to things one does that bring negative consequences back onto oneself and/or others. While the Buddhist philosophy of karma is different in some ways from the Christian idea of sin, the Buddhist lay person's understanding of karma is much closer in meaning. Thai lay people clearly understand and relate to the idea that "the wages of sin is death."

three Persons as in the traditional Western church. When asked about this, Pastor Somsak replied with a smile, "It's not my history." By this he means that the doctrine of the Trinity was articulated by fourth-century Christians who were very culturally different from the Thai, and because of this philosophical and theological explanations of the Trinity can be more confusing than helpful. The philosophical debates that gave rise to the doctrine were steeped in Greek philosophical categories that the Thai know nothing about. Speaking of three Persons, in the sense of "personae," is not easily rendered in the Thai language. The word usually translated for this Trinitarian concept of personae is *bukkhon*, which refers to an individual person (Martin email, September 4, 2020). It is no wonder that many Thai conclude that Christians worship three different gods. Consequently, the FJCCA teaches the Trinity in the course of inductive Bible study. As new believers grow in their faith, they read and learn about God the Father, God the Son, and God the Spirit in the biblical narrative.

Thai "Phi" and the Holy Spirit

A third contextual issue concerns being filled with the Holy Spirit in a cultural milieu that frequently observes people being possessed by spirits (*phi*). In this context, the FJCCA does not pray with new believers using the language of being "filled," since it can be quite frightening to a Thai to consider being "filled" (in their minds "possessed") by a spirit of any kind. Consequently, the role of the Holy Spirit in a Christian's life is taught later in the discipleship process.

Evangelism That Addresses Social Realities

The FJCCA addresses several social realities that can either function as obstacles or facilitate the movement to Christian faith. This section will describe how the FJCCA has engaged these social realities and some global forces in ways that pave the way for Thai Buddhists to become followers of Jesus and for the movement to continue to grow.

Moving with the Social Network

In 2019, the FJCCA had forty evangelism volunteer teams from seventeen mother churches that strategically went on a daily basis to villages without churches to share a simple gospel message. These teams consisted of five or more volunteer church planters. They begin by finding "a person of peace": a concept borrowed from the Southern Baptist International Mission Board. In the Thai context, this means someone who is friendly and open to hearing the gospel. They ask this person to introduce the team members to their relatives and friends in their village who might be interested in hearing a presentation of the gospel. They then ask permission from the village head man to hold a public meeting.

Evangelism meetings take place under someone's outdoor sitting area with a roof (a *sala*), attached to a home, or sometimes in Buddhist temple compounds—

making the event observable to anyone passing by. The event may be as small as ten or twelve people, or at times more than 150 people. Because most young people and men have left the villages to work in cities, the gatherings consist mainly of adult women, elderly retired men, and children.

In this way, the FJCCA teams are socially sponsored into new communities. Being introduced and recommended by a member of the community clearly helps remove the natural suspicion people have toward outsiders and naturally connects them to the community. By seeking permission beforehand from the local civil authority, they show "respect and gratefulness," or *khwamgatanyu* (Fleming 2014, 89). Thai authorities, when shown respect, have a long history of tolerating outsiders and foreign ideas. This is in part due to their confidence in the strength of their Thai Buddhist identity. This can be seen in Thailand's history of dealing with foreign powers and missionaries back to the nineteenth century.[8] Thus, Thai authority structures, which could be a significant obstacle, actually become the means by which FJCCA team members are sponsored into a community.

Thai-Style Meetings

The team intentionally addresses key Thai relational values, such as fun, respect for elders, relaxed but polite interaction, and the sharing of food. The meetings are highly participatory, with leaders who use a kind of Thai-style game-show host humor. The events qualify as enjoyable entertainment (*sanuk*). Team members act with polite humility (*suphab*) and show deference to local authorities and elders (*khawlop*). Team members speak with energy and confidence as they share personal testimonies and simple, short teachings. Each person speaks for no longer than five minutes; there is no hard sell. The atmosphere radiates relaxed hospitality. Everyone receives a small bowl of noodle soup served by smiling volunteers.

The team communicates a simple and clear message. They use short gospel presentations, with stories illustrated by old-fashioned colored poster pictures. Then two or three people share their testimony explaining why they follow Jesus. The last speaker asks if anyone would like to receive new life in Jesus. Everyone speaks of Jesus and thanks Jesus. One does not hear the typical Thai Christian phrase, *khawp khun Prachao* (thanks be to God), in these meetings.

Those who want to receive Jesus recite prayers to receive him, along with the team and the rest of the audience. Reciting prayers aloud and in unison is a traditional Buddhist temple practice familiar to everyone. New believers are encouraged to pray themselves and develop their own relationship with Jesus.

8 See Fleming's discussion of how King Mongkut (1851–68) and his song King Chulalongkorn (1868–1910), who were confident enough of the superiority of Buddhist philosophy that they sought to learn what they could from the West with little worry of losing Thai Buddhist identity (2104, 20–24). Aphornsuvan shows how the political and intellectual confidence of the Thai elite interacted with the challenge of Western science. The elite, she says, accepted Western science without abandoning their feudal social structure and remaining loyal to Buddhism and the king (2009).

They are taught that they can pray any time. To empower them to do this, they receive a paper with five short prayers printed in a large font. The prayers are for morning, noon, and evening, and confession and times of need. The large font is important in villages having many elderly people with poor eyesight and homes with poor lighting. The children have their own meeting, and are led through a short, simple explanation of the gospel as well.

Several social realities are dealt with here. First, the contemporary preference for short, entertainment-driven events is accommodated by using a style that is in stark contrast to the solemn and ritualized Buddhist temple meetings.[9] Second, the confusion over who Christians are praying to is done away with by only speaking of Jesus. Third, group participation overcomes the shyness that is typical of Thai villagers. Finally, large fonts overcome the lack of adequate lighting and the scarcity of eyeglasses among the elderly poor.

Socialization of New Believers

During these village evangelism events, typically ten or more adults show a desire to follow Jesus. The majority of converts are married, middle-aged, relatively poor village women. From this core of new believers, a house church is formed. Every week, one or more volunteers from the team returns to the village to teach the new believers. Team members return until a leader is raised up from within the house church. New believers attend the house church until they have grown in their faith. They have the option to attend a mother church on Sunday if they desire, but this is not encouraged at the beginning of their Christian life.

A mother church is a building strategically located in an area with a cluster of village house churches. It follows a typical contemporary Thai Protestant order of service, consisting of a welcome, announcements, singing of worship choruses, receiving an offering, and a sermon. The only somewhat unique thing is that three to five people share what they learned from Scripture during the past week or share how their life in Jesus is so different from their old life. This practice is common in their house-church gatherings as well.

FJCCA sees the first few months of a new believer's Christian faith as a crucial period in their spiritual lives. Typical Christian church services differ greatly from Buddhist temple community rituals. The experience of going directly into the social dynamics of a typical church can overwhelm a new believer. For this reason, new believers are encouraged to remain in their village house church for the first six months rather than to attend a mother church. Once they have grown in knowledge and confidence in their new faith, they can decide where they will worship. Most choose to attend both services.

New believers also decide when they want to be baptized. This can happen right after they identify themselves as a Christian or much later. They are taught

9 Some Protestant church services also fit the description of solemn and overly ritualized, rather than fun (*sanuk*).

that being baptized indicates a person has decided to abandon their former objects of worship and spiritual allegiances; they are now ready to only worship Jesus. The spiritual and social transformation of poor villagers, many of whom are women whose husbands have left for work in the cities, into confident and empowered disciples of Jesus is very evident in the testimonies and in their eagerness to volunteer space, food, and time to further the movement.

Local and Regional Organization

Churches are planted in clusters as the gospel moves from village to village through neighbors and friends. When they have about twenty to thirty house churches in an area (typically the size of a Thai sub-district), the FJCCA locates land and builds a one-room mother church large enough to hold between one hundred to five hundred people, depending on the size of the local house church network. They construct a kitchen area behind the building to accommodate the community's fellowship meals. The mother church serves as a central worship center and training center to strengthen and resource the surrounding house churches. In this way, training, resources, and encouragement become accessible to house churches in the area.

Transitioning from Buddhist to Christian Community

The FJCCA has made a key adaptation: they do not forbid new believers from going to a Buddhist temple or from fulfilling their family obligations to help family members make merit or care for the ancestors. Instead, they leave the decision to end participation in these Buddhist and traditional practices up to the new believer. They make space for new Christians to assure their loved ones of their love and respect and to decide when and how they will stop participating in merit rituals. This often takes place over time in discussion with family members. The FJCCA leaders have observed that new believers can and do make their own way through this issue as they grow in their knowledge of Christian faith.

At one mother church, I met the lay Buddhist leader from the temple directly across the street from the building we were in. He explained that he is a new believer in Jesus, but he still leads the Buddhist congregation through the temple rituals with the monks and will continue until he is able to find a replacement. This kind of easy accommodation to the needs of both communities is rarely found in Southeast Asian churches, and thus seemed refreshingly practical and kind. One would expect this kind of approach from Southeast Asian Buddhist-background people when left to make their own decision. It prioritizes a smooth transition that protects the feelings of family and friends in their community.

It is difficult to overemphasize how important this practice is. Thailand has seen a large number of evangelistic efforts come and go with little lasting result. Throughout Southeast Asia, most missionaries would agree that conversions are not the biggest problem. Rather, seeing Buddhist-background converts continue in faith long enough to be discipled and become witnesses themselves has been rare. The key obstacle to following Jesus has not been the inability to understand the message (although, as we have seen above, that can be an issue), but rather the inability of Buddhists to become followers of Jesus without forfeiting every important social relationship they have—relationships that are the anchor to their identity. The FJCCA seems to have found a way to allow converts to negotiate this path successfully, in their own way and time.

Many years ago, Donald McGavran defined a people movement as follows:

A people movement results from the joint decision of a number of individuals whether five or five hundred—all from the same people—which enables them to become Christians without social dislocation, while remaining in full contact with their non-Christian relatives, thus enabling other groups of that people, across the years, after suitable instruction, to come to similar decisions and form Christian churches made up exclusively of members of that people. (Visser 2008, 51)

What the FJCCA is doing here is similar to what David Martin sees happening in the global Pentecostal movement.

Pentecostals embrace a portable identity. People release themselves from wider ties embedded in the extended family and traditional community to emphasize the immediate family and fraternity of believers. At the same time local ties are not completely severed and Pentecostalism also services the need for place and territorial identity. (Martin 2006)

Lay Volunteer Evangelists and Leaders

None of the FJCCA leaders have any formal Bible or theological training. The movement is led completely by lay volunteers, the majority of whom are new to the Christian faith. This is significant in light of the history of church movements, which have almost always had high lay involvement. Lay people who are new in their faith often feel more comfortable and serve more effectively in non-church, missional contexts, simply because they come from those contexts.

The reliance on poor, socially marginalized lay converts to fuel growth fits with Paul Pierson's thesis that the expansion of the church historically has occurred at the margins of the church (Pierson 2009, 103). The missionary thinker, Ralph Winter, remarked at a Conference on Missionary Education for the 21st Century that "most missionaries are and always have been lay people. I refer especially to the women missionaries" (Winter 1993). In that same address, Winter argued that "missiological education for the lay person … outranks the strategic importance of training professional missionaries" (Winter 1993).

Winter based his arguments on his knowledge of the history of missions. Many of the great Protestant missionaries have been lay people (e.g., the Moravians, William Carey, D. L. Moody, and a vast number of Business as

Mission lay people today). Also, much of the on-the-ground work of evangelism on the mission field, even when instigated by a formally trained missionary, has largely been carried out by local lay people.[10] The famous missionary to China, John Nevius, wrote in his book, *The Planting and Development of Missionary Churches* (1888), that an ideal indigenous missionary church planting effort would be characterized by the following:

> *Believers stay in their own professions; unpaid lay leaders shepherd the churches; churches meet in homes or simple structures; missionaries and paid evangelists oversee several churches, give extensive training; churches plant daughter churches. (Visser 2008, 51)*

In one village that the FJCCA team took me to I met a woman who has led hundreds of people to follow Jesus. She makes and sells the classic Thai bowl of noodle soup called *kuay teow*. But when she isn't doing that, she travels on a small-engine motorcycle to other villages, sharing the gospel and doing discipleship. There are many lay people like her in this movement. Lay new-believer involvement is empowering and can transform individuals with relatively low social status into community leaders with influence that extends far beyond their own village.

The Discipline of Metrics

Software engineer Dwight Martin is the founder of the eSTAR Foundation in Chiang Mai (http://estar.ws). After ten years of owning his own software development company in the United States, Dwight sold that company fourteen years ago and returned to Thailand. Born in Thailand to missionary parents, Martin is fluent in Thai and serves as an advisor to the FJCCA.[11] He also provides funds through Reach A Village (http://reachavillage.org) to help accelerate the movement. The FJCCA provides over 50 percent of their financial needs from internal sources, but Martin sees his funding as helping to accelerate the movement by providing discipleship materials, mobilization and training, and occasionally the construction of a mother church. Martin is working on creating an app called "First Fruits," which will allow field workers to enter data on their smartphones instead of having to type data into the system in a main office.

The software Martin presently provides allows the FJCCA teams to update data in order do know where house churches are located and the names and addresses of all the believers. This enables following up for discipleship and tells

---

10 Andrew Walls makes a similar point in observing that for the first two generations of the modern missionary movement "the typical missionary long remained … a man of humble background and modest attainments. It was journeymen, artisans, and clerks who came to the mission field" (1996, 171). The role of laity in missions has exploded since the end of World War II. Dana Roberts also notes the door that opened for Catholic lay people in mission after Vatican II (2009, 114).

11 See these interviews with Dwight Martin about the FJCCA movement: https://youtu.be/6P3NMy7T24w and https://youtu.be/qn6kRKID434.

the team what material each disciple has studied. The most crucial thing seems to be that it allows their team to analyze the data and know quickly what is working and what is not and how close they are to their goals. It's inspiring to watch the map at www.thaichurches.org fill up with the green circles that indicate churches. It is fascinating to see relatively poor rural villagers practicing a disciplined assessment of the movement by means of the metrics that this technology provides.

Deliberate and Appropriate Discipleship

As already mentioned, it is not unusual in Thailand to see a lot of people "becoming Christians" who fail to become faithful disciples. A large part of this recurring failure has resulted from churches requiring Buddhists who come to faith to quickly renounce their family obligations in Buddhist and ancestor rituals. This effectively makes it impossible for new believers to show honor and respect to their families. This helps explain the delay between those who pray for salvation and those who get baptized (39 percent of new believers have been baptized) in the FJCCA movement.

Conversion in this movement is a process that includes: praying that Jesus will take away their bad karma, asking Jesus to come into their life, being discipled, becoming a member of a house church, learning to only follow and pray to Jesus, turning over household temple duties to family members, and, when they feel ready, public baptism.

Another issue related to the frequent failure of new believers to remain disciples has been the lack of follow-up to guide new believers into mature Christian lives. Discipleship is a labor-intensive and time-consuming effort. The task requires careful tracking of each new believer and a large number of volunteer laypeople capable of teaching others how to take the next step in their life with Jesus. FJCCA's data system and their army of willing, enthusiastic volunteers meet these demands.

The FJCCA pays careful attention to the discipleship process in two important ways. First, they follow up with new believers within forty-eight hours. The teams carefully record the new believer's name, address, the date they came to faith, age, gender, etc. They enter this data, along with the person's photograph, into a database that tracks new believers and the location of all their house churches.

Second, new believers are discipled in an easy-to-understand, step-by-step process. Initially, a new believer is given a small booklet called *Jesus' Plan for Us* (printed in a large font) that helps the person better understand the gospel. Each lesson is reviewed and taught again in their community meetings, and new believers are encouraged to practice teaching the lesson to others as well. This eventually results in believers having a firm grasp of the gospel and ability to articulate their new faith. Later, new believers enter a second level of discipleship that introduces them to the Gospel of John through a book called *The Water of Life*.

A third book, *Abundant Life*, covers basic doctrine. The third level of discipleship guides new believers in reading and studying the Bible in their house church.

Entrepreneurial Practicality and Flexibility

As stated above, Pastor Somsak has a background in business. He has infused the FJCCA teams with an entrepreneurial, practical, and flexible approach to ministry. They constantly assess and adjust what they do along the way. They consider using anything that helps people understand easily, helps people feel at home in the church, and helps facilitate the rapid and easy spread of the gospel. They discard anything that hinders this journey. During my first day with Pastor Somsak, he looked at me twice and said in Thai, "It's easy to win the Thai for Christ." I found this almost offensive because my experience had taught me that sharing the gospel in Southeast Asia was *not* easy. But as I watched him and the team, I saw they had a way of communicating the gospel that worked with the social realities that Thai live in and which have long made it difficult for Buddhists to come to faith.

In one village we visited, the gospel presentation was delayed because it was raining so hard no one could hear, even with the PA system. Because the rain did not let up for a long time, some of the audience left. Later, when the team tried to hold the event, the audience was small and inattentive. The team discussed later what to do next time. They decided to plan an activity for the group to do while they waited for the rain to stop, hoping they could keep the audience's interest and still get a hearing for the gospel.

This easy flexibility may also be related to the fact that they have no connection to any Western missionary or church organization. Without these outside theological, methodological, and historical traditions to guard, they have freedom to think outside the box, innovate, and read the Bible and apply it to their context in a way they feel is both faithful to the Scriptures and fits the social realities of the Thai.

Macro Social Factors

I asked Pastor Somsak about the potential for religious persecution in response to the rapid growth of their movement. After all, if this movement continues to spread through the country, some Thai might feel threatened. For now, at least, Pastor Somsak feels confident this will not happen. Historically, he says, Thailand has practiced a very open and tolerant kind of religious freedom. The Thai have long been noted for their tolerance and their confidence that whatever outside ideas come into Thailand, Thai Buddhist identity is strong and immoveable. If this is true, one wonders whether a movement like this could happen as easily in Cambodia, Laos, and Myanmar: countries that have not practiced that same level of religious tolerance.

Another macro factor that facilitates the FJCCA movement is the remarkably good roads that make many otherwise remote villages accessible. Roads to nearly every remote village and ubiquitous cell phones allow the team to coordinate and visit multiple house churches within a day, with relative ease. The other three neighboring Theravada Buddhist nations lack this ease of transportation.

A third macro factor that may contribute to the movement is the current political and economic malaise in Thailand. Pastor Somsak feels that the recent death of Thailand's beloved king has dealt a blow to national morale. The military takeover of the Thai democratic government in 2014 and ongoing lack of jobs in the countryside have added to the general discouragement. Some have also observed that Thai people today seem less committed to Buddhism than in the past. Perhaps this has been caused by the growing influence of education, wealth, and secularism. Given these macro factors, another reason for the success of this movement may be that this is an opportune time in the social and spiritual life of Thai society.

Implications for Missiology

After three intense days with the FJCCA team, I left thinking that perhaps it is possible for Christianity to meaningfully engage Southeast Asian Buddhists. Somewhat similar church planting movements are happening in Cambodia and Myanmar, and it would be worth investigating whether the social realities in Thailand might also be found to be facilitating those movements.[12] In the case of the FJCCA, it seems clear that something unique is happening that has not been seen in the 350-year-old effort to communicate the gospel among Buddhists in Thailand.

I have made the case that what drives the FJCCA movement is found in the way it has been able to work with the social realities to clear the path for Thai Buddhists to easily transition into the new social and spiritual setting of the church. The worship services and gospel explanations of the FJCCA mother churches are very similar to most Protestant churches in Thailand, while perhaps a bit more charismatic than some. But most Thai Christians would be comfortable in FJCCA church services. The FJCCA has done some contextualization of the gospel, but not as much as some other churches. The uniqueness of the FJCCA resides not in their mother church services or their teaching. It resides in their organizational discipline, their army of lay volunteers, and in everything they do to clear the path for Buddhists moving toward becoming disciples of Jesus. Everything about the engagement, communication, and discipleship of these Buddhist-background people not only affirms Thai identity but expands it beyond local family and community obligations. In fact, it empowers Thai identity by

---

12 A movement is happening in Laos among some minority groups, but it has not impacted the Buddhist Lao majority very much.

both affirming it and connecting it to the international plurality of the church.

The bridge that believers cross consists of relationships already in place, using well-known cognitive cultural categories and practices. To help them cross over into the social and religious world of the Christian church, time and social space are provided to new believers who decide themselves how to navigate the emotional and social anxiety that conversion brings. Chief among the social anxieties for converts is the need to deal with family and community expectations for Buddhist merit-making and honoring of ancestors. By courageously allowing new believers to use their agency to decide how and when they will follow Jesus, without dishonoring their families, the FJCCA has cleared the path to Jesus in a very Thai way.

Final Thoughts

If indeed the thesis of this chapter that dealing with social realities can be more crucial to movements than cultural contextualization is correct, then missiology would do well to update the model of culture it tends to use. A good deal of missionary effort relies on an essentialist theory of culture that is overly focused on culture belief systems and communication by means of choosing the right cultural categories. These are, of course, very important. But this view of culture may be keeping us from seeing that cultural meaning is always performed through social practices in very particular environments. The implication of this reality is that meaning is socially dynamic and negotiated to meet the demands of social circumstances. It is a bit like the difference between a word found in a dictionary and a word we encounter in speech. Speech is always performed in a context of social relationships that, given the right syntax, tone of voice, and circumstances, allows us to say new things with old words. This is why Paul Ricoeur wrote that meaning arises at the level of the sentence, not at the lexical meaning of the words (1976, 20).

If we only focus on the contextualization of meaning, we will miss out on the social transformation implications of following Jesus. Converts and churches live and act in social and natural environments that matter. In the FJCCA movement, this has meant affirming the cultural identity of Thai people while at the same time lifting it into another plane of relationship with the creator God and the diverse international church, where all our identities remain unique and hidden in Christ. This is social process as much as it is a spiritual process with social implications for relationships in the home and society. Thai Buddhists are using their God-given agency to expand and transform the meaning of being Thai in strategic ways they feel works best for them spiritually and socially. These decisions have political, economic, and familial consequences.

Charles Kraft, who championed contextualization in the 1970s and 80s, almost predicted this shift in understanding when he stated, "Social issues may turn out to be far more crucial than cultural issues in communicating the gospel"

(1997). Sherry Ortner offers us an understanding of culture that can be useful in today's missionary efforts. She sees culture as practice "within which neither 'individuals' nor 'social forces' have 'precedence,' but in which nonetheless there is a dynamic, powerful, and sometimes transformative relationship between the practices of real people and the structures of society, culture, and history" (Ortner, Kindle Locations 2491–93).

The FJCCA uses Thai logic and social strategies to make a path to Jesus that negotiates the challenges of traditional Thai identity, which is grounded in Buddhism and obligated to feudal social structures. As a result of the success of these strategies, they are seeing thousands of people follow Jesus. They are adapting global ideas and technology in some cases and rejecting them in other cases. In each case, it is a Thai practicality that decides to use and adapt things that fit their social realities. The resulting transformation is empowering poor central Thai by expanding their identities in ways that globally transcend their local situations to connect with the international network of World Christianity and cosmically in their new relationship with Jesus. Dana Roberts has explained the phenomena of World Christianity as:

> a system of meaning that allows for cultural adaptation and makes sense beyond one's own narrow ethnic or national boundaries. The universal vision transforms the local, and the local brings personal meaning to the universal. (2009, 177)

References

Aphornsuvan, Thanet. 2009. "The West and Siam's Quest for Modernity: Siamese Responses to Nineteenth Century American Missionaries." *South East Asia Research* 17, no. 3: 401–31.

Berger, Peter. 2013. "The Explosive Growth of Pentecostalism." Lecture at the Berkley Center for Religion, Peace and World Affairs. Available at https://www.youtube.com/watch?v=0tGXBuYXpwk.

Fleming, Kenneth. 2014. *Buddhist-Christian Encounter in Contemporary Thailand*, Religionswissenschaft / Studies in Comparative Religion Book 19, 89. Kindle edition.

Greetz, Clifford. 1973. *The Interpretation of Cultures*. New York: Basic Books.

Kraft, Charles. 1997. Class notes, Fuller Theological Seminary, Pasadena, CA.

Martin, David. 2006. "Pentecostalism and Changes in the Global Religious Economy." Panel discussion at the University of Southern California, Dornsife Center for Religion and Civic Culture, October 7, 2006.

Martin, Dwight. August 2019. "Free in Jesus Christ Church Association: August 2019 Status Update." Unpublished report.

———. October 2019. FJCCA baptism of 630 new believers. October 6, 2019. Available at https://www.youtube.com/watch?v=UdQzcmUirKg.

———. September 4, 2020. Personal email.

————. September 14, 2020. Personal email.

Ortner, Sherry B. 2006. *Anthropology and Social Theory: Culture, Power, and the Acting Subject*. A John Hope Franklin Center book. Durham, NC: Duke University Press. Kindle edition.

Pierson, Paul. 2009. *The Dynamics of Christian Mission History through a Missiological Perspective*. Pasadena, CA: William Carey International University Press.

Riceour, Paul. 1976. *Interpretation Theory: Discourse and the Surplus of Meaning*. Fort Worth, TX: Christian University Press.

Roberts, Dana. 2009. *Christian Mission: How Christianity Became a World Religion*. Sussex UK: Wiley-Blackwell.

Visser, Marten. 2008. "Conversion Growth of Protestant Churches in Thailand." Dissertation, University of Utrecht. Missiological Research in the Netherlands, No. 47: 51.

Winter, Ralph. 1993. "Missiological Education for Lay People." *International Journal of Frontier Missions* 10, no. 2: 75–81.

Movements in Iran and Algeria: The Second-Generation Challenge

Rania Mostofi and Patrick Brittenden

The last few decades have seen a remarkable number of movements of Muslims to Christ.[1] In his comprehensive survey, David Garrison identifies eleven movements that began at the end of the twentieth century and sixty-nine movements that proliferated in the first twelve years of the twenty-first century (2014, 18). While this extraordinary growth is cause for celebration, an important question that confronts these movements today is this:

> *How can we best participate in and with the work of the Spirit so that his wind continues blowing through to the second generation?*

Recent literature on movements sometimes refers to "generations" when describing the process of a movement catalyst who plants a church that goes on to plant another church and so on. These might be called spiritual generations. However, the term *generations* can also refer to a traditional familial category that describes the kinship that ties parents to their children, or to a social category, wherein a group of individuals have a similar age and live through shared historical events.

---

1   For the purposes of this chapter, our definition of a movement is "a Spirit-led process in which churches are planted, built up, and sent out on mission, reproducing fellowships and spreading the fragrance of Christ that brings *spiritual*, *social*, and cultural transformation." Movements include at least one thousand believers and/or one hundred church fellowships (Garrison 2014, 5).

What we have called the "second-generation challenge" is an invitation to reflect critically upon the faithfulness and effectiveness of movements as they move from the first to the second social and familial generation. While movements of Muslims to Christ have been underway for up to forty years in some contexts, there is a dearth of research addressing this second-generation challenge. Much of the literature to date focuses on the "How?" and "Why?" of movements, leaving questions about the "What's next?"—ecclesial identity, health, and mission—largely unaddressed. Given that every movement is only one generation from dying out, the temptation to push these issues into the category of "important but not urgent" should be avoided.

In what follows, we will explore the various dimensions of the second-generation challenge as it manifests itself in Iran and Algeria.[2] Through this discussion, our aim is to highlight key areas of ecclesial practice that need reviving in both movements so that they are positioned to experience a flourishing multigenerational future. Though our reflections are specific to Iran and Algeria, our hope is that the deliberations offered might also resonate with other contexts.

Iran

Today Iran hosts one of the fastest growing movements to Christ in the world. While estimates vary as to its size, the research suggests that Iran is home to between five hundred thousand and three million Iranian believers from a Muslim background (IBMBs).

As with Bahais, Sunnis, and Zoroastrians, IBMBs are considered a threat to Iran's Shia identity, and therefore experience persecution of various forms. Such persecution comes mostly from the government and includes discrimination in the education, military, job, and legal sectors—along with the frequent imprisonment of house church leaders, with sentences of up to fifteen years and forced exile. Up till now, four IBMB leaders have been killed.

With a few exceptions, foreign missionaries have been absent from the country since the revolution in 1979. Today, the vast majority of the church in Iran consists of the following three groups:

---

2   This chapter is a collaborative project, the fruit of rich dialogue and conversation. We write in the first-person plural throughout, except where each of us refers to personal experience or conversations (Rania in Iran, and Pat in Algeria), in which case we write in the first-person singular and indicate "I (Rania)" or "I (Pat)." We are both in different ways second-generation and "hybrids," attuned to the challenges facing the second generation in movements to Christ in Iran and Algeria. Rania was raised in the UK by her father, an Iranian BMB, and her mother, an Iranian BJB (believer from a Jewish background). Pat is the son of New Zealand missionaries who served the church in Algeria in the early 1970s, when there were only a handful of known believers in North Africa. He grew up in Algeria and later served as a mission partner in North Africa. Both of us are currently based in the UK, but we work full-time in theological education and leadership development among movements in Iran and Algeria.

(1) *Networks of house churches formed from previous building churches.* These building churches belonged to the three main Protestant denominations that continued to be active in Iran after the Islamic Revolution of 1979: Anglicans, Assemblies of God, and Presbyterians. Since the 1980s, they began to shift to a house church model due to increasing persecution and the perceived limitations of buildings for their long-term health and mission. This shift was accentuated by the gradual closure of all Persian-language building churches, beginning in 2012. Led by former lay leaders, these house church networks operate in close partnership with ethnic Armenian, Assyrian, and IBMB pastors now living in exile in the West.

(2) *Networks of house churches planted by Iranian leaders in exile in the West.* A significant number of former pastors of building churches in Iran have been forced into exile over the last thirty years. Since moving to the West, many of them began planting house churches in Iran, either through their own individual efforts and connections or through setting up parachurch organizations. These house churches make use of online technologies and small gatherings in countries neighboring Iran for pastoral care and training. Most members of these house churches have never set foot inside a church building.

(3) *Online churches formed by Farsi satellite TV programs.* Since their inception in the early 2000s, Persian-language satellite TV channels have played a pivotal role in the movement to Christ in Iran. Through the years, these channels have connected those coming to faith through their programs and websites to the two groups mentioned above. More recently, however, these channels have set up their own online churches. Such online churches consist of scattered individuals and families who watch prerecorded or live weekly services on various online platforms.

Within the IBMB church, one disciple making movement (DMM) strand has been active since 2005 and presently reports thirty thousand believers.[3] While DMM was introduced rather late in the history of the IBMB movement and has since influenced only a fraction of the movement, a number of characteristics identified in Garrison's definition of movements are nevertheless detectable across the three groups mentioned above (Garrison 2004, 172).

Algeria

Similar to Iran, Algeria has experienced a substantial movement to Christ. Broadly Protestant and evangelical, this indigenous church numbers anywhere from 50,000 to 380,000 believers (Brittenden and Sanders 2018, 9–13).[4] The public presence of Algerian believers from a Muslim background (ABMBs)

---

3 The widely promoted documentary, *Sheep Among Wolves*, portrays this thread within the underground house church movement of Iran.

4 Though there is a small population of indigenous Roman Catholic Algerian Christians (approximately 350), the vast majority of the indigenous Algerian church is broadly Protestant and evangelical.

has been met with opposition, and in some cases persecution. Recently, this has included state-sponsored oppression.[5] Though the pressure is considerable, an equally significant—though less publicized—threat to the future of the church comes not from external opposition, but from the church's own internal failure to successfully navigate long-term questions about individual and corporate Christian *and* Algerian identity.

On first inspection, one sees little evidence that a movement strategy has impacted the church in Algeria. Since the start of the Algerian "Revival" three decades ago, very few foreign missionaries have served in the country. My (Pat) own conversations with local church leaders indicate that their only contact with the phenomenon and methods of the "movements movement" takes place in the foyers and seminar rooms of regional conferences hosted by international organizations. When I reached out to experienced foreign CPM and DMM advocates and trainers involved in the NAME (North Africa and the Middle East) region, none could identify any known CPM/DMM practitioners in Algeria.

However, a brief overview of the catalytic event of the Ait Bouadou football camp in 1981 (LeBlanc 2006, 65–69) and the development of the Église Plein Évangile (the Full Gospel Church) into the "Jerusalem" of the contemporary Algerian church movement in the 1990s, indicates the presence of a number of elements that feature in Garrison's ten elements of a CPM. Seasoned pastor, trainer, and pioneer Youssef Yacob's personal reflection on the growth of the Algerian movement also contains numerous references to these elements (Yacob 2016).

The first five elements are particularly notable. *Extraordinary prayer* seems to have been a feature in the 1980s and through the bloody decade of civil unrest in the 1990s (Yacob 2016, 74–77). *Abundant* (and bold) *evangelism* unquestionably marked the movement throughout the 1990s and the early 2000s, even in the context of growing Islamist violence. While not viewed as a methodology, Algerian believers in the Kabylia regularly talk of a vision from the Lord for the *planting* and presence of churches in every village throughout the regions of Tizi-Ouzou and Béjaïa.

The *authority of the Bible* has served as a constant, especially across dividing lines between the majority Pentecostal evangelical stream and the older Reformed evangelical stream of the movement. From every stream of this movement, I hear the same message: "We do not want denominations. … We are Algerian Christians, and the Word of God is our authority in all matters of doctrine and conduct."[6] Finally, *local* and *lay leadership* has also been consistently encouraged since the 1980s, and especially in the 1990s, when almost all foreigners (including my own parents) were either expelled or forced to leave due to death threats.

---

5   In the past two years (2018–20), at least thirteen churches have been ordered to close. Additionally, as recently as October of 2019, two of the largest churches in Algeria were forced to close, with the Algerian police forcibly removing worshipers from these well-established places of worship.

6   Interview with Algerian church leader, n.d.

With regard to the last four elements of Garrison's ten universal elements of CPMs, the picture is far more varied. In the early years of rapid growth in Algeria, most believers met as *house churches*. However, over time the importance given to visible church buildings increased. Various reasons, both evangelistically and missiologically, were offered for the building of visible churches in Algeria. For example, the benefits of a visible place where Christians are known to meet and where Muslim seekers can make initial enquiries anonymously, which is sometimes felt to be less problematic (especially for women) than visiting private homes of those not in their wider family or social network. Nonetheless, research conducted by one Algerian pastor in 2012 demonstrably indicated a direct correlation between investment in the building of church buildings and the decrease in *rapid reproduction* of new churches and the hunger and passion for *church planting* and mission in and beyond Algeria.

The Second-Generation Challenge in Iran and Algeria

Of grave concern for movements in Iran and Algeria is evidence that the first generation is struggling to pass on the gospel to the next social and familial generation. In the case of Iran, while some second-generation IBMBs follow their parents' footsteps in leaving Islam and coming to faith in Christ, many others are drawn to ancient pathways such as Zoroastrianism or alternative spiritualities with New Age and occult influences. Perhaps more than anything else, the second generation is captivated by versions of Western secularism or exclusive humanism that promise a meaningful life without appeal to the transcendent.

In Algeria, some first-generation parents have the lingering presence of a mindset that assumes that because their children have been raised in a "Christian" family, they will by default be Christians. Contrary to such assumptions, many of Algeria's second-generation are either reluctant to embrace the faith of their parents or to abandon the faith they inherited as children immediately upon entering adulthood. Though many of them admire the costly witness of their parents' generation, some comment that the Bible teaching in many of their churches is superficial and disconnected from reality. Others point out that while churches uphold the authority of the Bible and seek to obey its teaching, many in this second generation find its application repetitive and pietistic, failing to address the socio-cultural and identity questions they face every day through social media and their Muslim-majority peer networks.

The factors underpinning the second-generation's disinclination to embrace the faith of their parents are undoubtedly varied and complex. To investigate these is a task that goes beyond the scope of this study. However, in our reflections on this persistent challenge, we have identified four important themes that shed light upon both what is lacking and what needs cultivating in these movements so that a vibrant multigenerational future is attainable. It is to these that we now turn.

Four Dimensions of Maturity for the Second Generation

1. Narrative

To find one's identity is to discover one's story. Struggles around identity unequivocally undergird the second-generation challenge as it plays out in Iran and Algeria. The concept of identity is vast and elusive, but a core element of it is in how an individual or community narrates the story of its existence. It is this story that shapes answers to core questions, such as "Who am I?" and "Who are we as a community?" as well as questions around *telos*—"Where are we going?" and "What purpose are our individual and corporate lives arranged around?"

A robust sense of belonging to a story is essential to communal maturity and continuity. Out of the competing stories that vie for allegiance in today's globalized Iran and Algeria, it is the story of God as revealed in the Bible that should orient the life of the BMB. And it is *this* story that will need to captivate the imagination of the second generation, forming how they perceive, assess, and act in the world, and equipping them with what Charles Taylor calls "existential bearings" (Taylor 2004, 2).

In my (Rania) work with different threads of the IBMB movement, I am intrigued by, on the one hand, the first-generation's sincere desire to believe and obey the Bible, and, on the other hand, their struggle to *see* or *feel* the world in biblical terms. A discrepancy is felt between the world they indwell and the world of the Bible. And thus it becomes increasingly difficult for them to *act* in biblical terms. This exhibits itself as a lack of integration and synthesis in the life of the believer. In other words, their lack of clarity about which story they belong to means a rigorous sense of identity as an IBMB remains unreachable.

Similarly, in my (Pat) work with ABMBs I have observed that the church is growing in the context of a battle of narratives within Algeria. As with the Iranian church, ABMBs struggle to relate their own story to the Bible's metanarrative. One believer described it to me this way:

The gospel that Jesus taught is very adapted to his context—very, very adapted to the context of the time. And now, today, when we read it we are far from Jesus' context, and here [in Algeria], we have a different context, and we have trouble linking the two."[7]

We have observed that believers in both these movements mostly engage the Bible in a disconnected and fragmentary fashion, treating Scripture as a series of individual stories, passages or books, and rarely as a unified story of redemption. Though DMM promotes the individual and communal reading of Bible *stories*— most notably through the Discovery Bible Studies—here more attention can be given to how sections of the Bible fit together, appreciating the thread that ties together the promises, covenants, events, people, and symbols. This is vital not only

---

7   Interview with Algerian student of theology, n.d.

because it gives believers the orienting story by which to live, but it ensures that their reading of the Bible conforms to what the Bible is: a unified whole with many parts. It also gives believers "canon sense" (Vanhoozer 2019, 117), by which they can interpret particular passages of Scripture in light of the whole Bible narrative.

Pockets of the Iranian church are taking steps to become more storytelling in their ecclesial practice. Individuals and house churches are choosing to read the entirety of the Bible over the course of a few years, rather than solely reading sporadic Bible verses or passages. Additionally, there are efforts to offer comparative teaching on the Bible story and other competing stories (i.e., Shi'ite Islam, nationalism, and secular humanism).[8] Finally, communal worship is being understood as, among other things, an opportunity to remember, enact, sing, and participate in the story of the Bible. This has resulted in extra care being given to how a worship service is structured, what liturgy is used, what songs are sung, and how the Bible passage spoken on is to be understood in light of the whole of Scripture's redemptive drama. Attempts such as these are not yet visible among Algerians, and we suggest that ABMBs might benefit from seeing and hearing how IBMBs are doing this.

2. Tradition

Another essential component of identity is in how members of a community understand their past. Roy Oksnevad identifies the "lack of collective memory" as the second of five of the greatest challenges facing the Iranian church today (Oksnevad 2015, 18). This he concludes on the basis of many interviews with IBMBs who repeatedly voice this concern, with one interviewee noting that the root of many IBMB struggles is that "'we [they] don't have any background of what church should look like" (U7M).

The role of church history and tradition is largely absent across Iranian and Algerian movements, albeit with a few exceptions. It is worth noting that in DMM literature, where tradition is cited, it is entirely negative. In *Contagious Disciple-making*, the Watsons adopt a rhetoric of "believing in Jesus but not in Christianity," casting a strong separation between Scripture and tradition (2014, 24–25). This posture represents a kind of primitivism that holds "a minimal commitment to God's action in history (in the life of Christ and usually in the apostolic activity) and makes only the New Testament church as normative for contemporary mission practice" (Smith 2006, 128–29).

Though space does not permit a thorough critique of this sensibility, some important deficiencies are worth delineating: First, such primitivism is weak from the standpoints of the doctrines of Creation (affirming the goodness of time) and Providence (affirming God's work by his Spirit through the church in time). Second, there is the danger of not taking seriously the incarnational nature of the

8 A helpful resource is Duane Alexander Miller, 2018. *Two Stories of Everything: The Competing Metanarratives of Islam and Christianity*. Grand Rapids: Credo House Publishers.

gospel, for to take the incarnation seriously is to take seriously the particularity of time and history. Third, a neglect of tradition is to misinterpret *sola* with *solo scriptura*, encouraging an unhealthy individualism in the local church's reading and application of the Scriptures that ignores the derivative authority of the credal tradition (Vanhoozer 2019, 183).

An embrace of tradition means that movements in Iran and Algeria can receive the gift of collective memory from history's communion of saints, allowing both the local community and "the convert's identity to have historical rooting" (Miller 2019, 2). It is important to note that "tradition neither supplements Scripture nor supplants its authority, it is simply the church's conciliar agreement as to what scripture says, means and implies." By this definition, tradition plays the role of an interpretative aid similar to the role of Philip for the eunuch in Acts 8. What we are suggesting here is not a move to become *traditionalist*, but rather to become *traditioned*. This is not an imposition of any tradition, rather an invitation for movements in Iran and Algeria to see themselves as part of the "great conversation," critically and creatively dialoging with, learning from, and adding to the different historical voices of the universal church.

One practical step in this direction is to embrace *conciliarism*—i.e., the use of councils with universal assent such as Jerusalem and Nicaea. Another step is to incorporate teaching on the Christian heritage of their respective regions in discipleship initiatives. In Iran, this would mean learning from the Nestorian Church, which experienced rapid church growth and persecution similar to today. In Algeria, this would involve rediscovering the Novatian and Donatists movements in the third and fourth centuries, perhaps unlocking why such a dynamic and influential church across North Africa completely died out.

3. Spirituality

In both Iranian and Algerian movements, spirituality is often limited to charismatic encounters on the one hand, or, on the other hand, rigid text-only Bible exercises. Most of the first-generation Iranian leaders that I (Rania) have encountered center their spirituality on direct encounters with the divine. Oksnevad names this a "super-spirituality … [that revolves around] supernatural experience … mystical connection[s] with God … [whose quality is] determined by the intensity of emotion generated" (2013, 164).

The residue of Sufism's dualistic mysticism is evident here. The direct encounters with Jesus—through dreams and visions—that many of the first-generation have as part of their conversion experience further heightens the expectation for recurrent meeting with the divine. When encounters of such emotional intensity do not occur frequently, many are left frustrated. Those in the second generation who do not have a "Road to Damascus" conversion experience are particularly disappointed when such encounters form the main content of the spirituality passed on to them. One second-generation IBMB described this to me as a feeling of "spiritual dissonance."

This dissonance also appears in the second generation of the ABMB movement. One pastor of a large Algerian church spoke to me (Pat) a few years ago about his church moving on from the "Pentecost era" to the "era of training." By this he did not mean that the charismatic practices associated with Pentecost had ceased. Rather, he meant that while the first generation was drawn to and nurtured by power encounters, the next generation hungers for deeper truth encounters. Of course, the former and the latter should not be seen as disparate experiences, and this itself raises a deeper tension found in some expressions of Iranian and Algerian spirituality, that of dualism.

Sadly, much of the church in Iran and Algeria has operated with a reductionist anthropology inherited from an enlightenment-infused evangelicalism that tends to view persons as purely thinking or feeling beings. This means that their spirituality has remained largely disembodied. A recovery of embodied spiritual practices and liturgical forms that attest to God's invisible presence and honor humans as whole persons are salutary as movements progress from the first to second generations. Of course, such practices should be seen as complementing rather than downplaying the importance of Bible exposition and charismatic encounters with the divine.

There is much that can be learned in this regard from the rituals and liturgies of other streams and eras of the world church. There is, for example, the *Spiritual Disciplines* tradition that is traced back to the early centuries, or the *Rule of Life* tradition that gives more structure to such disciplines as they are incorporated into one's daily rhythms. Similarly, the *Liturgical Year* tradition encourages specific embodied practices according to respective seasons of the church calendar, i.e., Lenten fasting and Eastertide feasting. Finally, there is the general use of the visual arts and multi-sensory experiences that encourage an integrated participation by the whole person in worship.

It is important to note that all of these practices are vulnerable to distortions and misuse. In applying them, one must be careful that they do not distract from the real yet invisible presence of Jesus Christ and his direct and unmediated action in his church. Nevertheless, both the positive and negative dimensions of global and historical patterns of spirituality can inspire Iranian and Algerian believers to reconstruct their own embodied rituals and liturgies, appropriate to their own context. As one elder shared with me (Pat), "I would like Algeria to invent its own model."[9]

---

9   Interview with Algerian church leader, n.d.

4. Community

Finally, there is the matter of interpersonal relationships. In his writing about IBMBs, Oksnevad describes the second-generation as disheartened by the "disharmony of interpersonal relationships exhibited by the lack of forgiveness and repentance" (2013, 163). Severe marital struggles are not uncommon within the Iranian movement, with many families struggling with different forms of abuse, often resulting in divorce or breakdown in relationships between parents, children, and siblings. The emotional trauma that many IBMBs have experienced in the past, combined with the dark side of their honor and shame culture, further magnifies the nature and impact of these relational tensions. Outside of the home, relationships in the public sphere are likewise tense and fractious. IBMBs are deeply suspicious and distrustful of Muslims, considering them enemies and themselves victims rather than neighbors.

ABMBs are also experiencing difficulties in living out the gospel in interpersonal relationships. Similar to Iran, this applies in marriages, particularly in the treatment of wives by their husbands. At a communal level, relationships between leaders and church members are also strained. One ABMB woman shared with me (Pat) that both phenomena convey lingering "Muslim" cultural attitudes to marriage and leadership. Concerning the latter, a couple told me that some ABMBs naïvely transfer their cultural concepts of leadership to the church, considering them sufficiently Christian. They disclosed that servant-leadership models were resisted both by leaders and their respective followers in part due to the *Zaim* (guru or strong man) complex prevalent in the culture: "Everyone plays the game … the little people and the leader … he doesn't like to be questioned, he doesn't like to be accountable and his word is ultimate."[10]

Likewise, it seems conversion has not brought deep changes to male hegemony within the Algerian church culture. In the words of the oldest known believer in Algeria,

> *Women are much more present and active, and very faithful too. It's just a case of letting them speak, listening to them, they have opinions to give… . It's clear that there is a Muslim heritage, and women suffer because of that. They tell us clearly that their husbands behave like Muslims toward them.*[11]

Alongside communal Bible reading and prayer, there is a great need for resources and training in areas such as conflict resolution, boundaries, marriage, parenting, abuse, interpersonal communication (especially between the genders), servant-leadership, and honor and shame. Having access to Persian and Arabic psychotherapy and counselling from a Christian perspective is also invaluable.

---

10 Interview with Algerian married couple church leaders, n.d.

11 Interview with Algerian mother and teacher, n.d.

Recovering a Healthy *Triangle* of Forces

To address the four themes above can appear an intimidating task. However, the Iranian and Algerian churches should not see themselves as walking this journey alone. By his Word and Spirit, the Lord has gifted them with a wealth of resources, including voices of the historic and global (universal) church. Indeed, addressing the second-generation challenge faithfully and effectively will require Iranians and Algerians to listen to and dialogue with such voices. Currently, the particular makeup of both movements and certain shifts in missiology throughout the last few decades might be limiting such fruitful interaction.

In the 1970s, much-needed critiques of the colonial "mission station" approach to church planting birthed the "people movements" anthropology, spearheaded by, among others, Donald McGavran. This perspective saw the various cultures of the world as distinct and separate pieces of a mosaic. Thus, the proper task of the missionary or church planter is to establish discipling communities (today we might call these DMMs) in each of these pieces of the mosaic. While the precise ways in which each church will worship, pray, and minister would vary as much as the pieces of a mosaic, they would all nonetheless be recognized as "our kind of show" (McGavran 1974).

Notwithstanding its many benefits, this missiological paradigm may have generated some unintended consequences over time. One of these seems to be the growing tendency to view any voice coming from "outside" the local culture as inherently negative: a corrupting, controlling, and dominating influence. Fearing the dangers of colonization, some local indigenous communities have been encouraged to silo themselves from outside voices and exercise independence and autonomy in ecclesial thought and practice. To lock out all voices of the *other* out of fear of domination may be contributing to an anthropology that places too much emphasis on the particularities of cultures, while ignoring the reality that though each are created unique and distinct, cultures are constantly intermingling, colliding, and integrally connected with one another. Only an anthropology that sees cultures as divorced and disparate pieces of a mosaic could accommodate such a turn.

The challenge for the Iranian and Algerian churches will be in how to healthily engage outside voices so that they do not dominate or control. It is here that the "triangle of forces" metaphor used by Lesslie Newbigin in the late twentieth century provides a helpful aid. Written as a critique of McGavran's mosaic metaphor, Newbigin's metaphor addresses the movement of the gospel from the first to the second spiritual generation of pioneering church planting. Newbigin presents the movement of the world church as a complicated and unpredictable "triangle of forces." In the first generation, these are: 1) the local culture; 2) the Christianity of the evangelist (or church planter); and 3) the Christianity of the Bible (Newbigin 1995, 147).

The dynamic of this triangle of forces addresses the development of the church as it is planted and grows in different contexts. It acknowledges the unavoidable distortion of truth that occurs when the church planter (or movement initiator), however carefully, attempts to communicate the gospel and biblical truth in cultural idioms and language that he/she seeks to use to reach the receptor community. It also acknowledges the unavoidable bias in the church planter's framing of the gospel that McGavran's people-movement approach sought to address. These distortions are addressed as the third element of the triangle, the Bible, is read (in the power of the Holy Spirit) and believed by the convert community and results in their beginning to raise questions about the difference between the Christianity introduced by the church planter and the Christianity of the Bible.

Crucially, however, Newbigin's triangle of forces not only addresses the need for the first generation to push back on the potentially unbiblical influences of the cultural outsider, it also identifies the priority of an ongoing dialogue between the indigenous church movement and outside streams of the church as the local movement grows. So, as the movement grows into the second generation, the three points of the triangle become: 1) the local church movement within the culture; 2) the Christianity of other steams and traditions of the world church; and 3) the Christianity of the Bible.

Because the spiritual DNA of the New Testament church, from its birth in Jerusalem via its cross-cultural transmission to new linguistic, cultural, and social terrain in later eras, is itself a constantly evolving movement, Newbigin's triangle metaphor seems highly appropriate for our discussion. In our view, the second-generation dimension of his triangle of forces metaphor addresses the constantly evolving dynamic in the relationship between the local and universal identity and mission of the world Christian movement better than the mosaic metaphor.

A constant dialogue between the local and outside streams of the church will seek to deliberately expose the first generation to questions of narrative, to the collective memory, traditions, and spirituality of other streams in the movement of the world church, past and present. This approach might address the subsequent tendency in some indigenous movements to reify their own cultural interpretation of the Bible into a kind of unfaithful localism or unconscious syncretism with the surrounding culture, such as the "Shiite Christianity" visible in parts of the Iranian movement (Oksnevad 2020) or in the myth of an unbroken "original" Christian Kabyle identity in Algeria (Guemriche 2011, 49, 105, 133).

Newbigin's model addresses this by suggesting that subsequent generations will benefit from further exposure to the wider global streams and influences of Christianity. With Newbigin, we see the vital importance of such a careful and constructive exposure, not as the icing on the cake or an additional dimension for super mature leaders in the movement, but for *all* believers. This might be one dimension of Bosch's "emerging ecumenical missionary paradigm" (Bosch 1991, 369) and is well defined by S. T. Antonio in his exploration of ecclesiology in frontier contexts. He writes,

> Biblical churches will reflect the essential components of a local church as well as its participation in the larger, universal community in Christ. This is a key point which qualifies any particular cultural expression of the church; every church should make room in its "church concept" for other cultural expressions of church besides its own. Cultural specificity must never deteriorate into cultural exclusivity, since Christ has reconciled people of all cultures into one new humanity. (Antonio 2020, 48)

We propose that church planters assist the first generation in seeking appropriate ways to engage with the wider streams of global Christianity and learn from both their successes and failures.

Conclusion

In this chapter we have sought to offer a critical engagement with the second-generation challenge as it pertains to movements in Iran and Algeria. To this end, we have painted a picture of the particular status and composition of movements in both our contexts, including the struggles they have confronted in passing the gospel to the next generation. By exploring the four themes of *narrative, tradition, spirituality,* and *community,* we have sought to provide a compass that helps practitioners judge the health and maturity of their movements as they pursue a flourishing multigenerational future. These four themes, though by no means exhaustive, invite movements to a reflective self-evaluation that asks the following questions:

1. **Narrative:** *Does our movement have a clear founding story that is faithfully lived out in word and deed? Do we intentionally let this story shape and order all that we do as a community?*

2. **Tradition:** *Is our movement rooted in history? Do we pay close attention to how the Spirit is speaking to us through the church's two-thousand-year history?*

3. **Spirituality:** *Are a wide range of formative and embodied spiritual rhythms, rituals, and practices promoted that honor our members as whole persons?*

4. **Community:** *Do we regard relational health as the lifeline of our community and take active steps toward promoting relational healing, reconciliation, and communal trust in private and public spheres?*

Our contribution ended with a discussion around the importance for movements to dialogue with global and historic voices of the universal church. This is a call to embrace a "glocal" hermeneutic that is at once biblical, transformative, and liberating (Van Engen 2006, 172).[12] In all of this, it is helpful to be reminded by Newbigin that

---

12 This term "glocal" is used by Charles Van Engen to describe the simultaneous and paradoxical relationship of the local and global church.

the Christ who is presented in Scripture for our believing is Lord over all culture, and his purpose is to unite all of every culture to himself in a unity that transcends, without negating, the diversities of culture. (Newbigin 1995, 149)

The journey that lies ahead of movements in Iran and Algeria as they seek to address the second-generation challenge will not be easy. Gratefully, the ongoing life of the church depends not primarily upon human actions but on the divine action of Jesus Christ by his Spirit; he is always the creator and sustainer of movements. Thus, the suggestions given above should be seen primarily as ways to improve our participation in and with the work Christ is already doing in Iran and Algeria by his Spirit. The road will still be long, with all kinds of twists and turns along the way. It is for this reason that we have called it a *challenge*.

References

Antonio, S. T. 2020. *Insider Church: Ekklesia and the Insider Paradigm*. Littleton, CO: William Carey Publishing.

Bauckham, Richard. 2003. *Bible and Mission: Christian Witness in a Postmodern World*. Grand Rapids: Baker Academic and Paternoster Press.

Bosch, David J. 1991. *Transforming Mission: Paradigm Shifts in Theology of Mission*. American Society of Missiology Series, 16. Maryknoll, NY: Orbis.

Brittenden, Patrick, and Paul Sanders. 2018. "Algeria," in the *Encyclopedia of*

Christianity in the Global South, edited by Mark A. Lamport. Lanham, MD: Rowman & Littlefield.

Garrison, David. 2004. *Church Planting Movements*. Monument, CO: WIGTake Resources.

———. 2014. *A Wind in the House of Islam*. Monument, CO: WIGTake Resources.

Guemriche, Salah. 2011. *Le Christ s'est arrêté à Tizi-Ouzou: Enquête sur les conversions en terre d'islam*. Paris: Editions Denoël.

LeBlanc, Jean. 2006. *Algérie, tu es à moi ! Signé Dieu*. Thoune, Switzerland: Editions Sénevé.

McGavran, Donald. 1974. "The Dimensions of World Evangelization," Lausanne Congress strategy paper. See https://www.lausanne.org/content/lausanne-1974-documents.

Mercado, Leonardo N. 1975. *Elements of Filipino Theology*. Tacloban City, Philippines: Divine Word University Publications.

Miller, Duane Alexander. 2019. "The Role of History in Pastoral Care for Converts from Islam." *New Wineskins Missionary Network*, https://newwineskins.org/blog/2019/4/2/part-2-the-role-of-history-in-pastoral-care-for-christians-from-a-muslim-background.

Newbigin, Lesslie. 1995. *The Open Secret: An Introduction to the Theology of Mission*. London: SPCK.

Oksnevad, Roy. 2013. "An Investigation into the Components of Disharmony in Iranian-Muslim Background Churches in the Diaspora." PhD diss., Department of Intercultural Studies, Trinity International University, Deerfield, IL.

———. 2015. The Iranian Diaspora Church: A Case Study, COMMA: https://pdfs.semanticscholar.org/d18c/7880ed7f80f0de214d74d10f1034c7d31f32.pdf.

Smith, James K. 2006. *Who's Afraid of Postmodernism?* Ada, MI: Baker Academic.

Taylor, Charles. 1989. *Sources of the Self.* Cambridge: Cambridge University Press.

———. 2004. *Modern Social Imaginaries.* Durham, NC: Duke University Press.

Van Engen, Charles E. 2006. "The Glocal Church: Locality and Catholicity in a Globalizing World." In *Globalizing Theology: Belief and Practice in an Era of World Christianity*, edited by Craig Ott, Harold A. Netland, and Wilbert Shenk. Grand Rapids: Baker Academic.

Vanhoozer, Kevin. 2019. *Hearers and Doers.* Bellingham, WA: Lexham Press.

Watson, David, and Paul Watson. 2014. *Contagious Disciple Making.* Nashville: Thomas Nelson.

Webster, John. 2006. "Discipleship and Obedience." *Scottish Bulletin of Evangelical Theology* 24 (1).

Yacob, Youssef. 2016. *As Fragile as an Egg? Lessons On Discipling, Training, Empowering and Sending Out Believers From a Muslim Background.* Alicante, Spain: Logos Ediciones.

PART V

MOVEMENT LEADERSHIP AND NEXT STEPS

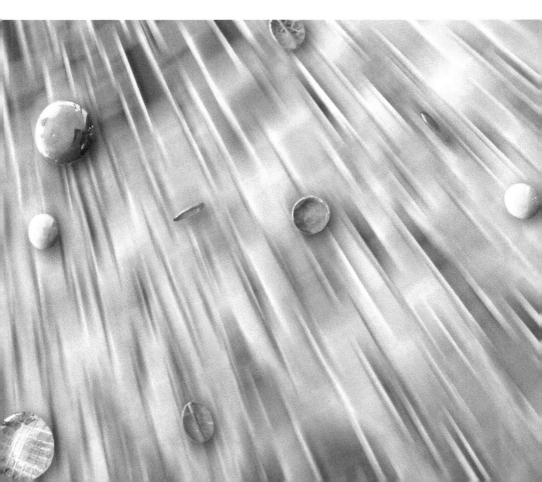

The Profile of an Effective Movement Catalyst

Emanuel Prinz

This chapter represents the first-ever empirical research into the qualities of effective movement catalysts. Prior to this study, there had been an intuitive understanding among movement thinkers as to the marks of effective movement catalysts. This intuitive understanding, however, was based either on the cumulative experience of a seasoned individual or on the analysis of a limited number of case studies. This chapter presents the findings of a strictly empirical research study that surveyed a representative sample of effective movement catalysts.

The study answers two questions concerning apostolic leaders effective in catalyzing a movement among a Muslim people group: Which traits and competencies do they self-report to exhibit? And which traits and competencies have contributed to their catalyzing of a movement? The outcome is a profile of an effective movement catalyst, verified with some conclusiveness.

The data of this study establishes a clear association between movement breakthrough and a certain kind of apostolic leader, exhibiting a set of particular traits and competencies. This finding should challenge the emphasis on movement methodology that has been commonplace among movement thinkers in recent years at the cost of emphasizing the role of character and personality of the movement catalyst. The data of this present research should lead to a paradigm shift in the field.

The profile provides us with a personality profile and a competency model for aspiring movement catalysts. As it is the first of its kind, developed strictly based on empirical data, it should be considered by Christian ministries committed to catalyzing movements.

This research used an empirical mixed-methods approach. The main research method utilized is the Delphi technique of iterative rounds of online surveys, with an expert panel of apostolic leaders who have catalyzed a movement themselves. Both qualitative and quantitative data are integrated, using statistical procedures as well as grounded theory in the data analysis. The research scope represents thirty-five movements in fifteen countries, thereby constituting a representative sample size. The resulting profile provides us with a personality contour and a competency model for aspiring movement catalysts.

What Are Movement Catalysts Like? The Massive Gap in Our Understanding

I have been involved with movements as a practitioner, mentor, supervisor, and trainer. I have wrestled with issues similar to those of many of my colleagues: What do we focus on when we only have one or two hours each month with the practitioners we mentor? How can we best train movement catalysts? What qualities and competencies do we cram into a training day? How does training on movement methods relate to training of the person and their personal development? Struggling to find answers to these and related questions led me on the journey of this research.

These questions have an answer! We need a better understanding of the qualities of effective movement catalysts. This will enable us to focus our mentoring, oversight, and training on those qualities, as they are a key to the movement catalysts' effectiveness.

However, up until now we have not had a clear understanding of the qualities that mark effective movement catalysts. Previous studies on movements affirm the critical role of leadership in catalyzing movements (Addison 2015). Apostolic leaders have been directed to important elements occurring in most movements and encouraged to implement these findings in their own work (Garrison 2004). Some publications (such as Woodberry 2011) have highlighted the fruitful practices that lead to breakthroughs. "Identifying the right leadership for the team" was highlighted as an effective practice in the *Fruitful Practice* research (Chard and Chard 2008, 174), in which 99 percent of the study participants considered the "right" leadership as "important" (174). What this "right leadership" looks like has not been addressed in a systematic way in the *Fruitful Practice* research, which surveyed "the qualities practitioners said they wanted in a leader" (175) listed below. These are the findings based on the most thorough research. Other publications suggest the existence of a vague understanding of the traits and competencies of an apostolic leader but are based merely on anecdotal evidence and intuitive insights. Empirical verification was needed—a gap that this study has filled. Therefore, the general research problem was summarized in the following empirical unknown:

The Empirical Unknown: The traits and competencies of apostolic leaders instrumental in the catalyzing of a movement

This led to the formulation of the following main research question:

The Research Question: What are the consistently exhibited and cited traits and competencies of apostolic leaders who were instrumental in the catalyzing of a movement among a Muslim people group?

The Research Design

The Effective Movement Catalyst: The Person Surveyed

All participants in the study have been effective catalysts of a movement in a Muslim people group. The participants comprised thirty-one apostolic leaders who have been effective in catalyzing a total of thirty-five movements. For the purpose of this study, a movement is defined as having occurred when more than a thousand individuals have chosen to become followers of Jesus Christ or more than a hundred churches have been planted in the third generation, meaning that one church planted a second church that in turn planted a third, following Garrison's definition (2014, 39).

For the purposes of this research, the apostolic leader is defined as an outside change agent; he is from a people group and culture other than the people group where he catalyzed the movement.[1] He was the first Christian to engage the people group with the good news, with his engagement resulting in the catalyzing of a movement. He is not an insider-innovator from within the community. Nor is he the man of peace (Matt 10:11ff; Luke 10:5ff) who is the first from within the people group to welcome the outside Christian worker, opening up his social network for the gospel. The effective movement catalyst may be an expatriate, or he may be a citizen of the country in which the movement happens, though from a different ethnic background than the target group. In the latter case, he may speak the same language as they do, and he may be from a geographically close area. The catalyst(s) may also be a pair rather than a single individual (following Luke 10:1).

The Movements Surveyed: A Representative Sample

This study surveys thirty-five movements among twenty-eight people groups in fifteen countries. Most of those movements (eighteen) happened in Indonesia. Other countries with several movements included in this study are India (three), Jordan (two), Ethiopia (two), and Bangladesh (two). Movements are currently underway in the countries of Burkina Faso, Cote d'Ivoire, Mozambique, Sudan, Pakistan, China, and Myanmar. Another movement has grown from Kenya across the borders into Somalia and Tanzania. This variety means that the

---

1   As all survey participants were male, with the exception of the spouse of one effective catalyst, masculine pronouns have been used throughout. The fact that only one female main catalyst was identified for the sample is likely due to the effect of male dominance in Muslim societies inhibiting significant influence from women more than on non-Muslim societies.

movements examined in this study represent the major regions of the Muslim world, including West Africa, East Africa, the Arab world, Turkestan, South Asia, and Southeast Asia (also referred to as Indo-Malaysia). Of the nine regions of the Muslim world Garrison describes as the different "Rooms in the House of Islam" (2014), only North Africa and the Persian world are not represented in this study.[2] This variety makes the sample quite representative.[3]

At the time this research was conducted, the pool of potential participants meeting the criteria to take part in this study globally was in the region of seventy catalysts. A total of sixty-nine movements were reported in the Muslim world, according to the most current survey (Garrison 2014). A few more probably occurred between the publication of Garrison's study in 2014 and the time of this research in 2015. Therefore, the precise number of living effective movement catalysts worldwide meeting the inclusion criteria could only be estimated, but that number was probably around seventy. Thus the participants in this study probably represent more than 40 percent of the potential survey pool of all living persons who met the inclusion criteria. Such a percentage constitutes a significant representation and gives the findings a high validity.[4]

The sample size combined with the wide variety of participants makes the findings of this study quite representative. The research approach of the Delphi technique that was utilized, with an expert panel building consensus, further augments the validity and reliability of this study.

The Foundational Literature Review

The empirical research aspect of this study was grounded in an extensive review of relevant literature. All publications on apostolic leadership and movements were surveyed (such as Miley 2003; Sinclair 2005; Allen et al. 2009; Dent 2011; Johnson 2009; Travis and Travis 2014; Smith 2014; Addison 2015, and more). Using these Christian understandings of apostolic leadership as the only basis of the empirical research would most likely have led to what is known as confirmation bias. This happens when participants, having been pointed to what is already

---

2   The reason is that the two movements in these two regions, one among the Kabyle-Berber of Algeria, and one among the Persians of Iran, were catalyzed in the 1970s and 1980s respectively (Marsh and Verwer 1997; Blanc 2006; Garrison 2014, 90–94, 130–41), and the initial movement catalysts are no longer living.

3   The movements examined differ widely in size. The number of fellowships reported to have been established in the different movements ranges from 46 fellowships to 23,000 fellowships, with a median of 430 fellowships. Likewise, answers differ as to the number of Muslims who have become followers of Jesus through the movements. The size of the movements surveyed ranges from 777 believers (for a movement with 146 fellowships, thus still meeting the inclusion criteria) to more than 100,000 believers. The median is 2,500 believers.

4   The largest research project on movements among Muslims to date has been the Garrison study (2014). The scope of Garrison's work includes a total of forty-five movements among thirty-three different people groups in fourteen countries (Garrison 2014, 231). Building on Garrison's key research, this present study becomes the second-widest in scope, based on the number of movements among Muslims surveyed.

believed to be known as "true," only confirm existing knowledge. The approach of this study, however, was to expose such biases where they exist. The starting point for this study, therefore, was the findings of secular empirical leadership research. All existing empirical studies (a total of over five hundred) were examined from the leadership theory called trait theory (Terman 1904; Stogdill 1948; Bass and Bass 2008),[5] as well as the leadership school called *Transformational Leadership* (Burns 1978; Bass and Avolio 1990; 1994; Bass and Riggio 2006).[6]

After more than a hundred years of researching the question, "What are the traits of effective leaders?" consensus has increasingly been reached that effective leaders, universally, have a number of traits in common. The understanding of what these traits are has become more clear too (Judge et al. 2002). The field of *Transformational Leadership* has validated the competencies of effective leaders.[7]

The findings from these empirical leadership studies differ somewhat from the common understanding of effective apostolic leadership. The results from empirical research in a secular context complement, expand, and indeed challenge some of the traditional beliefs about Christian apostolic leadership. This became clear when I produced a synthesis of all empirical leadership studies and all Christian publications on apostolic leadership and movements. This synthesis then formed the basis of the survey instrument that was administered to the participating effective movement catalysts. A synthesis of all publications relating to Christian ministry concerning apostolic leadership and movement research[8] is presented in the following tables, using the paradigms of traits[9] and competencies[10] from leadership theory. Table 20.1 presents all traits mentioned in the literature, showing which traits are listed by which author.

---

5   In summary, I addressed the field of trait theory from its first known publication in 1904 (Terman) to the present day. The literature review examined all meta-analyses and qualitative reviews that have been published, synthesizing more than five hundred empirical studies into what constitutes effective leadership. Special consideration is owed to the two meta-analyses of the trait literature, conducted by Lord, De Vader, and Alliger (1986) and by Judge, Bono, Ilies, and Gerhardt (2002). In addition, all major qualitative reviews are analyzed, which include those by Stogdill (1948; 1974), Mann (1959), Kirkpatrick and Locke (1991), Yukl (Yukl and Van Fleet 1992; Yukl 1998), Hogan, Curphy, and Hogan (1994), House and Aditya (1997), Zaccaro and colleagues (Zaccaro 2001; Zaccaro, Kemp, and Bader 2004), and Northouse (2010).

6   The field of transformational leadership was examined, since its first publication in 1973 (Downton 1973). The three streams of research that have contributed most significantly to the field of transformational leadership include the work of Bass and his associates (Bass 1985; 1990; Bass and Avolio 1990; 1993, 1994; Avolio and Bass 1991; 1999); the research of Bennis and Nanus ([1985] 2007); and the ongoing work of Kouzes and Posner ([1987] 2012). A strong correlation between the findings of these streams of research exists. The Multifactor Leadership Questionnaire, based on the research of transformational leadership, was selected and its questions integrated to the instrument put before the participants in this study.

7   A detailed review of the leadership literature can be found in Prinz 2016; 2019; 2021.

8   See in detail in Prinz 2016; 2019; 2021.

9   Understood as "patterns of personal characteristics that foster consistent leadership effectiveness" (Zaccaro 2007, 7).

10 Understood as "an area of knowledge or skill that is critical for leadership to be transformational."

Table 20.1 Comparison of Traits of Apostolic Leaders Identified in Publications

Traits	Publications by Author										
	Miley 2003	Sinclair 2005	Stevens 2008	Chard 2008	Nelson 2009	Dent 2012	Watson 2011 & 2014	Travis 2014	Smith 2014	Addison 2015	Larsen 2016 & 2020
Big picture thinking	X										
Strong personality	X										
Self-awareness	X										
Desire to initiate	X										
Independent	X	X									
Non-conformist	X										
Thrive on challenge	X	X									
Critical	X										
Impatience	X										
Tendency to overextend	X	X									
Hunger for depth with God	X	X			X				X		
Broad in their horizons	X	X									
Tenacity/not backing down	X	X						X	X		X
Want good handle on things											
Quirky/hard to get along											
Self-confidence											
Over-assertiveness											
Evangelistic heart											
Vision											
Praisworthy character/integrity											
Obedience to God											
Humility							X				
Determination to succeed							X				
Willingness to risk							X				
Ability to forgive							X				
Courage to change							X				
Passion				X							
Servanthood				X							
Love of people				X							
Availability				X							
Perpetual learner					X		X	X	X	X	
Reflective					X						
Sacrifice						X					
Focus						X				X	

Table 20.1 continues on the next page.

	Miley 2003	Sinclair 2005	Stevens 2008	Chard 2008	Nelson 2009	Dent 2012	Watson 2011 & 2014	Travis 2014	Smith 2014	Addison 2015	Larsen 2016 & 2020
Passionate urgency									X		
Single-mindedness								X	X		
Love for God									X		
Led by God									X		
Action-focus									X		
Results-orientation									X		
Perseverance								X	X		
Been with & called by Jesus										X	
Intentional spiritual growth		X									
Being a model		X									X
Strong work ethic		X				X					
Holy discontent		X									
Bible-driven		X									
Listening for God's voice		X									
Live the gospel										X	
Not fended in										X	
Aggressiveness											X
Boldness											X

Surprisingly, there is barely any overlap between different publications which examine the *traits* of apostolic leaders. The nine publications list a total of forty-one traits of effective apostolic leaders, revealing a lack of consensus in the discourse. Of these traits, twenty-eight are referenced only in one single publication. Only thirteen are mentioned by more than one author, seven of them by two different authors, three of them by three different authors, and only three of them by four different authors. The traits agreed on by three different authors are *evangelistic heart, vision,* and *integrity.* Those agreed on by four different authors are *hunger for depth with God, tenacity,* and *being a perpetual learner.* Even these three most-cited traits, however, are still only mentioned in fewer than half the publications (four out of nine). This means the discussion of traits that distinguish effective apostolic leaders is far from reaching a consensus.[11]

---

11 An exception is the relatively strong overlap of six traits between Miley (2003) and Sinclair (2005), simply due to the fact that Sinclair quotes Miley.

Table 20.2 Comparison of Competencies

Competencies	Miley 2003	Sinclair 2005	Stevens 2008	Chard 2008	Allen 2009	Nelson 2009	Dent 2012	Watson 2011 & 2014	Travis 2014	Smith 2014	Addison 2015	Larsen 2016 & 2020
Gift of faith	X	X		X			X			X	X	
Influence	X											
Gain following	X	X						X				
Initiate		X										
Make thing happen		X										
Vision casting		X	X							X		
Bible teaching		X										
Leadership		X								X		
Prayerfulness/intercession				X		X			X	X		
Experience in ministry				X								
Delegation/equipping			X	X	X			X	X	X	X	X
Recognize & catalyze gifts			X		X			X	X			
Evaluation of progress						X				X		
Leader development								X		X		X
Team building								X				X
Listening skills								X				
Knowledge of movements								X		X		
Strategize & implement plans								X				
Ethnographic learning									X			
Cross-cultural befriending			X						X			X
Miraculous gifts									X	X		X
Gift of evangilism									X		X	X
Advocacy									X			
Discipling										X	X	
Mentoring										X		X
Exercise accountability										X		
Cognitive ability										X		
Training		X									X	
Resource brokering		X										
Identify partners		X										
Connect with people											X	
Gather communities								X			X	X
Ask DBS questions												X
Guide multiplying groups												X

Table 20.2 continues on the next page.

	Miley 2003	Sinclair 2005	Stevens 2008	Chard 2008	Allen 2009	Nelson 2009	Dent 2012	Watson 2011 & 2014	Travis 2014	Smith 2014	Addison 2015	Larsen 2016 & 2020
Wholistic community development												X
Inner healing prayer												X
Group coaching												X
Assess health of groups & clusters												X
Multiplication of movements												X

To summarize the *competencies* of apostolic leaders, table 20.2 presents all competencies mentioned in the literature, and notes which competencies are listed by which author.

In analyzing the *competencies* of effective apostolic leaders, we again find very little overlap between different authors. Out of a total of thirty competencies mentioned in twelve different studies, only thirteen are referenced in more than one publication. Six competencies are listed twice, three competencies are listed in three publications, and three competencies are listed in four publications. Only one competency gains a near consensus: *delegating/equipping* is agreed on by seven of the ten authors. The competencies listed by four different publications are *the gift of faith, intercession,* and *the recognition and catalyzing of gifts.* Those listed by three publications are *miraculous gifts, vision casting,* and *cross-cultural befriending.* A total of seventeen of the thirty competencies listed are only mentioned by a single publication.

Concerning both competencies and traits of effective apostolic leaders, little consensus has been achieved. The traits and competencies which, comparatively, have the greatest amount of agreement among authors were included in the empirical part of this study to verify whether they are exhibited by effective movement catalysts.

The Research Method: The Delphi Technique

The subjects of this research were effective movement catalysts, in particular their traits and competencies, and how these are associated with catalyzing a movement. The research used a mixed-methods approach, combining quantitative and qualitative data analysis. The primary approach for this study, for a number of reasons, was a quantitative method, following the suggestions of Creswell (2008).

The research method selected as the most appropriate for the purposes of this research was the Delphi technique. The general usefulness of this technique is in fields where little certain or confirmed knowledge exists. It is an acknowledged method to explore future or new terrain (Borg and Gall 1983).

The Delphi technique is a structured research method that facilitates systematic communication among a panel of experts. The underlying rationale is that "two heads are better than one, or … *n* heads are better than one" (Dalkey 1972, 15). The Delphi technique is useful "to develop a full range of alternatives, explore or expose underlying assumptions, as well as [to] correlate judgments on a topic spanning a wide range of disciplines" (Hsu and Sandford 2007, 1).

The Delphi process can be broken down into a basic structure, summarized by the following diagram (McCoy, Thabet, and Badinelli 2009):

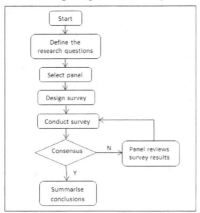

Figure 20.1 Delphi Technique Flowchart

Following this process, I began by defining the research question: What are the consistently exhibited and cited traits and competencies of apostolic leaders who were instrumental in the catalyzing of a movement among a Muslim people group? Then I selected a panel of subject experts knowledgeable about the area of research (who have catalyzed a movement themselves). I then designed the survey, based on the above literature review, and conducted the survey by asking the movement catalysts to fill out the questionnaire. This happened in three rounds. After each round, I calculated the mean or median of all answers given, collated any additional input, then fed it back anonymously to the participants. In passing along to the expert panel the results of the previous survey round, I pointed out incongruences and unexpected results, and invited further comments. This process continued until round three, when the panel reached a strong degree of convergence.

A Personality Profile and Competence Model of Effective Movement Catalysts

This study found that there are indeed a number of traits and competencies of the movement catalyst that can be associated with movement breakthrough. A total of eleven traits and competencies were exhibited consistently by virtually every single effective movement catalyst. A further twenty-two more traits and competencies were exhibited consistently by at least 80 percent of the effective movement catalysts who participated in this study—still a very significant portion.

To sum up, based on the findings of this study as presented in tables 20.3 and 20.4, a personality profile (that includes the traits) and a competency model emerge for aspiring movement catalysts. The personality profile of an apostolic leader can be depicted as follows:

Table 20.3 Personality Profile of an Apostolic Leader

PERSONALITY	Emotional Stability
	Confidence
	Initiative
	Dependability
	Adaptability
	Persistence
MOTIVATIONAL	Tangible Love
	Drive for Responsibility
	Drive to Achieve
	Desire to Excel
MENTAL	Perpetual Learning
	Intelligence
SPIRITUAL	Hunger for God
	Expectant Faith
	Fervent Intercession
	Evangelistic Zeal
SPIRITUAL CONVICTIONS	Confidence in the Bible
	Confidence in the Spirit
	Confidence in Locals
SOCIO-INFLUENTIAL	Inspiring Personality
	Sociability
	Boldness

A competency model can be derived from the same findings. This is the first competency model developed for Christian pioneer leaders based strictly on empirical data, and as such should be given serious consideration by Christian ministries. Most ministries develop their competency model, if they have one, from the process angle rather than from an outcomes angle. Christian organizations usually take the process angle and identify competencies that enable pioneers to fulfill their organizational role and lead their teams well. This needs to be complemented by the outcomes angle. This competency model identifies the competencies correlated with the outcome of movements catalyzed, presented in the following table:

Table 20.4 Competency Model of an Apostolic Leader

MENTAL	Complex Thinking
	Innovation
	Movement Knowledge
TRANSFORMATIONAL	Influencing of Beliefs
	Inspiring Vision
	Challenging Assumptions
	Personal Consideration
SOCIO-INFLUENTIAL	Discipling
	Coaching
	Empowering
	Partnering

Each of the traits and competencies is defined in the following tables. Table 20.5 lists the eleven traits and competencies verified as consistently exhibited by all effective catalysts. Table 20.6 lists the twenty-two traits and competencies exhibited by at least 80 percent of the effective movement catalysts in this study.

Table 20.5 Traits & Competencies Verified to Fit 100% of all Effective Catalysts

Hunger for God	Effective movement catalysts are hungry for depth with God, yearn to love Him more deeply; they seek to hear God's voice and be obedient.
Expectant Faith	Catalysts are expectant that God will grow a movement among their people group and save many soon, and they have great faith taht God will show His power through their lives.
Confidence	Catalysts feel confident in their spiritual gifts and skills and exhibit a sense of confidence.
Drive for Responsibility	Catalysts feel responsible for the people they serve and for engaging the with the Good News, and they are motivated by a sense of responsibility.
Dependability	Catalysts are reliable and trustworthy, so that others can depend on them.
Persistence	Catalysts are tenacious in spite of challenges and amidst difficulties, and they don't give up.
Empowering	Catalysts empower and enable locals to be the key players by putting responsibility and authority in their hands from the beginning and by developing their gifts.
Confidence in the Holy Spirit	Catalysts are confident in the Holy Spirit and have faith in Him to accomplish His intended work in the life of all God's children, as they are enabled to obey His commands.
Confidence in the Bible	Catalysts have a deep confidence in the Bible to be their movement guidebook, and a deep assurance in its power to accomplish what God desires.

Table 20.5 continues on the next page.

Influencing of Beliefs	Catalysts talk often about their most important values and beliefs, consider the moral consequences of decisions with people, and emphasize the importance of living toward the purpose one is created for.
Inspiring Vision	Catalysts articulate a compelling vision of the future, talk enthusiastically about what needs to be accomplished to see a growing movement, and express confidence that goals will be achieved.

Table 20.6 Traits & Competencies Verified to Fit ≥80% of all Effective Catalysts

Emotional Stability	Effective movement catalysts are emotionally mature and stable and are able to master their emotions in ways helpful for interactions with others.
Initiative	Catalysts take the first move when something needs to be done and initiate new enterprises.
Adaptability	Catalysts adjust their behaviors to changing situations and adapt their approaches as situations change.
Tangible Love	Catalysts genuinely care for the people they reach out to; they express love and genuine interest in their lives and welfare, because they truly love them.
Drive to Achieve	Catalysts are motivated by achieving goals and have a strong drive to get things done and atain results.
Desire to Excel	Catalysts give their very best effort to any work they do and strive to excel in their gifts and talents.
Fervent Intercession	Catalysts pray regularly and for extended time on behalf of their target people for many to be saved in growing movement.
Evangelistic Zeal	A passionate urgency drives catalysts to see the Good News shared with all the lost in their people group.
Confidence in Locals	Catalysts fully believe in the local worker(s) who lead the movement and have a strong sense of trust in them.
Perpetual Learning	Catalysts actively engage in experiences, expecting that in every situation there will be something new to learn.
Intelligence	Catalysts skillfully use intellect and reason, in order to understand situations and solve problems.
Complex Thinking	Catalysts use their mental capability and judgement to make sense of complex and ambiguous situations, in order to steer complex processes.
Innovation	Catalysts use their imagination to come up with creative ideas, innovative approaches and solutions.
Movement Knowledge	Catalysts are familiar with CPM theory and methods as well as other areas of knowledge relevant to the cataylizing of a movement and know how to apply them.
Sociability	Catalysts demonstrate culturally appropriate interpersonal skills and are characterized by pleasant conversation and companionship.

Table 20.6 continues on the next page.

Boldness	Catalysts are bold and brave to advance the gospel, even in the face of danger and threats, and are courageous to hold on to their convictions in spite of difficulty and resistence.
Discipling	Catalysts are intentional in disciple-making in the context of a relationship that leads to heart obedience, where believers actually grow in character and spiritual disciplines.
Coaching	Catalysts skillfully ask insightful and powerful questions which draw from other people's experience and learning, in order to facilitate their discovery of things for themselves.
Partnering	Catalysts initiate, build, and maintain trust relationships with partners, on the basis of which they foster cooperation to accomplish more together.
Inspiring Personality	Catalysts display a sense of authority and confidence, act selflessly in ways that build other people's respect for them, and instill a sense of honor in others for being associated with them and other Jesus followers.
Challenging Assumptions	Catalysts question people's assumptions to re-examine whether the assumptions are appropriate; they get others to look at realities from different angles, seek differing perspectives when addressing problems and suggest new ways of looking at things.
Personal Consideration	Catalysts consider an individual as having different needs, abilities, and aspirations than others in the group.

A Paradigm Shift:
From Movement Methodology to Personality

The empirical findings of this study affirm a large portion of the intuitive understanding of the traits and competencies of apostolic leaders, as shown in previous publications. Such understanding has been based on intuition, exposure to multiple movements, and case studies, but not previously proven through rigorous empirical research. The present study fills this gap and consolidates a large portion of the intuitive understanding.

This study verifies most traits and competencies that have been proposed repeatedly in the movement and apostolic leadership literature. The literature review identified a number of leader traits and competencies that have a certain degree of consensus among publications. All but one of these have a strong correlation with the effective catalyzing of a movement. The traits of *hunger for God* and *faith* are strongly exhibited by all participating effective movement catalysts. Most of them also strongly exhibit the traits *evangelistic zeal* and *fervent intercession*.[12]

---

12   One trait examined in the study that does not occur in the lists above—miraculous gifting—calls for comment. The result was a bimodal distribution. Some effective catalysts testified to having a miraculous gifting and stressed how significantly miracles had contributed to the catalyzing of their movement. A number of other effective catalysts, however, confirmed that they did not possess any miraculous gifting. Some even reported that no supernatural miracles at all occurred in their movement.

This study also identifies as significant several traits and competencies that have not received any attention in the previous literature. Some of these come as a surprise. These traits include *emotional maturity, dependability, adaptability, desire to excel, intelligence,* and *sociability.* These competencies include *challenging assumptions, coaching,* and *partnering.*

Apostolic leadership and movement literature has emphasized the spiritual traits of the apostolic leader combined with the right methodology. In *Church Planting Movements,* Garrison emphasizes characteristics of movements as well as methodology. He ascribes a crucial role to the apostolic leader (2004, 255), stating that "God has given Christians vital roles to play in the success or failure of these movements" (2004, 26). However, he does not look into their traits or competencies.

In DMM literature, Watson (2011; Watson and Watson 2014) and Trousdale (2012) also emphasize right methodology. Watson regards the role of the external catalyst as critical, since he is the one who sparks the process of a movement (2011, 114). Most of the traits and competencies mentioned by Watson are either verified directly in this research (for example, *perpetual learning*) or appear under competencies identified by this research, including *good character* (inspiring personality), *the ability to develop potential beyond boundaries, the ability to delegate* (empowering), and *listening skills* (personal consideration).

As for T4T, Smith and Kai (2011) likewise emphasize methodology overall. In the only publication so far addressing the exact topic of this study, Smith considers the person of the apostolic leader (2014). Based on multiple case studies of dozens of practitioners, Smith summarizes the traits and competencies of effective catalysts: "Each of them possesses a healthy combination of a set of characteristics" (2014, 38). Most of those characteristics were verified by the empirical data of this present research. Among the traits and competencies verified fully are *movement knowledge, radical learning, expectant faith, expectant prayer (fervent intercession),* and *mentoring.*[13]

The data of this research further suggests that effective catalyzing of movements, while almost always traceable to a movement ministry methodology, is not tied to any one particular movement methodology. Different effective catalysts employ different movement ministry approaches. The majority (53 percent) describe their approach as DMM, 18 percent as T4T, and 9 percent label it CPM. More than half of the effective movement catalysts use a hybrid of

---

13 Several other traits and competencies suggested by Smith are included within traits verified by this present research, such as knowledge of the Bible (under Bible teaching), tenacity and perseverance (persistence), integrity and spiritual authenticity (attributed idealized influence), loving God (hunger for God), being led by God, having vision from God, exercising faith (faith), bold discipling (discipling), ruthless self-evaluation (openness to experience and perpetual learning), training (Bible teaching, discipling, and mentoring), developing leaders (confidence in nationals, and mentoring), and vision casting (inspirational motivation).

two or more different movement approaches, which they have adapted to the uniqueness of their context.[14]

However, the overall emphasis of apostolic leadership and movement literature has been on the right methodology, with some attention to leader traits and competencies of the apostolic leader, particularly traits of a spiritual nature. The findings of this research go beyond these commonly established insights. The data demonstrates that a particular methodology is far less significant in the catalyzing of movements than may have been assumed, whereas certain personal traits and competencies are strongly associated with the effective catalyzing of movements.

This perspective has been voiced by only a few, most notably Neill Mims and Bill Smith, who formulated this significant insight after studying movements for twenty years: "At the end of the day, it is the man and woman of God and not the method that God blesses" (Mims and Smith 2011, 8). Another proponent of this perspective is Dave Ferguson, who concluded that "the greater the missional impact, the more obvious the pioneering apostolic leadership becomes" (quoted in Addison 2015, 12). The person of the apostolic leader is the key element that determines whether or not a movement is launched, not the method he or she employs. Again, Bill Smith is among the few who previously formulated the conclusion: "If someone says to me, give me the method or give me the curriculum, I know that they have not understood that this [the catalyzing of a movement] is accomplished through persons rather than methods" (Addison 2015, 19).

Simply put, the right leader will develop the right methodology for his particular ministry context. An apostolic leader with traits such as *openness to experience, intelligence, cognitive complexity, creativity,* and *initiative,* who also possesses the necessary socio-influential and transformational competencies, is a leader competent to develop as well as implement with his team the most effective methodology for his unique context. However, a person who is handed a certain methodology but lacks the leader traits and competencies identified in this study will not be capable of applying this methodology and will be highly unlikely to be effective. This stands in stark contrast to the conclusions of the vast majority of publications on movements that center around methods and principles rather than the person of the catalyst. The clear data of this research should jolt movement thinkers into a paradigm shift in movement missiology, away from an overemphasis on methodology to a focus on the personality and competencies of the catalyst.

---

14 Although the approaches used by effective catalysts differ in certain aspects, it is important to note that they are all reproductive movement approaches, and they all have certain principles in common, namely: cultural contextualization, obedience-oriented discipleship, house churches, reproduction, training of multipliers, and reproducible resources (Betts 2014).

Practical Usefulness and Outlook

This description of an effective movement catalyst provides us with a personality profile and a competency model for aspiring movement catalysts. As this is the first profile of its kind developed strictly on the basis of empirical data, I suggest it should be considered by every Christian ministry committed to catalyzing movements. The profile may prove invaluable as a tool for mobilizing and screening new candidates, for oversight and mentoring of movement practitioners, and for the development of movement training. Based on the profile, the most relevant traits and competencies can be selected for training programs and learning objectives can be formulated more precisely. Clearer learning objectives will lead to better training measures and higher quality training curricula.

Similarly, aspiring movement catalysts can focus on traits and competencies in which they want to grow and can identify specific learning objectives and steps which will serve as a roadmap toward becoming an effective movement catalyst. Movement breakthrough is not in our hands to achieve, but our personal growth is. The findings presented here show what kind of person we will want to become so God can use us to catalyze a movement.

More research is building on this study. A follow-up study with a larger sample size is currently being conducted by the Bethany Research Institute team to expand this research beyond the Muslim world, with the goal of verifying the universal nature of the findings presented here and of validating them further. The late Steve Smith (who endorsed the findings presented here) urged me to conduct a control group study to identify the traits and competencies that distinguish effective movement catalysts from other pioneers who have not catalyzed a movement. This control group study is being conducted simultaneously.

For more findings from this research and more details of the literature review, the research design, and best practices for many of the traits and competencies presented here, look for the publication of *Movement Catalysts* with William Carey Publishing (Prinz 2021).

References

Adams, Eric, Don Allen, and Bob Fish. 2009. "Seven Themes of Fruitfulness." *International Journal of Frontier Missions* 26: 75–81.

Addison, Steve. 2015. *Pioneering Movements: Leadership That Multiplies Disciples and Churches.* Downers Grove, IL: InterVarsity.

Allen, Don, et al. 2009. "Fruitful Practices: A Descriptive List." *International Journal of Frontier Missions* 26: 111–22.

Avolio, Bruce J. 1999. *Full Leadership Development: Building the Vital Forces in Organizations.* Thousand Oaks, CA: Sage Publications.

Avolio, Bruce J., and Bernhard M. Bass. 1991. *The Full Range Leadership Development Program: Basic and Advanced Manuals.* Binghamton, NY: Bass, Avolio and Associates.

Bass, Bernhard M. 1985. *Leadership and Performance Beyond Expectations*. New York: Free Press.

———. 1990. *Bass & Stogdill's Handbook of Leadership: Theory, Research, and Managerial Applications*. 3rd edition. New York: Free Press.

———. 1993. "Transformational Leadership: A Response to Critiques." In *Leadership Theory and Research: Perspectives and Directions*, edited by Martin M. Chemers and Roya Ayman, 49–80. San Diego: Academic Press.

———. 1994. *Improving Organizational Effectiveness Through Transformational Leadership*. Thousand Oaks, CA: Sage Publications.

Bass, Bernhard M., and Bruce J. Avolio. 1990. *Transformational Leadership Development: Manual for The Multifactor Leadership Questionnaire*. Palo Alto, CA: Consulting Psychologists Press.

Bass, Bernhard M., and Ruth R. Bass. 2008. *The Bass Handbook of Leadership: Theory, Research, and Managerial Applications*. New York: Free Press.

Bass, Bernhard M. and Ronald E. Riggio. 2006. *Transformational Leadership*. Mahwah, NJ: Lawrence Erlbaum Associates.

Bennis, Warren G., and Burt Nanus. 1985. *Leaders: The Strategies for Taking Charge*. New York: Harper & Row.

———. 2007. *Leaders: The Strategies for Taking Charge*. 2nd edition. New York: Harper Business.

Betts, Trevor. 2014. "Different Views of Essential Factors in CPMs." Unpublished paper.

Blanc, Jean L. 2006. *Algérie, Tu Es à Moi!, Signé Dieu*. Thoune, Switzerland: Editions Sénevé.

Borg, Walter R., and Meredith D. Gall. 1983. *Educational Research: An Introduction*. 4th edition. New York: Longman.

Burns, James M. 1978. *Leadership*. New York: Harper & Row.

Caldwell, Larry W. 1992. *Sent Out! Reclaiming the Spiritual Gift of Apostleship for Missionaries and Churches Today*. Pasadena, CA: William Carey Library.

Chard, Andrew, and Rachel Chard. 2008. "The Gathering of Teams of Laborers." In *From Seed to Fruit: Global Trends, Fruitful Practices, and Emerging Issues among Muslims*. 2nd edition, edited by J. Dudley Woodberry, 173–92. Pasadena, CA; William Carey Library.

Creswell, John W. 2008. *Research Design: Qualitative, Quantitative, and Mixed Methods Approaches*. London: Sage Publications.

Dale, Laurent. 2008. "Team Building in Multi-Cultural Ministries. Unpublished Paper submitted to the Fruitful Practices Narrative Review Fellowship.

Dalkey, Norman C. 1972. *Studies in the Quality of Life: Delphi and Decision-Making*. Lexington: Lexington Books.

Dent, Don. 2011. *The Ongoing Role of Apostles in Missions: The Forgotten Foundation*. Bloomington, IN: CrossBooks.

———. 2012. "Apostles Even Now." In *Discovering the Mission of God: Best Missional Practices for the 21st Century*, edited by Mike Barnett and Robin Martin, 355–69. Downers Grove, IL: IVP Academic.

Downton, James V. 1973. *Rebel Leadership: Commitment and Charisma in the Revolutionary Process.* New York: Free Press.

Fish, Bob. 2009. IC Leadership Study: Survey. Unpublished paper.

Garrison, David. 1999. *Church Planting Movements.* Richmond, VA: International Missions Board.

———. 2004. *Church Planting Movements: How God Is Redeeming a Lost World.* Midlothian, VA: WIGTake Resources.

———. 2010. *Leadership in Church Planting Movements.* Retrieved from https://churchplantingmovements.com/leadership-in-church-planting-movements.

———. 2014. *A Wind in the House of Islam: How God Is Drawing Muslims around the World to Faith in Jesus Christ.* Midlothian, VA: WIGTake Resource.

Garrison, David, and Senecca Garrison. 2008. "Factors That Facilitate Fellowships Becoming Movements." In *From Seed to Fruit: Global Trends, Fruitful Practices, and Emerging Issues Among Muslims,* edited by J. Dudley Woodberry, 207–18. Pasadena, CA: William Carey Library.

Geisler, Wilson. 2012. *Rapidly Advancing Disciples.* Retrieved from https://churchplantingmovements.com/wp-content/uploads/2012/01/Rapidily_Advancing_Disciples_RAD_Dec_2011.pdf.

Goldmann, Bob. 2006. "Are We Accelerating or Inhibiting Movements to Christ?" *International Journal of Frontier Missions* 28: 8–13.

Hogan, Robert, Gordon J. Curphy, and Joyce Hogan. 1994. "What We Know about Leadership: Effectiveness and Personality." *American Psychologist* 49: 493–504.

House, Robert J., and Ram N. Aditya. 1997. "The Social Scientific Study of Leadership: Quo Vadis?" *Journal of Management Yearly Review* 23: 409–73.

Hsu, Chia-Chien, and Brian A. Sandford. 2007. "The Delphi Technique: Making Sense of Consensus." *Practical Assessment, Research & Evaluation* 12: 1–8.

Johnson, Alan R. 2009. *Apostolic Function in 21st Century Missions.* Pasadena, CA: William Carey Library.

Judge, Timothy A., et al. 2002. "Personality and Leadership: A Qualitative and Quantitative Review." *The Journal of Applied Psychology* 87: 765–80.

Kirkpatrick, Shelley A., and Edwin A. Locke. 1991. "Leadership: Do Traits Matter?" *Academy of Management Executive* 5: 48–60.

Kouzes, James M., and Barry Z. Posner. 1987. *The Leadership Challenge.* San Francisco: Jossey-Bass.

———. 2012. *The Leadership Challenge: How to Make Extraordinary Things Happen in Organizations.* 5th edition. San Francisco: Jossey-Bass.

Larsen, Trevor. 2016. *Focus on Fruit! Movement Case Studies and Fruitful Practices: Learn from Fruitful Practitioners.* A Toolkit for Movement Activists: Book 2. S.l.: Focus on Fruit Team.

———. 2020. *Core Skills of Movement Leaders: Repeating Patterns from Generation to Generation.* A Toolkit for Movement Leaders: Book 7. S.l.: Focus on Fruit Team.

Lord, Robert G., Christy L. De Vader, and George M. Alliger,. 1986. "A Meta-Analysis of the Relation between Personality Traits and Leadership Perceptions: An Application of Validity Generalization Procedures." *Journal of Applied Psychology* 71: 402–10.

Love, Rick, and Greg Livingstone. 2005. *Apostolic Leadership: How to Influence Your Team to Fulfil God's Purposes in the Muslim World.* Frontiers.

Mann, Richard D. 1959. "A Review of the Relationships between Personality and Performance in Small Groups." *Psychological Bulletin* 56: 241–70.

Marsh, Daisy M., and George Verwer. 1997. *There's a God in Heaven: Life Experiences among North Africans.* London: Gazelle Books.

McCoy, Andrew P., Walid Thabet, and Ralph Badinelli. 2009. "Understanding the Role of Developer/Builders in the Concurrent Commercialization of Product Innovation." *European Journal of Innovation Management* 12: 102–28.

McGavran, Donald A. 1955. *The Bridges of God: A Study in the Strategy of Missions.* New York: Friendship Press.

———. 1970. *Understanding Church Growth.* Grand Rapids: Eerdmans.

Miley, George. 2003. *Loving the Church ... Blessing the Nations: Pursuing the Role of the Local Church in Global Mission.* Waynesboro, GA: Authentic Media

Mims, Neill, and Bill Smith. 2011. "Church Planting Movements: What Have We Learned?" *Mission Frontiers* 33: 6–8.

Nelson, J. 2009. "Fruitful Leadership Survey: First Glance Results." Unpublished paper.

Northouse, Peter G. 2010. *Leadership: Theory and Practice.* 5th edition. London: Sage Publications.

Patterson, George, and Richard Scoggins. 1993. *Church Multiplication Guide: Helping Churches to Reproduce Locally and Abroad.* Pasadena, CA: William Carey Library.

Pickett, J. Waskom. 1967. *Christian Mass Movements in India: A Study with Recommendations.* Lucknow, India: Lucknow Publishing House.

Prinz, Emanuel. 2016. "The Leadership Factor in Church Planting Movements: An Examination of the Leader Traits and Transformational Leadership Competencies of Pioneer Leaders Effective in Catalyzing a Church Planting Movement among a Muslim People Group." DMin diss., Columbia International University.

———. 2019. *Der Missionar, den Gott zu Großem Gebraucht: Eine Untersuchung der Persönlichkeitsmerkmale und der Führungskompetenzen von Pionieren, die Erfolgreich eine Gemeindegründungsbewegung Gestartet Haben.* Nuremberg, Germany: VTR.

———. 2019. *Exponential Disciple-Making and Church Planting: Practitioner Manual.* Nairobi: Bethany International.

———. 2021. *Movement Catalysts: Profile of an Apostolic Leader.* Littleton, CO: William Carey Publishing.

Sinclair, Daniel. 2005. *A Vision of the Possible: Pioneer Church Planting in Teams.* Waynesboro, GA: Authentic Media.

Smith, Steve. 2012a. "Getting Kingdom Right to Get Church Right." *Mission Frontiers* 4: 10–15.

————. 2012b. "The Bare Essentials of Helping Groups Become Churches: Four Helps in Church Planting Movements." *Mission Frontiers* 34: 22–26.

————. 2014. "A Profile of a Movement Catalyst." *Mission Frontiers* 36: 38–41.

Smith, Steve, and Ying Kai. 2011. *T4T: A Discipleship Re-Revolution*. Monument, CO: WIGTake Resources.

Stevens, M. 2008. "Focus on Next Steps … : Lessons from the Multi-Region Trainers Forum." Singapore. Unpublished paper.

Stogdill, Ralph M. 1948. "Personal Factors Associated with Leadership: A Survey of the Literature." *Journal of Psychology* 25: 35–71.

————. 1974. *Handbook of Leadership: A Survey of Theory and Research*. New York: Free Press.

Sundell, Jeff. 2014. "4x4 Movements Coming Soon to an Unreached People near You!" *Mission Frontiers* 36: 7–9.

Terman, Lewis M. 1904. "A Preliminary Study in the Psychology and Pedagogy of Leadership." *The Pedagogical Seminary* 11: 413–83.

Travis, John, and Anna Travis. 2014. "Roles of 'Alongsiders' in Insider Movements: Contemporary Examples and Biblical Reflections." *International Journal of Frontier Missions* 30: 161–69.

Trousdale, Jerry. 2012. *Miraculous Movements: How Hundreds of Thousands of Muslims Are Falling in Love with Jesus*. Nashville: Thomas Nelson.

Watson, David L. 2011. *Gemeindegründungsbewegungen: Eine Momentaufnahme*. 2nd edition. Schwelm, Germany: Deutsche Inland-Mission e. V.

Watson, David, and Paul Watson. 2014. *Contagious Disciple Making: Leading Others on a Journey of Discovery*. Nashville: Thomas Nelson.

Woodberry, J. Dudley, ed. 2011. *From Seed to Fruit: Global Trends, Fruitful Practices, and Emerging Issues among Muslims*. 2nd edition. Pasadena, CA: William Carey Library.

Yukl, Gary A. 1998. *Leadership in Organizations*. 4th edition. Englewood Cliffs, NJ: Prentice Hall.

Yukl, Gary A., and D. Van Fleet. 1992. "Theory and Research on Leadership in Organizations." In *Handbook of Industrial and Organizational Psychology*, vol. 3. Edited by Marvin D. Dunnette and Leaetta M. Hough, 147–97. Palo Alto, CA: Consulting Psychologists Press.

Zaccaro, Stephen J. 2001. *The Nature of Executive Leadership: A Conceptual and Empirical Analysis of Success*. Washington, DC: American Psychological Association.

————. 2007. "Trait-based Perspectives of Leadership." *American Psychologist* 62: 6–16.

Zaccaro, Stephen J., C. Kemp, and P. Bader. 2004. "Leader Traits and Attributes." In *The Nature of Leadership*, edited by John Antonakis, Anna T. Cianciolo, and Robert J. Sternberg, 101–24. Thousand Oaks, CA: Sage Publications.

21

Pursuing Movements:
An Organizational Paradigm Shift

Eric and Laura Adams _____

Can a traditional church-planting agency shift paradigms while remaining true to its original calling? Our agency is a missional community focused solely on under-engaged Muslim people groups. Our goal has always been to communicate the gospel in ways that result in gatherings of disciples which multiply. In 2017, we decided that the time had come to explicitly expand our faith horizon from "church planting" to "pursuing movements of disciples and churches." This decision was the fruit of more than ten years of exploration by leaders and field members, five years of wide-spread training and peer coaching related to disciple-making movements, and significant processing by representatives of the whole community during conferences. The impact of this gradual paradigm shift has become evident throughout the agency.

This chapter provides a snapshot of some of our field teams; we listen to how they describe their recent experiences, while trying to live out movement-related principles. These observations will help us continue to gain insight as we pursue this faith horizon. In presenting this chapter, we hope to engage with others wanting to join with God's harvest among Muslim peoples at this time in history. Perhaps other organizations who would like to integrate discipleship movements into their organization's ethos can learn from our experience.

Understanding the Context

How Has This Shift Happened?

The paradigm shift has taken place gradually over the past fifteen years. Initially, field members who were witnessing greater responsiveness in their regions shared their stories. The wider mission community's reports of movements added fuel to this growing interest. As our top leaders sensed that the time was ripe for this shift, they purposefully promoted and supported field initiatives.

Our agency has grown from a handful of American teams (back in the 1980s) into a multiethnic community numbering over one thousand field adults. Currently, teams are launched from sending offices in North, South, and Central America, West and East Europe, Australasia, East and South Asia, and Africa. Members have primarily joined in response to God's personal call to bring the good news to Muslim peoples. They form teams co-laboring in urban and rural Muslim-majority contexts, while maintaining residency by means of their professional skills.

Training takes place in many ways within our agency. One venue is conferences, where field members and outside experts collaborate to cross-pollinate what is being learned in field contexts. These whole-agency conferences are presented in English, with simultaneous translation in several languages. Since about 2005, conference workshops specifically addressing some form of movements began to be offered, led by field members working in more responsive regions.

At the main bi-annual conference in 2011, overseers and coaches met to discuss movement principles more deeply. About this time, our international leaders were also prompted by a promoter of movement thinking to provide widespread training in disciple-making movement (DMM) principles.[1] Within the next five years, 60 percent of our community took part in this training—starting with those in oversight or regional leadership roles, then primarily field members. In hindsight, field members alerted us to a significant mistake: this training happened only in English, so an important segment of our community had to process the information through interpretation or not at all.[2] As a result, some non-native English-speaking field members in some regions have been more reticent to adopt the paradigm shift.

On the positive side, though, along with DMM training, peer coaching skills were also taught, resulting in the emergence of informal networks of field members encouraging one another and sharing resources they develop. Over the past decade, trainers at many sending offices have upgraded pre-field

---

1　Training done in collaboration with David Watson. See *Contagious Disciple Making* (2014). Initial trainers came from agencies experienced in supporting movements in Muslim regions. Very quickly, a dozen trainers from our teams adapted these trainings and became the trainers.

2　In addition, some from non-Western backgrounds reported that the style of teaching did not allow adequate space to process new ideas.

preparation, integrating fruitful practices findings (Woodberry 2008) and movement-oriented principles.

The conference in 2015 proved to be pivotal, as we re-evaluated the agency's mission statement and core values. During this gathering, all participants spent time in small groups focused on these, first listening to God in prayer, then discussing each topic. Through this, we reached a consensus that we would all work toward movements of disciples and churches.

At the conference in 2017, every regional report included comments on their efforts toward movements. Many training workshops included movement-oriented practices. During governance meetings, the international board (made up of field team leaders) changed the wording of one core value from "church-planting" to "pursuit of movements of disciples and churches." Subsequently, during the conference in 2019, roundtable discussions probed more deeply into factors impacting the depth and breadth of movements throughout the regions.

During the years of this gradual paradigm shift, much room has been given for debate and evaluation. Our members openly express their reactions, skepticism, and resistance to movement thinking and how it relates to ministry efforts. These conversations continue to leaven the thinking of field teams as well as sending and support departments.

As a whole community, we have noticed changes in how we pray, how we partner, and how we measure progress. Our reliance on prayer has increased, especially prayer that deepens our responsiveness to God's presence. In every region, field members are asking God, "What will it take to see multitudes move toward Christ? What roles would you have us fill?" Field members partner more than before with national believers, near-culture believers, and other agencies. Each region has created new ways to observe and report on their priorities and progress.

As we have shifted to this new faith horizon, our hope as an agency has grown. We have rightly rejoiced over the past decades, as God has drawn households and groups to gather, Muslims worshiping Jesus for the first time in their recent history. Now we are expectant that God wants to do even more: he will breathe life into movements of believers in ways that will impact their societies and spill over into other cultural groups. In this decade we have already glimpsed this. God has used some teams to catalyze fresh movements. Other teams have joined in work supporting movements previously in progress (including movements that began decades ago), and many teams are reshaping their approach to ministry, hoping to lay foundations for future movements.

Why Was a Shift Necessary?

When our agency formed almost forty years ago, church planting among Muslim people groups seemed like an audacious goal. We aspired to communicate the gospel and disciple believers in such a way that the resulting fellowships would spontaneously reproduce and spill across cultural boundaries. Through decades of faithful praying, learning, sowing, and sacrifice, some fellowships of believers did emerge. Some have indeed spread, impacted their societies, and reached out to other groups.

However, in many locations, even if a group of believers emerged, this did not result in the gospel transforming those societies and spreading to other cultures. Although God's work through field members was indeed audacious and amazing, we sensed that something more was necessary for this time in history.

Through hearing case studies of God's work in other regions, we realized that building toward a movement requires different first steps than building toward a singular gathering of believers. As long as we kept "church planting" as our faith horizon, many field members would continue doing what they had been doing up to this point, with the same limited results. Worse yet, some of their practices might even prove counterproductive.

What Has Been the Impact So Far?

In 2018, the International Directors' Team wanted to assess the impact of this faith horizon and the DMM training among teams by listening to their stories. So we sought out field members' stories, listening for answers to three questions:

1. How is "movement thinking" changing or shaping how our community pursues its apostolic calling?

2. Which insights can serve as benchmarks, spurring us to go deeper in our understanding of how God works through us to produce healthy, long-lasting, Christ-ward movements?

3. What might help our community shift toward greater alignment with "movement-oriented behavior"?

We gathered thirty interviews of field members at various stages of movement efforts, ranging from "active movement" to "hoping for a movement." We then distilled our observations into this qualitative, inductive, and informal report. This report is "qualitative" because it is based on stories told by field members. It is "inductive" because we identified emerging themes and distilled them into representative statements. It is "informal" because we have not yet had these statements rated by other practitioners to identify ideas reflecting consensus of conviction.

Additionally, there are some weaknesses in this research project, which include:

- Eighty percent of the interviewees were Americans. A future study should include field members from a wider range of sending countries. However, the interviews do represent both men and women, six different field regions, and nineteen unique field locations.

- A variety of people conducted the interviews, using different questions. Some interviewees were interviewed multiple times, over a span of several months, revealing that much learning and change continued to take place. Thus these statements capture only the interviewees' perceptions at the time of the interview, not the endpoint of a journey.

- We had no initial "benchmark" to compare with, since we didn't conduct a study like this fifteen years ago.

- Paradigm shifts happen at multiple levels and over a very long time, based on experience and other evidence. Many of these levels will not be observable or verbalized.

Despite these weaknesses, we believe the observations direct us toward critical issues to explore as we align ourselves with what we perceive God is doing among and through us.

Question 1. How Is Movement Thinking Changing Us?

In listening to the answers to this question, we need to define "movement thinking," to discern differences between this thinking and the way we operated previously. We also need to discern how the interviewees identify what has changed for them.

What Is "Movement Thinking"?

Movement practices vary considerably from practitioner to practitioner. However, many practitioners consider practices in the following list to be important, even if they are all not unique to those pursuing movements:

1. *Pray.* Movements are catalyzed by God's Spirit and seem to be a significant part of God's work in this generation. We dedicate ourselves to individual and corporate prayer, deepening our relationships with the Prime Mover, tuning in to his plans for the groups to whom he has sent us.

2. *Learn.* Movements are propelled by the transforming and reconciling work of God within the communities on their cultural terms, not by outside (foreign) agendas. So we commit ourselves to long-term growth in understanding and involvement in the local community. We work within existing trust networks, respecting ways the community processes innovations and makes decisions.

3. *Partner.* Movements require more gifts and wisdom than any one person can provide. We lay aside personal ambitions, partnering with others in every aspect of this work. We partner with humility and grace, encouraging one another toward this vision of movements that will impact the community and beyond (2 Tim 2:2).

4. *Evaluate.* Movements can be slowed or stopped. Some of our ministry practices may disempower new believers from walking in the authority God gives them in Christ. (For example, if they defer to me as the leader and my ministry

practices are not easily imitated). So, along with our partners, we evaluate all that we do, to test whether it contributes to or hinders movement growth.

5. *Display faith publicly.* We express our personal spirituality daily and naturally. This encourages the community to approach us with their spiritual interest.

6. *Widen contacts.* We ask God to bring us into contact with yet more people who have spiritual interest and/or will welcome the gospel message into their family and relational trust networks. We discuss spiritual topics openly within these relational groups rather than teaching isolated individuals.

7. *Listen to God.* When we help others learn from the Word, we use discovery or participatory learning. Discovery style study encourages the group to ask questions, listen reflectively, and identify what God is asking of them, rather than having them rely on an expert to tell them what to believe.

8. *Obey God.* We expect those studying the Word to do what God is asking of them. This includes sharing with others what God reveals to them while they are still on their journey toward faith.

9. *Empower leaders.* Very early in the process, we encourage and empower an appropriately gifted member of the group to lead. We encourage group members to start new study groups within other trust networks.

These practices help cross-cultural messengers share the gospel in easily imitated ways, providing whole families and trust networks with many opportunities to interact with God in prayer and the Word. Such interactions can provide a context for God to reveal himself without extra barriers of foreigners and their cultures.

What Is Different about This Thinking?

Many of the assumptions and practices in this list are not new to us. Some line up with the core values inspiring us over the past thirty years. Some have been common practice among generations of those called to minister among Muslims, inside and outside our missional community (Woodberry 2008). The greatest difference between this list and earlier lists of core assumptions is that they are organized toward a vision of movements—groups of disciples that multiply rapidly—rather than a vision of a single church which may or may not have the potential to multiply.

Unless trained otherwise, field members default to the ministry practices which shaped their own discipleship. It is significant that many practices on this list are not the same as those of our home (sending) churches.

Our community has a continual influx of new field members from a range of cultural and church traditions. Thus, training shaped by the list above will play a critical role in uniting new members and seasoned ones under a common vision toward effective practices for cross-cultural communication of the gospel, which can support the growth of movements.

From Interviewees in Their First Years On-Field: How Have I Changed?

The newness of movement thinking to interviewees appears in their "aha" moments: the moments when their understanding deepens and allows them to embrace new ways of thinking and living. These moments of insight often include many predictable lessons, since all cross-cultural workers must adapt to the world as defined by members of the host culture. Soon after they arrive, field members realize that many aspects of how they learned to follow Jesus in their home countries prove to be counterproductive in their new context.

Fifty percent of the interviews involved field members who had lived among their host culture fewer than ten years. Here are some examples of this early learning curve evident in their stories.

Interviewees said, "*I have learned to shed …* "

1. *Assumptions about what constitutes the core of the gospel message.* I rediscovered what it means to follow Christ and to be the church.

2. *Preconceptions of how people should behave.* I learned how to communicate with love and respect within worldviews containing multiple layers of religious and cultural identity.

3. *Reliance on text-based communication.* I learned how to communicate with oral learners.

4. *Prescriptive (expert-led) ways of teaching.* I learned to use ways to study Scripture which allow seekers to hear God speak through the Word, to interpret the Word through their own cultural filters, and to deepen their cultural identity while following the commands of Jesus.

5. *Individualism.* I learned to live and communicate within societies that value strong relational networks.

6. *Expectation of instant results.* I learned that it may take thousands of hours to communicate the gospel across cultures, investing life-on-life, often experiencing the pattern of "three steps forward, two steps back." Deep-level responsiveness may commonly not become evident for many years.

7. *An unhealthy heroism or "lone ranger" mindset.* I learned to partner—with humility and respect—with other believers, both national and foreign.

8. *Personal blind spots.* I grew more self-aware, dying to pride and personal ambition, while responding to healthy correction from others.

9. *Reliance on formulas and strategies.* I learned to listen to God corporately, undergirding everything with prayer.

10. *Fascination with personal "bright ideas."* I learned to test the worth of my innovations.

Our home cultures and Christian traditions imprint us with deep biases. To effectively communicate the good news in a new context, we must become aware of these biases. Like the grain of wheat Jesus referred to, we have to die to our cultural assumptions, allow God to remove our husks, and rejoice as he plants us in new soil. Only in that way can the good news sprout in a uniquely relevant way among the people God has called us to join him in reaching.

From Interviewees More Than Ten Years On-Field: How Have I Changed?

One way to observe paradigm change within our community is to note how members on the field for more than ten years describe *recent* changes.

Here are representative paraphrases from the interviews:

- *We now partner with national believers.* After fifteen years of ministering among the Muslim majority while avoiding involvement with national believers (who are a minority), we are now starting to partner with them. Because we now have such long experience and deep understanding of the majority culture, we find that God is using us to draw the national believers into his heart for the majority people.

- *We now partner with believers from Muslim backgrounds.* After twenty years of ministering—with little response—we met some local believers from Muslim backgrounds who had already been discipled for years by others. God is calling them to join with us in this work. Now the seeds we planted over the years are coming to fruit.

- *We now avoid being the lead teachers.* For more than twenty years I used my giftings to preach and lead. During that time, a local evangelist also partnered with us and brought many to faith. Unfortunately, most new believers resisted discipleship (by me). Now God has shown me that I need to take on a different role. I am learning to step back and encourage from the sidelines, as God gives the emerging Muslim followers of Jesus and national believers gifts and anointing to disciple their neighbors.

- *We now avoid being the center of the gatherings.* After twenty years of ministry (during ten of which we were nurturing a small fellowship), we realized that as long as we stayed, they would rely on us for money and the pattern of how to do things. It was time to test what would happen if we left. So we left, with occasional visits. At the first visit, it seemed that the group no longer met together. But during a visit two years later, we saw a real change. Not only were they meeting, they were connecting with believers of their tribe in other parts of the country as well. They were taking ownership, making sure the gospel message was going out to their people.

These comments show that the long investment and faithfulness of these field members was vital, leading to depth of understanding and love. Their comments also reveal humility and willingness to be reshaped by God to fit in with his plans for a new season of responsiveness in their host communities.

In Broad Strokes ...

We can see from these interview themes that movement thinking encourages cross-cultural messengers to ...

- Be prepared to invest deeply and for a long time in the host community.
- Be active, authentic disciples themselves, eager to listen and be transformed.
- Become lifelong learners, willing to change.
- Communicate the gospel within natural relational trust networks.
- Become Bible-centric and expect God to speak through his Word.
- Expect God to work through their partnership with others.
- Be willing to take a role alongside, rather than up in front.

These principles push gospel messengers onto a steep learning curve, forcing them to grow beyond the preconceptions and cultural biases they begin with. Through this growth, the gospel is released to root deeply in incarnational ways.

Question 2. Which Observations Spur Us to Deeper Exploration?

Interviewees mentioned factors that seem to affect their ability to support movements. We have categorized these factors as: how we partner with others, who we are, what we do, receptive environments, ways we disciple, and how leadership and group identity are nurtured. Each of these categories raises yet more questions worthy of exploration.

Partnerships Can Contribute to Movements

Interviewees described a variety of things they are learning as they partner with other believers (from near cultures as well as foreign).

I have discovered that it is important to partner with ...

- Those who are willing to do the work of evangelism.
- Those who can move and adapt to new cultures.
- Those who already earn a living, so they are not dependent on me for financial support.
- Preexisting believers who are the fruit of someone else's efforts, already discipled and mature.
- Muslims who follow Jesus, while maintaining their Muslim identity.

I have learned to…

- Treat near-neighbor believers and new believers as key players in this ministry.
- Act with grace, respect, and trust with my partners.
- Care for my ministry partners as whole people, not as a means to accomplish my goals.
- Be alert to the potentially unique problems I bring as an outsider in the role of a trainer.
- Build structures to support the movement that is already emerging.
- Encourage reconciliation among divided local churches, so they will gain a heart to reach nearby Muslims.
- Expect ministry partners (especially cultural insiders) to come up with insights to move the ministry forward.
- Include near-neighbor believers when I talk with Muslims, as their presence changes the conversations.
- Accept a role at a distance after investing many years in learning within community.
- Develop resources with partners which make the Word accessible to group members (for example, using their mother tongue, phone apps, etc.), address their concerns, and enable them to lead the studies themselves, thus passing on the discovery process.

Additionally, while working with partners, interviewees described how their partnerships shaped both partners in many ways. This includes the next two categories: who we are and what we do.

Movements Can Be Strengthened by Who We Are

Interviewees described how God has changed them internally as they pursue movements, saying things such as, I have learned to …

- Acknowledge efforts others have made long before I joined the effort, rather than claiming credit myself.
- Become self-aware: recognizing my strengths, weaknesses, fears, hopes, expectations, and how others see me.
- Develop healthy rhythms of life for myself and my family.
- Encounter God in the Word and let him change my worldview.
- Humble myself to be a life-long learner, admitting that I don't know all the answers yet and that much of my learning will be "on the job."
- Live authentically as a disciple of Jesus myself—"walking the talk"—and expecting God to transform me as I minister to others and receiving more of God's love myself.
- Rest in how God sees me and my work, not striving for personal validation.

Movements Can Be Strengthened by What We Do
Interviewees also mentioned specific activities they have learned to value.

I have learned to …

- Avoid linking financial gain with the ministry.

- Build trust with local community leaders, especially "gatekeepers" who allow field members to become catalysts within their community. Open the Word in community settings. Persuade community leaders that the gospel blessing is for the whole community. Pray openly for their communities. Discern points of contact, where the gospel addresses community concerns.

- Carefully lay foundations for future growth. Persevere, even in the absence of responsiveness at present.

- Discover the host worldview; learn to see through their eyes. Persevere toward long-term participation in this community, through increasing fluency so that I can communicate gospel truths in contextualized ways from early on.

- Empower others to lead, to discern God's leading through prayer and community. Die to my ambition to have to be the one discipling key people. Recognize my role must diminish as local leaders' roles increase in this ministry.

- Prayerfully and regularly evaluate all we do: Is it fruitful? Is it worthy to teach to others? Welcome mentoring, to build trust and accountability.

- Express faith intentionally, naturally, and openly. Turn conversations into opportunities to read or listen to Scripture passages. Reveal the gospel message bit by bit over time through stories. End each spiritual conversation with a truth we have in common.

- Fast and pray toward breakthroughs.

- Focus on Jesus, not on religion. Grow in vision. Ask God, "What needs to be done to catalyze movements for this region and beyond?" Discover how God is catalyzing movements in other regions. Believe that movements are possible. Live and pray as if God wants to see a multitude—beyond counting—in our lifetime.

- Identify and resist spiritual attack, both personally and with partners.

- Invest more time in seekers who demonstrate obedience to what God asks of them, engaging in whole-life and long-term discipleship.

- Learn how to communicate like oral learners.

- Mobilize prayer from those outside our situation.

- Pray often with people in the host community, face to face and for their expressed needs. Expect God to confirm the truth with supernatural acts. Integrate inner healing prayer with the gospel message. Pray for healing and deliverance openly, as appropriate or prompted by God. Discover how God is already using dreams and visions among the host people.

- Pray, cry, be hurt, sacrifice.
- Pursue peace. Help seekers forgive and reconcile with those within their relational trust networks. Do this ourselves.
- Seek out new local people who will engage with the Word and share it with others. Share God's Word with their families and trust networks from the start. Use discovery study: question-discover-listen-obey personally and in groups.
- Take risks and experiment with new approaches. Admit mistakes, try things that may not work well, and learn from this. Discern the next step forward through listening prayer together.

Receptive Environments Correlate with Movements

The interviewees referred to factors they observe that affects the receptivity of host people to the gospel message.

Those who are most receptive include ones who have …

- Been traumatized or displaced.
- Become a mistreated minority, impoverished, or disillusioned with Islam.
- Been seeking a new identity or community.
- Been rejected by their own network or family.
- Been seeking a helpful political alliance with a Christian community (regional or foreign).
- Experienced practical help from Christians (regional or foreign) such as finance, employment, or protection.
- Encountered Jesus through dreams, answered prayer, miracles, healings, restored relationships, or witnessed Jesus transforming someone.
- Known people who have (or have themselves) been transformed by encountering God during Scripture study.

There are others, conversely, not seeking a new identity, family or community but experiencing spiritual hunger. Movements seem to be happening in such environments when the host people discover ways to follow Jesus while remaining culturally Muslim, remaining integrated within their community.

Discipleship Methods Can Fuel Movements

The interviewees described what they have learned about discipling in their contexts, saying things such as,

I have learned to encourage seekers to …

- Interact with God's Word themselves, discovering what it says and how it applies to their lives in all matters, including their lifestyle and religious identity.
- Do this together with other seekers or believers (not just one-on-one with a foreigner), preferably within a family or other preexisting trust network.

- Obey what they believe God is telling them to do through his Word (even if it seems counterintuitive to foreigners).
- Transparently share the real situation of their lives with other followers of Jesus. Pray for and encourage one another and love one another according to what Jesus taught (e.g., the "one another" practices of the New Testament).
- Identify and make use of the gifts God gives his community.
- Actively listen to God in prayer. Watch for and recount how God is answering prayers and showing his presence active among them.
- Share what they learn right away with those who do not yet know Jesus: through the Word, prayer, and action.
- Help shape which Scripture resources will be used by the group.
- Own the gospel as their message, for their people. The gospel motivates them to serve their community, and to take the gospel to the most difficult places.

Understand that we are saved by Jesus and not by religion or religious change. Additionally, interviewees observed as normative that some study groups do not continue long, but fall apart for various reasons. Groups sometimes grow rapidly for reasons other than spiritual interest. Early growth of groups of seekers (in numbers and maturity) seems slow, while later growth of groups of seekers seems quicker.

Leadership Development & Identity Choices Can Contribute to Movements
Some interviewees described what they have learned about their roles in leadership development, making comments such as,

I have learned to ...

- Be an encouragement to group leaders, showing them respect. Pray with and for them.
- Listen well, ask good questions, encourage them to make the decisions.
- Tap into what the leaders already value, ways they already learn, and stretch them using the discovery-listen-trust-God model.
- Model and teach reproducible leadership practices.
- Impart to leaders a vision for the power of the gospel to transform their region and all nations, a vision for 2 Timothy 2:2 and fourth-generation reproduction as the standard.
- Avoid emphasizing or pushing for a particular religious or group change of identity, but rather walk with new leaders as they determine for themselves what identity they feel God calling them to have.

In relation to this last, hugely important issue, some interviewees described how they have learned to encourage fellowships to wrestle with their identity change as believers, through Scripture study and prayer.

Groups need to make their own decisions about identity-related issues, including:

- What will we call ourselves, to communicate that we are followers of Jesus?
- Which previous cultural values and behaviors will we continue, using them to communicate gospel truth?
- Which previous cultural values and behaviors will we reject out of obedience to Christ?
- Which group structure will facilitate reproduction?
- How shall we relate to preexisting Christian groups in the region while retaining our cultural identity?

In Broad Strokes ...

God goes before us. In fact, he invites us to come join him in environments he has ripened for movements. As we enter these settings, we recognize that who we are in Jesus is as important as what we do in his name. We find that living as authentic disciples of Jesus ourselves allows the gospel to ring true and makes it easier for God to make his appeal through us with a message of reconciliation. We have learned that we become more effective when we partner with others, in a context of mutual respect and humility. We are more easily transformed toward Christlikeness as we function in community. We observe that Jesus meets each seeker on their own terms and within the context of their own culture. Their relationship with Jesus—and the love and power he brings—will naturally ignite and drive movements because it is genuinely good news. We are learning to give new believers the freedom to retain their cultural identity as they follow Jesus and negotiate their transformed identity into a compelling testimony for the society around them. We have discovered the importance of empowering emerging leaders and allowing them to be the center of God's work.

Question 3. How Can We Align Ourselves More with Movement Thinking and Practice?

This faith horizon of movements is gradually reshaping more than just the field teams in our agency. Overseers and mentors, both pre-field and on-field, are adapting their coaching to align with movement practices. Mobilizers are integrating this faith horizon in their recruiting strategies. We have changed significantly, but we realize that we still need even more alignment with this faith horizon within our agency.

To answer the question of how we can progress in realigning as a missional community, we will describe how the various parts of our community impact field teams, and then encourage each of these stakeholders to evaluate their contribution.

How Do the Various Parts of Our Community Shape Our Field Practitioners?

Within our community, some departments contribute in several different ways, so we have categorized our community by five functions rather than by departments. Here is a description of the functions and their impact on field teams.

Table 21.1: Functions and Their Impact on Field Teams

Parts which contribute toward mobilizing and recruiting
What they do: • Recruit, mobilize, vision-cast in sending countries • Screen and train candidates • Reports by mobilizers and pre-field trainers to International Directors *How this shapes field workers:* • People are recruited by a movement vision and narrative consistent with the realities of our fields. This helps them prepare for and enter the field with a healthy set of expectations. • Communication of the faith horizon to sending churches enables them to have reasonable expectations and adequately support those they send out.

Parts which contribute toward team building	Parts which contribute toward team upgrading
What they do: • Appoint team leaders • Evaluate vision and strategy papers and memos of understanding • Connect potential team members to team leaders • Train team leaders • Reports by team leaders to overseers • Train and coach • Reports by coaches and trainers to overseers *How this shapes field workers:* • Team leaders' expectations and skills are strengthened to align with a movement vision, consistent with field realities.	*What they do:* • Train field workers • Regional and international gatherings • Member care • Reports by trainers and member care providers to the community *How this shapes field workers:* • Team members' expectations and skills are strengthened to align with a movement vision, consistent with field realities.

Parts which contribute toward on-field partnering	Parts which provide overall direction
What they do: • Mobilize and train proximate believers • Coach teams and proximate believers • Form partnerships with other agencies and groups of believers • Reports by these entities to overseers *How this shapes field workers:* • Partnerships with proximate believers and field workers from other agencies are fostered, in ways that contribute toward movement.	*What they do:* • Monitor progress towards vision • Decide use of funding, manpower, and other resources • Communicate growth of vision (depth, bredth) to the whole community *How this shapes field workers:* • Movement-vision is cast throughout the community. • Lessons being learnt are cross-pollinated throughout the community. • Innovations and fruitful practices are encouraged throughout the community.

How Can We Continue Pursuing This Horizon?

To encourage our whole community to continue more fully embracing movement-orientated practices, *we suggest that each department …*

1. Continue discovering what field members are learning as they pursue movements, so these lessons can reshape the department's faith and vision.
2. Continue discussing the principles of movement thinking and being, asking God to show us more about what he is doing.
3. Evaluate current goals, usage of human resources and other resources against the principles and practices.
4. Identify areas where the department can strengthen its support of these principles and practices, reporting on this to the rest of the community.

Conclusion

While we have made significant steps toward a shift to movement thinking in our community, some members continue to have fundamental concerns about the validity of movement thinking. Their questions fuel important discussions and result in some of our best thinking and innovation. Our current paradigm shift seems driven by a combination of inspiring and empowering leadership practices, stories of progress from our own fields, candid sharing of failures and transformations, as well as cross-pollination of lessons learned. We add to these a willingness to honestly engage in discussion until we reach a deeper understanding of what God is doing in us, through us, and around us.

At each step deeper into this organizational paradigm shift, new issues become pertinent. Some of the questions we are currently asking ourselves include:

- How can candidates from every sending country be effectively recruited and trained so they can join in pursuing movements?
- Which factors shape our field members' expectations and on-field practices?
- How can multicultural teams bring out the best from each culture and perspective?
- How can we deal wisely with power imbalances that exist between different cultures as we work together and as we communicate the gospel?
- How can we avoid other powers—money, status, politics, education, etc.— replacing or eclipsing the genuine power of the good news Jesus brings?

What changes happen in the multiple layers of Muslim identity among followers that are part of emerging movements?[3] As a missional community, we are exploring what it takes to reorient ourselves so we enhance (rather than

---

3 This question is prompted by the concurrent need to study movements that have happened over the past fifty years, to see what remains, what impacts society, and what hinders healthy growth. See John Wilder, "Some Reflections on Possibilities for People Movements Among Muslims," *Missiology: An International Review* (http://www.asmweb.org/missiology.htm), July 1, 1977, Volume 5:3, pp. 301–20. Wilder suggested some movements may form Muslim-oriented Christian fellowships while other Christ-ward movements may take place with Muslims maintaining a Muslim identity.

hinder) movements of disciples and churches among Muslim people groups. This shift in faith horizon needs to continue to shape how we recruit, train and coach field teams. Through this interview project we have glimpsed a range of issues with which our field members—and thus all of us—must continue wrestling. We plan to continue reexamining all dimensions of our organizational practices, so we increasingly join with what we see our Father doing through Christ for his glory among all Muslim peoples.

References

Watson, David. 2014. *Contagious Disciple Making*. Nashville: Thomas Nelson.

Woodberry, J. Dudley, ed. 2008. *From Seed to Fruit: Global Trends, Fruitful Practices, and Emerging Issues Among Muslims*. Pasadena, CA: William Carey Library.

22

Maturing the Missiological Discourse on Discipleship Movements

Richard Grady, with the Symposium Listening Team

> *What exists now is what will be,*
> *and what has been done is what will be done;*
> *there is nothing truly new on earth. (Eccl 1:9)*

In respect to human behavior, there is nothing truly new on earth. Through ongoing academic research, we continually gain greater insight and understanding into what has always been. As our understanding of God's creation grows, so does our ability to minister effectively in his creation—in "new," yet also ancient, ways. Academic research is thus a unique form of worship, enabling us to gain greater appreciation for the Creator and his ways in his creation. Yet in respect to spiritual reality, there is something new—the kingdom of God breaking into the present.

In recent years, the global evangelical mission community has taken note of the phenomenon of small, rapidly reproducing communities of obedient Christ-followers. These communities of Christ-followers may look somewhat different than the churches with which we are familiar. Yet they are growing remarkably and are currently estimated to constitute about 1 percent of the world's population. If current growth rates continue, these kingdom movements will become an increasing percentage of the world's population in the very near future.[1] These are exciting times indeed.

---

1 Based on the research presented by researcher Justin Long during the symposium. The movements being tracked by the 24:14 research team currently consist of an estimated 75 million believers. This represents about 1 percent of the world's population. The average annual growth rate has been between 30 and 35 percent from the time the research team began tracking the growth of these movements. If that growth rate were sustained for the next five years, the number of believers in these movements would equal about 4 percent of the world's population.

To better understand the Lord's work in and through these kingdom movements, mission researchers, leaders, and catalysts gathered virtually in October 2020 for the Movements Research Symposium of the Motus Dei Network. As a function of the Symposium, a small team was commissioned to listen carefully to the presentations and conversations throughout the virtual event and reflect back to the broader community what we heard concerning four broad questions:

1. Where do we sense there is still confusion related to movements?

2. What are we hearing from the critics and what should we be learning from them?

3. What are the unanswered questions that require more research and reflection?

4. What don't we yet know that, if we knew it, might help movements to mature and accelerate the advance of the gospel throughout the world?

This diverse listening team, comprised of men and women representing five continents, summarized their observations into seven significant themes. Together, these themes capture the heart of our discussion on movements and suggest avenues for further research. Our intent in this exercise is to mature the missiological discourse related to discipleship movements today.

- **Movements need to have freedom of self-determination, to nurture their own development and theologies.** To a certain extent, this initial symposium primarily reflected academic research seeking to answer questions generated by those observing these kingdom movements from the outside. How can experienced academic researchers come alongside emerging leaders within these movements to help them with robust, credible research? Motus Dei is envisioned to be a five- to ten-year exploration of the Lord's work in and through these movements. We look forward to coming together to learn from local leaders within these movements as they take ownership, under the authority of Christ and his word, to answer their practical and theological questions in ways which make sense to their communities and enrich the global church and its ongoing mission.

- **The relationships and understanding must be improved between longer-established churches and emerging kingdom movements.** There is only one body of Christ. Jesus, in his high priestly prayer, prayed that his followers would be one as he is one with the Father, so the world might believe (John 17:20–23). Maintaining unity without demanding uniformity has always been a challenge for the body of Christ. In some contexts, longer-established churches may be able to facilitate the growth and sustainability of these emerging movements. Conversely, institutionalized churches can actually become a hindrance and stumbling block to growth. Movements can help revitalize longer-established churches when closer relationships are formed. As groups of believers within these movements mature, they need to be accepted and embraced as full members of the global family of Christ. Jesus tells us that new wine needs new wineskins, but that the new is often not accepted because those accustomed to the taste of the old wine prefer it (Luke 5:37–39). In light of this perpetual issue, how do we share what the Lord is doing through these kingdom movements, while continuing to honor what the Lord has done in and through his church throughout history? How do we do this without shaming the existing body of Christ or threatening existing structures?

- **In pursuit of improved relationships and greater mutual comprehension, we need more nuanced understanding of some commonly used terms.** Motus Dei needs to deepen and nuance our understanding of "church," "movement," "discipleship," and "conversion," both biblically and missiologically. At times, these terms are understood and used differently, which can lead to confusion. Rather than assuming common understanding, writers should briefly define their understanding of significant terms. Furthermore, research in Motus Dei should lead in the direction of deeper understanding of these realities, including the strengthening and refining of our biblical and theological framework for understanding and relating to CPMs. Sociology and other disciplines can also help to fill out the picture. We need "thicker" descriptions of these realities, not simply oriented to defend a movement's paradigm against critiques. We need constructive, holistic, multidisciplinary understandings of these realities.

- **We need to better observe the ways movements are transforming their broader communities.** Jesus instructed us to pray that the will of the Father would be done on earth as it is in heaven. What are the implications of that prayer as communities of obedient disciples in these movements continue to multiply? As disciples within these movements grow in obedience, how does their obedience bless their broader societies? As missiological researchers ask penetrating questions of established churches concerning their transformational effect on society, similar questions are being asked from within these movements. What is the personal, familial, educational, social, financial, and/or political transformational impact of movements in their societies?

- **Movements and the believers within them face ongoing questions about identity, longevity, and institutionalization.** Emerging identities in Christ are (re)negotiated as they are challenged by societal pressure on the children of first-time believers. This is especially an issue in non-Christian contexts. The identity of the believing community impacts social relationships and theological thought. Ritualistic patterns are developed. Identity impacts the ability of the movement to sustain continued growth within its context.

If found in the context, what is the appropriate role of longer-established churches in speaking into issues of collective new identity formation? How will these newly negotiated identities impact the ways these communities of obedient disciples interact with the broader body of Christ and their own societies? How will it shape the inevitable institutionalizing of these movements? And how can movements institutionalize and yet retain their movement DNA? What kinds of institutionalization stifle movements, and what kinds of institutionalizing help to preserve and enhance movements?

- **Robust sociological reflection is emerging.** Like the other major sciences, sociological research helps us better understand how the Lord created humans to live in community. What should we learn from previous social movements (both faith-based and secular) which have stood the test of time? Ongoing academic research in areas such as social network analysis, social change, social negotiation, intercultural competencies, ethnic studies, globalization, and ethnomusicology could help us better understand the Lord's work in movements. For example, how do secular sociological concepts, such as "boundary spanners," relate to "persons of peace," as often promoted in movement training? How do we identify strategic locations from which movements among multiple ethnic groups might emerge? How do we identify strategic ethnic groups which naturally cross boundaries to birth new movements in new geographic areas and among new ethnic groups?

- **God's sovereignty and supernatural work are foundational for the growth and multiplication of movements.** The best methodology can only nurture the emergence of a kingdom movement. We may plant and water, but only God causes growth. The rapid growth we currently see among previously unreached and resistant peoples appears to be a result of the prayers of many. Yet we still have much to learn. How is the Lord using dreams, visions, and miracles to sustain and accelerate the multiplication of movements? How are apostolic agents growing in spiritual discernment to hear the voice of the Lord at *kairos* moments, in ways which allow movements to cross into new areas and segments of society? How are spiritual gifts being manifested and utilized to strengthen these growing movements? How is spiritual formation and transformation taking place within men, women, and children within these movements? Is what we are observing in these areas unique to a particular context or common across movements? How does the emergence of the new "in Christ" spiritual family within an existing social structure empower and facilitate the growth of these movements?

These are exciting days. Many heroes of the faith prayed, served, and labored their entire lives hoping for spiritual fruit such as we currently see through kingdom movements. Motus Dei aims to honor their investment and ensure that their sowing continues to produce thirty, sixty, even a hundred times more fruit (Mark 4:8, 20). These movements continue to multiply as apparent authentic works of the Father among the nations. In response, the Motus Dei Network seeks to better understand how the Lord designed humans to live and interact in society and how he is working through this ancient divine design to multiply new creation communities in Christ. We hope that God's people in longer-established churches can clearly see, understand, and embrace these movements, and give praise to the Father in Heaven for such a harvest. We anticipate that robust research will provide insights that not only help us understand movements to Christ from other religious backgrounds, but also reveal clues to ways we can revitalize the faith of longer-established churches. We hope to see vibrancy of belief and purpose stirred up that will energize existing, emerging, and new generations of obedient disciples of Jesus. We long to see these disciples living out the reality of Christ's kingdom in diverse global societies, with confident boldness for the good of all.

We cannot ignore God's work in new kingdom movements. Let us rejoice in the new wine, even as it ages appropriately. It may not be our acquired taste, but it comes from the same vine. We can continue to celebrate the great harvest by raising our mutual cup and drinking in honor of the One who shed his blood—to create the new covenant symbolized by that cup in which we all are one. The Motus Dei Network intends to continue Christ-honoring research to that end.

AFTERWORD

I can't tell you how excited I am to read a book that is overfull of hard-won movemental wisdom and insight. I say this as someone who has spent the last three decades trying to engender movement thinking in primarily Western post-Christian, post-Christendom, and postmodern contexts. On many occasions I have lamented the sheer dearth of genuinely thoughtful, theologically rich, material on the topic. I wholeheartedly believe that implementing a movemental understanding of *ecclesia* is an irreplaceable key to reversing the decline of Christianity in the West. How is it that we have little collective wisdom on what is surely the most primal and most effective form of the church in history?! Any trip to the seminary library will reveal innumerable volumes written on some of the most obscure topics (e.g., *Presbyterian Polity in 18th Century New England* or *The Use of Subjunctives in Pseudo-Pauline Grammar*) but almost nothing of practical worth on movemental theology and phenomenology. This is an indictment to our historical scholarship and our apparent love of truth! Well, *Motus Dei* goes some way to reversing that deficiency in our thinking.

I have sought to bring the insights of missional theology into engagement with what can best be called *movemental phenomenology*. This means seeing the church and its functions through the significant paradigmatic shifts of what I call "movement thinking"—thinking from within the logic of a genuinely movemental ecclesiology. Movement thinking involves: (i) vigorous ongoing calibration/alignment around Jesus and his cause; (ii) the systemic importance of discipleship together with the design and implementation of disciple-making strategies and processes; (iii) activating and developing a ministry that is able to both *initiate and sustain* movements (the so-called APEST ministry typology described in Ephesians 4:1–16); (iv) developing genuinely incarnational forms of mission that are able to contextualize not only the gospel message, but also the ecclesia itself in different cultural contexts; (v) designing scalability and movemental capacities into the very organization from the get-go; and (vi) the ability to not only survive in the context of adaptive challenge and risk, but to be able to thrive and even flourish.

Not only are these necessary dimensions of movemental ecclesiology, but I am totally convinced they are already baked into the basic formula of church. There is a movemental *entelechy*—an inbuilt sense of direction and purpose—coded into the body of Christ. In his Ascension and at Pentecost, Jesus has already given his people everything they need to get the job done. We are literally designed for missional movement. Movement thinking is part of our deepest instincts.

We tend to lose touch with these latent potentials at the core of our being due to the various processes involved in the routinization of charisma that takes place in every organization as it moves further from its Founder and its founding ethos over time. Thank God, these entelechies are latent and can be activated. That's why they are triggered when the various historical institutions and institutional habits that can act as movement suppressors are removed—as in persecuted churches in various settings.

This is why this book is an incredible gift of grace to the church. I only wish that it was available thirty years ago. It is packed full of movemental wisdom, the kind of understanding that has been all but excluded from our paradigm of church for centuries (and even millennia) as we have found ourselves captive to the predominantly European, non-movemental, Christendom formulation of the church—the distinct, non-incarnational form of church that has been somewhat front-loaded into our missionary efforts in various non-Western contexts.

While I recognize that *Motus Dei* has been written by (and mostly for) reflective practitioners and missiologists operating in the Global South, there was little reflection on how their remarkable insights might impact Christian mission in distinctly Western and post-Christian contexts. Perhaps our next challenge is to integrate what we are learning in these contexts with the Motus Dei conversation. Until then, I am deeply grateful for the scholarship and devotion to our cause that has gone into this book. You should be too.

Alan Hirsch

ACKNOWLEDGMENTS

This compendium represents a colossal effort that transpired over the course of four years. As such, it will be impossible to thank everyone by name. For those names omitted here, let me remind you that your reward is in heaven!

The genesis for *Motus Dei* and the network (https://motusdei.network) occurred at a conference in East Asia in 2017. I was there with my boss at the time, L. Michael Corley. As we talked about the need for more insights into movements, there was one person I knew would be essential to the effort—Dave Coles. I had long admired Dave for his leadership in other mission networks and for his passionate involvement with movements globally. I am indebted to Dave for his skill in editing and networking—his influence on these pages is profound, and without him this book would not have come to pass.

At that same conference, the next person I spoke with was David Garrison, who provided a seasoned perspective and the emotional encouragement I needed for deeper missiological inquiry into movements. I quickly discovered that movements research, to different audiences, can appear to be either a threat or a waste of time. David's continued encouragement has been most welcome. I also connected immediately with Gene Daniels, with whom I had coedited a book previously and who knows a thing or two about research. Michael, Dave, and Gene then enthusiastically recommended Samuel Kebreab to also serve on what was shaping up to be our "facilitation team" (see https://motusdei.network/team).

The particular idea for our "Movements Research Symposium" originated from an event that James Lucas and Tim Martin helped facilitate at the Arab Baptist Theological Seminary (ABTS) in Beirut, Lebanon, in 2018, called the "Patronage Symposium." Their symposium was so fantastic that I approached Tim and James and asked if they would help us with something similar on movements. To my delight, they enthusiastically agreed. Later I learned that James was writing a theological book for InterVarsity Press, so I asked him to serve as an associate editor for this volume, along with Dave Coles. Through ABTS, I had also known Jonathan Andrews, and I am grateful that he helped round out our editorial team with his vast experience in publishing books and editing multicontributor volumes.

Tim Martin's organizational wisdom and experience in mission has helped lead our network to where it is today. As we pivoted to a virtual gathering due to a vicious microscopic organism in 2020, Tim and Daniel Brown are to be congratulated for pulling off an international virtual symposium that generated much more interest than we initially expected. We had twenty presentations on various aspects of movements, which later turned into the chapters you just read! I am grateful for all these authors and contributors who blessed me with their unique missiological insights into movements. I have learned so much from each of you, and I am incredibly grateful.

A heartfelt thank-you to my colleagues at One Collective and ABTS who have provided invaluable support and encouragement to complete this project. Finally, I would not have been able to network with so many people and edit this volume without the constant encouragement of my wife and children. Daily, they inspire me to "keep Jesus central."

WARRICK FARAH
Beirut, 2021

CONTRIBUTORS

Eric and Laura Adams have served with Frontiers for nearly forty years, as pioneer team leaders, mentors, translators, equipping, leadership development, knowledge management, research, field oversight, etc. Currently they serve the International Director Team as senior strategy associates. They led the research for Vision 5:9 for the "Fruitful Practices" sections of *From Seed to Fruit*, edited by Dudley Woodberry (2008). Eric also consults as a marine biologist and Laura as an expert in language acquisition.*

Steve Addison, DMin, is a catalyst for movements that multiply disciples and churches, everywhere. He is an author, speaker, podcaster, and mentor to movement pioneers. Steve is married to Michelle. They live in Melbourne, Australia, and have four children and two grandchildren. Steve and Michelle lead MOVE, a mission agency devoted to training and deploying workers who multiply disciples and churches. Visit Steve at movements.net.

Jonathan Andrews is a researcher and writer on the Christian communities of the Middle East and North Africa. He is the author of *Identity Crisis: Religious Registration in the Middle East* (2016) and coeditor of *The Religious Other: A Biblical Understanding of Islam, the Qur'an and Muhammad* (2020), among other works.

Pam Arlund, PhD, is a disciple maker and linguist. She previously served in Central Asia, where she helped ignite movements among several unreached Muslim people groups. She is now one of the members of the International Leadership Team of All Nations. She has written or edited several articles and books, including *The Pocket Guide to Church Planting* (2010), *Fruit to Harvest* (2018), and *Conversations on When Everything Is Missions* (2020).

Stephen Bailey, PhD, researches Christianity in Buddhist SE Asia and is President of SANTI Corporation, a nonprofit that provides training in the areas of religious freedom and peace-building. He is the author of "Death and Life Rituals in Buddhism and Christianity," in *Sacred Moments: Reflections on Buddhist Rites and Christian Rituals* (2018), and "A Short History of Christians in SE Asia," in *Emerging Faith: Lessons from Mission History in Asia* (2020).

Patrick (Pat) Brittenden, PhD, is a teacher, trainer, and theological midwife committed to encouraging believers of a Muslim background. He has published in various journals and written the *Introduction to the OT Designed for BMBs* (2014) and a few chapters, including "Mission in the North African Berber Context," in *Margins of Islam: Ministry in Diverse Muslim Contexts* (2018), and "Christianity in the Maghrib," in *The Routledge Handbook of the Maghrib* (2021). He coordinates the Hikma Research Partnership, a ministry seeking to amplify the voice of believers of a Muslim background through research, writing, and dissemination.

Bradley Cocanower, PhD, has served in a variety of cross-cultural roles over the past eleven years in Europe and Central America. Currently he lives in Southern Europe with his wife and two children, helping to train and equip Spanish speakers who are preparing for pioneer ministry in the majority world. He has published in journals, such as *Themelios* and *EMQ*, and recently coauthored *Terranova: A Phenomenological Study of Kingdom Movement Work among Asylum Seekers in the Global North* (2020).*

Dave Coles is an encourager and resourcer of church-planting movements among unreached groups, serving with Beyond. He has served among Muslims in Southeast Asia for twenty-four years. He has written over a dozen articles published (under a pseudonym) on topics related to contextualization, reaching Muslims, and the nature of the church. He is coauthor of *Bhojpuri Breakthrough: A Movement that Keeps Multiplying* (2019), and coeditor of *24:14 – A Testimony to All Peoples* (2019).

Michael T. Cooper, PhD, spent ten years as a pioneer church planter in Romania, ten years on the faculty of Trinity International University, and currently equips church planters and leaders around the world as Missiologist-in-Residence with East West Ministries International. He also directs the globally accessible MA in Missiology of Movements degree at Mission India Theological Seminary. His recent book, *Ephesiology: The Study of the Ephesian Movement* (2020) is a best seller at William Carey Publishing.

L. Michael Corley serves with New Generations, resourcing disciple-making movements with actionable intelligence as Director of Strategic Advancement. His family has served the people of the former Soviet Union since 1993, having led teams in Ukraine and Russia. He and his wife have been married for thirty years, and they have four children.

Gene Daniels, DLit et Phil, is a missionary and ethnographer whose specialty is qualitative research in Muslim contexts. He and his family spent twelve years as church planters in Central Asia among unreached Muslim people groups. Since that time, he has focused on research and training Christian workers for Muslim contexts. He is the author or editor of several articles and books, most recently coediting *Fruit to Harvest* (2018) and *Margins of Islam* (2018).*

Warrick Farah, PhD candidate, DMiss, serves with One Collective as a missiologist and theological educator in the Middle East. He coedited *Margins of Islam: Ministry in Diverse Muslim Contexts* (2018). His research interests include Muslim studies, frontier missiology, integral mission, and movements. He has published in journals such as *EMQ*, *IJFM*, and *Global Missiology*. Warrick is the founder and a facilitator of the Motus Dei Network (https://motusdei.network) and a researcher at the Oxford Centre for Mission Studies. His online accredited seminary course developed around this book can be found at: https://masterclasses.ephesiology.com/courses/foundation-movement.*

Regina R. Foard, PhD candidate, is a missiological researcher and practitioner in disciple-making movements among the North American diaspora. She has served as Director of Missional Engagement with a megachurch and as a translation intern in Kenya with CMF. Currently she facilitates DMM training and equipping of indigenous people within the North American diaspora context. Additionally, she is pursuing PhD research which examines the essential core factors required for establishing a baseline capacity for engagement between church leaders, congregations, and proximal diaspora.

David Garrison, PhD, is executive director of Global Gates, a ministry engaging diaspora communities through global gateway cities. Dr. Garrison has been a pioneer in the understanding of church-planting movements for more than three decades. He is the author, editor, and publisher of several books, including *Church Planting Movements* (2004), *T4T: A Discipleship Revolution* (2011), and *A Wind in the House of Islam* (2014).

Richard Grady facilitates the Global Church Planting Network (GCPN), a network of primarily non-Western indigenous church-planting organizations and networks. He has served with One Challenge in the Muslim world for over thirty years, working toward multiplying communities of obedient disciples among high-identity Muslim populations. He has published a number of articles (under a pseudonym) on various aspects of contextual missiology.

Alan Hirsch is the founder of 100 Movements, Forge Mission Training Network, and Future Travelers. Among his many books, he authored *The Forgotten Ways: Reactivating Apostolic Movements* (2016). Alan is cofounder of the M.A. in Missional Church Movements at Wheaton College. He is also an adjunct professor at Fuller Seminary, George Fox Seminary, and Asbury Seminary, among others, and he lectures frequently throughout Australia, Europe, and the United States.

Victor John was born in the state of Bihar in North India and has been a servant-leader in the cause of Christ's kingdom for more than forty-five years. He has a BA in Political Science and an MDiv in Theology. Victor is the founder and president of Asian Sahyogi Sanstha India (ASSI), he is also a founding member of Asian Parter International (US), and serves as a mission consultant with INTERACT (Sweden). He coauthored *The Bhojpuri Breakthrough* (2019).

Samuel Kebreab, MD, is a disciple-maker, trainer, and researcher of disciple-making movements. He previously served with New Generations as African Research Director. He is currently with Partners International and the Movement for African National Initiative (MANI) as the Horn of Africa regional coordinator.

Paul Kuivinen, PhD, is an ethnomusicologist, performer of twelve Central Asian ethnic instruments, studio engineer, and has led indigenous song creation workshops for twenty minority-language communities. He is a disciple-maker, DMM trainer, and researcher on the role of indigenous arts in DMMs. He has published a dozen articles (over half of them in Russian) and is the author of *The Garmun in the Traditional Culture of Kazan Tatars* (2020).

Trevor Larsen, PhD, is a teacher and "come-alongside coach" who is convinced of God's desire for all peoples. He and his wife live alongside the "Fruitful Band of Brothers" featured in his books on movements, which are available at https://focusonfruit.org.*

David S. Lim, PhD, is the President of the Asian School for Development and Cross-cultural Studies (ASDECS), which provides training programs for transformational development globally. He has written four books and writes articles for international journals, especially on Global South missiology and house church movements in Asia. He has also coedited five books published by William Carey Publishing, and a book by the Asian Society of Missiology: *Christian Mission in Religious Pluralistic Society* (2017).

Justin Long is the Director of Global Research for Beyond and stewards a global database of rapidly multiplying disciple-making movements. He has written articles for international journals, especially on the growth of movements and the places and peoples still lacking engagement. He produces the quarterly global dashboard of movements for the 24:14 Network.

James Lucas is involved in a number of projects developing Scripture resources in the Middle East. James and his family live in the region, where he is also involved in biblical and cultural research, church planting, caring for the poor, and cross-cultural training. He has coauthored a book on culture and theology with InterVarsity.*

Dwight Martin was born and raised in Thailand, and moved back to the country after a thirty-year career in the software industry. He has been the Research Coordinator for the Thai Church for over ten years. He also serves as the Free Church in Jesus Christ Association's (FJCCA) President of the Board of Advisors.

João Mordomo, PhD, is cofounder and vice chairman of Crossover Global, which has planted over 2,300 multiplying churches among unreached peoples. He serves on the Lausanne Movement's Global Diaspora Network and teaches adjunctively at several universities. João coauthored *Terranova: A Phenomenological Study of Kingdom Movement Work among Asylum Seekers in the Global North* (2020), was senior editorial consultant for the *Encyclopedia of Christianity in the Global South*, and contributor to *Scattered and Gathered: A Global Compendium of Diaspora Missiology*.

Rania Mostofi is the Associate Director of Pars Theological Centre, a ministry engaged in the education and formation of servant-leaders for the Persian church worldwide. She is also a Visiting Research Fellow at the Kirby Laing Centre for Public Theology in Cambridge and a convener of the Hikmat Research Partnership.*

Craig Ott, PhD, is professor of mission and intercultural studies at Trinity Evangelical Divinity School, where he also directs the PhD program in intercultural studies. He formerly served for twenty-one years in Germany as a church planter and educator and has taught or consulted in over forty countries. His numerous published works include *Global Church Planting: Biblical Principles and Best Practices for Multiplication* (2011, coauthored with Gene Wilson) and *The Church on Mission: A Biblical Vision for Transformation among All People* (2019).

Frank Preston, PhD, part of the Media to Movements team (mediatomovements.org) with Pioneers. He is a Media to Movements coach, trainer, and writer for material related to media in church planting. His work has been published in Christian and secular journals and book chapters on media in religious movements. His research in missions and the secular world is in the intersection of media, conversion, and high-identity social movements. He can be reached through the website above.*

Emanuel Prinz, PhD candidate, DMin, is a movement trainer and consultant to missions organizations and networks, including Bethany International and New Generations. He is the Associate Director of the Bethany Research Institute and Professor of Intercultural Studies at Bethany Global University, and the author of *Movement Catalysts* (2021) and *Exponential Disciple-Making and Church Planting* (2019). His Catalytic Leadership™ and EXPONENTIAL™ movement trainings have been translated into nine languages and are available at www.exponential-training.com. You can contact him at emanuel.prinz@gmx.net.

Pastor Somsak became a follower of Jesus at the age of twenty-four. Because there were no churches or any other Christians near where he lived in Thailand, he started studying God's Word on his own and faithfully following what the Holy Spirit taught him. Before the Free in Jesus Christ Church Association (FJCCA) movement started, he had planted thirteen "mother churches." He has a goal to plant house churches in villages based upon Mark 1:38. The FJCCA uses the book of Acts as their training manual.*

Aila Tasse, DMin, is a Muslim-background believer and the founder and president of Lifeway Mission International. He also serves as the Regional Director for New Generations East Africa. Lifeway is a mission organization that works among unreached people groups in Eastern Africa, making disciples and planting churches. Aila travels around the world doing DMM training, mentoring, and coaching church planters, with his greatest emphasis in the seven countries of East Africa, ranging from Sudan to Congo.

* Writing under a pseudonym.

INDEX